Design through Discovery

Reproduced on the cover:
MORRIS LOUIS. *Horizontal I* (detail). 1962.
Acrylic on canvas, 2′8″ x 9′7″.
Private collection,
courtesy André Emmerich Gallery, New York.

Marjorie Elliott Bevlin Otero Junior College

Design through Discovery

second edition

HOLT, RINEHART AND WINSTON, INC.
New York Chicago San Francisco Atlanta Dallas
Montreal Toronto London Sydney

Library of Congress Catalog Card Number: 72-85753
ISBN 0-03-072195-4 Text
ISBN 0-03-076480-7 Trade
Printed in the United States of America
456789 006 9876

Designer: Marlene Rothkin Vine

Preface

In writing *Design through Discovery* I have wanted to offer both an introduction to the visual arts and to the design elements that give the human environment, whether natural or man made, its order and coherence. The book's purpose is to reveal the links by which creative design processes maintain a vital continuum with the fundamental creative methods inherent in nature. My intention has been to demonstrate, for students eager to make their own contributions to the visual arts and for the general reader concerned about the quality of his response to the world surrounding him, that design is not a product derived solely, or originally, from the ideas and skills of professional technicians but a natural development whose genesis is clearly discernible in the universe—a structural principle functioning through all life that, once understood, can enhance for everyone the awareness and appreciation of the relationship between man and his environment.

There is a wholeness in life that can be made to give significance to all of man's experience. Thus, while I have concentrated here on contemporary forms, I have done so to express the continuity in modern vision of the traditions that nurtured it. In the same spirit, I have sought further to emphasize the close relationship that can be found between art and science, an affinity not at all dissimilar to that which allies art with nature. Within this context, it is not possible to examine the "major" arts of painting, sculpture, and architecture in isolation from such "minor" expressions as commercial art and the various studio crafts, or see two-dimensional design apart from problems of organization in three dimensions. Thus, the reader will find in the book chapters on forms that range from the handcrafts and their industrial applications, through advertising, fashion, and photography, to painting, sculpture, architecture, interiors, and urban development. In all these arts, I have urged the integrity of materials, of form, of function, and of ornamentation.

The first chapters explore the general principles of design found in nature, identify these elements, and assess their significance. This section of the book provides a survey of the general scope of two- and three-dimensional design. The concepts articulated in it are then applied to an examination, in subsequent chapters, of design in some fifteen different types of visual expression. In each of these chapters the highlights of artistic achievement are touched upon so that the reader may view his own time in its historical perspective and thereby understand more thoroughly both his creative heritage and the efforts of contemporary artists.

In writing about art and design I have endeavored to speak in basic English and avoid the abstruse terminology of art historical and critical commentary. However, to help the reader with whatever new language he may find in the narrative, I have prepared the glossary of terms that can be found at the back of the book. For those intrigued to read further about the topics introduced in the text, there are references for additional reading, along with certain notes to the text, which are also placed at the end of the book.

Since this is a revision of an older publication, I must say a word about the special character of the present version of *Design through Discovery.* Readers familiar with the first edition can perceive immediately the general improvement in the art and design of the book itself. There are many more illustrations—well over 400 in all—and 32 pages of full-color reproductions. In every instance, throughout the black-and-white series, the designer has established a close visual relationship between the text and its illustrations and, wherever possible, in the positioning of the color plates. New also to this edition are the sections on landscape and urban design, television, metal enameling, printmaking, and acrylics in painting. The color section is much expanded, with new material on light, as is the section on structural design. Everywhere in the book I have attempted to refine ideas, introduce new concepts, and discover greater relevance for art and design in modern life.

For many of the improvements that I have been able to make in *Design through Discovery* I must thank a number of people, primarily my students, who have taught me much about what it is to respond freshly and intelligently to visual phenomena, and the students of other teachers who have shared their knowledge of the first edition with me. Among the teachers I wish to cite especially Professors Charles Giordano of Syracuse University and Carolyn T. Stewart of the University of Alabama, whose critiques of both the old edition and the manuscript for this revision, commissioned by the publisher, were immensely helpful in their sympathetic candor and severity. Professor Zella May Case of the New York State University College at Buffalo also prepared a review of the old edition, and I am grateful for the detail with which she identified difficulties in both content and style.

At the same time, I acknowledge a major indebtedness to the artists whose work illustrates the premises the book is based on. Their cooperation and interest in my effort has been a continuing inspiration, and the consistency of their approach, despite the varied media and interpretations, has contributed in a very real way to the philosophical unity I have tried to make evident. I am also grateful to the museums, galleries, business organizations, and photographers all over the world for visual materials and the permission they granted for their use in *Design through Discovery.*

The staff at Holt, Rinehart and Winston deserve mention for their support of the enormous enterprise that is the production of an art book. Dan Wheeler visualized this edition and guided it to completion. Both Rita Gilbert and Joan Curtis have my warmest appreciation for the enthusiasm and expertise they brought to the vast responsibility for collecting illustrations and securing permissions, a task they appeared to transform into an adventure. John Kremitske, Carla Lord, and Robert Haycraft contributed their cultivated knowledge of art and its history as well as their copy editorial skills to the refinement and styling of the text. Rita Gilbert also served as project editor and deserves full credit for the final phases of preparing the manuscript for publication. Marlene Rothkin Vine designed the book, and I thank both her and John Macellari for the beautiful work they did in assembling text and illustrations into a functional and visually exciting format.

My personal thanks go to Dr. Dexter Hess, chairman of the biological sciences department, Jack Kappel and Kent Martin, instructors in biology, and William C. Andersen, instructor in chemistry, all at Otero Junior College, for guiding my way into the fascinating area where art and science meet. I am grateful to Mrs. Margaret Kolomitz, who took charge of the final typing and proofreading with skill and interest, and to Nanette Hoover, Judy Burns, Jo Olsen, and Shirley Mendenhall, who came to my aid when I needed it. I am indebted as well to my husband, Ervin W. Bevlin, whose help in countless ways made the book possible.

Eldora, Colorado
January 1970

M.E.B.

Contents

Nature and Design

I

Design and Life

chapter 1

The feeling for design is as old as mankind, but the materials for design are millions of years older. Design is considered a man-made expression, yet its roots reach back into the beginnings of the earth. When seen by the creative eye, the structure of a mineral deposit, the skeleton of a fish, and the veining of a leaf suggest designs of many varieties and great complexity, although, of course, they existed in primeval eras simply as the expression of natural laws of growth (Fig. 1). The Greeks gave a name to the hexagon and formulated the science of geometry of which it is an element; yet long before this recognition, geometry was being formed naturally by crystals of ice and volcanic ash and existed in the honeycomb and in the cornea of an insect's eye.

below: 1. The structural laws of nature are basically a plan for order with infinite manifestations. *left:* AARON SISKIND. *Rock by Ocean, Gloucester, Massachusetts.* 1944. *center:* WOLF STRACHE. *X-Ray Photograph of Sole.* 1956. *right:* WOLF STRACHE. *Leaf Skeleton of Black Poplar.* 1956.

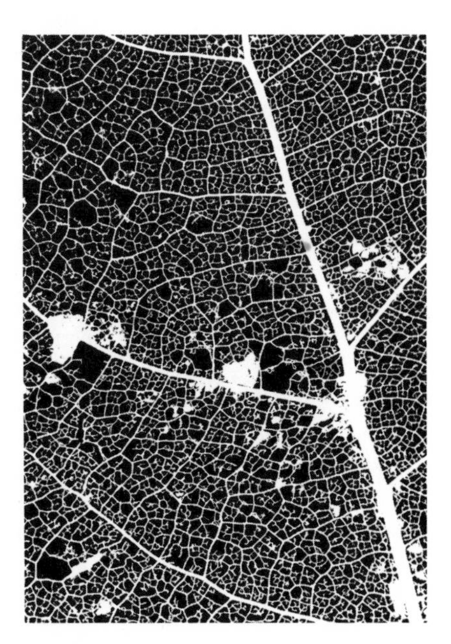

The understanding of the origins of forms and processes is of inestimable value to the designer. We live in a chaotic world dominated by the harsh impersonal face of industry and technology. Even in this modern environment, however, man remains a biological being with a spirit geared to the natural rhythms of which he is a part. An exploration of these rhythms and the ability to see not only the blighted scene about him but also the eternal forms which outlast all man's activities, are a challenge to the designer, whose very function necessitates the effort to see life whole and to contribute to it a sense of purpose.

CHARACTERISTICS OF DESIGN

The designer will find no rules or formulas to help him in his search for expression; he will not even find a simple definition for design. Being an expression of man's own reaction or experience, design is as individual as the person who creates it. There are, however, certain characteristics that can be associated with any good design.

A Plan for Order

From the beginning of time, order has been the cornerstone of creativity. The world began when order was created out of chaos. This is expressed not only in the Old Testament story but also in ancient Egyptian religion and in Greek mythology, where the entire complicated genealogy of the gods is traced back to ancestors who sprang from chaos and then sorted the universe into categories by taking upon themselves such identities as Earth and Love and the Darkness under the Earth. The ancient Chinese believed in a nebulous state that existed before the earth came into being. In all these versions the world as we know it began only when confusion or nothingness gave way to form and order—in other words, to design. As man evolved into an intellectual being, his need for order found expression in his habitat; the palace, the cathedral, and the skyscraper developed from a feeling of design not unrelated to the need which divided the simple cave into areas for sleeping and eating and which cleared the wilderness into fields for cultivating different crops. As Alexander Pope expressed it: "Order is heaven's first law."[1] Order, or design, can in fact be interpreted as the foundation of all living; consequently, *any good design is, first of all, a plan for order.* The study of the way in which design permeates life is an unending adventure in discovery.

Expression of the Material

The view from an airplane (Fig. 2) reveals one of the most spectacular of designs—the blocks of field and forest, of plowed ground and winter wheat, of towns and cities and cornfields all woven into a living tapestry that is the earth itself. This is not a superficial pattern laid upon the surface of the ground by climate and man's efforts. It is the very character of the earth coming to its surface from deep within: the areas of fertility yielding patches of feathery green or burnished gold; the towns and cities, with their deeply rooted networks of pipes, gas and electric lines, wells, and subways, marked by a richly textured area of concrete, glass, and trees, delineated by streets swarming with thousands of people and their perplexities. Thus, *any design should be an expression of its material, not an external attempt at decoration.*

---

[1] All annotations can be found in a special section at the end of the text entitled "Bibliography and Notes," which begins on page 367.

Fulfillment of Purpose

Purpose in nature is usually involved with survival. A tree grows in a certain shape in order to survive in a constricted area; the veining of a leaf results from the need of the tree for food. Fish develop fins for the purpose of moving through water, thereby allowing them to find food or safety from predators. Other species exhibit mutations that provide protection or the equipment for battle.

In man's designs, purpose is concerned with other levels of activity. Fulfilled purpose is seen in the totem poles created by the Indians of the Pacific Northwest (Fig. 3). Stylized characters of exciting variety are carved *into* the huge poles of the Northwest cedar, adding tremendous drama and meaning to the depiction of the

above: 2. An aerial photograph of the countryside shows the design created, inadvertantly, by man's pattern of living.

right: 3. Totem pole, Stanley Park, Vancouver, B.C. Coats of arms, tribal exploits, deaths, and even notices of debts are among the elements integrated into a unified design.

4. The distinctive forms of primitive art are abstracted to create a fabric design.

history of a clan. Nothing is stuck on for decorative effect alone; even the colors of the paint have meaning. The majestic tree clearly remains in the artwork, but in it is embodied the social and religious philosophy of a people, as well as the personal and familial legend of a proud individual. Yet, even to persons who understand nothing of the interpretation of the totem pole, the dramatic designs and colors have held enough esthetic attraction to be borrowed as motifs for paintings, for fabric designs (Fig. 4), and for various commercial uses. In these settings, it is still the intangible flavor of the Northwest and the mystery of the tribal philosophy *combined* with the native color and design which provide the interest; yet this peculiar flavor is secondary to the purpose for which the pole was originally designed. This fact gives us a third basic design principle: *an effective design will fulfill its purpose.*

One of the most functional uses of design is in the creation of architecture. It is a significant fact that a well-designed building will have a floor plan which makes a good two-dimensional design on paper. The linear ground plan which shows variety in the layout of space, harmonious arrangement of sizes and shapes representing rooms, and a pleasing rhythm in the flow of traffic from area to area will, when built, result in a structure that is satisfying and functional in its three-dimensional form. The plan of the Early Christian church was based upon the shape of a cross for symbolic reasons, and this two-dimensional figure has survived through the ages as the basis of varying three-dimensional forms of architecture—all related by this vital symbolism, yet fulfilling the needs of their congregations in diverse ways.

We have weathered the conglomerate, or eclectic, period of American architecture in which buildings were designed primarily for outward show (with all the periods of past glory getting a jumbled representation), and the interiors fell where they might. In the early twentieth century Frank Lloyd Wright revolutionized architecture with his organic designs springing from their native settings and expressing man's essential needs. Largely as a result of his teaching and example, contemporary architecture follows the principle found in nature, where shelters are constructed according to the vital requirements of the occupants, with the structure evolving outward into birds' nests or honeycombs or beaver dams. For integrity of design, buildings should be created for the life within them. The floor plan thus becomes all important, and the exterior is adapted to it in an attractive and functional way.

New Mexican architecture exemplified this principle long before the artists' colonies sprang up in its midst, for it was not art but necessity that fathered the design of adobe churches and pueblos. The designing of a pueblo church (Fig. 5) was simply a matter of laying out the size needed for the interior purpose, encompassing its congregation, sanctuary, and vestibule, and then enclosing this designed space. The method of enclosure was as expedient as the allotment of the space within. The ground is hard but malleable; with the addition of straw it was formed into bricks baked in the hot New Mexico sun, held together with mortar made from the same adobe mud, and the whole wall was then plastered with the same mud base to provide protection and a smooth finish. Cedar poles were brought from the nearby Sangre de Cristo Mountains to form rafters, or vigas, to support the roof. These poles, being long, stick out beyond the walls and create fascinating shadow patterns that change throughout the day. The mild New Mexico winters preclude the need to shed great quantities of snow; therefore the roof is flat. Meanwhile, the thick walls with their little windows not only provided a haven from enemies in the early days, but continue to achieve the cool dim interior, which is practical for climate reasons and also appropriate to the mystical rites of a church that is early Spanish Colonial with overtones of ancient Indian. Here is true design arising from the land and the people. It is not so much an erected structure as a flowering of the ground itself; from a distance, no strong line of demarcation between building and ground is discernible. And just as the adobe color is of the earth, one might say that the texture is of the people, for it was produced by the imprint of many hands, smoothing and patting, building flat-palmed with piety and devotion.

5. Mission St. Francis of Assisi, Ranchos de Taos, N.M. 1772–1816.

6. Ski hut in the resort region of Melchsee-Frutt, central Switzerland.

The high mountain valleys of the Alps have produced an architectural design entirely different but just as honest (Fig. 6). Built of heavy logs and boards from the larch-covered slopes below the timberline, the Swiss hut and chalet readily proclaim affinity to their dramatic surroundings. Powerful boulders from the mountain slopes form a solid foundation and serve decoratively for the fireplace so necessary for heat in this rigorous climate. The stone-slab roofs are steeply angled to shed the heavy Alpine snowfalls. Plaster chinking blocks the wind that would whistle through the cracks between the logs. After necessities have been provided for in such features as heavy doors and small-paned windows secure against high winds, colorful designs used on the shutters and interior frequently reflect the blossoms of the Alpine meadows above the village. This is decorative design applied to enhance the basic structure, but reflecting its surroundings and thus relating it more closely to them.

Relationship to Natural Laws of Growth and Order

Nature, of course, is the supreme master of inherent design. The smallest granite pebble has its patterns (Fig. 7), the result of centuries of building up and washing away until the round smooth core of design remains, each one different from the others. The trunks of trees are rich in design, drawn in concentric circles through the seasons, then twisted into writhing lines and textures by winds and snows and lightning, hostile elements which man could not withstand but which for the tree serve to improve its own intrepid character. The outer bark, too, has an individual design quality. The satiny gray-green of aspen trunks (Fig. 8), which turns to a black-streaked silver in winter, has little in common with the irregular roughness of fir or spruce but becomes more dramatic in contrast. Each has its own design—a beauty of color, texture, or line that has been part of the tree from its beginning, and that registers each scar from wind or the hand of man and molds it into its total being.

left: 7. Stream-washed stones exhibit individual textural characteristics that have been brought out by the impact of rushing water.

below: 8. New designs in nature reveal themselves with the changing seasons. As leaves fall, the white trunks of aspen trace patterns against the evergreens in the background.

Underlying the individual characteristics, however, there exist the eternal laws of growth and order. Each blade of grass unfolds in an orderly way characteristic of its kind. The leaves of every tree or plant, while limitless in variation, evolve in precise sequence: each becoming first a bud, then a tiny shape that emerges and reaches maturity and takes its place in the total design (Fig. 9). Granted that the effect of such growth is frequently disorder, that one plant grows on top of another and that the dead growth integral to the cycle of nature adds confusion to the scene, this is still a matter of quantity rather than quality. Although fertile soil and propitious growing conditions may create a tangled jungle, this does not alter the fact that each facet of that growth is accomplished according to basic and orderly procedures. From this, we deduce another of the qualities of creative design: *an authentic design is related to the basic natural laws of growth and order.*

9. The variety in plants is almost limitless, yet as each unfolds, a definite pattern of growth becomes evident. *above:* cryptocoryne, underwater banana plant; *below:* Florida moneywart, corkscrew vallisneria.

This order is found wherever we look. One may classify design into certain basic movements—the spiral, the circle, and similar symbols—but truly creative design is found not in standardized patterns but in individual variations. Each variety of tree is different in its characteristics, but each tree is also unique because its peculiar design is the outgrowth of its individual life. Trees in the same clump will be of varying shapes because of the way in which they crowd one another. A woodpecker will carve a hole in the trunk of one, a storm will rip a branch from another. Hail will pelt the surface of still another, while its neighbor may be sheltered from the direct beat of the hailstones. A basic shape and salient characteristics may be attributed to an entire species, but each tree has its own design story to tell.

Individuality

It is well known that snowflakes, though following basic patterns, are never exactly alike. Neither is any seashell exactly like any other seashell; nor is any tongue of flame, any ocean wave or cloud entirely like others. The artist who would create truly original designs must learn to see the individuality of his inspirations and to respect it. He must train his eye to look beneath the general shape of things to the variation that creates interest. *An interesting design has individuality.* For the creative artist this is the most important design characteristic of all.

It is a fundamental law of science that nothing new is ever created in the world of matter. This truth carries over into the field of design. Every design is based on age-old forms, whether these are found in nature or are simple geometric lines and figures used in an abstract way. Nonetheless, a new approach is like a spring bubbling out of a hillside; the water is the same as the water that has been used and drunk for centuries, yet it is always new, always fresh, always satisfying because it comes forth in its own way, in its own place, and with its own degree of coldness and freshness. A talent for design, using elements and methods long grown old, can bring forth freshness and originality in its own inimitable style.

DESIGN AND LIVING

Individual interpretations of design are not limited to the graphic artist. The creative mind is an orderly mind, a mind that sorts and arranges for creative use—whether it be figures, with the statistician; facts, with the historian; or theories, with the philosopher. The creative writer must have an orderly mind before he can build the design for a plot or a piece of poetry, and the musician must have an orderly vision of his themes and harmonies before he can set down original music so that it can be played by instruments.

The person who insists that he has no creative ability frequently builds his life on designs without being conscious of the fact. The handyman whose shop is a model of neatness, with nails sorted into jars and with every tool in place, is a designer in spite of himself, for his work is based on order and that order itself is pleasing to him. The woman who hangs her washing on the line in a certain way, with all the socks together and all the white shirts in a group, is creating design without realizing it; no doubt she feels creative satisfaction from her labors when she views the neatly hung rows. A clothing store has its stock hung according to sizes and forms of garments and by colors, because the merchant knows that if his stock makes an attractive design he is more apt to sell it. We plan our gardens in a certain order, not only so that plants will have sun and shade according to their needs, but also so that areas of pattern, color, and texture will be created. This is a part of landscape design. Design is not limited to attractive manifestations, however. Carefully planned crimes represent designs with a specific purpose, and there are probably no more thoroughly prepared designs than those governing military maneuvers involving life and death.

Even outside the realm of war, many people are realizing that, as life becomes more complex, man's very survival is going to depend increasingly upon design. The congestion in cities, air pollution, rapidly accelerating traffic not only on the ground but in the air—all these are basically problems which can be solved intelligently only by creative planning. Gyorgy Kepes, professor of visual design at MIT, stated the situation as follows: "The extended world revealed by science and the technical world of man's own making both require mapping by our senses, the disposition of our activities and movements in conformity with their rhythms, the discovery of their potentialities for a richer, more orderly, human life."[2]

Look around you and notice how many examples of design are created in your own day-to-day life. You will discover that most of life's activities depend upon design of one sort or another, for no one can live satisfactorily or creatively in confusion, either mental or physical. And, as soon as confusion gives way to order in any degree, you have design: design for living, design for working, design for creating.

SUMMARY

Design is considered a man-made expression, but the materials of design reach back to the beginnings of the earth. Understanding the origins of forms and processes is of great value to the designer, for it helps him to see beyond the harsh impersonality of the world today to the eternal values and forms which outlast man's efforts. One of the most basic functions of the designer is the necessity to see life whole and to assign to it a sense of purpose.

There are no rules for creating designs, nor any simple definition of design itself. Yet there are certain characteristics which can be found in any effective design:

1. A design is a plan for order.
2. A good design is an expression of its material.
3. An effective design fulfills its purpose.
4. An authentic design is related to the basic natural laws of growth and order.
5. An interesting design has individuality.

For the creative artist, individuality is the most important design characteristic, for it is his own identity that makes his work unique in the long history of artistic endeavor.

Design is important not only to the artist, however, but is also found abundantly in everyday living. Many people do not realize that they are unconsciously creating design in the orderly way in which they approach the tasks of everyday life. It becomes increasingly apparent, in fact, that man's survival in a complex world will depend upon his ability to design for the future.

Design and Nature

chapter 2

Design is implicit in nature in even its simplest forms. While everyone is conscious of the beauty of a flower, a leaf, or a seashell, the wonderful world of the microscope is frequently familiar only to the scientist. Yet in its magnifications are found some of the most fundamental truths about design and many of the most fascinating patterns and space relationships existing anywhere (Fig. 10).

Chapter 1 highlighted the fact that design began when chaos or formlessness was converted into order. Harlow Shapley states the approach of the scientist who senses a world beyond the realm of human knowledge when he says: "Chaos is but unperceived order; it is a word indicating the limitations of the human mind and the paucity of observational facts."[1] The intimation is that if we knew enough there would be no chaos, only form and meaning. It is frequently the function of the artist to see this form and meaning before it is obvious to others and, in any case, to search it out continually in his work.

10. Fern sporangium, when viewed through a microscope, reveals its basically circular motif.

RHYTHM

One of the most vital facts uncovered by scientific study is the existence of basic rhythms throughout nature. Any good design is based on some sort of rhythm, and the realization that not only the animal kingdom but also the plant and mineral worlds ebb and flow in a constant yet flexible rhythmic pattern can do much to make the artist realize that these principles are not restrictions imposed upon the designer but basic truths blending all of existence into a related whole.

Seasonal and Lunar Rhythms

We take for granted the rhythm of the seasons; much of our economy is based upon the sowing and reaping of the harvest. This has always been so, even with the most primitive peoples. The pattern of life has revolved around an eternally recurring cycle of spring festivals celebrating the sowing of seed, harvest celebrations in honor of the reaping and storing of crops, and winter festivities to relieve the long monotony of the barren months. Centuries before the Christian church translated such events into the holidays of Christmas and Easter, spring and winter festivals were annual occurrences with primitive tribes, with the Egyptians and Greeks, and in Oriental civilizations. Today, in our highly complicated lives such rhythms are taken for granted; yet most of us have some awareness of the miracle of growth and of the rhythm of seasonal change in landscape and weather.

In northern climates the sight of geese flying south for the winter is as much a part of autumn as are the falling leaves. Scientists have made detailed studies to relate the migrations of birds to weather, to the presence of insects and other food in certain areas, and to breeding habits; yet no conclusive reasons have been discovered for the obvious patterns followed by the individual species year after year. While the dates of departure and arrival may vary by as much as two weeks from year to year, the routes and the destinations are definite and unvarying for the most part, related to the changing seasons.

The reef heron is closely attuned to the cycle of the tides in its activity. Each day it leaves its Australian homeland to prey upon a reef as far away as thirty miles, arriving at low tide, when more food is uncovered. Even though the tide goes out fifty minutes later each day, the heron still alights at precisely the moment of low tide.[2]

The relationship of moon and tides has long led to theories about the effects of the moon upon human events. The *Farmers' Almanac* tells of the advantages of planting and harvesting crops according to the moon, and since the time of the ancient Mesopotamians the study of astrology has been undertaken in an effort to determine the fate of individual human beings according to the position of certain stars and constellations at a given time. These are fields that often defy scientific analysis, yet yield distinct rhythms to those who work closely with them. It is quite possible that much folklore may have valid bases stemming from the close association of primitive peoples with nature and their observation of and dependence upon cycles that tend to go unobserved in mechanized modern life.

Daily Rhythms

The rhythms of day and night have varying manifestations. When a bean plant is raised in darkness, it has no daily sleep movement in its leaves; but if exposed to a flash of light, it will show a definite natural reaction. When it is returned to darkness, the pattern remains; every day at the time of that single exposure to light the leaves will persist in elevating.[3] The fiddler crab starts to turn black at sunrise, wearing a protective cloak against the glaring sun and predators. At sunset it speedily blanches out again to a silvery gray. Even captured crabs, when kept in a dark room, will continue to exhibit this natural rhythm.[4] The movements of wild animals follow definite daily patterns; many animals emerge toward evening to seek water and food or, in the case of beavers, to work on their dams and lodges. Some of these patterns, of course, are conditioned by the presence of man or traffic during the day; yet even in isolated regions a natural rhythmic pattern can be detected among various species.

Man and Rhythm

From his first heartbeat, man is a creature of cycles—of the rhythmic contractions of the heart known as systole and diastole, of the beat of his pulse, of the regularity of breathing, of waking and sleeping, of eating and fulfillment, of activity and rest. His reproductive processes follow set patterns of fertility and sterility, and his gestation period forms a precise design of development that can be clearly charted from month to month.

It is only natural that when man celebrated the cycles of the seasons or his struggles and victories his festivities should take a rhythmic form in keeping with his own being. Primitive man's first expressions were his beating on a simple drum of animal skins, dancing to this beat, and chanting in monotonous rhythms. Gradually the structure became more complex, with narrations of events evolving into dramatic enactments and with new instruments added to accompany the drums. Voices began to vary and harmonize. From these beginnings emerged such divergent expressions as Greek drama, medieval morality plays, Elizabethan instrumental music, and the varied dances of the American Indian.

Graphic expressions follow much the same patterns. Anyone who has seen an electrocardiogram or a tracing of human brain waves can see immediately the relationship of natural rhythms to graphic representation. With its sharp peaks of systole and diastole, an electrocardiogram (Fig. 11) presents a definite design of heights and depths. The tracing of brain waves (Fig. 12) may be less marked in regularity, with calm impulses indicated by slightly varied lines and tumultuous impulses tracing patterns of greater angle. These are designs made unconsciously by man, designs based on the rhythms inherent in human life.

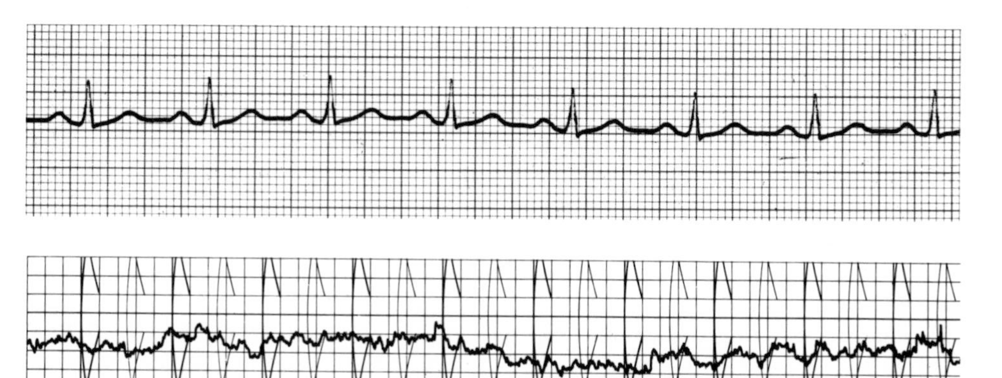

left: 11. The electrocardiograph creates a graphic design as it records the rhythm of a heartbeat.

below left: 12. Man's mental activity is seemingly random and unpredictable, yet when it is charted on the electroencephalograph, a definite pattern emerges.

13. The wings of butterflies are adorned with some of the gayest colors and most flamboyant designs to be found in nature.

VARIETY

Probably the most fascinating characteristic of nature is its variety. The existence of rhythm ensures variety, for it is the contrast of light with dark, of winter with summer, of height with depth, and of a loud beat with a soft beat that makes for rhythmic pattern.

Variation in nature is infinite and exciting. The green tree is enhanced by the tracery of black branches through its leaves. The variation in flowers, rocks, seashells, birds, and butterflies (Fig. 13) has caused people to travel the world over in search of specimens.

Variety in Size and Shape

The most obvious variations found in nature are those in *size* and *shape.* The landscape architect makes use of these in his planning, for a plot merely filled with shrubs and trees of the same size and shape would not be a garden but a nursery. In an area so small that it might well go unnoticed, the Japanese create an atmosphere of tranquil beauty (Fig. 14). Trees are pruned radically to present unusual shapes and to maintain scale with their surroundings. Foliage is combined for contrast, with lacy fronds of ferns accenting the shiny precision of azalea leaves, and the whole is interlaced with the tracery of branches. The supreme achievement of the Japanese landscape artist is his willingness to obscure his hand in the larger designs of nature. His surroundings are designed to look uncultivated and natural, and in this way they achieve the unity with nature that is the essence of good design.

Dramatic variations among trees have been noted earlier. Figure 15 shows how interesting a field of daisies becomes because of differences in size. Close scrutiny reveals a wide variation in scale, from the tiny flowers half hidden in the grass to the largest ones with their prominent button centers. A closer look shows that the shapes also vary, for some petals bend forward while others curve back. Again, notice the arrangement of pattern in the field. No area of grass between the clumps of flowers is of the same size and shape as any other area.

In astronomy, one finds similar variety of size and spacing. Although at a distance many stars may seem alike in size, the aspect of the heavens as a whole (Fig. 16) is one of infinite variety in distribution and brilliance.

Turning to the revelations of the microscope, one finds more evidence of the variety in nature. Figure 17 shows a section of cell structure taken from a glandular secretion in a guinea pig. Notice the varied character of the large cavities and of the dark round granules within them. The round areas are separated by different shapes and distances and by the textured pattern of the interior network surrounding

top: 14. Japanese landscape design stresses variety in textures and forms of plants, trees, and rocks. This typical garden was created by native craftsmen for the Museum of Modern Art in New York.

left center: 15. In a field of daisies, no two flowers are exactly alike.

below left: 16. The stars and planets that fill the night sky exhibit tremendous variety in size, shape, brilliance, and distribution.

below: 17. A study in textures and shapes is found in a cell of the guinea-pig pancreas.

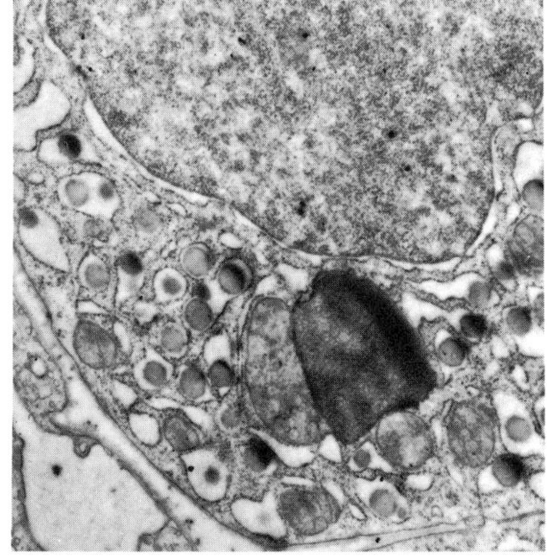

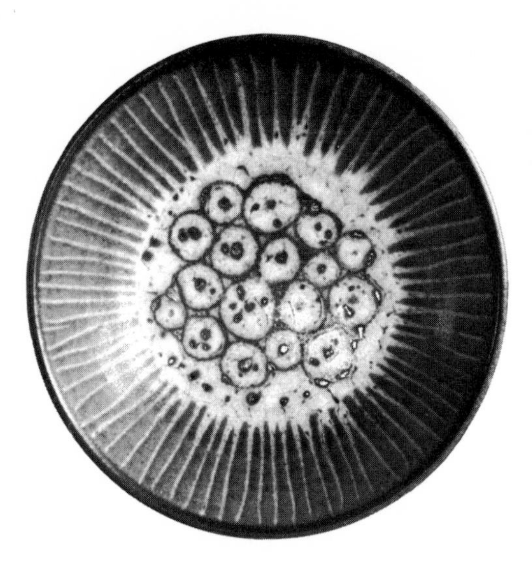

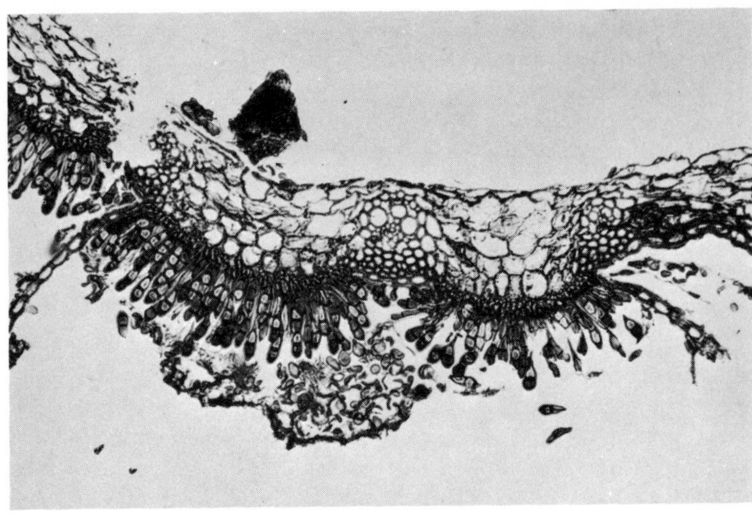

left: 18. Harrison McIntosh. Stoneware bowl with brush and sgraffito decoration. 1966. The design in this bowl is similar to that in the guinea-pig tissue.

right: 19. The powerful lens of a microscope reveals exciting forms and patterns in the cellular structure of black stem wheat rust.

them. That such cell structure can be translated from nature into effective man-made designs is shown eloquently in the ceramic bowl in Figure 18. Both the center and border designs have an organic quality that could easily have come from a tissue section viewed under a microscope. The microscopic view of black stem wheat rust in Figure 19 reveals the same variety in size, shape, and texture, asserting that even a parasite can have a share of beauty.

Variety in Color

Perhaps the best way to appreciate variation in *color* is to paint a landscape. To the beginning painter the most beautiful natural spots seem the best material for a painting, and thus he may select a peaceful meadow or a grove of trees. After an hour or so of work, however, frustration may set in. The green trees, the green fields, and the green bushes in the foreground have become an undifferentiated mess of bright paint that has taken control of the canvas and turned the scene of beauty into a gaudy jungle. It is only after scrutinizing his chosen landscape carefully that the artist discovers the infinite variety and subtlety of nature's greens, not only the differences between the green of leaves and the green of grass but of various areas within the leaves or grass, where a ray of sunlight brightens or a cloud shadow makes the green darker and cooler. The scene can be painted, but only with tremendous care in the mixing and use of the varied greens, and even then the finished work seldom has the interest and freshness of the original scene. The sky offers another pitfall, for there is no surer sign of an amateur painter than the garish blue of the sky he paints. To produce a sky with the convincing look of nature requires great subtlety and a willingness to see that what one may conventionally think of as blue is often green or rose. The same holds true for stone, with various mineral deposits giving it a wealth of earth tones and glints under changing lights. While color in nature is all around us, there is much that is hidden from us—not by outward circumstance but by our own blindness and preconceptions.

Before an artist can work creatively, he must learn to see. This is why the great Expressionist painter Oskar Kokoschka called his school in Salzburg the "School of Vision." Here he gathered together art students from all over the world and in four languages scolded, cheered, coaxed, and gestured in an effort to make students "learn to see." This ability to see is so vital to the young painter that the entire school was built upon this premise. Such perception is no less vital to the designer.

Variety in Texture

The exploration of texture is one of the major adventures in the artist's study of nature. Texture has two dimensions: *tactile* quality and *visual* quality. The tactile quality can be felt and appreciated with the fingers, like the ridges of an old log or the soft fur of a kitten. Visual texture can make one *feel* its quality without actually being in contact with the fingers. In Figure 7, for instance, one senses the hardness and roughness of the stones, a roughness of granite particles, sand, and ridges; yet if one could actually touch the stones, he would find that most of them felt very much alike because they have been worn smooth by centuries of washing in mountain streams. In design the tactile quality often comes from the nature of the material used, such as the roughness of a stoneware jar or the nubbiness of a tweed fabric, and the good designer takes his textural effects from the material itself.

Glance again at Figures 14 through 19, and explore their textural qualities. We spoke of the variation in size and shape of leaves in the Japanese garden. Large leaves make for rougher textural patterns, even though the leaves themselves may be smooth in surface and contour, whereas delicate fern fronds give the fine texture of lace. The field of daisies actually has three textural patterns: one comes from the knobby centers of flowers; another is created by the softly curving petals silhouetted against the dark grass; and finally, the textural quality of the grass and the plants makes a linear pattern of stalks and blades that gives us an instinctive feeling of combined prickle and smoothness. Great variation in texture can be found in the tissues of the guinea pig and in the black stem wheat rust, for in these, as in the Japanese garden, variety of size and shape contributes ultimately to perceptible differentiation in texture.

Weathering is the great creator of texture in nature (Fig. 20). Sometimes, as in the case of stones, old stumps, or metal, visual textures created by the elements

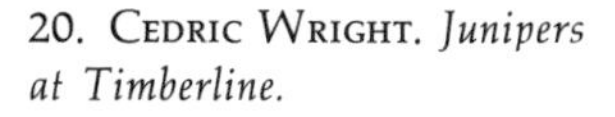

20. Cedric Wright. *Junipers at Timberline.*

remain after tactile textures have disappeared under the polishing action of wind, rain, sun, and snow. Leaves attacked by insects develop fascinating patterns as their cells disintegrate (Fig. 21); and even mineral deposits acquire texture from weathering, which can cause areas to flake off and roughen.

Look about you for other textures. The pattern on the tough skin of a pineapple, on the shell of a turtle, in the tuft of a dandelion (Fig. 22) or on milkweed pods, in a patch of cattails growing at a marshy roadside—these are but a sampling of the immensity of texture in nature.

BALANCE

When variety in nature is studied perceptively, a further discovery is made. Variations in size and shape, in color, and in texture provide esthetic balance to the natural environment. Visually, the blue sky is not an isolated area. Its color is repeated in the forget-me-not and the gentian, the pansy and the delphinium, as well as in the wings of a butterfly and the feathers of a bluebird. Somehow, one finds it difficult to imagine vast areas of red to correspond to the great areas of blue and green in nature. Because red is a brilliant and exciting hue and because man has become adjusted to the predominance of cool restful colors, such an environment would undoubtedly have violent effects on its inhabitants. Certainly, large bright areas would not be appreciated in the way that one now enjoys the sudden flash of a red bird or the brief glory of red leaves in autumn. This presence of bright color as an accent in the stretches of green field, forest, and blue sky is nature's way of counteracting great cool areas with small bits of exciting color. This is *balance.*

left: 21. Wolf Strache. *Feeding Pattern of a Caterpillar.* 1956.

right: 22. The seed carriers of a dandelion form a fascinating radial design that changes with each gust of wind.

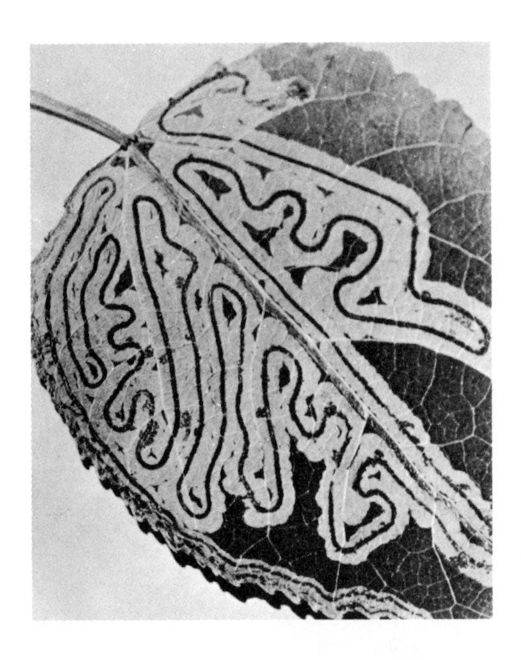

23. Wolf Strache. *Bark on the Trunk of a Plane.* 1956.

The rough bark of a tree (Fig. 23) is balanced by the smoothness of its leaves. Furthermore, one might note that the smaller flowers frequently have the greatest fragrance, whereas the showy blossoms of the tropics may have no noticeable scent. This, again, is another manifestation of nature's balance. In the animal kingdom, the porcupine has his protective quills, and the skunk his offensive odor, and tiny insects have a potent sting to compensate for their lack of size and ferocity. This is nature's balance of power.

In human life, balance is indispensable. For every intake of breath, one must exhale; and days of activity must be balanced by nights of rest. When the natural balance of our lives is disrupted, complications often ensue. Disease is an upset of natural balance, either by germs or virus or by the action of environment on our chemical makeup. Frequently, people are said to be mentally or emotionally "unbalanced," and recent research indicates that mental and emotional illness may indeed be upsets in body chemistry and that natural balance may be restored by proper medication. This is one of the great hopes for the future. Emotionally, also, there is a kind of pendulum action in the effort to achieve a state of balance. One does not experience serenity without knowing anxiety, and it is only after being involved in conflict that one appreciates the true meaning of peace.

FORM

The world around us is composed of forms, each with individual characteristics. When approached at close range, trees that had been flatly silhouetted against the horizon become three-dimensional *forms* that can be walked around and viewed

24. Edward Weston. *Grasses Against the Sea.* 1937.

from all sides. The contour of the land is a flattened shape at sunset when lighted from behind, but as one moves across it, he finds himself surrounded by hills and hollows—in other words, by forms. Even a blade of grass (Fig. 24) has form when it is handled or blown through to make a sound. Nature embodies all her animal life in form, from man to the so-called "shapeless" jellyfish. The round pebble that can be held in the hand and the mountain that requires days to climb are both natural forms. Form is involved with mass or volume, but it goes further. Mass or volume is delimited by *shape* and is contained by *size,* thereby becoming the form of an object. To understand the meaning of the word "form," imagine that the world is a stage set with all the scenery made of flats and the people and animals cut from cardboard. This would be a world of shapes and sizes, of *flattened* forms. However, as soon as these flats are rounded out into real trees, rocks, and buildings and the cardboard people into many-sided entities, depth and movement are achieved, as well as the capacity to view objects from all angles. Thus is attained true form, the identifying quality that makes objects distinguishable from their background, from the space around them, and from each other.

UNITY

Throughout this discussion of rhythm, variety, balance, and form, one fact has become increasingly clear. Nature, in all its parts, demonstrates a certain fundamental similarity. The life rhythms occur in weather, in the seasons, and in man—and all are interrelated. The rotation of electrons around a nucleus is not unlike the ordered movement in which infinite galaxies orbit through the universe, extending more than two billion light years from the earth in all directions. Variety is characteristic of nature in all its manifestations, whether it be in the hide of a hippopotamus or in the microscopic tissues of a guinea pig. The textured pebble, which one thinks of as inanimate, is actually a manifestation of centuries of living, in which it has been variously water, vegetation, and stone and then has become in part vegetation and waterborne sediment again as its roughness is washed away into the soil. This cycle of creation and disintegration illustrates the great basic fact of nature, the characteristic overall relationship of elements identified as *unity*, or harmony.

As physics and the other physical and biological sciences point more and more toward the oneness of the universe, one realizes that this is what philosophers have been trying to convey for centuries. The seventeenth-century philosopher Spinoza maintained that all reality is one substance, one in cause and one in origin, and that God and this reality are one. By substance, however, he did not mean the material content of nature such as hills and forests but an active and vital process involved, among other things, in the creation of this content. This is the eternal order, as opposed to the temporal order of things that exist in time and finally die; it points to the very structure of existence, underlying all events and things and comprising the essence of the world itself.

Two hundred years later, Arthur Schopenhauer pursued a similar train of thought in saying that only in time and space do we become separate beings, that space and time are the illusion hiding the essential unity of things. In his masterpiece, *The World as Will and Idea* (1819), he states:

> To understand clearly that the individual is only the phenomenon, not the thing-in-itself,[to see in] the constant change of matter the fixed permanence of form—this is the essence of philosophy.[5] . . . The true philosophy of history lies in perceiving that, in all the endless changes and motley complexity of events, it is only the self-same unchangeable being that is before us, which today pursues the same ends as it did yesterday and ever will. The historical philosopher has accordingly to recognize the identical character in all events . . . and in spite of all the variety of special circumstances, of costumes and manners and customs, has to see everywhere the same humanity. . . .[6]

These are comparatively modern restatements of a basic belief relating to one of the world's oldest religions, Hinduism. The Vedas, sacred Hindu writings dating back four thousand years, are believed to be the teachings of Brahma, who represents the totality of all creation; and stress is laid upon the underlying unity of all life and the presence in the universe of one great spirit called Atman, in whom all existence is a part.

THE CREATIVE ARTIST

The four principles found in nature and their resulting unity can be valuable guides to the creative artist as he strives to improve or to interpret what he finds. George Santayana says in *Reason in Religion:*

> He who lives in the ideal and leaves it expressed in society or in art enjoys a double immortality. The eternal has absorbed him while he lives, and when he is dead his influence brings others to the same adsorption, making them, through that ideal identity which is best in him, reincarnations and perennial seats of all in him which he could rationally hope to rescue from destruction.[7]

In Chapter 4 we shall explore ways in which artists have pursued that ideal by following the directions found in nature. First, however, we shall look into the ingredients or elements with which the artist works.

SUMMARY

In studying design in nature, we find four basic principles:

1. *Rhythm* The rhythm found in nature is usually based on cycles of the seasons or of day and night. In man there are other cycles, such as the brief cycle of the heartbeat or of breathing and various monthly cycles. Man's cycles are given graphic form by such devices as the electrocardiograph and the electroencephalograph machines.
2. *Variety* Variety is actually a concomitant of rhythm, for contrasts of rhythm make for the variety of day and night, winter and summer, height and depth. In nature variety takes many forms: size and shape, color, and texture. Texture, particularly, is one of the most varied elements to be found in nature and often results from the weathering process.
3. *Balance* Variety in nature leads to the principle of balance, for the large and the small, the bright and the dark, and so on, are intended to balance each other. In human life, balance is indispensible, for imbalance leads to illness, either physical or emotional.
4. *Form* The world is composed of diverse forms. Form is involved with mass and volume but goes beyond these, to become the quality of an object that distinguishes it from all other objects.

The four principles of design result in unity, the overall relationship sometimes called harmony. The study of science leads to an appreciation of the unity of matter, and an acquaintance with the great philosophers of various eras brings awareness of the unity of all things and of life. This unity comprises the essence of the universe. An appreciation of this essence and of the four principles which compose it can be a valuable guide to the creative artist seeking the ideal means of contributing to the field of design.

Man and Design

II

Basic Ingredients

chapter 3

In acknowledging the magnitude of design possibilities around him, man can assume that his environment is the result of definite methods on the part of nature. Such elements as color, texture, size, shape, and mass are combined through the principles of rhythm, variety, balance, and form into a unified whole in which he lives and finds his inspiration for work. Attractive as his natural surroundings may be, however, man feels the need to reflect their beauty in a more immediate way—in other words, to enhance his man-made environment by design and ornamentation. In the next two chapters we shall explore man's application of the elements and principles of design in his own creations.

MAN AND DESIGN

Man's earliest relics show signs of his creative need in the form of simple designs carved on the handles of tools and weapons. Other early manifestations are paintings on the walls of caves, such as those found in the Cantabrian terrain at Altamira, Spain (Fig. 25), and Lascaux, France. These paintings have been interpreted in many

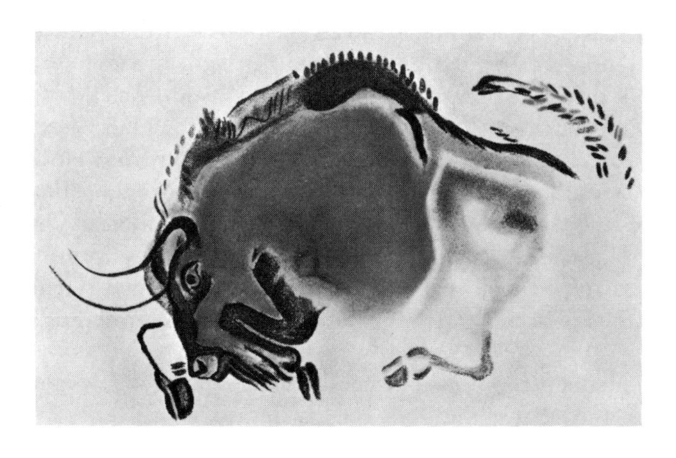

25. *Curled-round Bison,* cave painting from Altamira, Spain. c. 15,000–10,000 B.C.

ways: as superstitious talismen intended to ensure success in the hunt, as records of animals previously encountered, or as a kind of symbolic conquest of the animal needed for sustenance by capturing him in earth pigments and charcoal on the walls of the cave. Regardless of the motivation, the esthetic quality of the work is undeniable. The flowing line, the rich color, and the feeling for design that capture the spirit of the animal continue to awaken admiration in artists of each succeeding generation.

As man's shelter became more than a cave, his attempts to improve its design became increasingly ambitious. He discovered two ways of making his immediate environment attractive. First, he could use natural elements. He could plant trees and flowers, dam streams, and make clearings in the wilderness; he could use natural materials to build his shelter, combining wood and stone in their original state, merely shaping them to form the beams and corners needed. Second, he could produce new shapes and materials with his own hands, creating designs based on natural forms but indigenous to his own taste and creative ability. In this way, through the centuries he has produced all the textiles, tapestries, ceramics, glass, metalwork, painting, and sculpture with which he has enriched his surroundings.

The immediate problem for the creative artist is how to make his own contribution. It has been shown how nature creates an environment, but how does the human artist begin? He does not have time for a gradual development of his designs through evolution. He needs means of creating something which will be immediately effective and which will retain its original effectiveness throughout the duration of its usefulness or conservation. Using nature as his guide, he still needs to discover ingredients he can use in his own way. Some of these have counterparts in nature; one, however, does not—the element of *line.*

26. The meticulous brushwork of Chinese calligraphy is a particularly effective use of line. The characters illustrated here mean "face" (*above*) and "new wine" (*below*). Calligraphy by Helen Chiang.

LINE

In creative design, as in drawing, *line* is the artist's first ally. This is a man-made tool. What one thinks of as line in nature becomes on closer observation a joining of two surfaces, a dark form against a lighter one, a round vein in a leaf through which nutrients flow, a spider web that has a cross section under a microscope. Yet man uses line in his depiction of all these.

Man's very invention of line was to fill an urgent need, and it has a dynamic quality relating it to all his forms of expression. His buildings and machines take form on the drafting board through an elaborate scheme of accurately drawn lines, and his works of art originate in free and rhythmic strokes into which he pours his creative energies at the moment of conception. In all civilizations his communication has been a form of *calligraphy,* or handwriting, created through line (Fig. 26). Like a jet stream, line describes the wake of movement, of a hand wielding a guiding point that is a pen or brush or pencil. In his book *Vision in Motion* (1947), László Moholy-Nagy states that every drawing can be understood as a motion study since it is a path of motion recorded by graphic means.[1] Lines guide the eye by delineating shapes, for it is by the use of line that one encloses space and thus establishes the beginning of design (Fig. 27). Line may vary from thick to thin to convey form or shadow, thus showing what is referred to as the *quality* of line (Fig. 28). It is one of the most eloquent expressions of man's intent, guided to its destination through rhythmic movement.

If deprived of all other elements except line, one could still create a good design. Line itself can be the *motif,* or unit, that is the basis for the design, as in Figure 29.

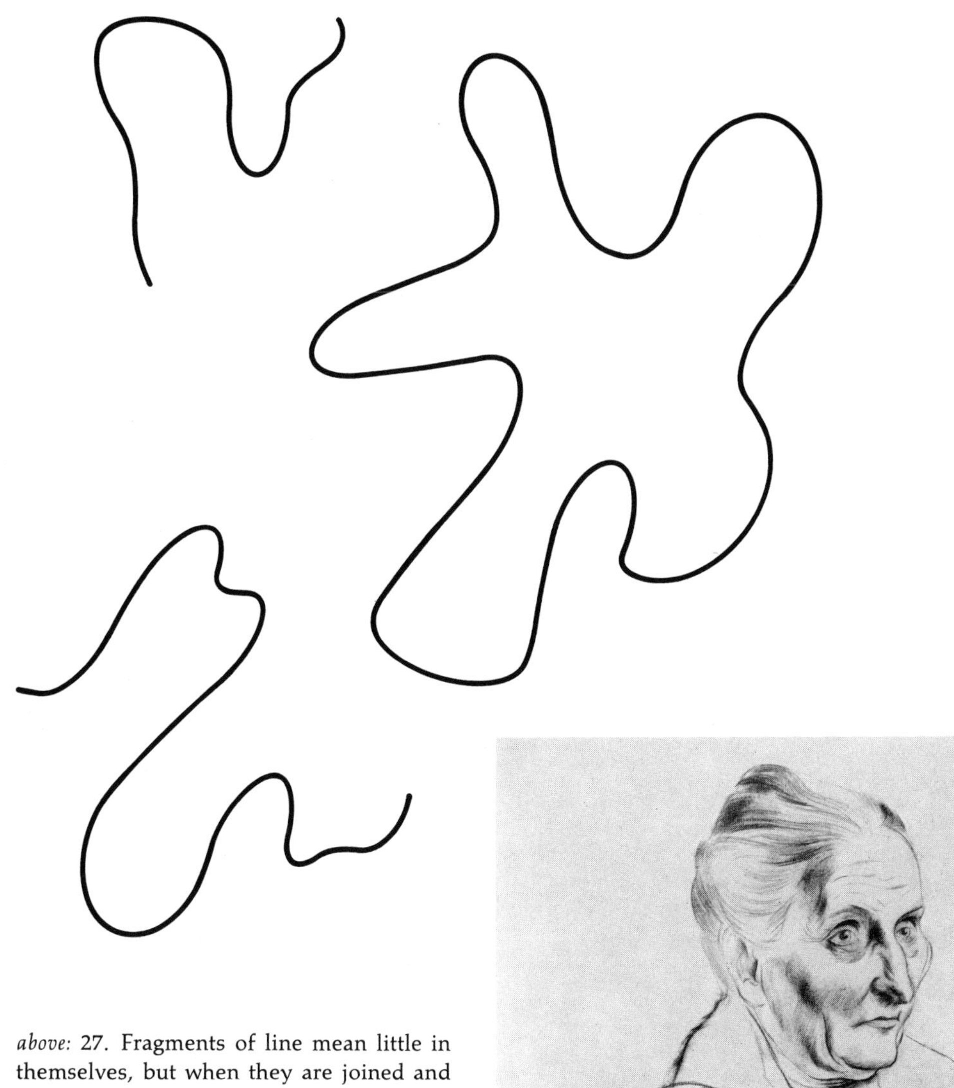

above: 27. Fragments of line mean little in themselves, but when they are joined and continued they create forms that are the beginning of design.

right: 28. GEORGE GROSZ. *Portrait of Anna Peter.* 1926–27. Pencil, $26\frac{5}{8} \times 21''$. Museum of Modern Art, New York (gift of Paul J. Sachs).

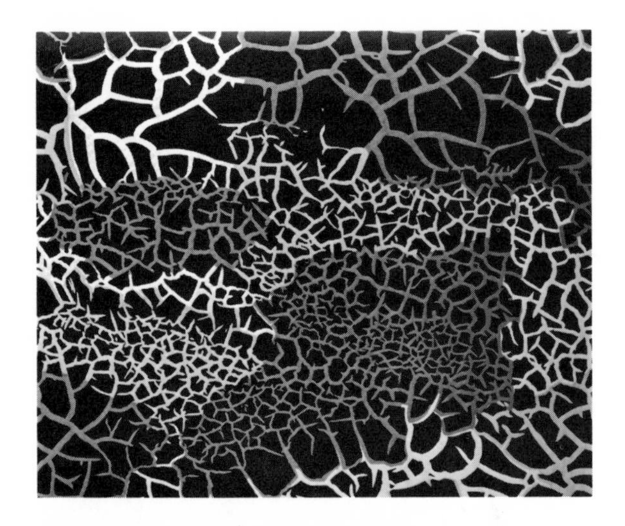

above left: 29. A design can consist entirely of lines, as in JACK LENOR LARSEN'S *Labyrinth* (1967), created for Caprolan stretch fabric.

left: 30. FRANÇOIS MORELLET. *Screen Painting: 0°, 22°5, 45°, 67°5.* 1958. Oil on canvas, 55⅛" square. Courtesy Galerie Denise René, Paris.

above: 31. GIORGIO MORANDI. *Oval Still Life.* 1945. Etching, 10½ × 11¾". Museum of Modern Art, New York (gift of James Thrall Soby).

Line can be used to simulate texture (Fig. 30) or tonal value (Fig. 31). Size and shape are the result of line enclosing space, and form can be created by carrying line a step further, into a three-dimensional treatment (Fig. 32).

Lines can also express the design principles found in nature. Lines express motion, leading to rhythm. The motion may be slow and flowing like a river, or short and frenzied like the brush strokes of Van Gogh (Fig. 33). Variety can be achieved with line: long lines, short lines, thick lines, thin lines, wavy or jagged lines, smooth straight lines. Balance can be achieved by the grouping of lines in certain ways. Line also can be used to achieve unity. Lines flowing in the same direction or moving in corresponding rhythm can be the unifying force that makes a composition a good design.

Lines assume expressive power and meaning through association with natural forms. Like a still lake or the far horizon, horizontal lines are considered to be generally restful. Trees and mountains reach up to pierce the sky, so that vertical lines are thought of as reaching and aspiring in effect and are used in buildings to create a feeling of awe or inspiration. Diagonal lines, on the other hand, call to mind lightning, falling timber, or sagging buildings in the process of decay (Fig. 34), and, therefore, these associations cause the slanting lines to be interpreted as suggestive of chaos.

Line, in the context of this discussion, has been treated as a specific element, drawn with a man-made tool. However, there is another connotation in which line does have existence in nature. In describing any artistic work, the word "line" is often used in a larger sense to express the feeling of the work, with an implication

below: 32. Josef Albers. *Structural Constellation: JHC II.* 1963. Engraving on plastic, 19¼ × 25⅞". Collection Mr. and Mrs. James H. Clark, Dallas.

right: 33. Vincent van Gogh. *Grove of Cypresses.* 1889. Pen and ink over pencil, 24⅝ × 18¼". Art Institute of Chicago.

left: 34. Ghost town in Colorado. The diagonal lines created by the sagging buildings intensify the feeling of decay.

of rhythm, unity, and balance. One may speak of the lines of a building, the flowing lines of a dress, and the interesting line of a painting or statue, just as one refers to the rolling horizon line or the rugged shoreline or the curved line of hills. This is a way of stating the overall feeling conveyed by a work of art or a scene, of describing its essence. It is the swirling, vertically rising lines of El Greco's *Resurrection* that give it its highly emotional quality (Pl. 1, p. 39). The balanced diagonals of bent arms, banner, swords, and extended legs form a counterpoint that effectively adds to the drama. The result is a feeling of great religious fervor, engendered by the fundamental structure based on line. This is line in its fullest sense, relating to the basic quality of any work of art.

TEXTURE

Texture provides man with a means of exploring his environment through his sense of touch. The variations in a surface can give a sensual pleasure as we run our fingers over them, and even when the texture is purely visual and we *feel* nothing, our eyes transmit a sense of variation to the brain and there is a sensory response.

Surroundings devoid of texture would deprive us of an important area of experience. When plastics first began to prove their versatility, a vast smoothness came into interior design, characterized by rooms with bare walls, concrete floors, and plastic and chromium furniture curved to fit the body. Simplified upkeep was extolled, for such rooms could be hosed down instead of vacuumed. Twenty years later, however, the sterility of such bareness brought a return to warmth and comfort, furthered by areas of rough-hewn fieldstone or used brick, planters filled with the textures of growing plants, wood paneling, and deep-pile carpets. It is as if some atavistic need draws us to the rough bark and thick foliage of the forest—something that makes us feel most at ease amid the natural textures with which early life developed (Fig. 35).

Perhaps the importance of texture lies in its relationship to variety. The variations of light and dark create visual texture, and changes in plane produce tactile textures. It is variety that we *feel* in an interesting surface. It is texture that makes us enjoy music as well—texture produced by the variation of sustained tones and staccato notes, flowing rhythms or sharp beats. Texture in literature results from characterization, figures of speech, conversation, and description, as well as from the use of certain words and their placement. Dance has texture depending upon the fluidity or violence of movement.

In the hands of the designer, as in nature, texture has two faces. *Visual* texture can be produced in many ways. A textured glaze can be achieved on pottery by use of a formula in which flecks of a substance hang in suspension. Visual texture can be printed on a fabric, woven into a textile, or created on a page by use of type. *Tactile* texture comes from the choice of materials: porous clay, nubby fibers, wood in which the soft grain has been worn away, thereby leaving interesting ridges. Tactile quality can also come from special treatment of a given material, as in sandblasting, etching, the carving of wood, the stamping or embossing of metal, or the incising of a design on plaster or pottery. The Impressionists used the textural variety of paint to express their dominant interest in light and color, applying an *impasto,* or thick layers of oil pigment, to catch the light and create shadows that emphasized the idea of sunlight (Pl. 2, p. 40). Instead of mixing their pigments on the palette, these artists relied upon the eye of the observer to mix the strokes of oil paint into the desired colors and forms. Consequently their painting is a study in texture, and since the forms are built up from the thickly applied pigment, the texture is an organic part of the painting.

Organic texture of amazing variety is seen in a Gothic cathedral (Fig. 36). Stained glass, niches, stone mullions in the windows, and sculpture in myriad forms all become a part of the surface richness that is one of the characteristics placing medieval religious architecture among the wonders of all time.

opposite: 35. The use of natural materials—wood and stone—in a modern house softens the effect of machine-made glass, metal, and vinyl, and provides a comfortable environment.

right: 36. West façade (detail), Amiens Cathedral. 1220–88 (façade 1225–36).

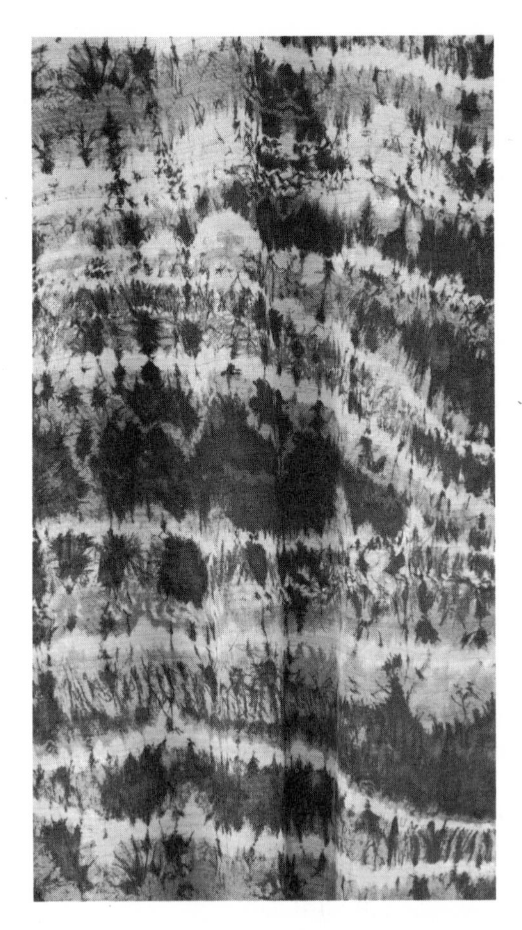

left: 37. A rich visual texture is printed on the smooth surface of *Nami* (1967), a silk screen fabric by Boris Kroll.

below: 38. Nik Krevitsky. *Mesa.* 1964. Felt appliqué and mixed threads on burlap, 26 × 34″. Collection Amphitheatre High School, Tucson, Ariz.

Two fascinating textures, one visual and one tactile, can be seen in the textiles in Figures 37 and 38. In Figure 37 is revealed a richly varied pattern that is printed on the material, purely visual yet exciting enough to provide a sensory reaction for the viewer. The textures in Figure 38, on the other hand, are just as eloquently tactile. Pieces of felt are appliquéd, or sewn on, in a pattern that is basically geometric, then enriched with an intriguing array of stitchery in mixed threads. Looking at the wealth of raised pattern arouses an urge to run the fingers over the surface in order to sense the design even more fully.

COLOR

It is possible to have a good design without using *color.* The title pages of books and magazines seldom use color, yet considerable artistry is involved in their effective layout. There are many striking allover prints in black and white on fabric. The use of color in design is not necessary, but it plays an important role in our psychological reaction. A design that is interesting in black and white becomes an exciting composition when done in warm bright colors. The same design becomes soothing and restful when executed in soft tones. People react differently in different color settings; this is why the psychology of color has become increasingly important in interior design. Soft colors are used in doctors' and dentists' offices to calm the nerves, and warm stimulating tones are painted on the walls of restaurants, where it is hoped that diners will enjoy their food and eat heartily.

Color is the most flexible of all elements used in design and can change the entire character of a design. It is never absolute but varies continually through its juxtaposition with other colors. Moreover, color does not exist without light. A closet full of bright-colored clothes is without color when the door is closed and the light turned off. Consequently, variations in light cause color to modify constantly and assume endless variations.

Because of the importance of color in everyday living, artificial restrictions about its use have made people afraid to combine colors without definite rules to follow. A careful study of color in nature should free anyone from such arbitrary limitations and open up a new and exciting world. A person who doubts that pink and orange can be used together has only to look at a field of poppies. Blue and green were once considered a daring combination in dress; yet bluebells and delphinium are surrounded by green leaves. The discovery of so-called "psychedelic colors" liberated most people from timidity where color is concerned, although it is doubtful if many would want to live for long periods in such highly stimulating surroundings as those produced by flashing lights and walls covered with psychedelic paintings. In using color for livable purposes, it is safer to follow nature, with large areas of cool or restful colors accented by occasional spots of brilliance.

Color is a broad and exciting subject, which has been explored from many angles. Most artists have an intensely personal feeling about it and express this feeling in their work in ways as individual as handwriting. To emphasize its importance to the designer, color will be discussed more fully later in a separate chapter.

SIZE

The relationship of parts within a design is dependent upon *size.* Scale is another term, implying a similarity between the sizes of various parts which leads to proportion, the principle of relationships between sizes. Designers are guided by the

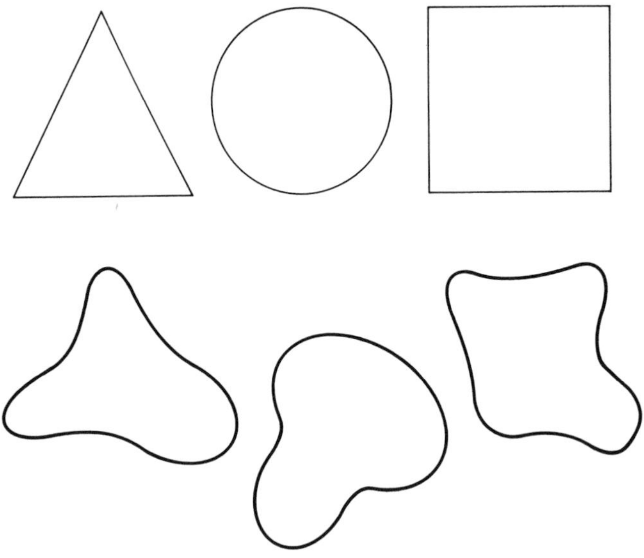

39. The precise forms of triangle, circle, and square can be relaxed to create nonobjective shapes.

"Modular," a set of ideal proportional ratios originally promoted by the French architect and designer Le Corbusier and since called *modular units.* These are dimensions and ratios based upon the human body and its parts, and by the use of their multiples a designer can create a building, a park, or a city based on fundamental human proportions. A modular unit will help the designer to make his chairs or door openings in correct relation to the human form. Since man's interpretation of environment is keyed to human perception and consciousness of his own size, the use of modular units in design can result in a unity between man and his surroundings. Modular units can also be a matter of shape, forming recurrent basic units such as are combined in erecting a wall of cast building blocks. Such modular units are seen in a honeycomb, in biological tissues, or in geological structure.

Similarity, however, is not always the most striking solution to a design, either in shape or in size. As with a clash of color, exaggerated size may be used for emphasis and impact. In *Black Cross* (Pl. 3, p. 41), Georgia O'Keeffe has expanded a section of a cross into a monumental form, dwarfing the rolling dunes of the country around it. To the people of New Mexico, where this painting was created, this is a symbolic dramatization, for large wooden crosses are associated with the Penitentes, a fanatical religious group that flourished in New Mexico until the 1930s. Characterized by vigils and acts of self-flagellation, the rites of the Penitentes reached their climax on Good Friday, when the events of the Crucifixion were reenacted. Whenever a black or blue cross appeared in a stretch of wild or lonely country, it usually meant the Penitentes were not far away and also frequently indicated the presence nearby of a *morada,* or Penitente church. In her dramatization O'Keeffe manages to impart a feeling of the ominous mystery associated with these people.

Size is always determined by the original area within which the designer starts to work. Although the use of modules will scale it to the human form, the size of a house will be prescribed in large part by the size of the lot, combined with the consideration of how much garden and open space the client wants around it. The size of elements in a fabric design will be affected by how the fabric is to be used and how much of it will be seen at one time. Larger elements will be used in a design for draperies than will be used in material for a small girl's dress. Sizes in a mural will be amplified in relation to those of the same elements in an easel painting. The eminent twentieth-century architect Eero Saarinen wrote: "Every object, small or large, has a relationship to its neighbors. . . . If the problem is an ashtray, then the way it relates to a table will influence its design. If the problem is a chair, then its solution must be found in the way it relates to the room cube. If it is a building, the townscape will affect the solution."[2] The designer may find color and rhythm more exciting, but none of the elements and principles of design is more basic than the problem of size.

SHAPE

The universe is composed of shapes of infinite variety, shapes that have meaning for man, often in a symbolic sense. Giving them connotations from his past experience, man learns to read shapes as we read handwriting.

Shape results from line or mass, line enclosing *space* or delineating the shape of a mass and the shape of the area around it. Whenever two masses overlap, a new shape is created. Man's use of shape has four sources.

Natural Shapes Although direct imitation of natural shapes is seldom effective, nature offers endless possibilities for whimsy, for formal stylization that eliminates extraneous detail, and for imaginative distortion of shapes into original designs.

Abstract Shapes Shapes can be abstractions, that is, familiar objects simplified or distorted to enhance their design qualities. In an abstraction the point of departure, although radically changed, is still recognizable. The essence of the original object remains the basis for the design evolved from it.

Nonobjective Shapes The difference between abstractions and nonobjective shapes is that nonobjective shapes rarely resemble any recognizable object. Even such geometric shapes as a triangle, a circle, or a square, under certain circumstances can become nonobjective (Fig. 39). Although nonobjective shapes do not resemble *objects,* they are often found in nature, for instance, on the surface of water (Fig. 40),

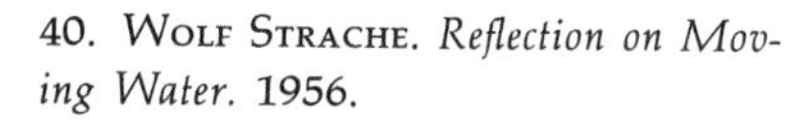

40. Wolf Strache. *Reflection on Moving Water.* 1956.

41. Ben Nicholson. *Relief.* 1939. Synthetic material, painted, $32\frac{7}{8} \times 45''$. Museum of Modern Art, New York (gift of H. S. Ede and the artist).

the bark of a tree, or in weathered textures. Such shapes are called *biomorphic,* a term that is of Greek derivation, meaning "with a form based on life." Thus it becomes evident that categories are seldom final. A shape can be both *nonobjective* and *natural* in the strictest sense, for a nonobjective shape could very well be the shape of a rock or of a cloud. In fact, nonobjective shapes are seen to have a close relationship to nature, since they are usually fluid organic shapes that express growth and flexibility.

Geometric shapes If nonobjective shapes show an affinity to nature, geometric shapes express the man-made environment. Geometric angles and curves are found in buildings, bridges, automobiles, and machines. A relief composition created entirely from pure geometric shapes is seen in Figure 41. Although most of the shapes in this work are square or rectangular, no two are exactly alike. Even the two circles, used for variety and balance, differ in size. Combining similar shapes effectively can present more of a challenge than working with varied ones, for if any two areas are identical, a composition may become monotonous. In the rug designs by Dorothy

Plate 1. El Greco. *The Resurrection of Christ.* 1600–05. Oil on canvas, 9′$1/4$″ × 4′5″. Prado, Madrid.

Plate 2. Claude Monet. *Le Basin d'Argenteuil.* c. 1875. Oil on canvas, $21\frac{3}{4} \times 29\frac{1}{4}''$. Museum of Art, Rhode Island School of Design, Providence.

Plate 3. GEORGIA O'KEEFFE. *Black Cross, New Mexico.* 1929. Oil on canvas, $39 \times 30\frac{1}{16}$″. Art Institute of Chicago.

Plate 4. DOROTHY LIEBES. *Fiesta.* 1961. Area rug designed for Bigelow-Sanford, Inc.

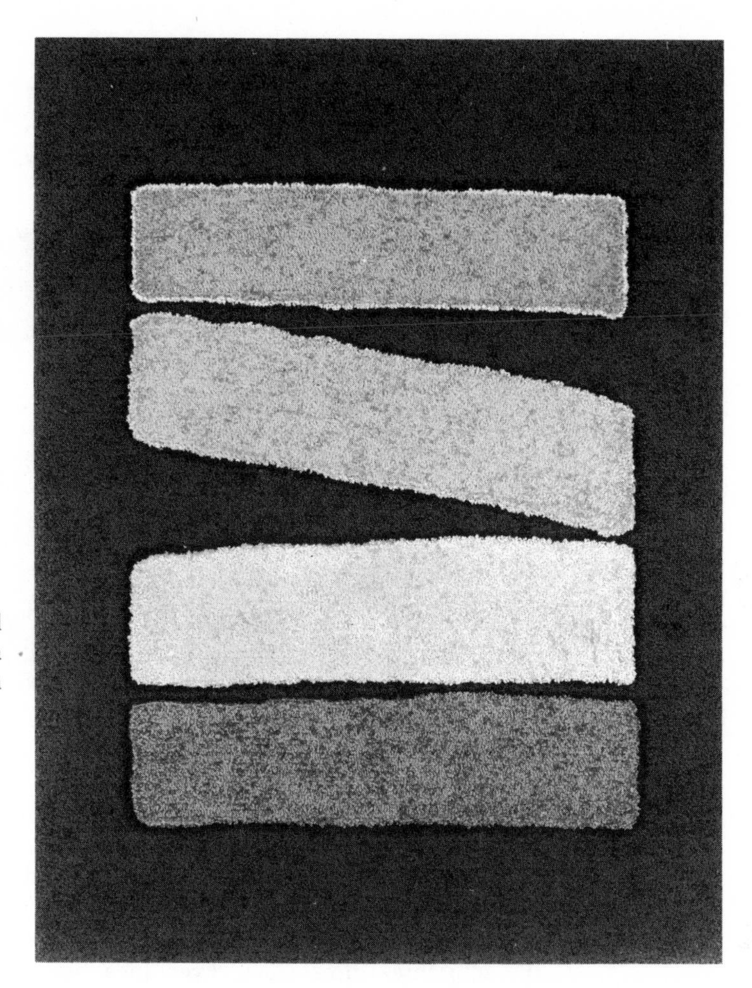

42. *Futural* (1960), an area rug created by Dorothy Liebes for Bigelow, is an example of contemporary design based on geometric forms.

Liebes (Pl. 4, opposite; Fig. 42), identical repeated shapes are used, but variation in other elements creates interest. In Plate 4 the colors and values are varied, and the circles are divided into varying segments. Notice that there is no regular formula for the variations, that similar circles are not placed in any definable relationship. In Figure 42 the design consists simply of four elongated rectangles, but the tilting of one creates an intriguing diagonal. Here again, the colors of each area are different, and the feeling of variation is thereby enhanced.

MASS

One cannot discuss shape without becoming involved in its three-dimensional counterpart, *mass.* The earth is a mass, and much of our environment is concerned with mass, matter that has weight and solidity. The human body is a mass that resists the force of gravity, and consciousness of this fact causes one to interpret other masses according to his experience. Whenever a shape acquires a third dimension, it becomes a mass that is perceived as something to be lifted, pushed, or walked around; yet there are also fluid masses, which change shape constantly, such as clouds or ocean waves. A waterfall is a mass that to the observer seems to have a constant shape yet which changes from second to second in actual content.

43. HENRY MOORE. *Two Forms.* 1934. Pynkado wood, 11″ high. Museum of Modern Art, New York (gift of Sir Michael Sadler).

In the arts, the emphasis on mass varies with the medium, or the material with which the artist works. Mass is one of the most important elements in sculpture (Fig. 43) and is a major attribute of pottery, architecture, interior design, and many objects in wood and metal. In painting it is indicated only by symbols, except in the case of experimental forms of painting that approach sculpture and extend physically into three dimensions. Even in a two-dimensional painting, however, the symbolic representation of mass is important. The viewer wishes to feel that the objects depicted do exist in space and could be seen from the opposite side if he were to walk around them. Even in discussing nonobjective paintings, one speaks of the interesting masses and the feeling of solidity in certain areas. At any given moment mass may have form, size, weight, shape, and/or volume; yet the concept of mass is more flexible than any of these, being the total substance which is given these attributes through the design of the artist.

Mass in *motion* can be a continuum, as in a river or a waterfall, or it can be an explosive movement, as in a meteor or the sudden eruption of flame. The Italian Futurists were interested in depicting motion through multiple images, in which the same form was shown in a superimposed sequence of different positions to indicate a physical progression. Radiating lines and flowing lines are also used to depict a sense of motion. Multiple-exposure images of a moving mass photographed successively at short intervals create fascinating designs as well as define the overall pattern in which the mass is moving. Various instruments are used in this kind of photography: notably the stroboscope, which shows successive images, and the oscillograph, which records distinct movements in a continuous pattern giving an illusion of motion.

These, then, are the ingredients that the designer has at his disposal. Just as the scientist does not use all the materials in the laboratory in mixing every chemical compound, so it is not necessary that the artist invariably use *all* the elements of design. He must be able to understand the possibilities of line, texture, color, size, shape, and mass and to decide which will be important in each of his works. These are his tools, and he can choose among them to suit his particular goals. Acquiring the knowledge to choose wisely is a fundamental part of the process of becoming a designer.

SUMMARY

The fact that man needed to create from earliest times is evident in the carvings on early tools and weapons, as well as in the cave paintings of northern Spain and southern France. As his living conditions became more complex, he found two ways of making his environment attractive: (1) by using natural elements and (2) by producing new shapes and materials with his own hands.

The artist today finds in nature all the elements that he needs for his work, except for line, which is a basic instrument of communication.

1. *Line* A man-made tool, line is a dynamic expression of man's thoughts and dreams. Line can also mean the essence of an object, as when one speaks of the "lines" of a painting or a building.
2. *Texture* Texture is that physical aspect of environment related to the sense of touch. It may be visual texture, which gives a consciousness of texture without actually affecting the surface plane, or tactile, a texture that can actually be felt by the hands.
3. *Color* Although color is not essential to a good design, it is one of the most exciting elements, for it can convey flavor and emotion.
4. *Size* Size must be considered in any work of art, for it determines the area in which the designer can function. Scale is another term, implying a relative similarity in size among the various parts of a work.
5. *Shape* Shape follows from line and mass, with line enclosing space and mass being suggested through carefully disposed areas of light and dark. There are four kinds of shapes: (1) natural, (2) abstract, (3) nonobjective, and (4) geometric.
6. *Mass* The three-dimensional counterpart of shape or contour, mass is concerned with weight, solidity, and resistance to gravity. Some masses are fluid and change continually, however, as in clouds or water.

The Magic Touch

chapter 4

It has been shown that there are six basic ingredients or elements with which to work in creating a design: line, texture, color, size, shape, and mass. This does not mean that these are to be put into the category of *rules* for creating, for in art it is necessary to remain flexible, with only an outline of possibilities to guide conception. There have been artists who reduced their work to three basic considerations—line, form, and value—and considered anything further as confusing and extraneous. Others have listed as many as 13 basic elements of design, breaking mass into space and volume, and color into hue, value, and intensity. There is no conflict here, just a shift of emphasis. Some people prefer to catalogue information as minutely as possible, whereas others like to think and work simply and with large areas of understanding. The important characteristic of the artist is a creative flexibility, which allows him to work intuitively with elements and principles as his raw materials.

When one realizes that the entire world of design, in architecture, painting, sculpture, clothing, industrial and commercial design, and all their many ramifications, is based on these six ingredients, he can only marvel at the variety that is achieved.

SECRET OF CREATIVE DESIGN

If so much diversity can be created through the use of six or fewer simple elements, only one conclusion can be drawn: the determining factor in a design is not so much the elements used as the magic touch of the creative designer who uses them. In this touch lies the secret of exciting design.

One of the most important differences between art and science lies in the role of the artist. Although the scientist undoubtedly has feelings and emotions about his experiments, he works primarily with rules and formulas in such a manner that the same experiment can be performed in the same way by any number of people. The artist, however, is such a potent part of his work that even his own assistants or disciples will not achieve the same results as he would. There are many instances of paintings done in the workshops of the Old Masters in which experts can distinguish the work of the helpers from the touch of the master himself, even when the master had given direct instructions about how the work was to be handled. There is inspiration to be derived from working in a studio with other artists, in seeing the varying approaches and the diverse viewpoints toward a single subject or model. For instance, set up a still life and tell a class to paint it; no two finished paintings will be entirely alike. Even such a simple object as an orange will be depicted in diverse sizes and colors, depending upon the viewpoint of the observer. The type of composition selected and the emphasis placed on various elements can actually provide a key to the personality of the painter. This realization obliges the artist to develop his taste and knowledge to the fullest, for not only does he reflect the social and spiritual climate of his age but also he reveals what he is himself in the intangible quality of his art. His artistic skills express what he is: a person who has mastered a technique and who uses it not as an end in itself but to say something to the world.

PERSPECTIVE AND PERCEPTION

The artist's individual representation will depend primarily upon what he sees and how he perceives it. This is involved with physiological and psychological theories, as well as with the laws of physics and the opinions of philosophers and critics. Without making a thorough study of the subject, however, it is possible to understand several important aspects. First, what we see depends upon the presence of light all about us, filling the air and being reflected and diffused by the surfaces that we see. Light changes from moment to moment throughout the day, and from point to point as the observer moves. This brings us to the matter of perspective. Most art students are familiar with linear perspective as it was formulated during the Renaissance (Fig. 44), in which the outlines of geometric forms are projected from one plane to another plane by use of a grid of lines intersecting at a vanishing point. Even in this type of perspective, of course, the entire set of lines changes

44. RAPHAEL. *School of Athens.* 1510–11. Fresco, c. 26 × 18′. Stanza della Segnatura, Vatican, Rome. Lines converging at a vanishing point create the illusion of three-dimensional space on a two-dimensional surface.

above: 45. EUPHRONIUS. *Herakles and Antaeus,* Attic red-figured vase. 5th century B.C. Louvre, Paris.

right: 46. LUDWIG WILDING. *Kinetic Structure 5/63.* 1963. Tempera on wood with plastic cord, $33\frac{7}{8} \times 26 \times 3\frac{1}{4}$″. Collection the artist.

every time the person representing the "eye level" changes position. This is the perspective of the architect and mathematician. However, there are other kinds of perspective involved in seeing. The philosophers and psychologists, for instance, speak of perspective based on color areas. Colors seem to grow cooler and grayer as they recede from the picture plane, brighter and warmer as they approach the observer. This is sometimes referred to as *atmospheric* (or *aerial*) perspective, since it is the action of the volume of air intervening between the observer and the object seen that causes the apparent modification in color. The atmosphere causes a similar diminishing of the sharpness of contours, therefore making objects at a distance softer in outline and less detailed. Textures grow blurred and less distinguishable with increasing distance and finally become nonexistent to the human eye, and shapes become more ambiguous. Long before mechanical perspective was formulated, the Greeks gave the effect of distance and change in plane to their relief sculpture and paintings by superimposing nearer figures over the far ones and by making the more distant ones smaller (Fig. 45).

Children and primitive peoples have their own approaches to perspective, such as arranging figures vertically to denote differences in plane, with the highest on the page usually intended to be farthest from the viewer. The flat patterns of Oriental art are not concerned with the third dimension and have influenced many artists to realize that design quality is often more important than a sense of depth.

Not all perspective is concerned with distance. Objects seen from above are quite different from the same objects as seen from eye level or below, such change arising not from distance but from orientation, that is, viewpoint.

Perception is a selective process, dependent upon the viewer, for it consists of visually gathering knowledge about the world through attention to something that he considers important and of interpreting its meaning. The painting in Figure 46 is the result of the "perceptual images" of Ludwig Wilding, who has based his work on the patterns perceived in *moiré,* the French word for watered silk, which consists of two layers of finely ribbed silk laid face to face with one set of lines embossed in a slightly off-parallel relationship. *Moiré* patterns occur in many places: through overlapped screens or the folds of thin window curtains or wherever two fine grid patterns overlap. Both artists and scientists are fascinated by the perceptual illusions that result and by possible explanations of them.

It is important to realize that perceptual images are not always a matter of the eye alone. There is a perceptual intelligence, which varies in different individuals; and there are also influences from memory and past experiences unremembered, which affect what we see when we look at things. Optical illusions result from the discrepancy between what the eye sees and preconceived ideas in the mind of the observer. *Figure-ground perception* is a primal capacity to distinguish between an object and its background—between the picture on the wall and the wall on which it hangs, between printed words and the page on which they appear. Figure-ground relationships are an important consideration in any design and can be readily perceived by people with normal eyesight (Fig. 47). However, there is apt to be a difference between individuals in *visual acuity,* the ability to perceive fine differences in the details of the visual environment.

Nature attempts to diminish our visual acuity when she camouflages her creatures according to the principle of *disruptive coloration.* The success of this method relies not only upon optical principles but also upon a psychological factor. Patches of color are used in a way that catches the eye and draws the observer's attention away from the shape or form which bears them. The patterns themselves may be conspicuous, but since they contradict the form on which they are superimposed, they fasten attention on themselves and so masquerade as part of the general environment.

The person who has traveled about has seen the world from many viewpoints, and if he is perceptive he is able to sift his impressions to find those which are invariable, which reveal the world as a whole with all its parts related. It is the particular talent of the artist, however, that he often perceives the realities with very limited personal experience. Sometimes this involves probing more deeply into the minutiae of everyday life to perceive details that go unnoticed by the average person. The novelist Marcel Proust lived his entire life within a small radius in France, yet his analytical character studies based on painstaking perception of detail are revealing of mankind not only in Proust's own era and place but also in all times everywhere. To the visual artist, such perception could reveal the wholeness of life by making him aware of similarities in forms and patterns—for instance, the resemblance

47. In this example of figure-ground ambiguity, the viewer might perceive a white pedestal on a black ground or two black profiles on a white ground.

48. In closeup, the forms assumed by a broken automobile windshield suggest an abstract painting, the patterns of frost, or plant growth.

between plant forms, frost patterns, and the shattered windshield of an automobile (Fig. 48). A concise statement of the importance of perspective and perception to the artist is given by James J. Gibson, a psychologist: "The artist is a perceiver who pays special attention to the points of view from which the world can be seen, and one who catches and records for the rest of us the most revealing perspectives on things."[1]

NATURE POINTS THE WAY

Knowing that the ultimate result in a work of art depends upon the philosophy, personality, and mental and spiritual qualities of the artist, one can nevertheless look for some general guiding principles. Earlier, the six elements of design found in nature have been related to man's own efforts; it is logical, then, to turn to the principles discovered in Chapter 2 and see how these can guide the artist's activities toward effective design.

RHYTHM

In design as in nature, the underlying principle is rhythm. Unlike color or texture, rhythm cannot be added to a design (that is, decided upon later) but must be a part of the creative process from the very beginning. Some artists create to the accompaniment of music in the hope that the rhythmic sounds will be transmuted into the visible forms of their work. Others have a natural sense of rhythm that they express visually without conscious effort, much as rhythm is expressed physically by a dancer or in the gyrations of a jazz band. There are, however, some specific procedures for achieving rhythm.

A natural rhythmic cue is found in the heartbeat, with its *repetition* and *emphasis.* Simple visual rhythm can be created just as African natives achieve a simple rhythmic sound by repetition of one motif at regular intervals (Fig. 49). This might be compared to the human heartbeat under a condition of relaxed regular breathing. However, when anything of interest occurs, this regular pulsation varies perceptibly, changing to a pattern of a strong beat and a lesser one. When a strong element is introduced into the simple visual rhythm to accent the original motif, there is an immediate increase in interest. When a strong element is balanced with two lesser ones, the visual attraction increases even more (Fig. 50). Kay Sekimachi has created

above: 49. The simple rhythm of a drumbeat can be interpreted visually as a series of dots. Here the beats are all of equal intensity.

below: 50. A more complex rhythm is expressed in varying sizes of dots, with the larger dots representing the accented beats.

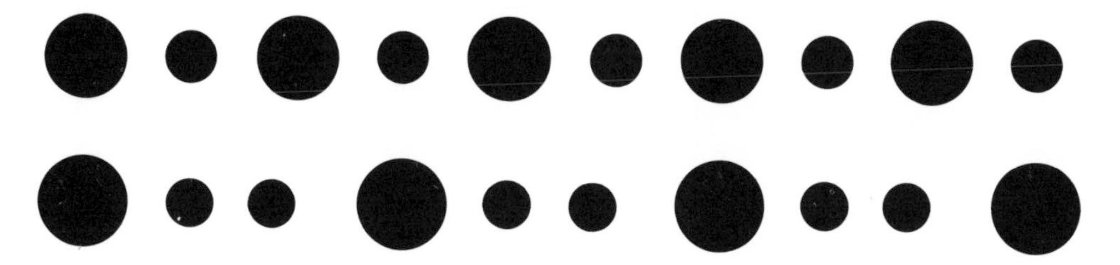

a textile into which she has woven just such a rhythm, varying not the size of the repeated motif but its value and texture (Fig. 51). One may notice the way in which she has omitted the motif entirely from some areas, thus giving a surprise to the rhythm much as one finds in modern music. In the screen in Figure 52, on the other hand, the rhythm derives from a change in the size of the basic motif—the square—and the interlocking small squares superimposed on the large square units. This type of rhythmic design presents a visual blend, a kind of graphic counterpoint.

It is possible to design in the same way as a dance is developed, by starting with a simple rhythm and then developing a sequence of repetition and emphasis until a degree of complexity is obtained. The emphasis gradually increases in importance until it reaches a *climax* toward which the whole composition is focused. The

below left: 51. KAY SEKIMACHI. *Square Variations.* c. 1962. Warp brocade tapestry, $19\frac{1}{2} \times 32''$. Collection the artist.

below right: 52. A Karvalum screen by Morris Kurtzon, Inc., illustrates a variation on the square motif.

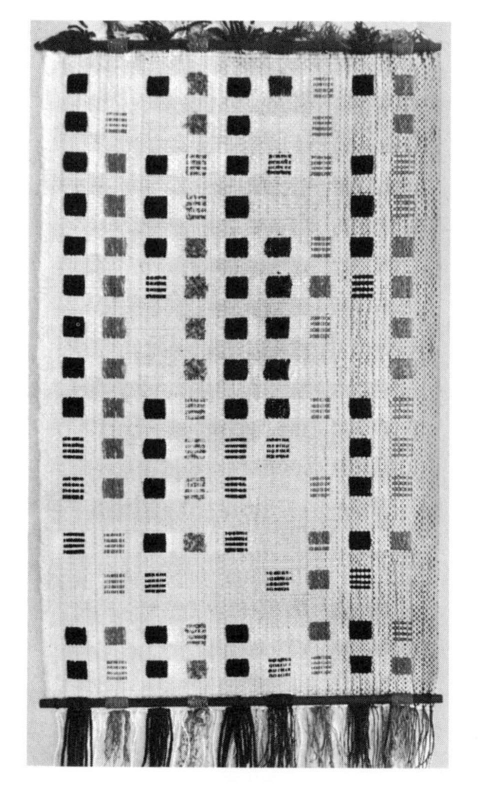

53. West façade, Amiens Cathedral. 1220–88 (façade 1225–36, towers 1366–1420). (See also Fig. 36.)

Gothic cathedral provides us with a visual example of this sort of rhythm (Fig. 53). When one approaches the portal, interest is awakened by the succession of carved figures in their niches, and the eye is carried upward to the elaborate sculptural compositions in the tympanum, the semicircular area above the door. Suspense mounts as the gaze goes upward through the clerestory arcades and statues, and a point of major emphasis is reached in the intricate tracery of the rose window. Further carvings and finials lift the eye to the bell towers, with their series of arches serving to emphasize the repeated rhythm. The final emphasis or climax is attained in the tapered pinnacles, with their upward surge carrying the eye and mind still higher until one achieves a feeling of infinite space, a visual and spiritual transcendence toward which the total design is directed. The esthetic and emotional experience of a Gothic cathedral is similar to that of the drama, which builds toward the climax in the plot. The final unravelling of the plot, in the case of the cathedral, would consist of a more searching scrutiny through which the viewer recognizes that the statues are saints, that the carving is rich in symbolism, and that the stained glass window is symbolic as well as beautiful. Such a full appreciation of what this façade embodies is a graphic realization of the importance of the cathedral to a civilization. During medieval times, the cathedral provided the focal point of the community for miles around, commanding the horizon as a sheltering monument around which the lesser buildings of the town clustered. It served, too, as a focus for all the arts. Dramas were performed in the ambulatory, music was composed for the Mass, craftsmen came from great distances to take part in the building and decoration, lavishing upon it their skills in carving stone or wood and making stained glass. The cathedral was also the vehicle for unifying Christian teaching, the heritage of Christianity passed on largely by word of mouth until the medieval monks recorded it on parchment. Thus, the cathedral served as a dominant organic component of its epoch culturally as well as visually.

Rhythm, as discussed in the preceding paragraphs, has been shown to be composed of repetition and emphasis, leading to a focal climax; to many people, however, rhythm has a more flowing quality, such as the measured rhythm of breakers rolling toward the shore or of draperies swirling about a dancing figure. While repetition and emphasis remain a part of these rhythms, their flowing quality is derived from the use of more fluid motifs (that is, units) and a less rigid placement of them. Such rhythm is found repeatedly in nature, even in such an unlikely place as the bacteria of crown gall (Fig. 54). Designer Ted Hallman has exhibited a feeling for this sort of rhythm in an acrylic screen, which achieves a linear flow in light and dark areas that are not too far removed from forms apparent in the crown gall and the ocean waves (Fig. 55). Alfred Manessier has expressed the same kind of rhythm in painting (Fig. 56). Here the peaks are flattened out, but the flowing quality is unmistakable. There are other related features in the works of these two artists and in the crown

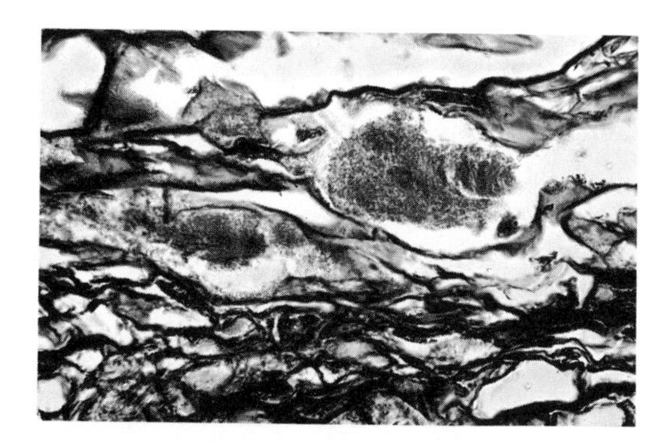

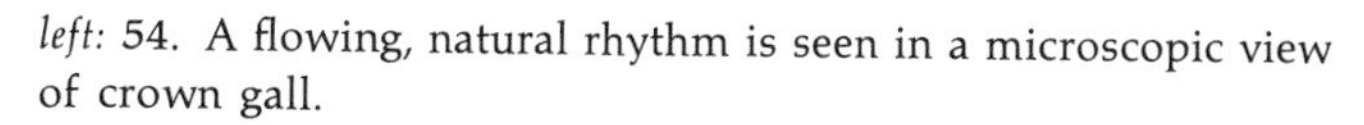

left: 54. A flowing, natural rhythm is seen in a microscopic view of crown gall.

below left: 55. An acrylic screen (1960) designed by TED HALLMAN exhibits fluid rhythms similar to those found in the crown gall.

below: 56. ALFRED MANESSIER. *Plain-chant.* 1955. Oil on canvas, $22\frac{1}{4} \times 32''$. Courtesy Galerie Anne Abels, Cologne.

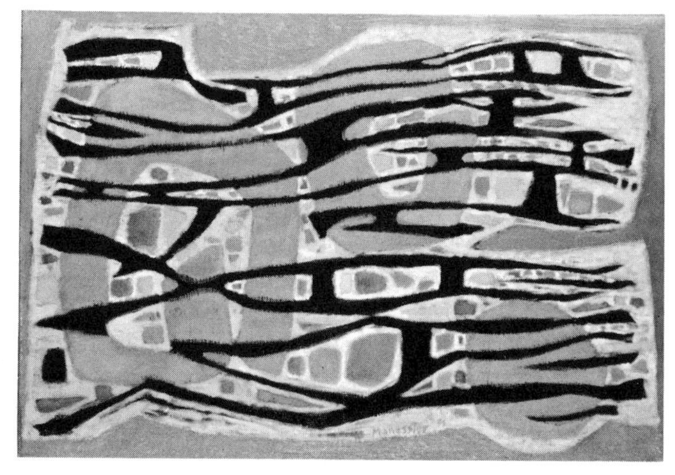

gall. There is a similarity of texture and a like pattern of light and dark. It is interesting that Manessier titled his painting *Plain-chant,* thus extending the field of reference into music.

These, then, are three approaches to the use of rhythm in design: the simple rhythm of repetition and emphasis, the rhythm in which repetition and emphasis build to a climax, and the flowing rhythm in which a less pronounced repetition and emphasis are submerged in fluid forms.

VARIETY

Just as variety is one of nature's most endearing qualities, it should be the designer's key to interesting design. The more one studies design elements and principles, the more it is possible to realize their interrelationships. For instance, the repetition and emphasis that make for rhythm are basically a matter of variety in beat, and variety is achieved through all the elements of design. As in nature, line, color, texture, size, shape, and mass all provide the designer with endless opportunities.

The contemporary artist has greater possibilities for variety through texture than anyone before him. He has more materials with which to work, and the spirit of experimentation typical of art today leads him to new uses for old textures. He can embed stones or glass or sticks in concrete, carve out holes in plaster, eat grooves in wood with acid, use plastics in ingenious and unconventional ways, and weave pods and grasses into fabrics.

The means for achieving variety in color are almost limitless. With one paint manufacturer now advertising 1322 different colors of paint available for home decorating, the problem becomes not so much one of finding the right color as of knowing it when one sees it. Paradoxically, the reaction of most customers to such infinite choice is one of confusion rather than delight. Deciding beforehand that you want a blue room instead of a rose one is comparatively simple, but when faced with hundreds of samples of variations of blue, blue-green, and blue-violet, your decision becomes extremely difficult. Of course, the artist has always had all these colors to work with, and possibly even more. They are his for the mixing, and endless subtleties and variations are at his fingertips if he has the knowledge to blend them. What he needs to decide first in any specific work is just what he wants to accomplish with color.

Sometimes works that have little else to recommend them are lauded for their "vibrant" color. Other works are described as exceptional for their "subtle" colors. Textiles and ceramics are frequently executed in "earth tones"—the browns, ochers,

57. Pottery bowls and jars from the Zuni pueblo in New Mexico. Fired earthenware, height of largest jar 10". Collections of the Indian Arts Fund, School of American Research, Santa Fe, N.M. A vivid symbolism is responsible for the varied designs found in the arts of the North American Indian.

58. Cup in the form of an open lotus flower, from Egypt. 19th–20th Dynasty, 1350–1090 B.C. Faience, height 5¾″. Metropolitan Museum of Art (Carnarvon Collection, gift of Edward S. Harkness, 1926).

and dull reds found in natural rocks and soil. These colors are particularly appropriate to arts in which some affinity to the earth remains apparent, such as unglazed pottery and weaving done with natural vegetable fibers. The rugs and blankets of the early American Indians are examples of this sort of color range. In this case no deliberate artistic choice was made, since there were no dyes to be had other than those found in earth pigments and plant colorings. The same is true of the pottery made in early periods. Brown, red, and black designs on neutral grounds were esthetically suitable, since these express intrinsic qualities of the earth from which the vessels themselves were made (Fig. 57).

Variety through Symbolism

The varied *visual* texture of the Zuni pots in Figure 57 is the result of a highly decorative use of symbolism. The world of primitive man has always been rich in symbols, for *symbolism is the means of representing what is not known or not seen.* Each stylized bird and animal and each geometric shape conveys a story or signifies a wish or prayer to be fulfilled. Sigfried Giedion describes symbolization as arising "from the need to give perceptible form to the imperceptible."[2]

Typical use of symbol was made by the Egyptians. Like the American Indians, the Egyptians believed primarily in nature gods, and their religion was expressed through a wealth of representations of plants, animals, and birds. The lotus blossom, with its waxy petals, was a favorite motif; on the Lotiform Cup (Fig. 58) it is presented with its most usual symbolism, that of birth or evolving life. Its petals reach up to enfold all forms of life—the fish in the river, man, and animals. In an Egyptian poem, however, its aroma is associated with drunkenness and with death:

> Death is before me today
> As the odour of lotus flowers,
> As when one sitteth on the shore of drunkenness.[3]

With or without symbolism, variety can be achieved by working with the elements of design in a spirit of exploration. As in all other aspects of the designer's art, it is necessary only to experiment to find new and effective means of expression.

BALANCE

There are many ways of accomplishing a state of *balance.* In chemistry an equation is balanced if the same number of the same kind of atoms appears on each side. Algebraic equations are also balanced quantitatively. In art one does not follow a rigorous formula, and the condition of balance is not always so obvious. The rigid symmetrical balance represented by the clock centered on the mantelpiece with a candlestick on each side is familiar to most people. This is balance by formula, and a person who designs in this way can be certain that his compositions will be balanced. However, he may find that they are not particularly interesting. Moving the clock to one end of the mantel and placing the two candlesticks together with a pot of ivy at the other end may achieve a balanced effect that is more unusual. It will also give this mantelpiece arrangement a closer affinity with the sort of balance one finds in nature and the human body. Perfect symmetry is seldom found in our natural surroundings. People are never exactly the same on both sides of their faces or their bodies. For instance, most people find their right foot bigger than their left. Evergreen trees may look perfectly symmetrical at a distance, but closer inspection reveals that their branches do not grow out of the trunk in precise symmetry, even though the overall contour of the foliage gives this impression. Leaves, though regular in outline, are not symmetrical in their veining; stones, though perfectly round, have differences in grain on opposite sides. In photographs of landscapes, balance is achieved by the placement of large elements such as trees, bodies of water, rock formations, and hills, as well as by the textures of rocks, bark, grass, and foliage. Nature achieves balance in a varied and flexible manner.

In working for balance in design, the artist should work for the same fluid treatment found with rhythm, for which principles are used as guides but not as rigid formulas. He can follow nature in balancing a large area of dark or subdued color with a spot of bright color or by balancing a bulky undifferentiated form with

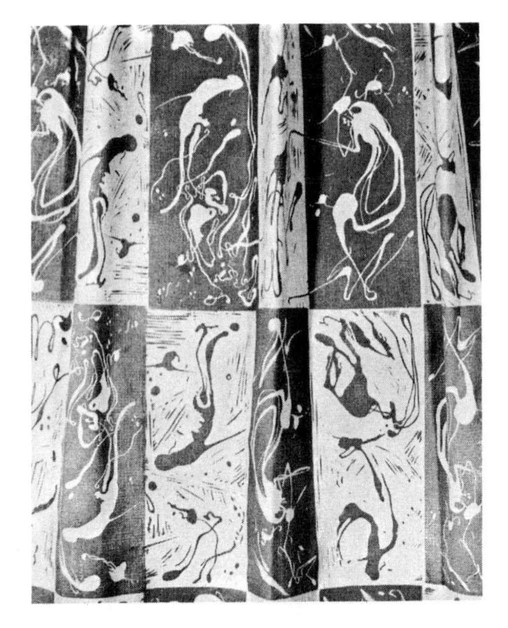

right: 59. *After Pollock,* a hand-blocked print by JANET ERICKSON.

far right: 60. A stoneware bottle (1961) by HARRISON McINTOSH combines visual and tactile textures.

a smaller, more interesting one. He should think of balance as a control over variety, through which variety is kept from becoming too complicated by the simple measure of keeping the various colors, shapes, sizes, and textures in balance with one another.

The textile in Figure 59 shows balance of value in the alternate dark and light background panels and the corresponding reverse treatment of the figuration on them. The allover effect would not be nearly so interesting if the ground were not broken into areas of dark and light. In the bottle in Figure 60 the balance of texture is effective. The larger, rougher area of the vertical striations is balanced by the finer visual texture of the neck. The concavity of the neck area also provides contrast to the convex shape of the body of the piece. Moreover, the heavier texture gives a feeling of stability by being located near the base, where it seems to hold the bottle firmly on the table. This sort of visual balance gives esthetic pleasure, and satisfies as well the viewer's sense of gravity.

The Brazilian Ministry of Education Building is an excellent example of beauty in architecture achieved principally through balance (Fig. 61). One may see many skyscrapers with long bands of windows reaching upward, some of these having esthetic effect and others purely functional merit. The particular attractiveness of the Rio de Janeiro skyscraper lies in the balance of extended vertical line by horizontal louvers, which creates a striking pattern rather than an unrelieved series of immense verticals. One of the most important aspects of the building is that the louvers are designed in horizontal groups of four, interspersed with open spaces, and are recessed in a way that gives striking shadow patterns.

FORM

As the artist works with rhythm, variety, and balance, *form* emerges. This, more than any other consideration, establishes the identity of the design. The physical qualities that we see, smell, touch, or feel reach us through the senses, but the form of a work derives from the mind, which organizes the messages of the senses into a material embodiment, much as one gives significant expression to the potentialities of pen and paper in the content of a letter. The form of sculpture or a piece of pottery

61. Le Corbusier, Oscar Niemeyer, and Lucio Costa. Ministry of Education, Rio de Janeiro, Brazil. 1937–43.

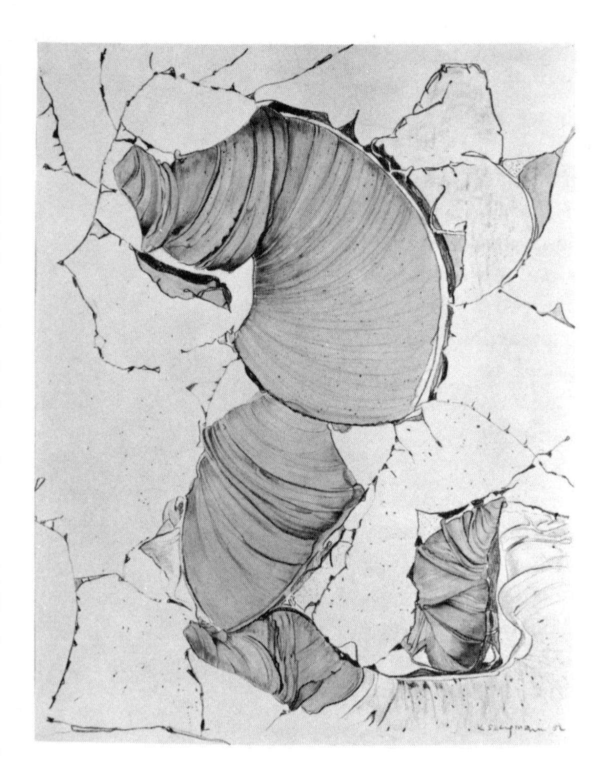

left: 62. Kurt Seligman. *Caterpillar.* 1952. Varnish, crayon, and wash, 28 × 22″. Fogg Art Museum, Cambridge, Mass. (bequest of Meta and Paul J. Sachs).

right: 63. Miriam Sommerburg. *Menorah Triptych.* 1963. Mosaic, 30 × 29″. Collection the artist.

is obvious; yet a fabric design or a body of type also has form. The form is the particular combination of sizes, shapes, and masses that compose the whole and that cause the design to exist in the space around it. The intellect of the artist organizes these elements into an integrated entity. The drawing in Figure 62 reveals an artist's interest in a natural form, which he has then translated into an artistic form. Such form embodies his total effort. At the moment of its conception he visualizes his work in a certain form, and when he has completed his labor, form is the ultimate result.

UNITY

Encompassing all the principles involved in creating a design is *unity*, the quality that makes the design consistent and complete. In a mosaic, unity is achieved in one way by the grout that is used between the varicolored tesserae (the individual pieces), weaving its way among the various colors and shapes and tying them into a relationship with one another (Fig. 63). Some contemporary painters leave scattered patches of canvas unpainted as a means of unifying their painting. Unity can be created by using the same color or variations of it throughout a design, much as the musical composer might use variations of the same theme throughout an entire symphony.

The most important means of arriving at unity in any work of art is *to create with a definite objective in mind.* If the artist maintains a singleness of purpose in all his work and successfully fulfills that purpose, his work will have a basic unity. The painter who sets out to express an experience will find that he must achieve some degree of unity before he can feel that he has succeeded. The writer who is determined to convey a certain message and devotes an entire work to that end will have unity of content. The same artistic unity may be true of the sculptor or the musician or the choreographer. Devotion to his work as a means of accomplishing a certain objective will make the artist himself the strongest possible unifying influence.

Limiting what the artist uses in his work is another help in achieving unity. This refers to the actual materials as well as to the colors, textures, sizes, shapes, and lines. It is more effective to choose a few elements that will best express his feeling and to repeat these in variations than to clutter the work with too much diversity. Some of the most striking compositions are monochromatic; that is, they use variations of one color only and bring out that color in all its ramifications. One or two colors threaded through a painting or design are more satisfying than a patchwork of many colors that fight for emphasis. The designer must learn to compose, by manipulating colors, lines, sizes, and shapes over and over; varying, emphasizing, and diminishing them where necessary; choosing a motif and then developing it to fullest effect, leaving other ideas for another design—just as the writer polishes his work, cutting words, phrases, and even whole sections to eliminate extraneous matter and maintain the basic unity of his writing. When the artist has accomplished this, he too will have achieved unity or harmony, the intrinsic quality of any successful creation, which results from rhythm flowing through it, variety contributing interest, balance giving control, and form establishing individuality.

EVOLUTION OF A DESIGN

To most people the word "design" means a graphic representation, something created with lines and forms to express a certain feeling. The uses of graphic design are many: book jackets and billboards, plates and silverware, fabrics, carved panels, mosaic walls and surfaces, and innumerable others. In short, graphic design is the basis for all facets of creative work, and it is well to understand its general evolution before delving into individual aspects of it. Such understanding will guide the artist in constructing and evaluating his own designs.

The first approach, referring back to Chapter 1, will be through the requisites of a good design. Even before the artist begins to think of elements and principles, he must, of course, consider the purpose for which the design is to be used and the material from which it is to be made. Then, by using the elements at his command and combining them according to such principles as balance and rhythm, he will develop a plan for order, which will evolve according to the natural laws of growth and which, through a distinctive use of variety and form, will display his individual touch.

Using line as his basic tool, the designer should consider size and shape. How big a pot does he want, or how large a piece of textile? A page of type, a book jacket, or a design for a record album will each have a predetermined size. When this is established, he can decide which of the four kinds of shape he wants to use (natural, abstract, nonobjective, or geometric) and, through the instrument of line, begin to sketch some possibilities.

The four kinds of shapes can also be combined in imaginative ways. In other words, because the designer chooses to create a *nonobjective* design, he is not limited to nonobjective component shapes. An effective nonobjective design could very well include geometric shapes, abstract shapes, and even a natural shape if used with imagination. What makes it nonobjective will be the total effect of the combination, the predominant feeling of the finished design. The stained glass panel in Figure

64 is a good example. The allover impression is of a nonobjective design; yet, of the 21 panels shown, 14 are essentially geometric. The seven panels that deviate from strict geometry lend interest, which is heightened by the interplay of textures. The small dark shapes within the lighter textured areas echo the larger shapes, and the heavy outlines of the leading contribute to a strong sense of unity. It is equally possible to create an *abstract* design using geometric shapes; the fact that it is an abstraction indicates that natural forms are the point of departure.

Conceptual Images

Perceptual images that are seen by the selective eye of the artist have already been discussed. Before the process of abstraction is analyzed, it would be helpful to understand what is meant by a *conceptual image.* A conceptual image is a kind of symbol, a shape or form that represents something in the artist's mind rather than what he actually sees with his eye, the image that is based on external sensory stimuli. One thinks of the eye as being like a camera because the camera is designed upon the theory of the eye, but the eye does not actually register complete and separate pictures like those which appear on photographic film. Instead, it registers a continually changing kaleidoscope of images, colors, shapes, sizes, textures, and lines, many of which are superimposed upon others or rearranged from the order in which they actually appeared. From this wealth of material the artist often creates his original image, a combination of visual experiences that is distinctively his own. Such images have been used by Mildred Fischer in her tapestry in Figure 65. Through her title, *Canto,* she gives us a clue to what she had in mind, but visually

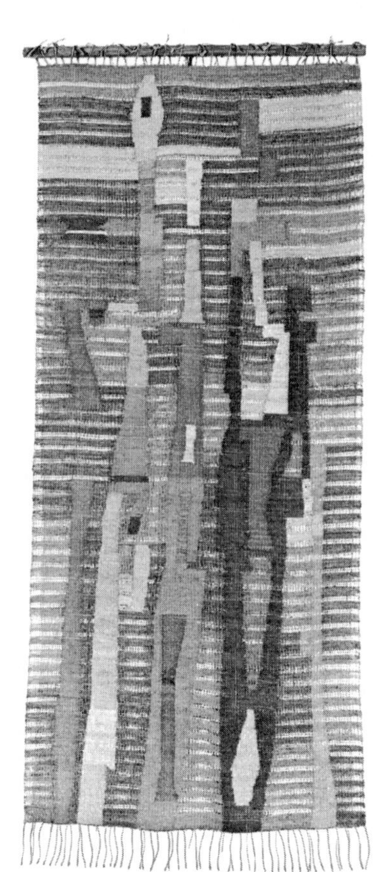

far left: 64. Both geometric and nonobjective shapes are used in this panel of fused and painted glass designed and executed by Joseph Meert.

left: 65. Mildred Fischer. *Canto.* 1965. Linen and silk yarns, 52 × 22″. Collection the artist.

she has used an entirely personal mode of expression. Are the elongated forms people who are grouped together singing? Or are they visual representation of the sounds of the song itself? These are fascinating questions that allow the viewer to play with various interpretations, but which do not require an explicit answer in order to appreciate the work. The forms and textures of the work are enough in themselves, particularly when seen in color. The conceptual images of the artist have resulted in a work of great individuality.

The Process of Abstraction

Some of the most effective designs used in contemporary art media are those which have been abstracted from a recognizable object. This is true particularly in advertising and packaging, where it is important that the design be identified with the product in question without being merely a realistic representation of it. A completely natural depiction of a product is rarely good design unless it is imaginatively used as a component of a photographic composition. In most fields, for that matter, purely naturalistic interpretations are seldom effective as designs. The reason for this is that, from a design standpoint, nothing has happened to them. A fabric strewn with natural-looking flowers is not a product of the designer except for the placement of the fllowers. Understandably, the more the creative touch is reflected in a work, the more successful a design will be. For this reason, the ability to abstract is vital.

As a noun, the word "abstract" means something that concentrates the essential qualities of a larger, more detailed whole; for instance, in literature the abstract is a summary or short form giving the essential argument or plot structure of a book. This is what one attempts to do in "abstracting" an object to make a design—to pinpoint its essential feeling or flavor and translate it into simple forms that may or may not resemble the original object. As mentioned earlier, the term "stylization" is often used when the object is still identifiable but has been simplified to give it a design quality.

Now suppose that the artist is going to abstract an object to make a design. The beginning step in any abstract design is to find a point of departure. It should be emphasized that anything can be used as design material: for instance, such natural forms as leaves, shells, vegetables, trees, birds, and fish. Man-made objects can be adapted just as effectively, such objects as keys, lampposts, kitchen utensils, or buildings. The designer should, however, choose something that holds a personal interest, an object that has meaning for him. It is only through feeling enthusiasm and excitement about his work that the artist is inspired to create something that is significant.

Once the subject has been chosen, the next step is to look at it in an entirely new way. The designer should attempt to catch the essence of this object, to express things about it that heretofore he has not suspected. To do this he must submit it to a painstaking critical anaylsis in which he takes it apart to explore all its possibilities and those of its components.

In the creation of an advertising design for an aquarium, one point of departure is an actual fish. The first thing to do is to select a particular fish. The end result may become so abstract that it will not seem to matter; yet an authentic starting point could very well make the design come through in a more convincing way. The next step it to draw the fish exactly as it appears, in a realistic manner, and then to sketch its parts—the head, the eye, the tail, the fins—each as a separate unit. One should draw the bone structure and make sketches of the texture of the

left: 66. A highly abstracted fish design is the focal point in this poster for the John G. Shedd Aquarium, Chicago.

right: 67. STANLEY KAPLAN. *Fish.* c. 1960. Polychrome Philippine mahogany, 24 × 48″. Collection Dr. Jack Sherman, Bethpage, N.Y.

scales. When the designer is convinced that he has drained the original fish of all design possibilities, he can begin to put the materials back together, working as imaginatively as he wishes. If the designer wants to use a cross section of any part, that is his privilege, and he may repeat any unit as often as his design requires. Although the fish has only two eyes, the designer may repeat the circle of the eye a dozen times if that suits his needs.

As the designer experiments, he should keep in mind the elements and principles of design and make decisions concerning his application of them. Will his rhythm be the beat of a drum or the flowing rhythm of a river? Different shapes will emerge according to what he decides. There will be positive shapes drawn with lines, and the negative shapes formed by the space outside the lines. In general, like shapes should be of varying sizes, and elements similar in size should be varied in shape. There is the matter of texture, which in a graphic design is visual rather than tactile. But will it be crosshatched, for example, or stippled? If the designer applies crosshatching to a large area, he may want to echo it in a smaller section of interesting shape elsewhere in the composition. Or he may find it more creative to work for *balance of interest,* complementing the interesting texture with an area of bright or unusual color. Any of the elements of design can be balanced by any other element, provided that both elements are applied in a similarly interesting way.

One solution to this hypothetical problem can be seen in Figure 66. It is evident that a complete fish has not been depicted, for in the more detailed representation the head has been cropped off. A flowing rhythm is created by the overlapping of fins and tails from the two shapes; yet the strong underlying motif is not a fish at all but simply some bold stripes over which is superimposed the more naturalistic fish, with its detailed line and texture. The texture is the most important element, dramatizing the qualities of the fish rather than its essential shape. Fins and tails are merely indicated with accents, and the whole upper shape looks as if it might have been printed from a painting on glass. In a strict sense, there is no fish literally portrayed here; yet no one would doubt the presence of fish as the dominant motif in the composition. Only when one analyzes the design carefully does he realize how imaginative a treatment of the subject has been used.

An approach just as abstract and original but entirely different is seen in the wood panel by Stanley Kaplan in Figure 67, which could be a suitable wall decoration for the home of a fisherman. Here the eyes, gills, and fins make strong decorative elements that are repeated in a rhythmic pattern throughout the composition. One may notice also the rhythm produced by the juxtaposition of light and dark areas and the fascinating texture, which not only exploits the qualities of wood as a medium but which also imparts a feeling of the sea. Certain areas are stained with green, blue, umber, and white, with gold leaf accents giving an impression of underwater lights and patterns. One can analyze the plaque for all the elements and principles of design and notice the effective way in which each has been used.

Using this same approach to create a fabric design based on leaves, it would be possible for the artist to arrive at something like the design of Janet Erickson in Figure 68. Here the rhythm is a drumbeat, repeated at intervals throughout the fabric. The leaf has been dissected and put together again, with its vein structure forming a strong and imaginative part of the design. One may observe how the veining flows free of the leaf itself in certain parts. Of course, neither leaf shape nor vein structure in the finished design is naturalistic; each is a personal statement by the designer, as is her use of geometric forms to vary the motif, and their variation in value and placement.

In making his own design, the artist will find color an important consideration. If he has not decided in advance on the colors to use, he should review his basic design idea before making the decision. If he wants a feeling of gaiety, as in a travel poster for Spain, he may use various warm colors. If he is designing a jacket for a book about the English countryside, he may choose more subdued colors, but with an effort to retain a feeling of freshness. Posters advertising cosmetics will be more subtle in color than billboards proclaiming the merits of gasoline, which should suggest speed and power. If he is designing for printed fabrics and wallpapers, he has an advantage—and an added consideration—because his design will probably be printed in several different color combinations. The designer may, of course, want to experiment and see which colors are best suited to the forms of the design.

68. A hand-blocked print by Janet Erickson carries a repeated motif of stylized leaves.

Creating abstract motifs will give the artist a firm foundation for most areas of design, but perhaps more important is the way in which it will open his eyes to the design opportunities in the world around him. He will become acquainted with a whole new field of inspiration, that of the natural abstraction. This does not mean abstractions found in nature alone, but abstract patterns that occur in all kinds of materials and situations where design was never consciously considered.

A concrete sidewalk cracks and makes a design. A mud puddle dries up, a coil of rope falls to the grass, paint peels off a wall—all form their own designs (Fig. 69). Next time you walk by a building incorporating glass blocks, notice the light patterns made by the translucent glass. Look for patterns on old walls where the bricks are broken or the plaster is cracked and flaking. Notice the color and interesting shapes of oil floating on puddles and the patterns formed in flagstones by mineral deposits and wear. Investigate in close-up the way that blades of grass divide space into shapes (Fig. 70). Even the worn wooden steps of old buildings have design possibilities. The importance lies not so much in using *things* for inspiration as in learning to see the patterns and designs inherent in one's surroundings.

When you have opened your eyes and mind to the fascination of the world around you, there will never be any problem in finding inspiration for your work; and the more you see, the more you will develop the sensitivity and magic touch that will convert such inspiration into striking, original designs.

SUMMARY

In accepting the elements and principles of design as materials with which to work, it is important to realize that these are not rigid rules but simply guides for creativity. Seeing the variety of design in the world and recognizing that it is all created with the same basic elements and principles, it may be concluded that the determining influence is the imaginative touch of the designer, which depends upon his perspective and perception—the viewpoint from which he sees the world and those parts of the world which he chooses to see. Perception is a gathering of visual knowledge of the world through observing those things which the individual considers to be important.

Using nature as his guide or reference, the artist can see how the principles of design may be applied in his own work by studying their application in works of others, in both the past and the present. One way to achieve variety is through symbolism, a device that has been used by man since primitive times. Primary among the principles of design is unity, the quality that makes a design consistent and complete. Unity can be achieved in two ways: (1) by creating with a definite objective in mind, and (2) by limiting what the artist uses in his work.

A successful graphic design is evolved through application of the requisites of good design given in Chapter 1, which are supplemented by use of the elements and principles of design described thereafter. The distinction between visual and conceptual images is important in creating contemporary works. Developing the esthetic method of abstraction is a vital basis for design today.

left: 69. AARON SISKIND. *Peeling Paint: Jerome, Arizona.* 1949. This photographic composition is so full of form, texture, and balance that it might easily be mistaken for a modern abstract painting.

right: 70. BRUCE ROBERTS' photograph of grasses proves that the creative photographer can find design in the simplest forms of nature.

The Glow of Color

chapter 5

Color is the music of the graphic arts. Great art can be created without color, but its presence brings a mood and a depth of experience that cannot be achieved in any other way. Furthermore, like the notes of the basic scale when played by a symphony orchestra, it has seemingly unlimited variation and enormous capacity to manipulate our emotions. It is therefore one of the most powerful assets, or tools, of the designer.

Color may be approached both as a science and as an art, and the designer must have some knowledge of both aspects. The physicist can tell him much about the abstract theories and sources of color sensation, about the optical principles involved; the chemist formulates rules for mixing and applying color; and the psychologist can provide information about emotional response to certain colors. The artist should seek to understand all these aspects and then go further, endeavoring to coordinate the discoveries of science and to develop his own variations, which fill the needs of and distinguish his work.

COLOR IN NATURE

In nature color is often a matter of life and death. In high wild country, what seems a lichen-covered rock suddenly ruffles its feathers and moves, revealing instead a ptarmigan. In winter this same bird turns white, along with the snowshoe rabbit and the ermine, thus becoming indistinguishable from a drift of snow when danger threatens. This is a characteristic found throughout the animal kingdom. In the White Sands of Alamogordo, New Mexico, all the common forms of insect and reptile life take on the natural whiteness of their habitat (Fig. 71). Lizards and horned toads

71. A lizard whose natural habitat is the New Mexican desert changes color to adapt to its background.

become albinos, thus protected from detection against their background. Fish are usually a kind of silver-gray, with flecks of green or blue, to match their watery habitat. Most aquatic species are light on the underside, so that they will not be obvious when seen against the sky by predators from below, and dark on top to camouflage them from attack from above. With so much importance given to color in nature, it is logical to expect it to have an overwhelming influence on man-made environment as well. None of the elements of design is more deserving of mastery.

THE ESSENCE OF COLOR

The perception of color is a *neurophysiological process,* which means that it involves both the nervous system and the physiological apparatus of seeing. Although it is not fully understood, we do know that color is actually light broken down into electromagnetic vibrations. Variations in the wavelength of these vibrations cause the viewer to see different colors. The longest wavelength, which is 32 millionths of an inch, is perceived as red; the shortest wavelength, 16 millionths of an inch, registers on our vision as violet.

The vibration wavelengths are made visible by passing a beam of sunlight through a prism, thereby breaking the light into hues that correspond to those seen in the rainbow—usually listed as violet, indigo, blue, green, yellow, orange, and red (Fig. 72). Although the artist may think of his pigments as man-made materials, color itself cannot actually be manufactured. Instead, it is caused to occur by the manufacture of materials which absorb or reflect certain rays of light. When a particular substance is exposed to light, it will absorb all the rays but those creating a certain color, and the rays that are not absorbed will constitute the color attributed to the substance. When the manufacturer makes green paint, he actually puts together the materials that will absorb rays of violet, indigo, blue, yellow, orange, and red. The green rays are not absorbed, and one perceives these and says the paint is green. Thus the process would seem to be in reverse, putting into the paint the rays of colors that will not show, with the one that is left out giving the paint its identity.

It was mentioned above that vibrations with the longest wavelengths are seen as red, whereas those with the shortest become violet; hence, these two colors are at the opposite ends of the scale insofar as wavelengths are concerned. About 1666 Sir Isaac Newton, in studying color, realized that violet and red have a relationship, since together they form purple—a deeper variation of violet. Following this reasoning, he made a circular chart in which he placed the seven colors of the rainbow side by side, thus bringing the violet at one end of the range to a place beside the red at the other end and unifying the chromatic scale into a continuous whole. This was the first *color wheel.* Color experts have devised other wheels, in which the colors are varied according to the theories of physics, visual perception, or pigments.

Probably no aspect of art has created more opposing theories than the study of color. Both scientists and artists have developed color systems, and people working

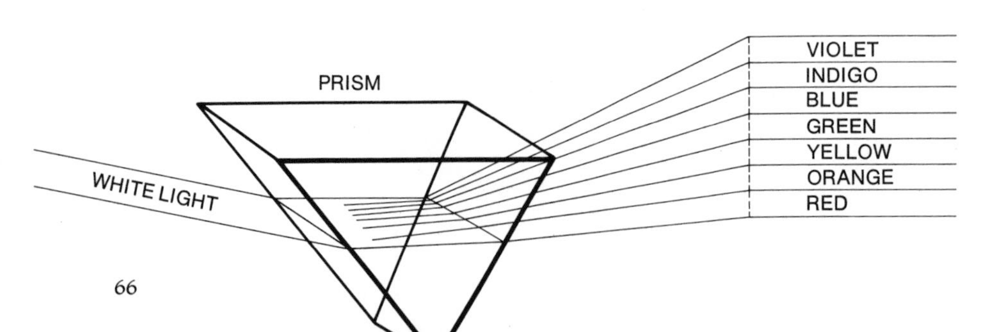

72. A ray of white light projected through a prism separates into the hues seen in a rainbow.

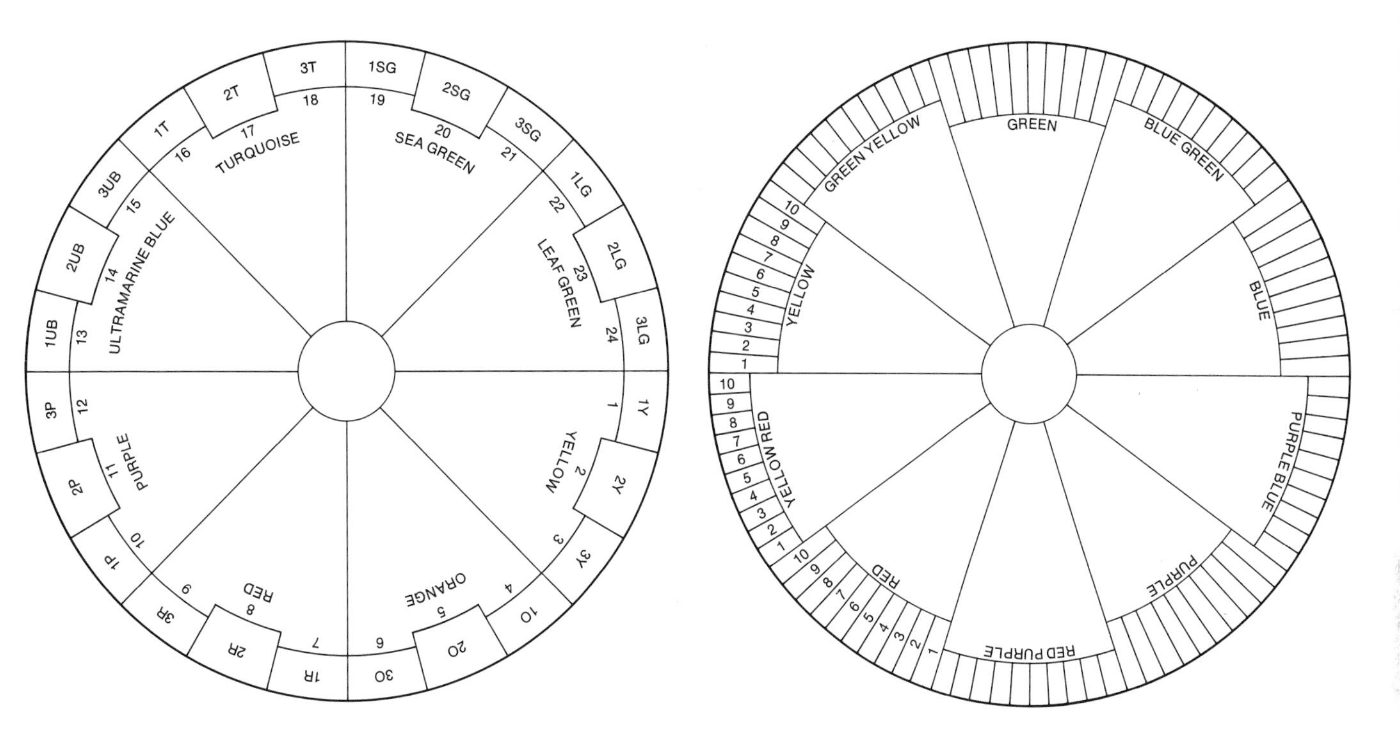

in the field tend to feel strongly about which one is "correct." As in any series of experiments, there is no absolute right and wrong, but simply a variety of approaches. The very fact that people do feel intensely about the matter attests to the importance of color in art and design.

left: 73. The Ostwald color wheel considers red, yellow, green, and blue to be the primary colors, with all other hues deriving from variations of these four.

right: 74. The Munsell color wheel is based on five key hues: red, yellow, blue, green, and purple.

COLOR WHEELS

For many years the color theory taught to students was based on pigment and the three *primary colors* of red, yellow, and blue. These colors were considered basic, because it was thought that they could not be mixed from other colors. By mixing these traditional primary hues together a new group of *secondary colors* was created: green from yellow and blue, orange from yellow and red, and violet from red and blue. Going a step further, the artist can extract a third group of colors sometimes called *intermediaries:* yellow-orange, orange-red, red-violet, blue-violet, blue-green, and yellow-green. When these three groups are placed in such a way that they seem to flow naturally, or modulate, into one another, we have the basic color wheel (Pl. 5A, p. 75). This wheel, best known through the work of Herbert E. Ives in America, is of value as *a system of mixing colors.* However, Ives discovered that red actually can be mixed from magenta and yellow and that blue can be mixed from turquoise and magenta; accordingly, for use in mixing dyes and pigments, he designed another wheel, which has for its primaries magenta (which he called achlor), yellow (zanth), and turquoise (cyan). Physicists who work with light use a color wheel based on red, green, and blue-violet. Still other color wheels are widely used, concerned both with human vision and with the sequence in which we see colors, or afterimages. One such wheel, designed by Wilhelm Ostwald, uses yellow, green, blue, and red as the basic colors (Fig. 73). Another, known as the *Munsell system* because it was worked out by Albert Munsell, establishes five key hues: red, yellow, green, blue, and purple (Fig. 74).

Still another pioneer in the study of color was the Frenchman M. Chevreul, who early in the nineteenth century formulated propositions that subsequently became cornerstones in the discussion of color harmony. Among these propositions was the statement that complementary assortments are superior to all others; he also suggested that colors not too harmonious when placed side by side may be improved by the addition of a black or white outline or separation. It was in Chevreul's system that the terms *complements, split complements, adjacents,* (analogous colors), and *triads* became accepted color usage (Pl. 5, p. 75).

For a thorough understanding of color, all possible systems should be studied and analyzed. Each is valuable according to the medium for which it was designed. A good exercise is to design a color wheel. Like the number of elements in design, the number of colors can vary according to temperament. A forthright, impulsive personality will probably find a few basic color "steps" sufficient, whereas a meticulous individual will work out a more expanded series of closely related gradations. Both approaches are equally valid. Rather than being regarded as a strict formula, the color wheel should be used to increase the designer's flexibility and sense of excitement about the possibilities of color.

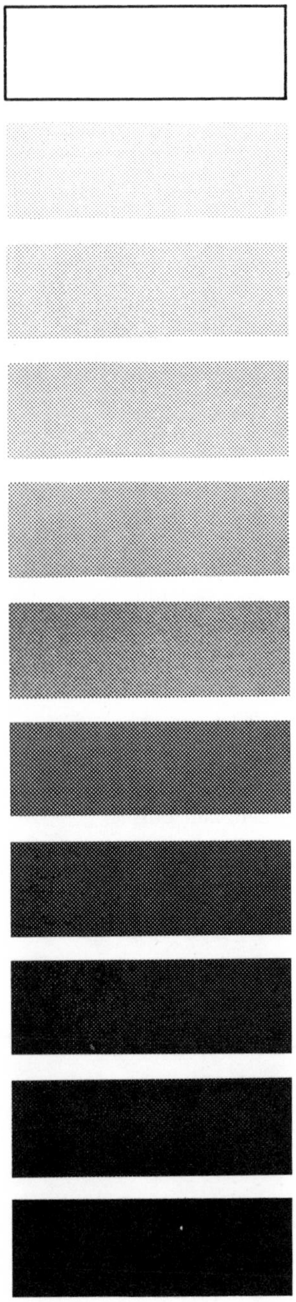

THE DIMENSIONS OF COLOR

Regardless of which theory of color is accepted, the dimensions, or properties, of color remain similar. *Hue* is the pure state of a given color, as well as the name by which we identify that color. Red as a hue means a pure red, unmixed and unmodified. Hue is the basis for the other color dimensions, much as shape is the foundation for form. Once such a color as red or yellow or violet has been established, one can go on to explore its other dimensions.

Intensity, sometimes called *chroma* (the Greek word for color) or *saturation* refers to the relative purity or grayness of a color. Magenta and orange are colors of *high* intensity (or strong chroma), whereas pink and beige are colors of *low* intensity (or weak chroma). Colors of high intensity are those which approach pure hues, while those of low intensity have greater similarity to natural gray (Pl. 6, p. 76). *Saturation* is the term usually employed by scientists.

The third dimension of color is *value,* defined as the lightness or darkness of a color. Every hue has a range of values, running in opposite directions from a middle value equivalent to a medium gray: on one side through the *tints,* which are all the variations lighter than middle value, and on the other through the *shades,* which are darker than middle value. Strictly speaking, it is incorrect to say "a shade of pink," since pink is one of the lighter values and must therefore be a tint.

The subject of value can best be understood through a study of the "gray" scale (Fig. 75), in which one sees all the value gradations from white to black and can relate these to the gradations of any other given hue. According to psychologists, the average person can distinguish nine steps from white to black, with middle (or "medium") gray as the fifth value in the scale. Theoretically, then, he should be able to differentiate at least as many values for any hue. A useful assignment for the student is to make a value scale for each of several hues in order to determine how many gradations he can distinguish. He should then combine these variations in different ways to study their effects upon one another. He will find that any two colors will harmonize if appropriate values are used.

75. The gray scale shows variations in value from white to black.

In addition to tints and shades, there is a third category of values known as *tones,* formed by mixing pure colors with white *and* black, or with gray. The result is a range of grayed hues that are extremely useful in the blending of colors, because tones will frequently go together where pure hues will not, since they are related by this common admixture of gray. Examples of tones to which names have been given are beige, rose, and taupe.

There are two more terms referring to color generally. *Chromatic* colors are colors with the quality of hue in them—in other words, any colors that originate with pure color. *Achromatic* colors, on the other hand, are the so-called "neutrals" such as black, gray, and white (Fig. 76). Black and white should not be considered as being entirely apart from color, however, since they have a definite influence when added to hues. Black, in particular, can change a hue radically, such as converting orange into brown, or yellow into olive green.

COLOR AND PIGMENT

Colors that are in some way related will be harmonious when combined and, thus, establish *color harmonies.* The possible harmonies are almost limitless, for even colors that are not related in hue can be made harmonious if certain values or intensities are used. The artist should be aware of the ways in which colors relate to one another, and the color wheel is helpful for putting these various relationships into graphic form. For purposes of describing these methods, the traditional color wheel based on primary colors of red, blue, and yellow will be used. One should recognize, in this case, that the wheel is simply a chart for mixing pigments and is not a formula in any sense. After considering the methods of mixing pigments, one may look into the effects of color as light and see how the results differ.

Fundamental to the mixing of color is familiarity with *complementary* colors, those which appear opposite each other on the color wheel. On the traditional wheel these include such pairs as red and green, orange and blue, and yellow and violet (Pl. 5B, p. 75). Theoretically, mixing equal parts of complements will produce a neutral gray, although with some pigments the result is closer to brown; at any rate, the addition of a small amount of a complement will gray or soften a color. Some painters use solely the complements for modifying colors into darker values or into tones, because they feel that addition of black has a deadening effect upon pure color.

76. WILLEM DE KOONING. *Painting.* 1948. Ripolin enamel and oil on canvas, $42\frac{5}{8} \times 56\frac{1}{8}''$. Museum of Modern Art, New York.

Paradoxically, in spite of the graying effect when complements are mixed, when placed side by side they intensify each other. Red placed next to green looks brighter, but when mixed with a little green, it becomes a soft rose. In the various other color wheels, turquoise will soften orange, green-yellow will soften purple, and red will soften blue-green.

Notice that every pair of complementary colors consists of a warm color and a cool one. The warm colors are the yellows, oranges, and reds, which are associated with the sun and fire; the cool colors are the blues, greens, and violets of water and deep woods. Gray may be warm or cool, depending on whether more of the warm complement or of the cool one is used. If mixed from black and white, gray will be neutral. This knowledge expands the possibilities of gray alone from one rather drab tone to a whole family of vibrant variations. Colors softened by their complements retain the lively quality of both the original hue and the complement; the result is a subtle color, not a dull one.

Colors next to each other on the color wheel are called *analogous* (Pl. 5C, p. 75). Because of this proximity, such colors are always related and harmonious. Many such analogous combinations are found in nature, as in the blue of a lake turning blue-green at the water's edge or the blue-green of fir trees seen against a turquoise sky. Analogous colors on both sides appear also in the highlights and shadows of any given color. An orange nasturtium or marigold will have yellow highlights and red-orange shadows; a green leaf shows yellow-green in the places where light hits it but turns to blue-green when in shadow.

The effects of analogous colors are only a step removed from a *monochromatic* treatment, in which variations of a single color are used. Working with one color can be challenging and enlightening, for the process of modulating a hue into all its possible variations can reveal qualities otherwise unsuspected.

Still another way of combining colors is through *triads*. A triad is composed of any *three* colors equidistant on the color wheel (Pl. 5D, p. 75). Here the principle of balance comes into play, for any triad represents a balance of colors touching all areas of the spectrum. According to the traditional color wheel, the primary colors (red, blue, yellow) form a triad, and the secondary colors (orange, green, violet) are a triad as well. Other triads include the intermediaries. On different color wheels triads may consist of magenta, yellow, and turquoise or of yellow-orange, purple, and blue-green—or any other combination of colors located on an equilateral triangle within the circumference of the wheel. Such balanced color combinations are abundant in nature. The scales of a fish may contain the entire spectrum, and a red geranium with yellow highlights and green leaves presents a basic triad. Other triads can be seen in the feathers of a hummingbird and in the coloration of tropical birds, fish, and butterflies.

A further source of color harmonies is the *tetrad*, which consists of *four* colors located at equidistant points on the color wheel. These can be established by inscribing a square within the circumference of the wheel and turning one corner to any particular color. The colors indicated by the other three corners of the square will be harmonious with the original one. For example, if one corner of the square is pointed at red-orange, the other three hues will be yellow, blue-green, and violet.

The *split complementary* should be mentioned as one of the traditional combinations of colors. A color is chosen and then instead of using its complement, the color on each side of the complement is selected. On the traditional wheel this would create such alliances as yellow, blue-violet, and red-violet, or blue, red-orange, and yellow-orange.

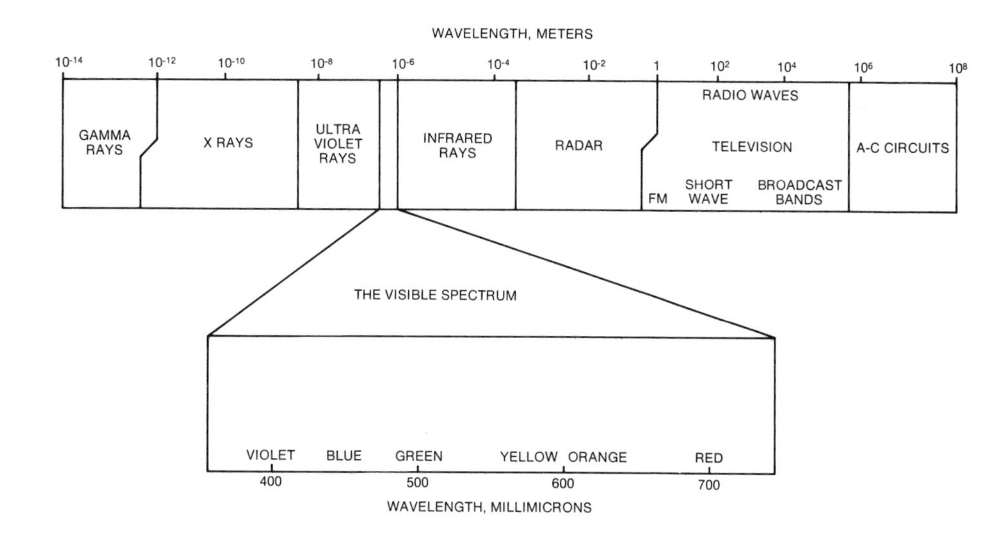

77. This diagram of the electromagnetic field demonstrates the portion of the spectrum that is visible to the human eye. The designation 10^{-6} indicates wave lengths of .00000010 meters. A millimicron is one thousandth of a micron, which in turn is one millionth of a meter. The part of the spectrum that is visible is what we call light.

A WORD ABOUT PIGMENTS

Since we have been discussing ways of combining pigments, it might be interesting to look into the nature of pigments and some of their origins. Pigments are substances of various kinds that have been ground into a fine powder which can be used for coloring paints and dyes. Originally, pigments came from the earth or from other natural substances. The so-called "earth tones" got their names during the Renaissance when they were dug from the soil around Siena and in Umbria in Italy. These pigments have been known ever since as *raw sienna* and *raw umber* or, when baked, as *burnt sienna* and *burnt umber.* In either case they are variations of brown or tan that are basic to the artist's palette. Alizarin crimson was ground from the red root of the madder plant. Blues come from various sources. Ultramarine blue was originally made from powdered lapis lazuli, which had to be brought to Europe from the Orient—hence the name "ultramarine," or "beyond the sea." Cobalt blue is ground from cobalt aluminate; cerulean, a greenish-blue, is a form of cobalt stannate. The ancients ground purple pigment from the glands of a mollusk, the *Murex brandaris,* which was found off the coast of the Phoenician maritime city of Tyre (modern Lebanon). This bluish-red pigment, known as Tyrian purple, required so many snails to produce even a small amount that it was restricted to the use of the nobility. It was because of this convention that the term "royal purple" arose. Many of the familiar pigments are now produced by chemical means, which increases their supply and also improves their durability and vividness. Dyes need special reinforcement, for they must do more than color the fiber; they must become a part of the fiber chemically. Only in this way will they wash and wear satisfactorily, lasting the life of the fabric to which they are applied.

Pigments are made into paints by grinding into a medium that binds them in a plastic form which can be applied with a brush or palette knife. The pigments themselves remain the same; it is the binder that determines whether they will be used as oil paints, watercolors, casein, tempera, or acrylic.

COLOR AND LIGHT

What is called light represents only a very small portion of the electromagnetic field, that part which is visible (Fig. 77). The adjoining sections of the field are the ultraviolet, where wavelengths are shorter and have a higher frequency and higher energy radiation, and the infrared, where the electromagnetic vibrations have a longer wavelength, lower frequency, and lower energy. In all these regions light travels at the same velocity and carries energy, even though it may not be seen. When light strikes organic molecules, some of its energy is absorbed and the molecules show different effects. When molecules absorb light within the visible region, the effects of such change are seen as color.

A mixture of all colors results in the effect of white light. This is true only of color in light, for when all pigment colors are combined they give an approximation of black or gray. In dealing with light, any color can be duplicated by a mixture of varying quantities of red, blue, and green. For this reason these colors are called *additive primary colors.* Colors that absorb the light of the additive primary colors are called *subtractive primary colors;* these are magenta, yellow, and turquoise, which absorb green, blue, and red, respectively. Complementary colors, when mixed together in pigment form, result in gray; but light complements result in white light when combined. Such complements are violet and yellow-green, blue and yellow, green and purple, yellow and violet, orange-red and green-blue, and red and blue-green. The mixing of subtractive primaries takes place in color photography and in printing colored illustrations in magazines, where successive impressions of red, blue, and yellow inks build up a final image in the desired color.

The means (i.e., the mechanism) by which substances absorb light to produce color is still unexplained, although it is assumed to be a function of molecular structure. It is known that if colored light is focused on a pigment in the complementary color the result will be black; for example, casting green light on a red surface will produce such an area of black "light."

Today artists are using light itself as a medium in new forms of construction and painting. The theory of light thus becomes increasingly important in the field of art, with light gradually taking its place beside pigments, dyes, and colored inks as one of the physical materials of the artist.

COLOR IN HISTORY

Now that a brief outline of color theory has been presented, the discussion may be expanded into a study of ways in which color has been used in the past. Choices of color tell a great deal about individuals, and one can learn much about cultures as well through their use of color. Museum models of Greek and Roman buildings in sterile white plaster and the colorless casts and copies of ancient sculpture belie the passionate natures of the people who created the originals. Ancient Egypt, Greece, and Rome all favored brilliant hues such as peacock blue, lemon yellow, carmine, tangerine, and vivid greens to embellish their temples, homes, and wardrobes. Roman togas and Greek chitons, so often shown as white in pictures and statues, were actually woven in the richest hues and trimmed with gold and silver.

The sophisticated artists and patrons of the Renaissance, while borrowing to some extent rich colors of the past along with Classical art forms and philosophy, modified the brightest colors into more subtle bronze and olive greens, yellow-oranges, and purplish-blues. Similar colors persisted through the Baroque period, especially in Italy. In France, where the Baroque became the style of Versailles and Louis XIV, esthetic emphasis was increasingly on the feminine and delicate, culminating in the extravagances of the Rococo during the reign of Louis XV. The colors of the garlanded interiors and dainty furniture were pastel: woodwork was painted in white, soft blues, pinks, violets, and grays, and gold and silver gilt were liberally applied to furniture.

In England, in keeping with traditional British reserve, colors have been generally more conservative until recent years. During the period of the great cabinetmakers—Adams, Chippendale, Hepplewhite, and Sheraton—the individual pieces of furniture were frequently so elaborate that accessory colors were limited to soft tones to complement them. Misty greens, beige, dove gray, carnation pink, and hazy blue were typical of eighteenth-century England.

Oriental and Near Eastern peoples have long been associated with opulent color. The Persian and Chinese silks and other Eastern treasures brought back to Venice gave it a reputation as a center of far-reaching commerce, especially in luxury items, and as a city of rich color. The Chinese are acknowledged to have been expert colorists from very early times. In the Han dynasty, before the Christian era, colorful paintings of great beauty were collected by at least one Chinese emperor, and the T'ang dynasty (A.D. 618–907) has left evidence of vividly colored panels and mural paintings. The high point of Chinese beauty in the realm of pure color, however, is found in the exquisite glazes for ceramics (see Chapter 8).

A knowledge of historical use of color is basic to the designer of costumes or sets, whether for the stage, motion pictures, or television. It is also essential to the interior designer who may be asked to reconstruct a period room or an entire home in period style for a client.

THE PSYCHOLOGICAL USE OF COLOR

Before considering the ways in which the designer can use color, one should be aware of the psychological aspects of color selection. The effects of (i.e., human responses to) color are so important that color styling has become a career in its own right. The stylist, who may design color schemes for anything from subways to factories, maintains a counseling service for industrial concerns and small businesses. His services are based on a thorough knowledge of color and its relationship to people. Many interesting facts have been disclosed through the experiments of the color stylist—facts that are of particular interest to the designer.

In general, warm colors stimulate and cool colors relax. The terms *warm* and *cool* are well chosen. Green can actually make people feel cold, and office workers have been known to have chills when they worked in rooms with blue walls. With the room temperature kept at the same level, the chills abated when the walls were repainted in yellow or the chairs slipcovered in orange. Knute Rockne, the famed Notre Dame football coach, had the locker rooms for his own team painted red and those for the visiting teams painted blue. The reason? When halftime came, the visitors instinctively relaxed in their soothing quarters, while the home team remained keyed up and ready for a winning second half. Similar psychology has been adopted in painting the stalls of racehorses.

Warm colors tend to make objects look closer than cool colors do. For instance, a red chair seems closer than a blue one placed at the same distance from the observer. Knowing this effect, the designer will use vivid colors to cut down the apparent size of a room or to lower high ceilings and will employ soft cool colors to make a small room seem larger. Color can be an important factor even in traffic situations. Study has shown that most automobile drivers, when driving along the highway, feel a greater urgency to pass a red, maroon, cream, or yellow car than a black, blue, or green one.

Although cats and dogs are color-blind, insects react emphatically to color. Mosquitoes avoid orange but will approach red, black, and blue. Beekeepers wear white to avoid being stung, for they have found that if they wear dark colors they are besieged. The knowledge that flies have an antipathy to blue has helped the meat-packing industry, in which many plants now have blue windows.

An interesting aspect of color psychology is observed in the field of synesthesia, in which sounds are given visual form. Many musicians hear music in color; for instance, Beethoven considered B minor a black key, and Schubert described E minor as "a maiden robed in white with a rose-red bow on her heart" and C major as sunlight. Liszt is said to have used phrases in his conducting such as "That is too black," "More pink here, if you please," and "I want it all azure."[1] Some people associate musical instruments with a color: the French horn has been characterized as yellow, the brass family as red, the flute as blue, and the oboe as green. This intermingling of the senses works in other ways, as when one speaks of a "loud" color or a "black" look, a "cold" glance or a "warm" smile. All these associations hold more than a passing interest for the designer. They form a kind of symbolic background to which he can refer when choosing colors to express his own reactions to his environment.

COLOR AND THE CONTEMPORARY ARTIST

The spirit of experimentation typical of art today frees the artist to follow his personal color sense into new areas. When he studies color theory, it is not as rules that must govern his work but as background that will encourage further exploration on his part.

Johannes Itten, in an experiment with students, discovered that individuals have distinctive conceptions of color harmonies, each valid and based on personality characteristics. Furthermore, he found that some students are inclined toward crisp, clearly defined color areas, whereas others, more apt to be emotional and sentimental in temperament, tended to interpret colors in blurred haphazard patches. Some people paint color areas vertically; others orient shapes horizontally or diagonally.[2] Itten's teachings have undoubtedly done much to develop the attitudes of freedom and individuality in the use of color and form that are typical of today's artist.

Color Dynamics

Some of the truly fascinating aspects of color may be approached by experimenting with the effects that colors have upon one another. Such effects are related to *subjective vision,* that is, the psychological interpretation of color relationships by an individual according to his own peculiarities of vision and perception and the past experiences which contribute to his color associations. For centuries the color yellow was associated with the sun. In China it was reserved for the emperor, and no one else was allowed to wear a yellow garment. On the contrary, the Expressionist painter Wassily Kandinsky had a horror of yellow and called it the color of madmen. It is commonplace to speak of a cowardly person as being "yellow." These are three very different interpretations of the same color, all based on subjective response or associations.

There are, however, certain observations concerning yellow that follow similar patterns for most people. For instance, if you gaze for several minutes at a yellow object and then close your eyes, you will probably see the same object in its complementary color, violet. If you turn your glance to a sheet of white paper, however,

Plate 5. Four variations on the color wheel. (A) The traditional color wheel begins with primary colors of red, yellow, and blue. From these three hues are formed the secondary colors orange, green, and violet. All other variations derive from these two groups. (B) Complementary colors are those opposite one another on the color wheel. In this example each pair of complements is shown connected by a different type of line. (C) Analogous colors are those adjoining one another on the color wheel. Various types of lines here show some of the analogous ranges possible. (D) Triads consist of three colors equidistant on the color wheel. Various triads can be traced by following the different types of lines designating each. Red, blue, and yellow (the primary colors) form one triad, while violet, orange, and green (the secondary colors) form another.

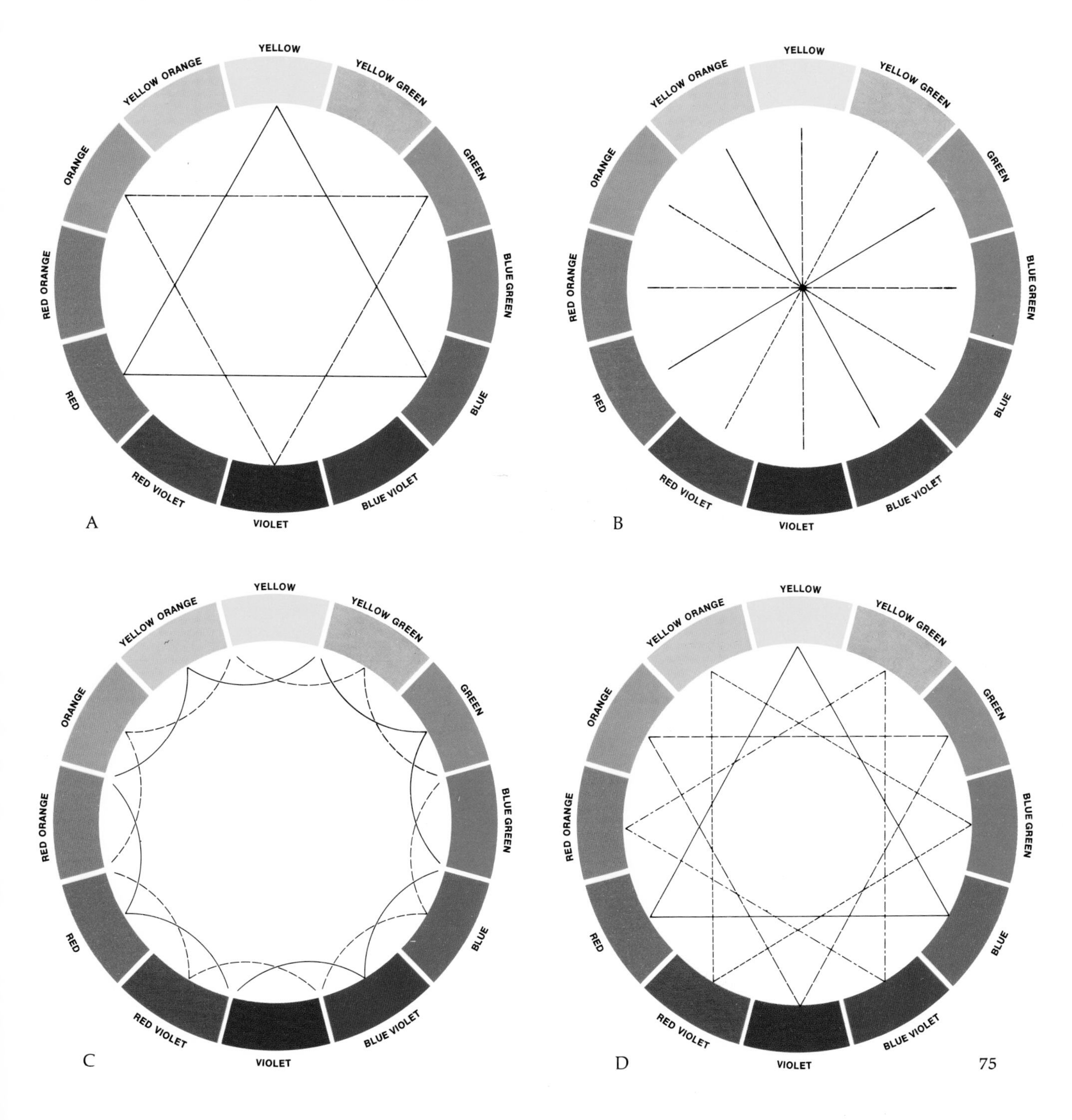

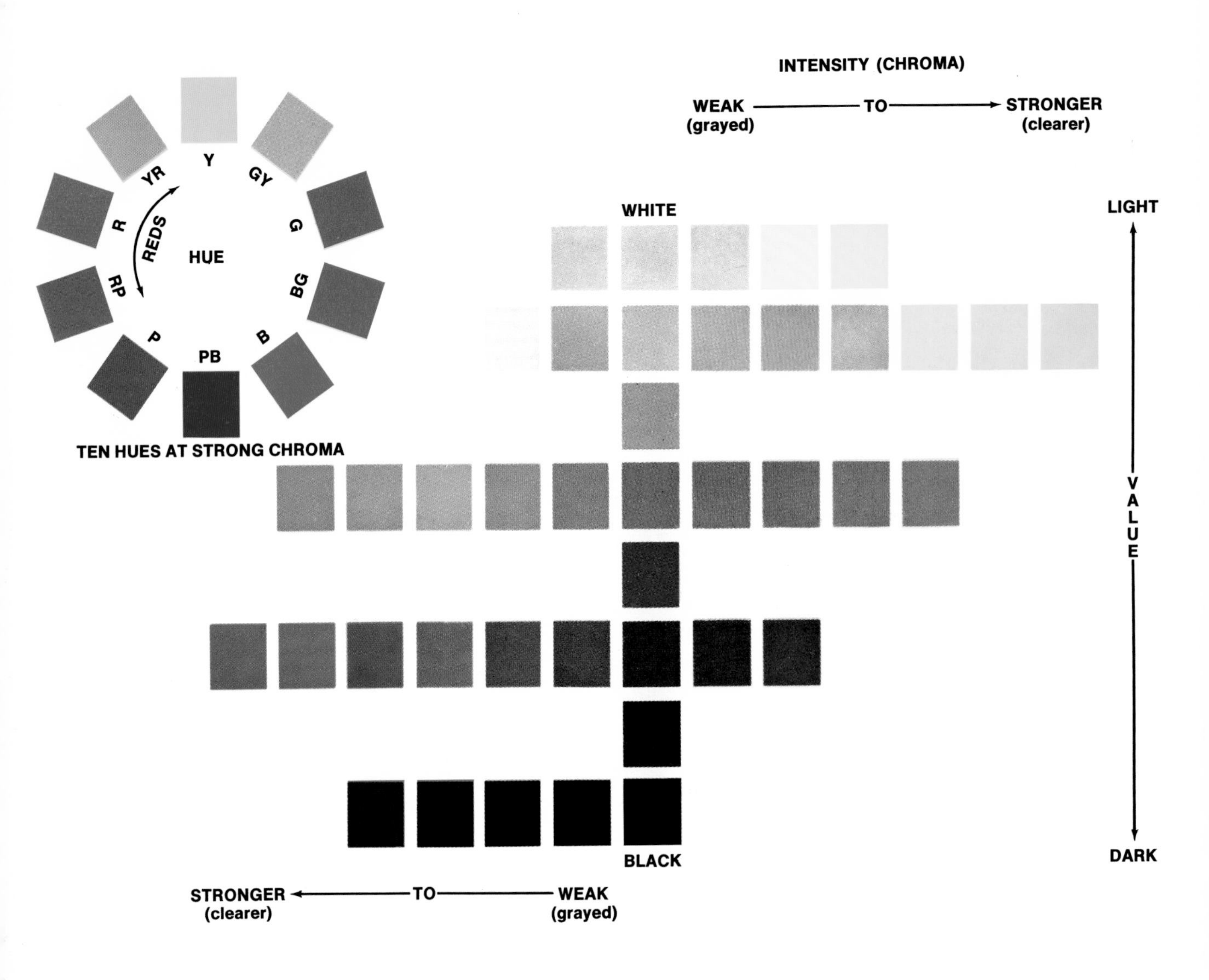

Plate 6. The chroma scale is a device for showing variations in intensity for any given hue.

Plate 7. Mildred Fischer. *RedGoldBlue.* 1966. Linen yarns and wool, 4′10″ × 5′10″. Collection the artist.

Plate 8. PIERO DORAZIO. *Where Is the Way Where Light Dwelleth.* 1966. Oil on canvas, 7′6¼″ × 5′2½″. Courtesy Marlborough-Gerson Gallery, New York.

the yellow object will reappear in blue. In both cases, what you see is the *afterimage.* In looking at the color yellow, the sensitivities of the red and green receptor systems in the area of the retina where the yellow object is seen are reduced by prolonged exposure to a mixture of red and green light. When the yellow object is replaced in the line of vision by neutral white paper, red and green are subtracted from the white, and a blue image appears. As the receptor systems recover their sensitivities, the afterimage fades. This is the theory of local color adaptation, which can occur with any color, producing the afterimage in the complementary color. For a red object, the afterimage may be green or blue-green, whereas for a violet object it may appear as yellow or yellow-green. This phenomenon, known as *successive contrast,* is a means by which a color when separated from its complement strives to compensate in the human eye, as if the two complements formed a whole that is incomplete when only one is seen. The reason for this is that any pair of complements embraces the entire spectrum. The complement of yellow, a primary color, is violet, a secondary color composed of blue and red; and the complement of blue is orange, a combination of yellow and red. Hence each pair of complements that includes a primary color actually encompasses all three primary colors.

To return to yellow: if a shape in neutral gray is placed on a yellow background, the gray takes on a violet cast. If the gray is placed on violet, the gray then has a tinge of yellow. This is another phenomenon that holds true for all the complementary colors; with every hue, gray tends to take on the color of its complement. This is referred to as *simultaneous contrast.*

The dynamics of color include experimentation of many kinds to discover what effects colors produce under varying conditions. The same color will produce quite different results when displayed against black and against white. Two hues will react in varying ways when made into tints or shades. Also revealing are contrasts between light and dark, starting with yellow, the lightest color on the color wheel, and contrasting it with violet, the darkest. The tendency of warm colors to come forward and of cool colors to recede has been mentioned. Warm and cool colors should be placed side by side and the effects studied. The artist can learn ways of making one color look like quite a different color by juxtaposing it with various other hues. These are discoveries that should be made by the artist himself, for while there are certain results that can be expected, the possibilities are limitless, and only firsthand experimentation will convince him of the infinite range of color at his command and allow him to make the best choices for the medium in which he is working.

In Plate 7 (p. 77) Mildred Fischer has created a striking textile from the basic colors of the traditional color wheel; but she has devised a distinctive variation by adapting them to three nonobjective shapes of her own design. Instead of the primary yellow, she has used a soft gold that enriches the chord formed by this basic harmony. The gold of this textile is quite different from the yellow of the wheels in Plate 5. It is different also from the yellow of a daffodil, the yellow of sunlight, the yellow of a canary's feathers, the amber of a glass of Rhine wine, or the color of brass. The color in this tapestry differs also from the yellow hue of a piece of suede or velvet or satin. It is, in short, something that the artist has created in relation to her own medium and her particular vision.

Expansion of Color

The uses of color can be expanded by experimentation with such effects as iridescence, luster, luminosity, and transparency. *Iridescence* is the rainbow effect evident

left: 78. Georges de La Tour. *The Education of the Virgin.* Late 1640s. Oil on canvas, 33 × 39½″. Frick Collection, New York (copyright).

below left: 79. Hans Holbein the Younger. *Sir Thomas More.* 1527. Panel, 29½ × 23¾″. Frick Collection, New York (copyright).

opposite: 80. El Greco. *The Virgin with Saint Inés and Saint Tecla.* 1597–99. Oil on canvas, 76⅛ × 40½″. National Gallery of Art, Washington, D.C. (Widener Collection).

in a raindrop or the inside of a seashell, where the play of light or surface color gives the appearance of including all the hues of the spectrum. This is the result of *diffraction,* in which some circumstance causes the surface to split a ray of light into its component parts, so that the eye sees the various hues of the spectrum separately. This is a difficult effect to achieve with paint, but it can be created through careful control of the background. The use of a soft gray ground will give an illusion of mistiness, against which vivid pure colors will seem to have a luminous quality, as in Figure 78.

Similarly, *luster* can be achieved by using bright colors on a deep navy or black background. There are many kinds of luster, and considerable experimentation is necessary to master the technique. The Old Masters arrived at lustrous effects through the use of glazes—colors thinned with a paint medium and applied in successive semitransparent layers (Fig. 79). A vase or pot was made lustrous by painting its highlights in a pure hue rather than in a lighter one, thus maintaining the effect of brilliance.

Luminosity, another accomplishment of the Old Masters, was often achieved through the use of glazes; but this was not always the case. El Greco usually painted with spontaneity, yet his works have a great deal of luminosity. In *The Virgin with Saint Inés and Saint Tecla* (Fig. 80) is seen one of the reasons for this. His use of color in this painting is typical of many of his works, in which three colors appear again and again: the rich blue of the Virgin's robe, the orchid pink of her gown,

and the lemon yellow of the robe on the lower left-hand figure. These are El Greco's distinctive variations of the three primary colors of the traditional color wheel. The luminosity has much to do with the background that is also typical of El Greco's works (see Pl. 1, p. 39). Gray-toned and full of movement, some of his backgrounds are much darker and more dramatic; yet the use of these three sharp color accents against the neutral ground is instrumental in creating his luminous effect.

Transparency is a quality that fascinates many contemporary artists. The use of cellophane or colored tissue paper within a painting is not unusual, giving areas of color with a feeling of great depth below. Transparency can be achieved with more lasting effect in paint by the simple device of placing colored cellophane over a color area and then fabricating the color made by the cellophane. An intriguing and difficult feat of transparency has been achieved by Piero Dorazio in *Where Is the Way Where Light Dwelleth* (Pl. 8, p. 78). A series of transparent stripes has been laid over other transparent stripes, and the effect of their crossings and interlacings has in turn been painted with considerable skill. This is typical of the work of artists today, who are trying all kinds of new techniques and combinations in an effort to find original ways of using color that are as boldly experimental as the age in which they live.

SUMMARY

The importance of color cannot be overrated. Not only can it be a matter of life and death in nature, it is vital to man as both an art and a science. The artist should know something of both the scientific approach, through physics and psychology, and of the artistic or esthetic approach to color. There are many theories, and he should realize that each is valid in its own terms without excluding all the others as being incorrect. It is important to study all these theories in order to use them as springboards for his own color experiments.

Color has three dimensions: hue, value, and intensity. There are also tones, which are grayed hues achieved by mixing with gray pigment or the complementary color. Chromatic colors have the quality of hue in them, whereas achromatic colors are neutral.

Color harmonies result when related colors are combined. Color relationships are based on the color wheel. Harmonies can be built from complementary colors, analogous colors, triads, tetrads, and split complementaries. A harmony can also be attained monochromatically, with varied gradations of one hue being combined.

The pigments used in paints and dyes have many origins. Color in light is also important to the artist, who makes skillful use of additive and subtractive primaries. Although complementary-color pigments give gray when added together, complementary combinations in light result in the effect of white light.

Throughout history, colors have told much about the cultures that used them. The uses of color tell a great deal about human psychology also. Color styling for psychological and visual effect has become a career in its own right, serving industrial firms and others who need expert advice on how to increase the comfort or efficiency of their employees or the effectiveness of their operations.

The contemporary artist has a new and experimental approach to color and its uses. He is more interested in color dynamics—the action of color upon other colors—than in traditional rules for mixing. He has become involved in many methods, including successive and simultaneous contrast, as well as in the expansion of color possibilities into iridescence, luster, luminosity, and transparency.

Structural Design

chapter 6

As knowledge of the principles of design is applied to specific projects, the work falls into one of two categories. First, the artist must be involved in the *structural design* of the piece he is working on, and, second, he must concern himself with the development of the object's surface, which can be termed *decorative design.* The interrelationship of these two categories of design is basic. While decorative design is sometimes used like counterpoint in music, structural design usually determines the decorative design in all its aspects: the shape and size, the techniques used, and the nature of the design applied, which must be related intrinsically to the materials and the basic structure of the object.

MEANING OF STRUCTURAL DESIGN

Paul Weiss, now professor emeritus of Rockefeller University, once stated that if there is one lesson to be learned from the study of organic nature, it is that there is order in the gross (or large) forms, with freedom and diversity in the small.[1] Birds have an orderly growth pattern and a definite vertebrate structure, but there is infinite variety in the color and pattern of their feathers. The mountain is built up over the centuries, layer upon layer of glacial deposits, fossilized vegetation, and alluvium, growing with the rhythms of fire and ice into an orderly structure; on closer inspection, however, its surface is a treasure house of variety, in textures of stone, alpine vegetation, and tundra, each with its own growth pattern. Even the smallest fern (Fig. 81) unfolds in its own way, revealing a structure different from that of other varieties of fern, yet consistent in general with the members of its own species.

81. Ferns, like trees, display an orderly growth pattern, but there are obvious differences in individual specimens.

Just as the configuration of the mountain shapes the glaciers and snowbanks, so should man build his edifices from the inside out. Function should be the first concern, with the structure itself dictating what form the surface detail will take. However, the architect should not make a finished design for a building and then call in the muralist or mosaicist or sculptor to decorate its surfaces. The architect and the artist should work together from the inception of the design, in mutual respect, sharing the original vision and combining their talents for the creation of a beautiful building. This sort of relationship can result in the highest form of art.

Structural design embodies the most fundamental aspects of any object: its purpose, its function, its very nature. If the structural design is not successful, no beauty of decorative design will save it—any more than a symphony can be given form by harmony alone. Frank Lloyd Wright once commented that the doctor can bury his mistakes but the architect can only plant vines over his. Obviously, even the most beautiful vines cannot hide from the occupants the fact that a building does not fulfill its function.

STRUCTURAL DESIGN IN NATURE

We have only to look around us to observe nature's amazing structural designs, particularly in the animal world. Some of her most ingenious solutions to environmental conditions are seen in the following examples. The mountain goat has sharp ridges around his soft foot pads, enabling him to climb rapidly on ice, snow, and bare rock. The female penguin, living in barren arctic wastelands, carries her eggs with her in a special pouch until they have hatched and the young are old enough to endure the outside world. The bat, seeking its food in darkness, has been found to guide itself with a special sonar system, emitting ultrasonic cries and then following the echoes to avoid colliding with obstacles.

For centuries, the shells of snails have fascinated biologists and mathematicians alike because of the orderly growth pattern, which follows the logarithmic spiral and can be reduced to the very same mathematical formula as the "golden section" of the Greeks. This precept was expressed philosophically by Aristotle as the "golden mean," the virtue that is the median between two vices, as courage is the mean between cowardice and foolhardiness. The golden section, a formula on which

below: 82. WOLF STRACHE. *Shell of Marine Snail.* 1956.

below right: 83. Central staircase of the Hôtel Terminus-Grüber, Strasbourg.

left: 84. The spiral shell of the oyster drill facilitates propulsion through water.

below: 85. Valvular intestine of the skate, *Raja,* shown in cross section.

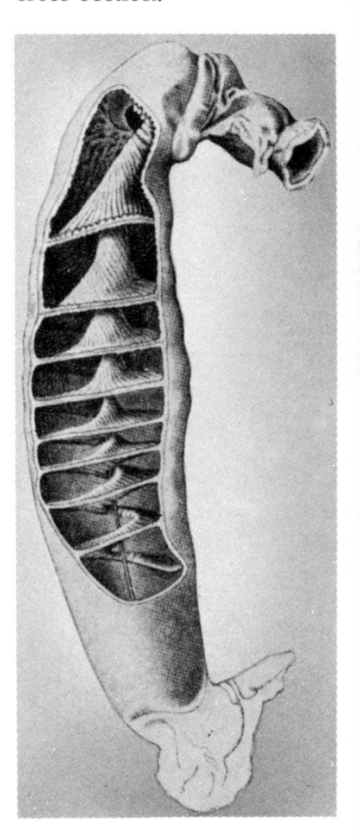

Greek temples were based, can be stated mathematically as $a:b = b:(a + b)$. Assuming that a is the width of a temple and b is the length, the relationship between the two sides becomes apparent. The same mean rectangle that determined the floor plan of the classical temple has been found to circumscribe Greek vases and sculpture as well. Its mathematical ratio, which has been the subject of intensive study, was no doubt an influence on Leonardo da Pisa (Leonardo Fibonacci), medieval Europe's greatest mathematician, who in the early thirteenth century developed the "Fibonacci series." This is a series of numbers that has been found to reveal the secret of much of nature's structural design, particularly in the field of botany. The numbers run as follows: 1, 1, 2, 3, 5, 8, 13, 21, 34, 55, 89, 144, and so on. It is evident that each number is the sum of the two numbers preceding it. It has been found that pine cones have 5 and 8 rows of seeds, pineapples have 8 and 13, dandelions 13 and 21, daisies 21 and 34, and sunflowers 55 and 89. These same numbers are expressed in the spiral shells of snails (Fig. 82), and their relationship to each other is almost exactly the same as that of the golden section, which can be shown[2] as the ratio 1 : 1.618. With such a firm mathematical basis, it is not surprising that the spiral shell has been used as inspiration for architectural structures such as the central staircase of the Hôtel Terminus-Grüber in Strasbourg, France (Fig. 83).

Still more dramatic than the snail shell in Figure 82 is the pointed spiral of the oyster drill (Fig. 84), which facilitates rapid movement through water. This is only one of many examples of the spiral found in marine life. Externally, the spiral shell causes the water to swirl, thereby propelling the animal to its destination; internally, the spiral is used to move food through the body of the fish (Fig. 85). The spiral is not limited to sea forms, however; it is evident in whirlpools, in plant life, and in human fingerprints. Like the human body, with its marvelous ability to adapt and recover, the forms of marine life are the result of millions of years of adaptation, during which organisms gradually evolved to fit their changing environment.

Unfortunately, the artist can neither wait for such prolonged evolutionary change nor, usually, for further knowledge based on a trial of his designs. A designed object must be right from the time it is put to use, whether it is a building or a piece of power machinery or a fabric. In machinery and appliances, of course, later models profit by the failures or shortcomings of the previous ones (as well as from controlled trial runs); nevertheless, each successive design must be right for its own time, or the manufacturer will be flooded with complaints and the designer will have failed. It is imperative that the professional designer know his field thoroughly before he begins. His only protection against error is a sure knowledge of what is needed,

what the object is expected to do, what has already been done in the field, and how he might improve upon previous models. Beyond these considerations, he must know the structural limitations of the sort of object or mechanism he intends to design.

POSITIVE AND NEGATIVE SPACE

Any solid structure exists in and occupies space and shapes the space around it. Space flows throughout a building, defining the living areas as well as influencing many of the decorative elements. The walls and solid forms of the structure are positive elements, which can be referred to as *positive space;* the areas enclosed and shaped by the walls are termed *negative space.* Similarly, in a piece of sculpture, the sculptured material itself is the positive space, and the space established around it (and perhaps within it) is negative. Such negative space is created by the angle of an arm or leg or the inclination of a head, or by definite openings within the positive forms. Positive space is constructed in a painting by the persons or objects painted, or by the dominant forms, while the background areas or other unoccupied spaces become negative space. In the creation of any art form negative space should be considered, for it is sensitive interaction of the negative space with the more pronounced positive space that makes a successful design. A particularly effective interplay of positive and negative space is used in Stanley Kaplan's wooden panel shown here (Fig. 86). In a pine plank, the artist has created a composition expressing the faceless moving crowd of modern urban life. With the wood stained in some areas for contrast, it is carved on both sides so that it might be used as a room divider. Varied textures make the positive relief figures interesting, but the stark white void of the negative forms gives the dramatic touch that makes the composition a truly striking design.

COMPOSITION

In painting and in two-dimensional design, structural design is frequently referred to as *composition.* Although actually decorative designs in one sense, such works, in order to be successful, must have a structural basis that is carefully coordinated.

opposite: 86. Stanley Kaplan. *People.* c. 1960. Carved planks of pine, 4 × 5′. Collection Mr. and Mrs. Paul MacLean, Louisville, Ky.

right: 87. The sea urchin (*arbacia punctulata*) grows around a vertical axis with radial symmetry in the arrangement of its spines.

A basic consideration in composition is a sense of *symmetry.* Symmetry involves the balance of parts among themselves as well as between individual parts and the whole, a primary aspect of proportion. Bilateral symmetry, in which both halves of an object are identical, is only one of seventeen kinds. Nature has created symmetry in both plant and animal life, often with a symmetrical arrangement of leaves or tissues around a vertical axis. This sort of *radial symmetry* (Fig. 87) is found in the cross section of almost all roots, as well as in many plant and animal structures.

Like the logarithmic natural spiral, symmetry in nature has been reduced to a mathematical formula—an approach that has been carried over by some artists into the field of composition. The theory of composition so constructed mathematically is known as *dynamic symmetry* (Fig. 88). This is a system with which a rectangle can

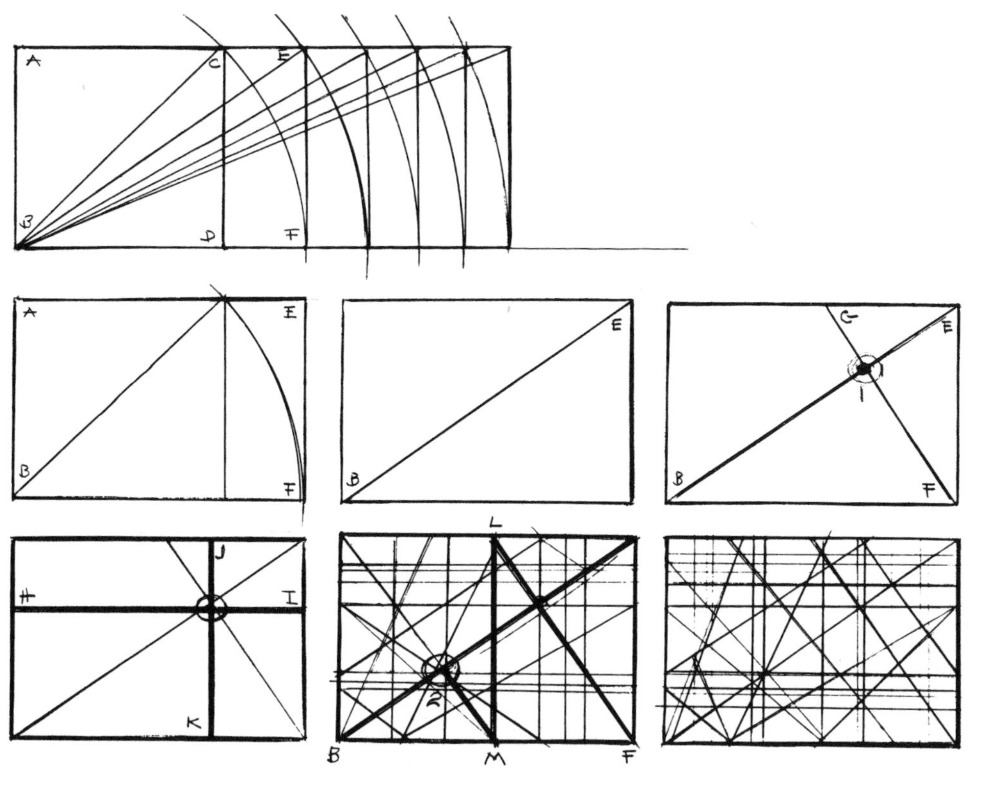

88. The development of structural design through dynamic symmetry can be seen in this series of diagrams by Thelma Winter. The artist begins with a square, constructs a related rectangle, and establishes verticals, horizontals, and diagonals by geometric methods.

left: 89. THELMA WINTER. *Christ and Apostles.* 1956. Enamel on steel, 5′ × 7′6″. Bethany Evangelical Lutheran Church, Ashtabula, Ohio. (Executed in collaboration with EDWARD WINTER.)

below left: 90. Diagram for Fig. 89, *Christ and Apostles.*

be logically divided or expanded into similar and proportionate areas by means of geometric progression, thus achieving the measured recurrence by which all things in nature grow. Related to the golden section, dynamic symmetry was applied by the Greeks in their temples and vases, and it still provides the contemporary artist with a method of achieving natural rhythms in his designs. The picture plane is divided into proportionate geometric shapes, and the resulting lines form a structural web that will determine the dominant shapes and spaces of the composition, creating rhythms that propel the eye through and around the design in ever-changing propor-

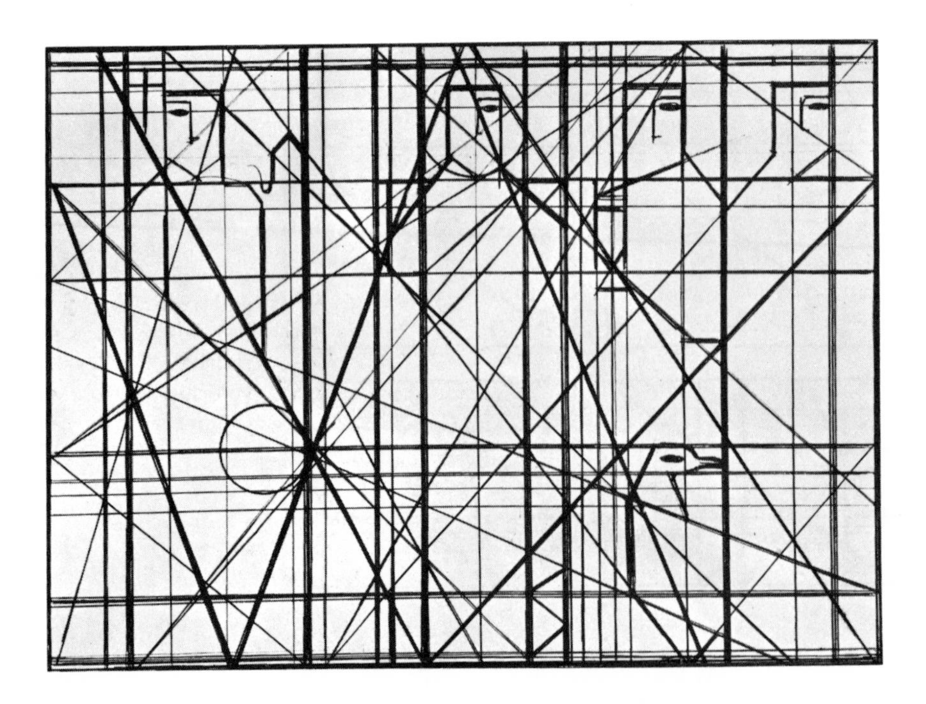

tions and spacing. Thelma Winter's enamel panel *Christ and Apostles* (Fig. 89) is an excellent example of these compositional principles. Although the structural lines are readily apparent in the finished panel, the artist has also provided a schematic diagram to give us a clearer idea of how she created her design (Fig. 90). Intersections of lines determine salient points in the details of the figures. The main verticals bounding the figures intersect horizontals and diagonals and thereby determine the height and width of the figures, the size of the heads, the placement of the hands, and the folds of the drapery. The wings of the eagle are outlined along diagonals that strike across the picture plane to the midsection of the first figure, with other strong diagonals determining the width of his head. The central figure has a crisscross grid of lines delineating the folds of his garment, the size of the halo, and so on. The longer one studies this design, the greater are the number of linear relationships that become apparent. In this kind of dynamic arrangement the possibilities for creating combinations of line and shape are endless, and the subtle interlocking relations of the parts of the composition to one another and to the whole ensure a rhythmic and unified design.

ART AND SCIENCE

Differences between art and science are many and are easily recognized. As technology becomes more dominant in human life, however, it becomes increasingly clear that both art and science must play major roles in the design of environment. The artist, too, must acquaint himself with scientific knowledge and new developments. Both the artist and the scientist must grasp the wholeness of existence, instead of succumbing to the traditional pigeonholing of one pursuit in opposition to the other. Since the Industrial Revolution, human life has been affected by major developments in technology with such great rapidity that no one has been able to keep any systematic control over environmental conditions. The result is that the present-day designer is faced with a vast "landscape" of ugliness and confusion. A trip across America today is dominated not by scenic wonders but by gaudy billboards and junkyards. The marked increase in mental illness and emotional disturbances attests to the inadequate housing, the noise, the dirt, the seemingly insurmountable traffic problems and hazards, and the myriad irritations and annoyances that plague the individual in his struggle to lead some semblance of a rational, humane life in the urban culture of the twentieth century. All this can be overcome, but only by sound study of the biological, physiological, and psychological needs of the individual and a concerted effort to provide for them. Comparatively little can be accomplished by the artist or the scientist alone. Never before has it been so necessary for experts or specialists to contribute to the whole of existence, to work together and to pool their knowledge for the benefit of civilization in general. It has been said that genius consists of the ability to see apparently unrelated elements as parts of an integrated whole. This sort of genius is always essential to an understanding of one's own time, but it is particularly urgent in a period of such rapid change as the twentieth century, for without this overview the delicate balance that holds all elements of society together would be destroyed.

Nowhere is the need for such a gift more important than in the crafts. An intelligent and creative interdependence of the artist and the machine is now acknowledged for the first time since the Industrial Revolution replaced the craftsman with the power-driven loom, glass blower, and pottery mold. After decades of mediocre machine-made products, industrial engineers have come to recognize a dependence upon the artist-designer to create prototypes of distinctive and esthetically satisfying pottery, glassware, and fabrics that can be reproduced in quantity by the machine. The artist who understands the technology of the glass factory or the textile mill can thus be a significant influence in improving the taste of his generation.

THE MEANING OF INTEGRITY

The importance and lasting value of a designer's contribution will depend in large degree upon his *integrity.* Here again is encountered the need to see a situation whole—indeed, "integrity" stems from the Latin *integritas,* meaning the quality or state of being whole. In the artist-designer it involves a personal realization of the relevance of his individual design to its own time, the necessity of its being honest in its use of materials and in expressing its function, and a forthright choice of decorative design, using ornamentation as an integral part of the structural design rather than as something to alter or camouflage it. In short, the integrity of a work of art will hinge in large part on the artist's sincere desire to create something significant and pertinent for his own time and his reaction to it. This concept is so basic to contemporary design that it is imperative for the artist to consider the matter of integrity in each of its separate applications: to materials, form, function, and ornamentation.

Integrity of Materials

Integrity of materials is the first requisite of structural design. Not only must the designer know what materials are available, but he must also be aware of their advantages and limitations. If he is designing buildings, he must know which materials are strong in compression (when pressed under weight) and which have more strength in tension (when stretched). If he is working with clay, he must know which clays are more plastic and how much weight or pressure they will bear before he can design a specific shape or form. If he is creating textiles, he must understand animal, vegetable, and synthetic fibers. A warp that will respond favorably to contact with water combined with a weft that will mat or shrink when wet can mean a textile unsatisfactory for daily use.

Generally speaking, materials fall into eight categories: wood, metal, paper, ceramic, glass, stone, fiber, and plastic. Each group has distinct characteristics, and

91. Triglyphs and metope on the Parthenon, Athens. 448–432 B.C. Metope 4′8″ × 4′2″.

92. Ludwig Miës van der Rohe and Philip Johnson. Seagram Building, New York. 1958.

the designer should make the most of these. Thus, wood should not be used where great tensile strength is needed, and stone cannot be effectively employed when the resiliency of wood is required.

Spearheaded by the architect Louis Sullivan in this country and the Bauhaus School of Design in Germany, drastic steps were taken to jar designers into using steel for its inherent qualities, instead of simply as a structural frame to be camouflaged by other materials. The first skyscrapers were characterized by accretions of Renaissance stone ornament and Greek columns stuck on *after* the basic steel structure was completed. Of course, this is not a fault of the nineteenth century alone. Even the Greeks may have imitated the ends of wooden beams when they began to build their temples in stone, as is seen in the triglyph of the Doric frieze (Fig. 91). If this were true on the part of the Greeks, however, how meaningless it was still to be using triglyphs to embellish the tops of 14-story buildings more than 23 centuries later! While Sullivan himself encased his steel skeletons in stone and concrete and even decorated his skyscrapers rather lavishly, his work clearly disclosed the essential structure of the building, and ornamentation was planned as an integral part of the structure rather than stuck on as an afterthought. Moreover, ornament was expressly designed for its own period instead of borrowing Greek moldings and Gothic gargoyles, so that Sullivan's finished work did not look like a hybrid medieval castle or a cathedral raised high above the ground. Much controversy flared about these early innovations, but they led more or less directly to the simple functional beauty of many modern high-rise buildings (Fig. 92).

93. Dominick Labino. *Rendez-Vous IV.* 1969. Cobalt blue glass with enclosed silver-glass forms and gold veil, height 11″. Collection the artist.

Whatever material the designer chooses for his work, he must explore all its possibilities to achieve the maximum effect. If he is to work in wood, he should know the characteristics of the various types of wood—which are hard, which are soft, which will carve well, which will splinter easily, and which will provide the most beautiful grain. In using metal, the artist must know which will corrode rapidly, which can be molded or hammered, and the comparative weight to be expected in the finished product. Above all, he must be willing to accept the limitations of his materials, for there is nothing to be gained by imitating one material with another. Bricks painted to look like plaster, plastics grained to resemble wood, and the proliferation of plastic flowers, vines, and shrubs all over America today are glaring examples of a lack of integrity with respect to materials, which has no place in good design. The intrinsic qualities of the original materials are completely missed in the imitations—the warmth and fresh odor of wood, the growth cycle and oxygen-giving property of plants, and the scent of flowers. Only a superficial visual similarity is achieved, and such unfortunate creations indicate a complete insensitivity to integrity of materials.

An excellent example of integrity of materials is found in modern glass, such as the piece shown in Figure 93. Here glass as a material is exploited to the fullest, and decorative use is made of its fluid and transparent qualities. There is no attempt at applied external decoration, no effort to make it look like anything but a piece of glass. Yet the beauty of this piece could not be approximated in any other material.

One of the most challenging fields for the designer is the relatively new area of plastics. The term "plastic" refers to any of numerous substances composed of organic molecules in certain predetermined complex combinations. The physical and

94. Vinyl provides a floor covering that is both attractive and durable.

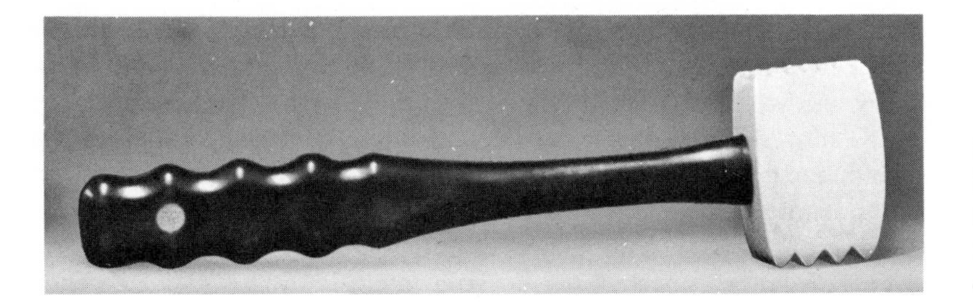

95. The handle of this kitchen utensil demonstrates how plastic can be molded to fit the fingers and ensure a firm grasp.

chemical properties of an individual plastic are determined by the structure and weight of the component molecules. The present-day field of plastics was anticipated in 1860 when the wild elephant herds began to be decimated; this caused a sharp increase in the price of ivory. A prize of $10,000 was offered for a satisfactory substitute to be used in the manufacture of billiard balls, and although it did not win the prize, celluloid was developed, the forerunner of plastic. The use of natural resins, which developed at about the same time, started the experimentation that led to the plastic materials of today. Numerous resins, with widely varying characteristics, are now in use. *Acrylic* resins are components of Lucite and Plexiglas, which are used not only for lenses but also for decorative objects, handles on brushes and mirrors, and reflected illumination in highway signs and advertising. Acrylic plastics are unusually clear and warm, lend themselves to high polishing, and effectively withstand weathering and hard use. Orlon is an acrylic textile fiber. *Polyamide* resins are responsible for nylon, used for bristles in brushes as well as for a textile whose fibers were originally designed to replace silk during World War II. Because of its great strength and wearing qualities, nylon has increased in popularity ever since. *Vinyl* resins, formed from vinyl chloride and vinyl acetate, which made possible unbreakable phonograph records, are used for many items of clothing and for hard-wearing floor coverings that are designed in a variety of textures and patterns (Fig. 94). Attractive designs in vinyl—which is impervious to stains, heat, and most ordinary wear—are much in demand for working surfaces in kitchens, laboratories, and studios. A great variety of plastics are used for insulation, airplane parts, paints and other finishes, and industrial purposes. Plastics have replaced metal and glass in many of the containers used for food, drugs, and cosmetics. No other material is so easily shaped and manipulated. Rolling into thin sheets, molding, shaping by means of dies, or pouring as liquids are all possible methods of forming objects from the materials in this category.

Such versatile new materials have brought a wealth of possibilities to the designer, some of which were not fully realized at first. For years, conventional shapes from older materials were fabricated in the new materials without any attempt at adaptation. Plastic handles on utensils and irons were made in exactly the same shapes as those which had been turned on wood lathes and thus retained all the same limitations. When designers discovered they could mold plastic in any desired form, they began to create handles that lent themselves to a firmer grip (Fig. 95). Much plastic design was called *streamlining*—design built to move rapidly through the air with a minimum of resistance, since all corners and sharp edges were smoothed out and projections were reshaped to hug the body. However essential these smooth lines may be to rockets and automobiles, they are not particularly necessary to vacuum cleaners and electric beaters. Nonetheless, there resulted a certain simplicity of design that gradually became incorporated into forms which expressed the individual object.

The possibilities of a class of materials such as plastics would seem almost infinite; yet there are limitations to be recognized in any area. The enthusiasm with which designers welcomed these new opportunities in plastics led them to produce also such failures as measuring cups that melted under heat, couplings that broke under strain, and toys that did not withstand the hard wear of children's play as well as wood or metal might. Such problems are being solved as new attributes are added to plastic materials. Although continuing experimentation is necessary and adjustments are to be expected, the designer must know his materials thoroughly before he can be certain that his design will be effective both in purpose and in esthetic truth to the material.

Mass production of objects in plastic has had much to do with the increased interest in crafts made by hand. Ease of acquisition tends to diminish the value of consumer goods, and objects sold in great quantity do not satisfy the innate longing of many people to surround themselves with belongings that indicate an exclusive and refined taste. For this reason handmade pottery and textiles, carvings, mosaics, sculpture, and painting are enjoying a wide public appeal unprecedented in our era. Individual design and the handcrafted look have become cherished symbols of a world in which man's talents and his dreams remain impervious to the pressures, the lack of beauty, and the standardization of a mechanized modern society.

In keeping with the search for individuality, many artists are finding new and exciting uses for old materials. Recently, some young artists have been exploring the possibilities of paper and have fashioned it into objects never before associated with this material, considered so fragile and disposable. Paper products today offer new versatility, for they combine brilliant color with varied textures and great

opposite left: 96. ERIC RENNER. *Hanging Structure.* 1967. Brown paper tape, wrapped and glued; height 18″. Collection the artist.

opposite right: 97. HIROSHI OGAWA. *Untitled Sculpture.* 1966. Scored, folded, and glued paper; height 8″. Collection the artist.

right: 98. Fantastic animal, from Mexico. 20th century. Painted papier-mâché, height 4′7″. National Museum of Popular Arts and Industries, Mexico City.

strength, as well as such attributes as being waterproof, wrinkleproof, and fire-resistant. The Japanese have long used paper in lanterns, masks, kites, screens, and even partition walls, but contemporary papers are even more adaptable to imaginative use. Furniture composed of paper tubes, toys ingeniously devised from colorful cartons or egg crates, and sturdy but decorative cardboard wastebaskets are some of the many objects now made from paper. Many paper inventions are geared to a mobile population, which prefers change to durability and which welcomes such items as paper pile rugs that last a single season at a summer cabin or dresses to be discarded after one wearing. These are, of course, a logical extension of the viewpoint which has long accepted paper towels, dishes, and napkins for their convenience and practicality.

A particularly noteworthy example of the possibilities of paper was created by students at the Parsons School of Design in New York City, where an entire playground was constructed of corrugated paper, including trees as well as play equipment, for the use of mentally retarded children who might injure themselves in an environment of wood or metal. Another highly practical use of paper is to combine it with polyurethane foam and coat it with polyethylene as was done to build lightweight fire-resistant homes for migrant farmworkers in California, after the design of the Canadian Herbert Yates.

Experiments with paper for decorative purposes have produced some highly imaginative results. Even as prosaic a form as brown gummed tape has been made into a surprisingly ornamental creation by Eric Renner (Fig. 96); Hiroshi Ogawa, inspired no doubt by the Japanese tradition of paper folding and cutting (*origami*), has created striking paper sculpture from scored and folded paper (Fig. 97).

Quite a different approach to paper is found in papier-mâché (from the French, meaning "chewed paper"). Soft absorbent paper is moistened to a pulp and mixed with glue, size, or resin and then molded into desired forms. Papier-mâché has long been used for masks and for display props, but the artists and craftsmen of Mexico have now revived the art in a new style. Using many coats of bright lacquer which give a high gloss to the finished object, they have produced papier-mâché works with the gay, whimsical expression that has been associated with so many Mexican techniques and art forms. The grotesque animal in Figure 98 is typical of the fantasy

above: 99. Chrystya Ivanivna Olenska. Necklace. 1966. Painted papier-mâché, width 9½″. Collection the artist.

right: 100. Jean (Hans) Arp. *Human Concretion.* 1949 (after original plaster model of 1935). Cast stone, height 19½″. Museum of Modern Art, New York (gift of the Advisory Committee).

and imagination displayed in this medium. Different in origin, yet reminiscent of Mexican folkloristic color and gaiety, is the necklace in Figure 99 designed by Chrystya Ivanivna Olenska of New York City.

Integrity of Form

Simultaneously with consideration for materials, the designer must devote himself to *integrity of form.* The form will determine the materials, and the materials will in turn affect the form, so that it cannot be said that either consideration takes absolute precedence.

Integrity of form has been summed up for years by the expression "form follows function." This term has long been associated with the evolution of the skyscraper into a building that is frankly functional; yet it is a concept that has always existed in nature—in birds' nests, beehives, and beaver dams, which are all forms evolving strictly from function, with minimum expenditure of effort and material. Raul France, who has made extensive biotechnical studies, states that if we could use in a skyscraper the same structural principles that appear in the stalk of a plant we could erect a building seven hundred stories high with the same material used in our present building.[3]

Jean Arp's sculpture *Human Concretion* (Fig. 100) has no function but to please the eye, yet it has great integrity of form. As cast stone, it makes no pretense at anything but a simple massive form, smooth to the touch and the eye, with a fluid rhythm that makes it appear different from each side. The title indicates something that is solid and real, as opposed to an abstraction. Arp himself has written: "I believe that nature is not in opposition to art. Art is of natural origin . . . spiritualized through man's sublimation."[4]

Integrity of Function

Function in Environment If man's environment is to be improved, and the idea of integrity of function implemented, it is necessary to go one step beyond "form follows function," and to make certain that function follows man's physiological, sociological, and emotional needs. Rooms without windows, however well air-conditioned, can bring out latent feelings of claustrophobia; yet numerous offices and school buildings are so designed in order to utilize space to the maximum. On the other hand, houses with large expanses of glass may look open and free in plan, but they may spell chronic frustration for the housewife who must keep every room ready for continual inspection by anyone approaching the front door. Although both of these forms fulfill their principal function, they could easily contribute to nervousness on the part of their inhabitants. The simple functionalism of the skyscraper is one of modern man's great achievements; yet this same functional simplicity may seem rather impersonal and sterile when applied to individual residences. The very fact that man usually works in such austere surroundings may accentuate his need for warmth and comfort at home.

It is also true, however, that the interior of the modern skyscraper is becoming more suited to human needs. Murals, mosaics, and sculpture now appear in the lobbies and hallways, and thick carpets adorn offices in which tropical plants soften the lines of walls paneled in beautifully grained woods. For every executive installed in such offices, nevertheless, there are hundreds of employees working side by side in large open rooms whose principal concessions to modern design are adequate lighting, air conditioning, and the latest-model office machines. These ordinary employees are also compelled by economic status to go home to boxlike houses placed side by side on treeless land, with only two or three basic designs alternated, so that every third family lives in an identical house with the same yard, and a different colored roof or shutters becomes their sole claim to individuality (Fig. 101).

below: 101. Tract housing near San Jose, Calif.

left: 102. Electric iron, 1910.

below: 103. Electric iron, 1967.

A child reared in surroundings so similar to those of his peers cannot be expected to exhibit strong traits of imagination, individuality, or willingness to break away from the "average," whether it be an idea or a way of life. Standardization may have its economic advantages, but monetary gain alone must not be allowed to force human beings into molds that warp their best innate qualities. The great challenge of the future is to find a way of providing for the tremendous increase in population without stifling man's needs for self-expression, privacy, and at least some contact with natural surroundings.

Function in Industrial Design While the idea of form following function and function satisfying man's various needs is a more sweeping consideration in architectural design, this principle is just as pertinent to the smallest designed object. As for the use of materials, technology has opened up new ideas with respect to function. The use of old-fashioned flatirons (Fig. 102) was associated with the idea of weight combined with heat, and for years after the advent of the electric iron a certain amount of weight and pressure were still exerted in the task of ironing. Since then, however, it has been discovered that, with the proper temperature of the iron and dampening of the clothes to be ironed, a weighty appliance and strong pressure are not necessary. Consequently, the newer irons (Fig. 103) weigh only a fraction as much as the older ones, and the job of ironing requires less energy. With lightness came the possibility of shaping for more skillful manipulation, combined with

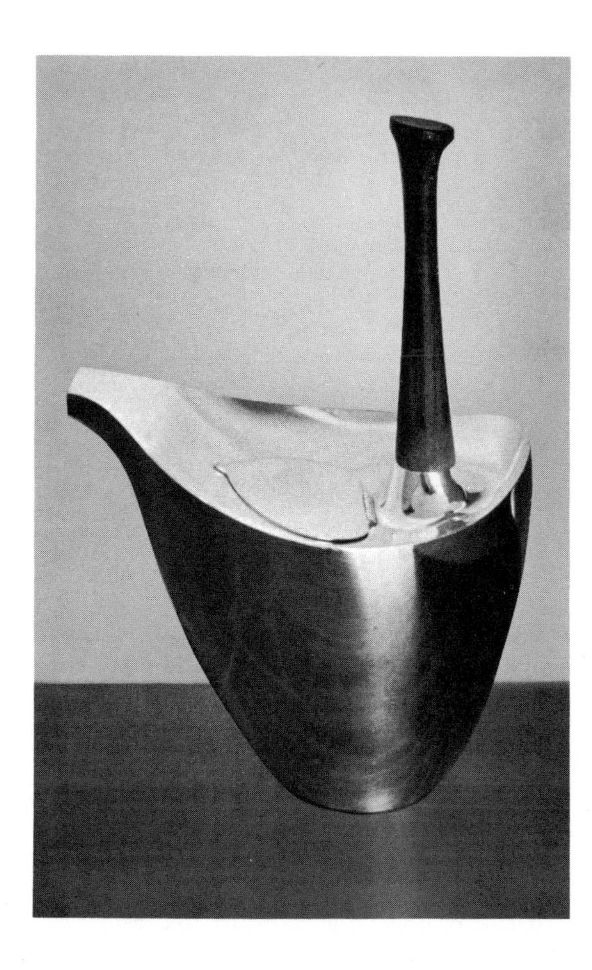

left: 104. Hans Christensen's coffee pot (c. 1960) exploits to perfection the qualities of silver and teak.

below: 105. Karen Karnes. Demitasse set. 1958. Stoneware with orange glaze, height of coffee pot 8½". Everson Museum of Art, Syracuse, N.Y.

intelligent use of plastic shapes for the handle, so that on the whole the newer models not only perform their function more efficiently but do so with far less human output. Similar changes have occurred in vacuum cleaners. With early models the housewife had the feeling that she was extricating dirt by sheer force as she bore down on the carpet while maneuvering the machine. With careful experimentation in shapes and forms, modifying the body of the cleaner has increased the ease of manipulation, and the lightness of the later models has proved that the suction works just as well when the machine skims over the surface.

Function in Decorative Design Design does not have to involve working mechanisms, however, to achieve integrity of function. Hans Christensen's coffee pot, (Fig. 104), for instance, shows both beauty of form and integrity of materials. It has an original but dignified form that displays the silver to advantage without applied ornamentation, the teak handle being the only accent. Yet there is an innovation in function, for the pot can be emptied without having to be turned upside down.

A different material and a different form, but with a similar function, is seen in Figure 105. More traditional in design, this pot is noteworthy for its solidity and for the interesting texture which adds decorative qualities. The stoneware, which is heavy enough to protect the hands against the heat of the coffee, also provides color and texture. The cups echo the honesty of design, with their functional handles balanced against the body of the cup and curved to allow for grasping them.

106. GERTRUD and OTTO NATZLER. Ceramic bowl. 1956. Stoneware with blue-turquoise "crater" glaze, height 8¼". Collection the artists.

Integrity of Ornamentation

There is one more aspect of structural design to be considered: *integrity of ornamentation*. Like many other aspects of design, this question has undergone radical changes in recent years. Moholy-Nagy has stated: "Texture is, at least for our time, the legitimate successor of ornament."[5] (See Fig. 106). However, before the problem can be dismissed so easily, it is necessary to review the field and study the developments that have led to our present-day approach. This will be done in Chapter 7.

SUMMARY

In applying knowledge of design to specific projects, it is necessary to consider two categories into which the work falls: structural design and decorative design. Structural design is fundamental to decorative design, determining all its aspects and embodying the function and very identity of the object designed.

One of the most fascinating structural designs in nature is the spiral shell, which has been reduced to a mathematical formula related to the golden mean of the Greeks. The Fibonacci number series is also closely related to natural phenomena, as evidenced in pine cones and numerous other botanical specimens.

Any structure involves positive and negative space—the positive space occupied by the object itself, and the negative space around it. The designer must be aware of both to create a truly effective design. In two-dimensional works, structural design is frequently referred to as composition. Structural design in nature is often based on symmetry, and some artists use dynamic symmetry as a basis for their work. This system too is related to the golden mean and can be worked out mathematically.

Now more than ever before it is important for the artist and the scientist to work together to produce a satisfactory environment for human life. The artist must be aware of new developments in science and technology in order to make his designs adaptable to the uses of his time. His most important characteristic is integrity, which refers to his ability to see his work whole and in relation to the universe around it. There are four areas in which integrity is vital to design: materials, form, function, and ornamentation. It is essential to make an honest approach in each of these areas if a design is to have genuine value.

Decorative Design

chapter 7

Decorative design is frequently thought of as ornament, but in its true sense it goes deeper than mere ornamentation. Ornament is commonly regarded as something that is not essential to the form of an object, something that is stuck on after the object is otherwise completed. Decorative design should be part of the object from its inception, something that could not be removed without destroying its unity. In its true sense, good decorative design simply brings out the structural design by enhancing it and playing up its most interesting features. It should never be an independent entity.

107. Helmet mask, from New Guinea. 20th century. Barkcloth, cane, and raffia; height 37¾″. Museum of Primitive Art, New York.

HISTORICAL SYMBOLISM

The first decorative designs were symbols carved into the handles of tools and weapons, either to ensure success in their use or to record success that had already occurred. Some historians believe that primitive carvings had much the same purpose as the notching of a gunstock to record the number of killings. From these beginnings developed the decorative motifs applied to pottery and masks. In Figure 107 is seen a mask of a sea spirit from New Guinea made of painted barkcloth, cane, and raffia. The design around the border repeats the simple tribal rhythms of the drumbeat and native dances.

In more advanced societies, the element of symbolism in decorative design has remained strong. The Greek vase decorators incorporated paintings as a part of the basic form, shaping them according to the body of the vessel. Designed for practical use, these vase types included amphorae, for holding wine or olive oil, and lekythoi, for containing funerary ashes. For both, the decoration consisted of human figures in scenes depicting everyday occurrences, battles, and athletic events. Often the artist painted himself at work on the vase, thus turning the design into a form of self-portrait. Several ornamental styles were employed, starting with archaic animal forms on a yellow ground, through a black-figure style on red clay adopted by the Athenians in the sixth century B.C., and, a hundred years later, a red-figure type

108. *Herakles and the Cretan Bull,* Attic red-figured and black-figured amphora (black-figured side not visible). c. 530 B.C. Height $20^{15}/_{16}$″. Museum of Fine Arts, Boston (Pierce Fund).

painted on a white ground. The Athenian amphora in Figure 108 bridges a century of artistic development by showing the red-figure technique on one side and the black-figure style on the other. No matter what the subject or the technique, each vase is an epic poem singing the history of a people. The figures are combined in a stately rhythm comparable to the Classical Greek chant.

The Early Christian church, in its conscientious avoidance of anything resembling idolatry or ostentation, evolved one of the most pragmatic manifestations of symbolism in its mosaics (Pl. 9, p. 111). Although statues and figural paintings were not allowed in Byzantine churches during the iconoclastic controversy of the eighth century, in other periods the telling of Bible stories through mosaics became an important part of the teaching of the church. Entire walls were covered with compositions of inlaid stones or small glass or ceramic tiles, which, while decorating the surface, far transcended the usual conception of purely decorative art. Vaulted ceilings, arched niches, and broad wall panels were planned specifically for the combined decorative, structural, and instructional function of these mosaics.

This Christian symbolism continued as a dominant force in the decorative design of Western art for six more centuries, just as the symbols of Buddhism and Mohammedanism dominated much of the art of the East. Painting, sculpture, mosaics, textiles, and ceramics all attested to the strong part that the Christian faith played in the lives of the people. The Renaissance, with its dedication to the Classical heritage, brought about the combination of Greek and Roman mythological motifs with Christian symbols in decoration. These Classical themes retained a symbolic meaning, though with a somewhat different interpretation than that of the original symbolism 14 centuries earlier. Along with the idealization of the human form, Renaissance Classicism was an expression of the importance of man as an individual and his striving for renewal as a result of increased learning.

After the Reformation the uses of Christian symbolism were modified in Northern countries, and their original vigor and relevance were never to be fully restored. The external gestures were continued and still persist sporadically, but the artistic embodiment of Christianity as a driving force of humanity has not found the strength that it achieved before and during the Renaissance and again, briefly, in the Counter Reformation. The Baroque period is remembered mostly as a flowering of exuberant and elaborate decoration, often applied with little regard for underlying structure (Fig. 109). The French refined this tendency into the more delicate and fragile Rococo style. Wall decorations consisted of pastel-colored murals depicting dimpled princesses or shepherdesses swinging or cavorting with youths in flowing shirts and satin trousers (Pl. 10, p. 112). Cupids, sheep, garlands, and shells were the motifs that symbolized the frothy existence that led to the French Revolution. Similar decorative elements were found on porcelain, silver, tapestries, and embroideries, as well as in carved wall panels and furniture.

The use of animal elements was characteristic of the furniture of the eighteenth century, possibly because of the popularity of hunting as a pastime. The dainty hoofed leg of Rococo furniture grew into the heavy ball-and-claw foot of the English cabinetmakers. Interest in decoration for its own sake grew gradually until the Victorian era, when humanity all but stifled under the excrescences of ponderous furniture, heavy tapestries and draperies, thick carpets full of Oriental design, and murky paintings, all housed in buildings heavily ornamented with classic moldings. Renaissance medallions and Baroque archways were admittedly stuck on for the purpose of making an "imposing" dwelling. Commercial buildings suffered from the same ailment. Architects of this era did not question the necessity of basing their designs on books of patterns drawn up by students of Classical and Renaissance art. The best architect was the one who could most faithfully represent these symbols of bygone eras while adequately fulfilling the purpose of his building.

109. Gianlorenzo Bernini. *Cathedra Petri* (*Throne of St. Peter*), St. Peter's, Vatican, Rome. 1657–66. Marble, bronze (partly gilt), colored glass, and stucco.

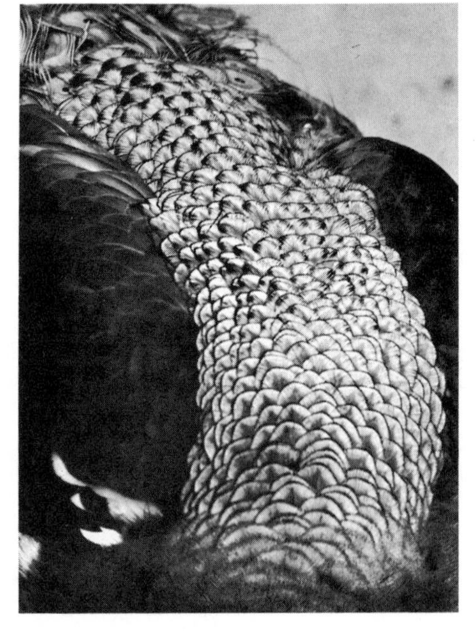

above left: 110. Antoni Gaudí. Casa Batlló, Barcelona (detail of roof). 1905–07.

above right: 111. Wolf Strache. *Back View of Peacock.* 1956.

right: 112. Aubrey Beardsley. *The Peacock Skirt,* from *Salome.* 1907. Drawing, $8\frac{7}{8} \times 6\frac{1}{4}''$. Fogg Art Museum, Harvard University, Cambridge, Mass. (Grenville L. Winthrop Bequest).

ART NOUVEAU

At the end of the nineteenth century, a movement was started by young artists who felt that the machine was dominating the position formerly held by the artist and craftsman. Known as Art Nouveau in France and Jugendstil in Germany, this movement was an effort to counteract the machine esthetic—or lack of it—by incorporating biological symbolism into the arts. Borrowing from the Orient and certain peasant cultures, these artists scorned straight lines and rigid geometric surfaces, turned to woman as the symbol of perpetual genesis, and incorporated the curving lines of the female body, fruits, flowers, and other sinuous organic forms into their paintings, architecture, and crafts as ubiquitous reminders of natural life and growth. Lighting fixtures became metal sprays of flowers, iron blossoms adorned bridges, and even the Eiffel Tower showed Art Nouveau forms at its base. Buildings and architectural ornament were made to resemble plants unfolding or the forms of fruit or birds, as in the fantastic work of Antoni Gaudí (Figs. 110–111). It has been theorized that the movement was short-lived because it emphasized the ornamental forms of nature rather than the structural principles. Whatever the reasons for its decline, it is presently enjoying a resurgence of interest. Art Nouveau crafts have become collectors' items, and the drawings of the Englishman Aubrey Beardsley (Fig. 112), who illustrated books in the Art Nouveau style, have again become popular in advertising, in decoration, and through reissued volumes of his work.

BAUHAUS INFLUENCE

Reacting against the organic ornamental influence of Art Nouveau, the Bauhaus School of Design established its own program for dealing with the dominance of the machine. Established in 1919 by Walter Gropius in Weimar, Germany, the Bauhaus was hailed as a liberator of esthetic thought because it stood squarely for stern unadulterated design and carried out its teachings in its own buildings and interior furnishings (Fig. 113).

Gathering students from all over the world, it accepted the fundamental importance of the machine in modern civilization and sought to bridge the gap between artist and industry by finding a common ground upon which fine art, handicrafts,

below: 113. WALTER GROPIUS. Bauhaus School of Design, Dessau, Germany. 1925–26.

and industrial design could flourish by interaction. The basic course involved a three-step principle of experience, perception, and ability. Various exercises were carried out to give the beginning designer visual experience, followed by intellectual explanation and comprehension, and finally the execution of a specific, individual project. Assignments covered the entire scope of art, including figure drawing, color study, analysis of space, familiarity with materials and tools, and the study of nature and form. Individual students were carefully observed and analyzed and led to find their own distinctive expression, through a process known as *subjective forms.* It was believed that there was a relationship between the shapes of man and the forms which he designs and that, if a man is genuine in his expression, everything he does becomes a reflection of his formative powers.[1]

In addition to being a radical architectural-industrial school, the Bauhaus had a worldwide influence on painting. (The name derives from the German *bau,* meaning structure.) Artists such as Wassily Kandinsky, Paul Klee, and the American-born Lyonel Feininger made it the world center for experiments in painting.

Installed in new quarters in Dessau, Germany, in 1925–26, the Bauhaus was finally suppressed by the Nazis for its radical teachings. However, some of its adherents emigrated and started a school in Chicago that has carried on its basic concepts: the Armour Institute of Design, predecessor of the present Illinois Institute of Technology. It would be difficult to estimate the number of Bauhaus disciples who have been an influence in raising the standards of industrial design throughout the world.

RETURN TO PATTERN

The Bauhaus influence is usually associated with precise, unornamented surfaces that clearly express the function of the object designed. About five years after the founding of the Bauhaus, however, Frank Lloyd Wright began a trend back toward pattern by casting concrete building blocks in decorative forms, which he used in the construction of houses (Fig. 114). Interesting singly, when assembled with metal rods and poured concrete, these blocks carried a recurring motif throughout the building, inside and out, in a fluid rhythmic pattern that was not only decorative, but also served to unify the structural design. Here the design *was* the structure as well, since it was cast into the very walls.

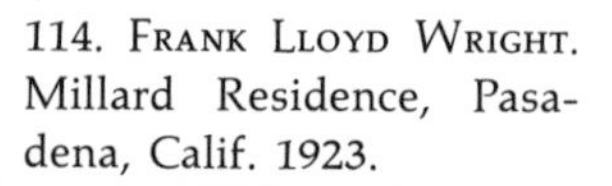
114. Frank Lloyd Wright. Millard Residence, Pasadena, Calif. 1923.

115. Maori house, New Zealand. 19th century.

Wright's principle is a later manifestation of an approach that had been used by Maori tribesmen in nineteenth-century New Zealand. In the house in Figure 115 the exterior structure is enlivened by symbolic carvings that are carried over into the interior of the building.

The obvious difference between these last two examples of buildings and those to which the Bauhaus objected so strongly lies in the integrity of the decorative design and its application. The Bauhaus sought to free architecture from the accumulation of the past, from conventional designs copied through the centuries for no apparent reason and applied as an inappropriate accretion to the basic structure. In the Millard house and the Maori house, the decorative designs were created specifically to enhance one particular building and are as much a part of the architecture as are the structural members themselves.

Wright's emphasis on decorative design and patterned wall surfaces certainly affected the increasing incidence of mural art, both indoors and out. Murals were encouraged by the Federal Government in the Depression years, when artists were commissioned to paint the walls of public buildings as a means of livelihood. In these a symbolism of sorts emerged in stylized depictions of the history of a region, its geographical assets, or the activities for which the building was intended. Artists who disapproved of the sterility of modern buildings were happy to create designs in a variety of media to add beauty and interest to contemporary architecture (Fig. 116).

116. THOMAS HART BENTON. *Agriculture and Lumbering,* detail of *New School Mural.* 1931. New School for Social Research, New York.

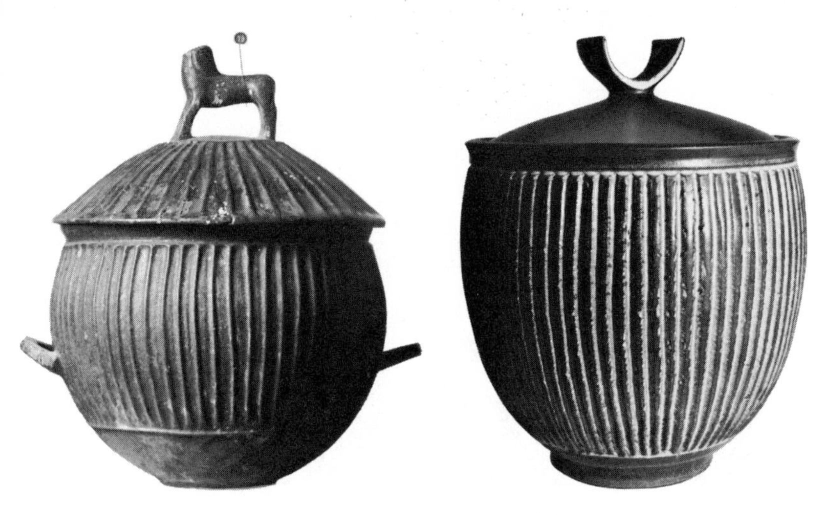

left: 117. Etruscan jar. 6th century B.C. Clay. Vatican Museums, Rome.

right: 118. HARRISON McINTOSH. Ceramic jar. c. 1960. Stoneware, height 12″. Collection the artist.

Walls are not the only surfaces that lend themselves to pattern. In Mexico and in various South American countries vast areas of pavement are inlaid with colorful tile mosaic. In these countries paving blocks are specially designed to add texture to garden areas or patios. Pebbles, gravel, washed stones imbedded in concrete, or concrete laid in patterns outlined by strips of redwood are all accepted ways of achieving decorative effects in pavements.

What of the decorative design of small objects? The use of texture in lieu of symbolic content for visual interest is not restricted to the twentieth century. The two jars in Figures 117 and 118 show a similarity in shape and texture that is particularly noteworthy when one realizes that they were conceived over 26 centuries apart. There are differences, of course, and it is not hard to guess which of these objects was made in pre-Roman times and which is an expression of an age of streamlining and fast movement; yet one sees the same basic principles in both, the careful combining of smoothness and texture, the sturdy shape, and the use of the handles as a decorative accent. While such discoveries make known the eternal fellowship of creative artists, they can also have a disquieting effect on a young designer aspiring to make his own contribution. If the same basic principles are valid and effective through the ages, can there really be new visual forms? Are there actually any new emotions or sensations to express? What can the twentieth-century designer do to make some distinctive contribution?

CONTRIBUTION OF THE DESIGNER TODAY

First, *the designer should make the most of materials that are typical of his time.* Plastics can be made in many forms and textures and will be made in many more as designers

119. A series of lamps designed for Lightolier is characteristic of forms made possible by the use of plastics.

continue to innovate. Contemporary decorative lighting fixtures (Fig. 119) are only one example of designs that would be impossible without plastics and their capacity for being spun into thin sheets and molded into many varied forms. New metal alloys are opening doors from the standpoint of both durability and design potential, and revolutionary paints and sculptural materials make possible techniques never before explored by the artist.

Second, *the designer should concentrate on a sincere expression of his own reaction to his world, rather than lean on the past or imitate symbols that have no meaning for him.* The construction in Figure 120 could not have been created in any era prior to the mid-twentieth century. The material is Plexiglas, discovered during World War II; it is stronger than glass and shatterproof and has a more subtle sheen. Formed as it is from the edges and surfaces of the material, the decorative design is an inseparable part of the construction and seems to move as it is watched—reflecting, interweaving, rotating from light to shadow as the viewer changes position. In spite of its depth and the fact that the construction can be viewed from all sides, this is not so much a sculpture as a kind of multidimensional painting, composed of a multiplicity of reflective surfaces arranged on many planes. There is almost a scientific approach here, an invitation to the viewer to participate in an experiment in visual and perceptive imagery, to move about and see what happens in this ever-evolving interplay between the composition and the human eye.

Last, *the student of design should realize that the fact that something has been expressed before does not diminish its importance for his own era.* Just as words of kindness are welcome in any age, so also a beautiful object is always acceptable. If the artist is true to his own interpretation and speaks in his own idiom, his work will have a distinctive quality, no matter how many centuries of creative predecessors have done the same sort of thing. A fresh interpretation of decorative design is apparent in the stoneware casserole by James McKinnell shown in Figure 121. The free forms

left: 120. FRANCISCO SOBRINO. *Unstable Transformation: Juxtaposition, Superposition B.* 1963. Plexiglas, $32\frac{3}{8} \times 16\frac{1}{8} \times 16\frac{1}{8}$". Courtesy Galerie Denise René, Paris.

below: 121. JAMES MCKINNELL. Ceramic casserole. c. 1960. Stoneware, diameter $13\frac{1}{2}$". Collection the artist.

on the cover may suggest plants or fish. Each viewer can apply his own associations and experiences in interpreting them, but he should not be overly concerned with *what* is represented. The visual texture is carried throughout with smooth flecked areas repeated on the lower section and again around the handle; the solid tone of the handle and rim lends an effective accent.

Perhaps this is the symbolism of an era in which man has come to realize how much lies beyond his knowledge. Even the natural forms he sees every day have aspects which he does not fathom and which can result in dramatic new developments affecting his very life. The relationship of common mold to the triumph over disease and the overwhelming consequences of splitting the atom are only two indications that there is much beyond what we see. Man's symbols can no longer be final statements, because his reactions to his environment are no longer clear-cut, nor is his knowledge conclusive. Practically each day brings some new discovery affecting human life, and the contemporary artist depicts the ever-uncertain status of his world by decorative design that is flexible and that sometimes appears unfinished by previous standards. The viewer is thus encouraged to carry through his own interpretation according to his feelings at the time. There are those who insist that the artist today is a vague, lost personality, who has found no relevant symbolism. Perhaps these very qualities of vagueness and ambiguity are the symbols of an age in which science, philosophy, and art have been unable to provide conclusive statements.

SUMMARY

Decorative design should be a part of the object to which it is applied, not something added afterward. Historically, decorative design has often had symbolic meanings.

With the advent of the machine, a movement known as Art Nouveau in France and Jugendstil in Germany rose to counteract the influence of mechanization by incorporating biological symbolism in the arts. This elaborate natural ornament in turn inspired a reaction from the Bauhaus, an architectural-industrial school in Germany, which was instrumental in promoting architecture with clean lines and unadorned surfaces, as well as similar qualities in its initiation of industrial design.

The return to some ornamental effects came with Frank Lloyd Wright and his patterned building blocks for use in houses. During the Depression, murals, usually stressing historical or social consciousness, were painted by many artists on government buildings as a part of a program to help artists find work. Today, interesting textural patterns are found not only in or on buildings but in decorative pavements, particularly prevalent in South America and Mexico.

The contemporary designer should follow three guidelines in making his own contribution. First, he should make the most of the materials that are peculiar to his own time. Second, he should strive for sincere expression of his own reaction to his world, without leaning on the past or imitating conventional symbols that have no meaning for him. Third, he should recognize the fact that although something has been said before its importance is not thereby automatically diminished for his own era.

Plate 9. *Empress Theodora and Retinue.* c. 547. Mosaic. San Vitale, Ravenna.

Plate 10. ANTOINE WATTEAU. *Fete in a Park.* 1720–21. Oil on canvas, 4′1″ × 6′2″. Wallace Collection, London (reproduced by permission of the Trustees).

Plate 11. Beaker vase, from China. Ming Dynasty, 16th century. Porcelain with turquoise glaze, height $8\frac{1}{4}''$. M. H. de Young Memorial Museum, San Francisco (Avery Brundage Collection).

Plate 12. Bottle vase, from China. Ch'ing Dynasty, c. 1662–1722. Porcelain (Lang Yao ware) with *sang-de-boeuf* glaze, height $7\frac{1}{4}$". M. H. de Young Memorial Museum, San Francisco (Avery Brundage Collection).

Expressions in Design

III

Design in Pottery

chapter 8

The fascination of clay is older than recorded history. The same instinct that makes children fashion mud pies perhaps also moved primitive man to dig in the mud of the riverbanks and then pat, roll, mold, and shape this basic substance until he found he had created a vessel that could hold something. That his actions would someday evolve into a process for fashioning some of the most beautiful objects known to civilization probably never occurred to him.

DEVELOPMENT OF POTTERY

The discovery of clay led to exciting explorations from the beginning. The earliest pots were patted and pinched into shape and left to dry in the sun. Later the clay was rolled into coils or ropes the diameter of a man's finger and laid coil upon coil to form a vessel wall, after which it was smoothed with a piece of shell or gourd.

As pots grew more ambitious in size, a piece of mat or woven basket was used to support the work, and to make it possible to survey the results from all angles as the potter progressed. Eventually, someone placed a pot on a smooth stone and found that it could be turned *while* working, thereby achieving a more uniform smoothness and symmetrical form. Thus evolved the potter's wheel. Such wheels, which were devised independently by many cultures, have ranged from those turned by donkeys to the Renaissance version driven by a cord strung over a pulley. Today, even with numerous kinds of electric wheels available, many potters still prefer the ancient method of propelling the wheel by moving the foot. Body and wheel work together, relating physical and creative energy in a single concerted operation, during which hands and clay become almost indistinguishable until the final separation of creation and creator (Fig. 122).

It is interesting to imagine what accident caused the first clay pot to fall into a fire and harden. The increased durability and the fact that the material would no longer melt when wet apparently were recognized as improvements, for firing in an open fire soon became an accepted practice.

122. The intimate connection between the potter's hands, the clay, and the wheel is evident in this photograph, showing the final stage in throwing a lid.

123. Hippopotamus, from the tomb of Senbi at Meir, Egypt. 12th Dynasty (2000–1788 B.C.). Faience, height $4\frac{3}{8}''$. Metropolitan Museum of Art, New York (gift of Edward S. Harkness, 1917).

There remained the matter of making vessels waterproof so that they could be used to hold liquids. Early man painted his fired clayware with plant resins and animal fats as a protective coating. Although we are not sure when the process of glazing was discovered, it was probably the result of an accident. We do know, however, that it opened up one of the most challenging fields of artistic endeavor and, by the time of the Egyptians, raised potterymaking to the level of a true art (Fig. 123).

THE NATURE OF CLAY

Clay is the very substance of the earth's crust, the result of weathering and change, a process that has taken place over the centuries through the action of ice and snow, wind and water, air and decomposition. Most frequently the decomposed matter is feldspar, which contains alumina, silica, and other minerals in varying combinations that finally evolve into clay. Geologically, there are two varieties of clay. *Residual* clay has stayed in the same spot since its formation. *Sedimentary* clay, on the other hand, is the product of many movements, of wind and storm and rushing streams, which have carried it from its starting point and finally deposited it in the bed of a lake or along the bank of a river. It is worn fine by its adventures, and it may pick up fascinating colors. It may be red from iron, green or blue from copper

124. The ridges of the coils are left unsmoothed to lend surface texture in this pot (1967) by DONALD CYR.

opposite: 125. Two ceramic pieces by Ed Traynor illustrate the flexibility of the slab technique, which can be used to create open, abstract works such as *Slab-cut Form* (1969), *right,* as well as finished, functional objects like the bottle (1969), *far right.*

content, white or gray or yellow, depending upon its own individual history. It can be mixed with other clays and left to age in damp crocks for weeks at a time, since clay, like wine and cheese, improves with aging.

From the standpoint of use, clay falls into one of four categories, each of which is fired at a different temperature, depending upon the origin and innate qualities of the clay itself. *Earthenware,* which fires at the lowest temperature of all clays, has a heavy porous quality. It includes the "baked earth" known as terra cotta, which is used for sculpture and tiled roofs. *Stoneware,* which fires at a higher temperature, is a favorite of contemporary potters for its solidity and for its affinity for textured glazes. *China* is made from a combination of clays and is widely used in commercial pottery. *Porcelain* fires at the highest temperature of all, and is a specially prepared clay that becomes extremely hard and vitreous as a result of firing. It contains *kaolin,* a fine white clay named after the Chinese term for "high hill." Each type of clay requires a different approach to bring out its creative possibilities.

METHODS OF MAKING POTTERY

Today pottery is made by one of five methods. *Pinch pots* are formed by pinching a ball of clay into shape, much as was done by the earliest potters.

Coil pots start with a flat base consisting of a circle of clay one-half inch or so in thickness. On this base a rope of clay is placed, much as one would lay the bottom row of bricks in a wall. A second rope is placed on the first one, and the walls are thus constructed in whatever shape the potter wishes, varying the form by the length of the rope as the walls rise higher. The coils may be smoothed together with a metal scraper until no ridges are discernible or they may be left rough to give surface texture. This is the method used by the Southwest Indian potters, as well as by many potters who work in a contemporary style (Fig. 124).

Slab pots are built as one would build a box of wood, with the sides cut from a flat sheet of clay that has been rolled out to the desired thickness. Special care must be taken to smooth the joints and edges together so that no cracking will occur when the object is dried and fired. Joints are reinforced with small rolls of clay that are then pressed into the crevices between the adjoining pieces. Slab pottery is usually geometric in form and is utilized for planters, square ash trays, or boxes in various sizes (Fig. 125).

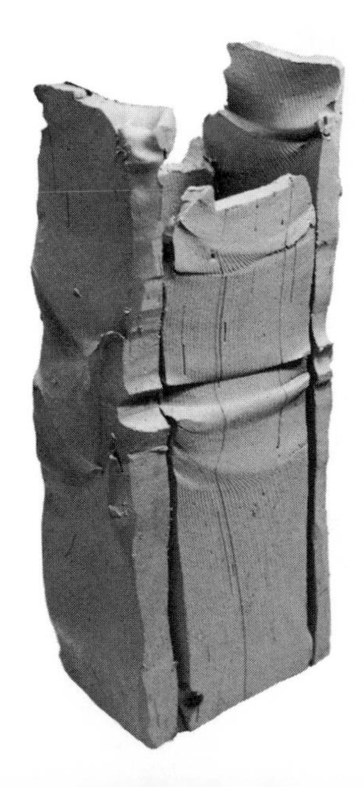

Commercial potters make use of *molds* from which similar pieces can be made in quantity. The clay in this case is a liquid known as *slip*, made by dissolving a powdered clay in water to the consistency of cream. The slip is poured into a two-piece mold of plaster of Paris; when the clay has dried, the mold is opened and the finished object removed and set out to dry.

The most difficult method of making pottery is by use of the *potter's wheel*. This is a highly skilled technique requiring months of practice in order to achieve complete control. The wheel can be powered by electricity or by foot pedal, but in either case a ball of clay is centered on the wheel and then is gradually raised in the potter's hands as the wheel turns (Figs. 126–28). It is necessary to keep the clay wet at all times in order to prevent dragging or sticking. When the form has been raised,

126–128. The skilled hands of the potter exercise absolute control in all the stages of throwing a pot.

above left: 126. The ball of clay is centered on the wheel and "opened up" in the middle.

above right: 127. The potter begins to draw up the sides.

left: 128. Potter Richard M. Lincoln creates texture with his fingernails.

various tools can be employed to help with the shaping, and such simple devices as a comb, a fork, or the potter's fingernails can be held against the turning pot to give a band of texture. One finishes the operation by smoothing the edges. The pot is cut from the wheel with a thread or wire and is set aside to dry. This method of making pottery, like weaving, is one of the few fields in which the artist still works with his material in a close and rhythmic interaction.

DRYING AND FIRING

Clay that has never been fired is known as *greenware.* All greenware, whether still in process or completed, must be protected from drying too fast, so that it will not crack. This danger varies with the humidity of the air, and the precautions taken depend upon the climate and the current weather. Generally, a *damp box* is used for the first stages of drying. This is a cupboard lined with zinc, in which a block of plaster of Paris has been placed. The plaster is kept wet by pouring water on it, and the zinc keeps the air inside the box moist enough to allow for gradual drying. When the pottery has lost most of its dampness, it is called *leather hard.* At this stage it can be decorated and removed to open shelves where exposure to air will complete the drying process. Placing the piece against the cheek is the accepted test for dryness. If the clay feels cold, it is still damp; if not, it is ready for firing.

Today's kilns are fired by gas or electricity, but in either case the temperatures required for pottery are much too high to be measured by thermometers. Consequently, pyrometric devices must be employed. The most usual device is the pyrometric cone. This is a small pyramid of hardened clay to which fluxes have been added in order to make it melt at a given temperature. Cones are numbered according to the temperatures at which they melt. The cone is placed before a peephole in the kiln, sometimes being flanked with a higher cone and a lower cone to help the potter determine the exact moment that the kiln has reached the proper temperature. When the cone bends, the kiln is turned off.

Most pottery is fired twice. The first firing is the *bisque* fire, to which the greenware is subjected after it has dried. Ware that has been fired once is known as *bisque.* The second firing is the *glaze* firing, after the glaze has been applied.

THE GLAZE

A glaze is actually a superficial layer, or layers, of molten material that has been fired on the clay body of the pot, becoming a part of the original clay. Glazing has two purposes: to make the vessel waterproof and to increase its attractiveness. It also provides imperviousness to dirt and moisture and strengthens the piece. The glazing materials must be appropriate to the particular clay used in the pot; otherwise, fusion will not be complete.

There are three essential ingredients in all glazes: *silica, alumina,* and *flux.* It is the silica that vitrifies under high fire, giving a glassy appearance to some glazes. Alumina, or aluminum oxide, is necessary to keep the silica from becoming liquid at high temperatures and from running off the piece to which it is applied. Flux, on the other hand, lowers the melting point of the silica so that it will vitrify without melting the clay itself.

Glazes can be classified as *high fire* or *low fire.* Because of the effects of the high temperatures, high-fire glazes are harder and more subdued in color. Normally, they are used on porcelain clay. Low-fire glazes are principally of two types, depending

above left: 129. Plate, from Italy. c. 1515–25. Majolica, diameter 16⅜″. Metropolitan Museum of Art (gift of V. Everit Macy, 1927, in memory of his wife, Edith Carpenter Macy).

above right: 130. HARRISON McINTOSH. Compote. 1964. Stoneware with pale green mat glaze, height 5½″. Collection the artist.

upon the flux employed. *Lead glazes* take a flux of oxides of white or red lead. *Alkaline glazes* use borax, colemanite, soda ash, or similar substances as flux. They make possible more brilliant color effects than in the lead glazes.

A glaze may be transparent, translucent, or opaque. There are various special glaze effects that contemporary potters use, some with interesting textural effects and speckles. One of the favorites is the *mat glaze,* formed by adding an excessive amount of alumina or by substituting barium carbonate for some of the flux. The effect is soft rather than glassy, and it lends itself well to the contemporary potter's interest in form and subtle color. The *crackle glaze* is sometimes used for visual texture. It is the result of tensions developed when the glaze and clay expand and contract differently, causing a network of tiny cracks.

Glazes come in powder form, which is mixed with water to achieve a smooth consistency. Colors are added through the use of metallic oxides: copper carbonate for turquoise or green, rutile for yellow or brown, tin oxide for white, and so on. Combinations of oxides will cause different colors and interesting effects. The glaze may be brushed on, sprayed on, or the piece may be dipped in a large receptacle containing glaze. The glaze dries almost immediately, and the pottery is then ready for the glaze firing.

HISTORICAL EXAMPLES

The Chinese are considered to be among the world's greatest potters, and several of their glazes are especially noteworthy. The rich *Ming blue* (Pl. 11, p. 113), seen in much of their porcelain, resulted from the use of cobalt, which the potters of the Ming period found would endure the high temperatures needed to melt their glazes. Cobalt is still an effective colorant.

Celadon is another type of glaze often associated with Chinese porcelain. It is a thick translucent glaze, varying from gray and blue-green to sea green and grass green. It is produced by firing black oxide of iron under *reduction,* in which extraneous material is burned in the kiln to *reduce* the amount of oxygen; thus unusual effects are created from the reactions of the chemicals in the glazes. The *sang de boeuf* (Pl. 12, p. 114), or oxblood, widely used by the Chinese, is also a product of reduction from red oxide to copper. The Chinese used other glazes combined with elaborate designs. *Cloisonné* is a combination glaze and mosaic technique that is seen in much Chinese

above left: 131. Harrison McIntosh. Compote. 1963. Stoneware with blue-green mat glaze, height 3⅜″. Collection the artist.

above right: 132. Harrison McIntosh. Compote. 1963. Stoneware with dark-brown and black mat glaze, height 6¾″. Collection the artist.

work. Small areas of glaze are separated by gouging, applying clay-coil ridges, or by carving grooves that are then filled with contrasting glaze. The usual method of separation is by thin strips of brass, which give a rich linear unity to the design.

Majolica is a ware that was developed in Italy during the Renaissance (Fig. 129) and is still made by many potters today. It consists of earthenware coated with a glaze containing tin oxide or zirconium, which produces the opaque white background that differentiates majolica from other ware. The tin glaze is highly receptive to lustrous metallic pigments. The name is derived from a process used in the fifteenth century for wares exported to various countries in Majorcan trading ships, and the pottery was mistakenly supposed to have been made in Majorca. There is evidence that majolica may actually be an imitation of Chinese porcelain that was brought into Majorca from China by Moslem traders. Designs have varied in different periods, from fruit and arabesques to complicated narrative subjects.

Faïence is an elaborate type of majolica, incorporating gold as well as colors in its decoration. It originated in Faenza and Florence in the late fifteenth century and later blossomed in France, where it was called faïence ware instead of the Italian *porzellana di Faenza.* Spain and Portugal have their faïence ware; the blue-and-white Delft pottery of Holland is faïence as well. Technically the term faïence, like the term majolica, applies to any earthenware of coarse texture covered with an opaque glaze and fired, then decorated and fired again. The difference between the two lies primarily in the style of decoration.

There have been many well-known potteries in Western Europe, each renowned for a particular type of ware. In addition to the Delft ware of Holland, German Meissen, English Wedgwood, and French Sèvres all are known for their individual treatments of blue-and-white glazes. English Royal Doulton and Staffordshire are other familiar names in fine pottery. Both of these are known for figurines as well as for dinnerware, as are the Meissen potteries in Dresden, where the so-called Dresden figures are made.

STRUCTURAL DESIGN IN POTTERY TODAY

The contemporary potter is primarily concerned with honesty of form, and his glazes complement the structural design rather than overshadow it. A variety of compotes can be seen in Figures 130 through 132, all of them straightforward and honest in design. They have little in common with pottery that is shaped like tomatoes or pineapples. These forms have been used by potters in the past, but today the function of the pot and its material are more important than whimsical imitation. The jar in Figure 133 is completely forthright, yet it has a flair that makes it highly original. The combination of interesting structure and unusual textural treatment give it the distinction characteristic of the best in modern pottery.

Honesty of form implies honesty of function. Lids must fit, spouts must pour; cups, bowls, and pitchers must be balanced for stability and for active use. Casseroles must be ovenproof, and teapots should have an escape vent for steam. Neither beauty of line nor subtlety of glaze is sufficient to compensate for a piece that does not serve its primary purpose.

DECORATIVE DESIGN TODAY

The subtle glaze is characteristic of contemporary pottery, yet there are other methods by which the potter can create decorative design. While the clay is still wet, he can create design as it turns on the wheel, or, letting it stand still, he can use dies of various materials and press them into the side of the wet pottery. When the clay has dried to the leather-hard stage, the potter can *incise* designs, cutting out pieces of clay and filling the spaces with clay of a contrasting color. *Slip trailing* is another device by which contrasting clay in liquid form is poured through a glass tube or syringe, making a raised design on the surface. *Sgraffito* may be used: the piece is coated with glaze, which is then scratched through in a design that shows the natural color of the basic clay underneath. *Sprigging* consists of applying designs made of cutout clay, or rolls of clay, onto the surface.

below: 133. HARRISON MCINTOSH. Vase. 1967. Stoneware with gray mat glaze and sgraffito decoration, height 6″. Collection the artist.

right: 134. In this contemporary Dutch pitcher the forms of the vessel and of the applied decoration are beautifully integrated.

135. RICHARD M. LINCOLN. Bottle. c. 1962. Clay with sgraffito decoration, height 20″. Collection the artist.

EXPRESSION OF THE MATERIAL

The potter working at his wheel is not merely forcing clay into shape through the exercise of will and fingers; rather, he is creating a symbol of the very essence of the earth and its eternally changing history. For a few moments he becomes an extension of the clay, experiencing its plasticity, feeling its willingness to go in certain directions, sensing how far and how long it can be worked without collapsing. He cannot arrive at his conclusions through facts or logic; no amount of discussion will tell him as much as his intuition can when he feels the clay. This is skill, but with a deeper connotation. It is hands and mind and spirit concentrated on extracting from the clay its most poetic possibilities.

The creation of a piece of pottery is a complete and totally related process from beginning to end. The type of clay is determined by the function of the piece, the form is decided by the qualities of the clay, and the decorative design must be integrated with the form. Thus the design is never something stuck on as an afterthought but is a continuation of the form and clay. There are many ways that this can be done. The Dutch pitcher in Figure 134 has a fluid form with a smooth glaze. The decorative design is painted with overglaze in a soft blue with variations of gray and violet on a subtle background of blue and white. A fine mist of the same blue is sprayed at the base and around the lip and handle. The use of the bird form as a decorative motif is not arbitrary. The bird and form of the pitcher are integrated and treated with the same flowing quality. The graceful posing of the body, the uptilt of the beak, and the sweep of the decorative tail feathers serve to emphasize the form of the pitcher in such a way that it would seem incomplete without them.

In contrast, many contemporary American potters rely more on texture and sgraffito than on meticulous painting in overglaze. They scratch through glazes, or they use broad strokes that express an affinity with the clay or a suggestion of natural form. The piece in Figure 135 displays the best traits of such pottery. Interesting

136–137. Clean lines and subtle glazes give a contemporary feeling to these two lines of dinnerware by Dansk Designs Ltd.

right: 136. Fluted Flamestone, designed by JENS H. QUISTGAARD.

opposite: 137. Generation Mist, designed by NIELS REFOGAARD.

yet honest in shape, it achieves distinction through both structural and decorative design. The motif is nonobjective, yet there is a feeling of natural form that arouses the viewer's imagination and allows him to develop his own interpretation.

THE POTTER AND INDUSTRY

Even though creative pottery is associated with the craftsman's studio, the potter himself is made more and more aware today of the proximity of industry and of the relevance of industrial procedures and methods for his own efforts. The machine is fast and efficient, but it has one fatal deficiency: it cannot produce beautiful objects by itself. The artist must realize, however, that the machine has two great advantages over the craftsman: it does not tire, and its output does not vary in quality once the standards are set. In the field of pottery this mutual need of craftsman and industry is producing results that are increasingly beautiful. Fluted Flamestone (Fig. 136), designed by Jens H. Quistgaard, is strikingly contemporary in its clean lines and subdued earth colors, yet because its pattern is classic and elegant, it would be equally at home on an antique table. Like the Flamestone, Generation Mist (Fig. 137), designed by Niels Refogaard, is made of durable stoneware which resists chipping and breaking. It also permits the creation of a unified design in cooking and serving accessories, for the sturdy casseroles can be carried directly from the stove to the table. Both designs illustrate the benefits that result when art is allied with technology.

SUMMARY

Pottery making is an ancient art, practiced even before the time of the ancient Egyptians. Made from clay, pottery involves the very substance of the earth. Geologically, there are two types of clay: *residual,* which has stayed in the same spot since its formation, and *sedimentary,* which is the product of displacement caused by wind and water.

From the standpoint of use, clay falls into one of four categories, each of which has distinctive qualities and a different firing point: *earthenware, stoneware, china,* and *porcelain.* Pottery today is made by one of five methods: by *pinching,* by *coils,* by *slabs,* by use of *molds,* and by the use of the *potter's wheel.* Clay that has never been fired is known as *greenware,* whereas ware that has been fired once is *bisque.* The firing used for glazing is known as a *glaze* fire.

A glaze becomes a part of the clay by firing; it contains three essential ingredients related to the clay itself: *silica, alumina,* and *flux.* There are different kinds of glaze which vary according to their chemical content and the temperature at which they are fired. Historically, the Chinese are considered among the world's greatest potters, and their ceramic works are exceptional for their beautiful glazes.

Contemporary potters are concerned primarily with honesty of form and decorative design. Decorative design can be applied by one of five methods: *incising, inlay, slip trailing, sgraffito,* and *sprigging.* The most popular practice among modern potters is to enrich the surface by *sgraffito* and other textural variations. The potter of today realizes the interrelationship of artist and industry by frequently designing pottery that can be produced in quantity by the machine.

Design in Glass

chapter 9

138. Harvey K. Littleton. *Stylized Growth.* 1969. Blown glass, height 31½″. Courtesy Lee Nordness Galleries, New York.

The unique characteristics of glass have endeared this material to artists for a number of reasons. Its transparency, fluidity, and sparkle are a challenge for the designer to exploit glass to an extent hardly possible in other media (Fig. 138). The affinity of light with glass results in a fascinating beauty, and the expression "clear as crystal" indicates a purity not associated with any other material.

COMPOSITION OF GLASS

The earliest glass was obsidian, a shiny black substance created by nature and similar in analysis to some bottle glass manufactured today. The chief raw material in glass is sand, which must be silica in its purest possible state. Basically, glass is composed of silicon dioxide that is fused with metallic oxides and then supercooled to a brittle solid. Various other materials may be added to produce the qualities necessary for different uses.

The glass most important to the designer is *lead glass,* a complex of potassium-lead silicate; it is indeed the heaviest type of glass. Its high refractive index makes it useful for lenses and prisms, and because of its brilliance when cut, it is the type used for crystal chandeliers, decorative cut glass, and fine table crystal. The subtle facets of Ursula stemware (Pl. 13, p. 131) catch and reflect every ray of light, and no applied decoration is needed to enhance their gleaming beauty.

Windows, lighting fixtures, and glass containers are usually made of *lime glass,* consisting of potassium silicate, sodium silicate, or a mixture of the two, with a small amount of lime added to make the ingredients insoluble.

Pyrex cooking utensils and laboratory equipment come from *borosilicate glass,* which is largely a mixture of silica and boric oxide, usually with the addition of sodium silicate.

Various compounds are added to molten glass in order to color or decolorize it, to improve its texture, and to lessen its tendency to form bubbles. Iron oxides, often present as impurities, give glass an undesirable greenish or brownish cast, and manganese, nickel, and selenium are used as decolorizers to eliminate it. Coloring agents, on the other hand, give the jeweled tones that distinguish stained glass windows and mosaics, as well as the various hues that are used in colored tableware. Copper oxide is used for red and blue, cobalt salts for blue, nickel oxide for purple and brown, selenium or uranium oxides for yellow, and chromium oxides for yellow and green. Ruby-red glass is usually produced by the addition of selenium. It is an interesting fact that although silica is a basic component in both glass and ceramic glazes, the oxides used as colorants produce colors in glazes that are quite different from those they cause when added to molten glass. This is the result of the action of other chemical substances present in each case.

METHODS OF MAKING GLASS

In order to understand the art of designing in glass, it will be helpful to have an idea of the five processes by which glass is made. The oldest method is *pressing,* in which semifluid glass is taken from the melting pot and worked into shape by means of paddles or other tools. As early as 3000 B.C. the Egyptians discovered that the glazes they put on stones and pots for decorative purposes would stand alone, and as a result they began making containers for cosmetics by pressing the molten glass into crude forms. Today machine-operated presses are used, forcing the glass into molds that form the outsides of the objects, while plungers are inserted to smooth the inside.

Casting is a common technique for reproducing the work of the designer. This is a process much like pressing, except that no pressure is applied. The glass is simply poured into molds to the desired thickness and allowed to cool until it hardens.

One of the most fascinating methods of working glass is the ancient art of *blowing,* believed to have been used first in the century before the birth of Christ. The blowpipe is usually an iron pipe about four feet long with a mouthpiece at one end. The glassblower dips up a small amount of molten glass with the opposite end, rolls or presses it against a paddle or metal plate to cool it slightly, and then blows into the mouthpiece, producing a bubble of glass. He shapes the bubble by twisting the pipe while blowing and by rolling with a paddle, often adding more molten glass as the work progresses. When the desired shape is obtained, the glass is cut away from the pipe with shears. For the past several centuries most glass blowing has been done in molds (Fig. 139). More involved forms are achieved by *lampworking,* in which the artisan uses rods and cylinders of preformed glass, shaping and joining the forms after heating them in the flame of a glass lamp or Bunsen burner.

Such rods and cylinders, as well as fibers and window glass, are made by the process known as *drawing.* Sheets of glass are formed by lowering a long narrow trough with a longitudinal slit in the bottom into a tank furnace containing molten glass. A sheet is forced upward through the slit and caught by a series of asbestos-covered rollers, during which process the glass is *annealed.* Annealing is a necessary process for all objects made of glass, for it relieves the strains that are set up within the glass as it cools. This treatment generally consists of reheating the glass and allowing it to cool slowly so that very little additional strain is produced. After it has been annealed, the sheet of glass is put on a flat table where it is cut into smaller sheets. Tubing is produced by drawing out a cylindrical mass of glass and blasting air through a nozzle into the center of the cylinder.

Drawn window glass cannot be made of a uniform thickness; consequently minor distortions may result. Plate glass is made by *rolling* the glass sheet between two water-cooled rollers; then, after it is annealed and cut, the glass is set in a level bed of plaster of Paris. The sheets are ground with successively finer grades of sand

below: 139. This photograph illustrates the technique of blowing glass in a mold. The hot glob of glass at the end of the pipe is placed in an open mold. When the mold is closed the glob is blown out against the walls of the mold, thus determining the shape and dimensions of the piece.

140. This glass vase has as its sole ornamentation a laid-on design in clear crystal.

and emery and are finally brought to a high polish by buffing with rouge. This, of course, is the fine glass used for mirrors and display windows. Windshields are now made of *safety glass,* produced by laminating a sheet of transparent plastic between two sheets of plate glass. When safety glass is broken, the pieces of glass are held in place by the adhesive plastic layer between them. This prevents shattering, even under the impact of a violent blow.

DECORATIVE DESIGN IN GLASS

Although the inherent beauty of glass makes ornamentation unnecessary, the temptation to combine this quality with decorative design has led artists and craftsmen to many distinctive effects.

Laid-on designs consist of separate shapes of glass applied to an object for added interest. In the past the shapes were often of contrasting colors, sometimes gilded for a luxurious effect. The contemporary application is usually simple and without color, as in the vase in Figure 140.

Etching is often used as a means of decorating less expensive glassware, resulting in a frosted texture. Parts of the glass that the craftsman intends to leave undecorated are coated with wax, and the glass is submerged in hydrofluoric acid, which eats away the exposed surfaces and creates areas of texture that form the design.

Examples of *enameling* and *gilding* can be seen in museums, although these forms of decoration have not been used in recent years to any significant degree.

Heavy crystal may be ornamented by *cutting,* a method of decoration that has reached considerable popularity in past eras. Cutting is done by means of various wheels onto which a stream of wet sand drips from an overhanging funnel, with the sand performing the actual cutting. Smaller wheels are used for smoothing or for cutting intricate designs; wooden wheels of willow, cherry, or other soft woods are employed for the final polishing, although acid, rottenstone, or pumice may also be used. Hand polishing can be applied for a softer luster.

Engraving is probably the most adaptable of the decorative processes for glass, principally because it enhances the surface without detracting from its inherent qualities of brilliance and clarity. Since the process is painstaking, however, it is limited to the finest crystal. Motorized tools, consisting of copper wheels of many

Plate 13. Ursula stemware, designed by JENS QUISTGAARD for Dansk Designs Ltd.

Plate 14. EDGAR BRITTON. Stained-glass window, Chapel of the Holy Family, St. John's Church, Boulder, Colo. 1967. (Executed by HANS and ELLIE GALLUS.)

sizes and shapes, are revolved rapidly while the glass is pressed against them. A masterpiece of the engraver's art is seen in Figure 141. *The Great Ring of Canada* was designed as a gift from the people of the United States to the people of Canada on the one hundredth anniversary of Canada's nationhood in 1967. It stands 40 inches high and 28 inches in diameter, and consists of a ring of 12 cut and engraved crystal plaques, one for each of Canada's ten provinces and two territories. Each plaque is beautifully engraved with the armorial bearings and flower of the area that it represents. The smaller ring above consists of four crystal plaques, two engraved with the Arms of Canada, and two with a natural maple leaf enclosed in the formal maple leaf of the Canadian flag. In each quadrant the ring is engraved with the motto of Canada: *A mari usque ad mare* (from sea to sea). At the top a many-faceted sphere symbolizes the nation as a whole, while the base is designed of rhodium-plated steel.

right: 141. Donald Pollard and Alexander Seidel for Steuben Glass. *The Great Ring of Canada.* 1967. Cut and engraved crystal, height 40″. Property of the people of Canada.

far right: 142. Angelo Beroviero (?). Goblet, from Venice, Italy. c. 1475. Deep blue and clear glass enameled in colors, height 7½″. Toledo Museum of Art, Toledo, Ohio (gift of Edward Drummond Libbey, 1940).

HISTORICAL STYLES IN GLASS

One of the first distinctive styles of glass was the *cameo glass* of the ancient Romans, involving a technique also used by the Chinese. A design of contrasting color, carved or molded to form a *bas-relief,* is overlaid on the glass vessel, and the whole is reheated until fusion takes place. The design then stands out, resembling a cameo.

The discovery of soda lime glass early in the fifteenth century made possible the use by Venetian glassblowers of the famous clear glass known as *crystallo,* which was particularly suited for blowing the elaborate forms in demand during the Renaissance. This was a period of extensive maritime activity for Venice, a key port where all the color and exotic forms of Eastern art were brought together.

The glass industry in Venice probably developed after the arrival of skilled Syrian glassmakers, who were deported following the fall of Damascus to Tamerlane in 1401. The Crusades had been an earlier force in bringing Eastern influences to Venice, as well as to other parts of Western Europe. As a result of these influences, the fifteenth and sixteenth centuries in Venice saw the rise of several distinctive practices in the design and execution of glass. One such practice was the use of metallic oxides to produce richly colored goblets with pedestal feet (Fig. 142). These goblets were

left: 143. Covered jar and two vases, from Venice, Italy. 16th–17th century. Lace-glass (*center*) and Latticinio glass (*left* and *right*); height of covered jar 11¼″. Toledo Museum of Art, Toledo, Ohio (gift of Edward Drummond Libbey).

below: 144. Wine decanter, from the area of Pittsburgh, Pa. c. 1815–35. Blown glass, height 9⅜″. Corning Museum of Glass, Corning, N.Y.

often elaborately enameled with figures, or embellished by gilding or *gemming,* which is the application of jewellike spots of colored enamel. Sometimes the glass was colored to imitate streaked stone, such as agate or onyx. *Aventurine,* a kind of glass containing copper particles that created a golden effect, was frequently used.

Milk-colored glass known as *lattimo* was made in variations from dull opaque white to a more or less transparent opalescent glass, which was often garnished with gilding, painting, and splash decorations.

Crackle glass was made by the sudden cooling of a hot half-blown piece that, once cooled, was reheated, expanded, and finished with cracks or fissures covering the surface. Sometimes glass fragments were rolled into the surface, and the glass was fully blown and finished as usual.

Vitro di trina, or lace-glass, was one of the most distinctive of Venetian innovations. Starting as a spiral threading of opaque white enamel, the design expanded into multiple threads that were worked into lacy bands, often covering the bowl and foot or even the entire vessel (Fig. 143). The climax of this development came in the intricate *netzglas,* which resulted when two layers of lace-glass were fused in such a way that the threads formed a net pattern of tiny squares, each containing a miniature bubble. Eventually the lacy effect was produced in colored glass as well, often with ruby threading.

Enameled coats of arms on drinking bowls and vessels were a favorite with the German nobility, who ordered their glass from Venice.

Masking was a device borrowed from the Romans, in which medallionlike faces were attached to the glass. The Venetians often attached a lion's head, symbolic of St. Mark, the patron saint of Venice.

Festooning, fluting, ribbing, and many other methods of decoration were applied in profusion to Venetian glass. Glassmakers of most other European countries were influenced to some degree by Venetian craftsmen.

Pressed Glass was prepared in molds in Europe prior to its introduction into the United States; yet we usually associate its finest expression with the American glass factories of the nineteenth century. The first American pressing machine was made

far left: 145. T. G. Hawkes & Company. Plate in the "Russian" pattern. c. 1900. Blown and cut glass, diameter $13\frac{1}{4}$". Corning Museum of Glass, Corning, N.Y.

left: 146. Louis Comfort Tiffany. Table lamp. c. 1900. Bronze and favrile glass; height 27", diameter of shade 18". Lillian Nassau Art Nouveau and Tiffany Glass, New York.

in 1827 by Enoch Robinson in Cambridge, Massachusetts. From this invention developed Sandwich Glass, named for the Sandwich Glass Company, which improved the methods and developed many of the designs that later were widely used. Although this company originally made large quantities of hand-blown tableware, its fame rests on the variety of pressed designs in every range of color. Lacy Sandwich was characterized by a stippled background that gave a fine lacelike pattern. Pressed candlesticks, saltcellars, wine decanters (Fig. 144), and lamps with overlay were some of the most popular items made, with designs ranging from animal and flower forms to geometric shapes.

The method of decorating glass by cutting it with rotating wheels was known in Syria and Egypt in early times. *Cut glass* was later made in England and Ireland; yet it, too, reached a peak of excellence and popularity in nineteenth-century America. Although red, blue, green, yellow, and amber cut glass were made, the colorless clear variety is now better known to collectors. Patterns used in cut glass were listed in the dozens, ranging from bowknot, Grecian with strawberry-diamond, and star, to elaborate chrysanthemums and roses, in which each artist tried to achieve something increasingly more delicate or luxurious. A complete service in the "Russian pattern" (Fig. 145) was ordered for the White House during the administration of President Grover Cleveland. This was a variation on the star-and-hobnail design that was executed especially for a banquet service ordered by the Russian embassy in Washington, D.C.

Among the American followers of the Art Nouveau movement (see p. 105) was Louis Comfort Tiffany, son of the famous New York jeweler. After traveling to Paris and the Orient, he established a studio in New York City and became known for his interiors designed in the Art Nouveau style. He also achieved recognition for fine metal crafts, pottery, and especially for stained glass. Much of his glass was used in architecture and reflected the Art Nouveau characteristics—biological symbolism with fruit and flower designs, vines, and tendrils, combined with elements from Oriental and French paintings. His stained glass lampshades (Fig. 146) and elegant vases have recently enjoyed an enthusiastic revival.

CONTEMPORARY GLASS DESIGN

Like the contemporary potter, the glass designer of today is concerned primarily with an expression of the full potential of his material. Most contemporary designers in glass express their ideas through structure and the exploitation of the inherent qualities of glass, rather than by using decorative devices. At the same time, some of the most unusual effects in modern glass have resulted from the adaptation of traditional techniques for the creation of contemporary forms. The prism in Figure 147, for instance, is cut in three planes with curving edges. A sprig of vine is engraved on one plane, while a single wing of a butterfly is engraved on each of the two far planes. Because of the prismatic effect, both engravings are reflected in reverse. As the reflections appear and disappear, the vine seems to spread within the crystal, and the butterfly's wings actually seem to move. Such works confirm the contemporary designer's respect for traditional forms, as well as his capacity for innovation, a combination that often leads to unique expressions.

Swedish designers were among the first to appreciate the inherent beauty of glass itself, and to utilize the fluidity of glass to the fullest. The design by Mona Morales Schlidt in Figure 148 is typical of fine Swedish glass. Also consistent with the developments in modern glass design is the bottle in Figure 149, which was conceived by Andries D. Copier of the Netherlands. The American designer Marvin Lipofsky also shows a sensitivity to his material, yet places more emphasis on its plastic quality (Fig. 150). Even a Venetian artist, with the strong influence from the past still upon him, has embraced the contemporary approach in an entirely individual way (Fig. 151). All of these works are eloquent in their integrity, displaying a correlation between material and form. No other material makes possible the transparency, fluidity, and totally organic quality that these artists have achieved in glass.

STAINED GLASS

Stained glass derives its effect from the variations in the light that strikes and shines through it. Once stained glass has been illumined by natural or artificial light, it glows with a gemlike irridescence. Gothic cathedrals present the most splendid array of stained glass still in existence. The earliest surviving medieval example apparently

147. George Thompson and Alexander Seidel. *The Butterfly*. c. 1964. Cut and engraved crystal, height 8″. Steuben Glass, New York.

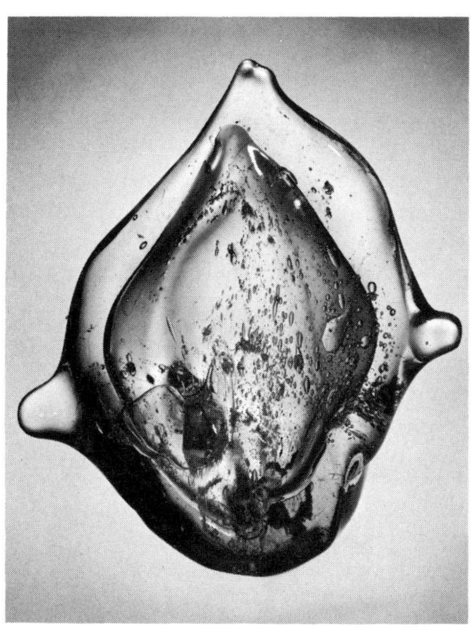
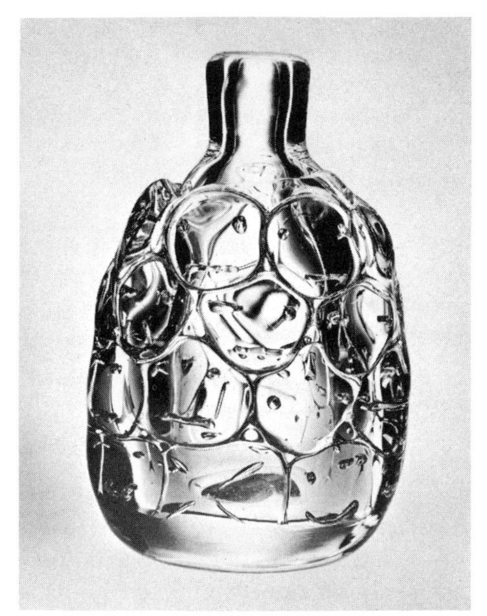

top left: 148. MONA MORALES SCHLIDT for Kosta Glassbruk. Vase, from Sweden. c. 1961. Cased and cut glass, height $5^{15}/_{16}$". Corning Museum of Glass, Corning, N.Y.

top right: 149. The fluidity of glass is expressed in a contemporary design (c. 1960) by ANDRIES D. COPIER for N. V. Knoinklijke Nederlandsche Glasfabriek Leerdam, Netherlands.

above left: 150. MARVIN LIPOFSKY. *Glass Form with Two Knobs.* 1966. Clear green glass with brass bubbles, height 10". Corning Museum of Glass, Corning, N.Y.

above right: 151. The influence of a rich history in glassmaking is evident in this bottle (c. 1960) by the Venetian designer FLAVIO POLI.

dates from the eleventh century, coming from the Abbey of Wissenborg. Medieval artists painted the individual pieces of glass with metallic oxides and then fired them in a kiln to fuse paint and glass. Shading was added in a monochromatic effect called *grisaille,* made of a metallic oxide and powdered glass in a gum medium. After the individual pieces of glass had been completed, they were joined together with H-shaped strips of lead. When the glass was completely leaded, the strips were soldered at their intersections, and the spaces between glass and lead were filled with putty. Frequently the window was supported further by metal rods installed in strategic positions. Breathtakingly beautiful windows were created in this way, windows that cast their jewel tones into the cool dark interiors of most European cathedrals. The windows at Chartres and St. Denis near Paris have long been cherished by lovers of stained glass.

Originally, the great windows of the Middle Ages served a didactic purpose. They were meant to illustrate pictorially for an essentially illiterate congregation the moral teachings of the Bible and the Christian tradition. The windows at Chartres were indeed the "gospels of the uneducated," and their beauty was a visual demonstration of the glory of God and Heaven.

Not since the Middle Ages has stained glass received the attention it engenders today. Following the example of a few European craftsmen who have preserved the old techniques, the contemporary artist is experimenting with stained glass not only as an ecclesiastical art form but as a secular one as well. This can be seen in Joseph Meert's panel in Figure 64.

Even in a liturgical adaptation, the artist today shows a new approach. In Plate 14 (p. 132) Edgar Britton started with the figure of the Virgin and developed it into an effective abstract design. With a literate congregation it is no longer necessary to use paintings and windows as a medium of instruction. Instead the artist endeavors to create an atmosphere of worship and contemplation by means of the soft light that filters through the sumptuous patterns of colored glass. The mind is allowed to follow its own direction, as thoughts weave through the colors and forms of the panel without intrusion by realistic shapes.

MOSAICS

Hand in hand with the renewal of interest in stained glass has come the revival of mosaic as an art form. As enthusiasm has increased for the integration of decorative design with architecture, mosaic has come to hold a place no other art can fill. The color, sparkle, and texture produced by a panel or wall of mosaic cannot be obtained in either painting or sculpture. Furthermore, mosaic is quite durable and easy to maintain, and it often outlasts the structure to which it is applied. Many of the examples of Roman mosaics found in the past several hundred years have been uncovered from the debris of crumbled walls.

There are two methods of creating mosaics, the direct and the indirect. In the direct method the pieces of glass or ceramic material (*tesserae*) are inlaid directly on a wall of wet mortar. The artist works with the realization that irregularities of surface will add to the interest of the total design, catching the light, casting tiny shadows and making a tapestrylike pattern that emphasizes the subtleties of the design itself. In the indirect method, the work is done from a full-scale drawing, or *cartoon,* which is a representation of the design in reverse. The tesserae are placed on the paper with a special paste, and much of the mosaic composition is completed before the mortar is applied to the wall. When the mortar is ready, the paper-backed mosaic is placed face down against it and pressed gently into the mortar. When the mortar has dried, the paper is peeled off, revealing the mosaic as it was originally designed. At this stage a grout of glue and cement may be applied to fill in the crevices between tesserae. When it has become firm, the excess grout is wiped off with a damp cloth or sponge. White or colored, the grout can serve to accent the design; in either case it is a unifying element, relating each tessera to the whole.

The truest mosaic quality is currently achieved by individuals who are reviving the technique as a method of expression rather than as a means of covering a wall. Some designers glaze their own tile or make their own glass tesserae. Others combine mosaic with wood carving. Since color is already in the structure of mosaic and, in the case of glass, goes all the way through it, mosaics have an advantage that few other media enjoy. Some artists have given this quality full play by creating transparent mosaics of stained glass, designed to be suspended with the light shining through from both sides. Others mount their mosaics on sheets of Plexiglas with a special transparent adhesive, illuminating them from behind for richer color.

Varying the technique, some mosaicists use colored sands attached to Masonite with glue, or they set rock, glass, or terrazzo in concrete walks or terraces. A soft plastic called Pyracon makes possible the formation of tesserae by hand, which gives an irregular, handcrafted appearance to the finished work.

The first integration of mosaics and architecture in the twentieth century was seen in Juan O'Gorman's monumental designs for the library of the University of Mexico in Mexico City (Fig. 152). A total of 4000 slabs, each a meter square,

152. JUAN O'GORMAN. Mosaics, University of Mexico Library, University City. Completed 1953.

comprise a full acre of exterior walls, on which the history of Mexico is depicted in millions of colored stones gathered from many parts of the republic. Since no separation is visible between slabs, the panorama unfolds in uninterrupted progression around the building. Thus the mosaics are not only ornamentation but are integral with the form of the building itself.

In contrast, Figure 153 shows a mosaic designed for the outside wall of a thirty-story office building in Lower Manhattan. In a space approximately 86 by $12\frac{1}{2}$ feet, artists Lee Krasner and Ronald Stein attempted to retain the quality of handmade mosaic in a panel scaled to monumental proportions not attempted before in modern times. They achieved this effect by procuring glass plates from Italy, which they smashed into tesserae, and by letting the spirit of the glass determine the shapes. They carefully supervised the imposition of the pieces and sought, above all, to dramatize the light-reflecting characteristics of the broken and varied surface of mosaic. As a result, a rather drab commercial district now has a colorful accent, while the building itself has acquired a face that can weather all seasons and retain its brilliance as long as the building stands.

Another example of contemporary mosaic design is found in Joe Testa-Secca's creation for the exterior wall of a building at the University of South Florida in Tampa (Fig. 154). The shapes in the design are nonobjective and have a general relationship to the forms of the building, but they are free enough to permit the viewer to interpret them for himself. The whole of the composition is enhanced by its reflection in a quiet pool surrounded by plantings, for the mosaic catches the sunlight both directly and from the surface of the water below. Here, then, are exhibited the best qualities available in the mosaic technique. The mosaic is formed by the wall it articulates, and this constitutes an interrelationship that is indicative of the highest function of decorative design.

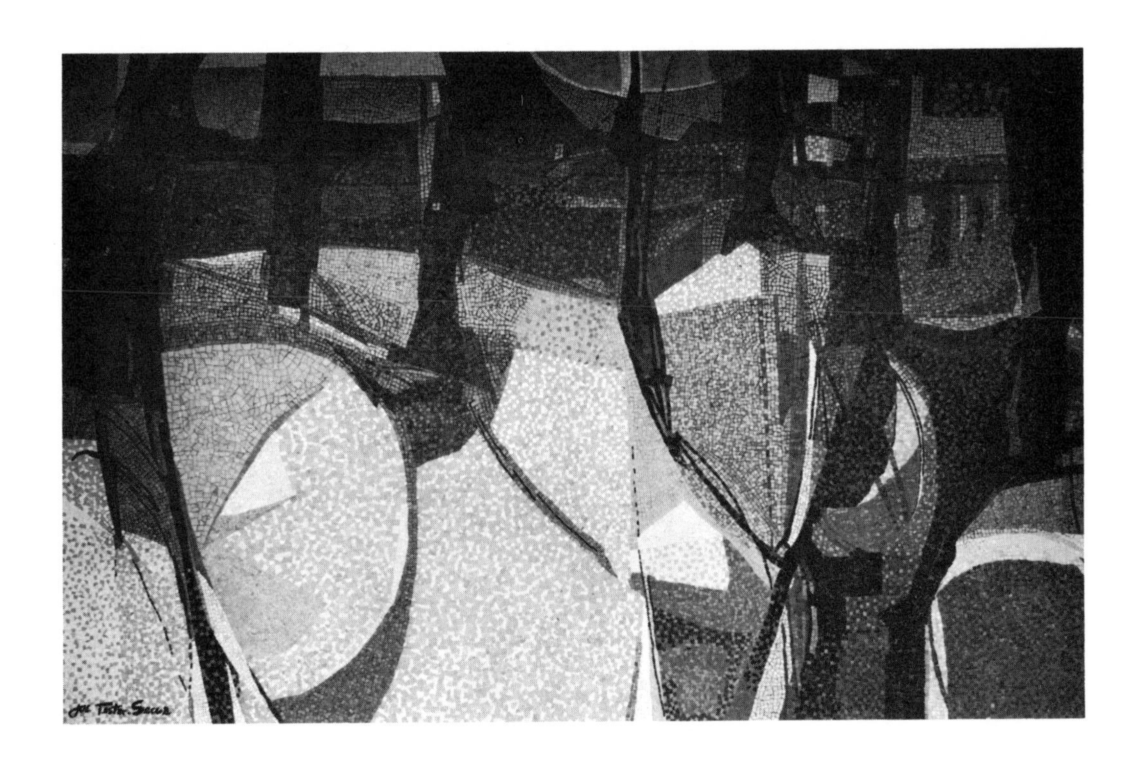

SUMMARY

Glass has unique characteristics that the designer exploits—transparency, fluidity, and sparkle. Its chief raw material is silica, with variations for the different types of glass made. The main types are *lead* glass, *lime* glass, and *borosilicate* glass. Glass is colored by various oxides added to the molten material.

There are five principal methods of making glass: *pressing, casting, blowing, drawing,* and *rolling.* Decorative design in glass can be achieved by use of *laid-on* designs, *etching, enameling, gilding* and *gemming, cutting,* and *engraving.* There are many historic styles in glass, beginning with the crude Egyptian containers for cosmetics. Venetian glass was highly developed, and it encompassed a variety of different techniques and styles. Pressed glass and cut glass are both well known as American techniques. Tiffany glass is an American style associated with Art Nouveau.

Contemporary designers in glass prefer to exploit the fluidity and plastic qualities of the material, rather than to work in elaborate techniques, although some use is made of traditional processes, particularly that of engraving. The Swedish designers were among the first modern craftsmen to appreciate glass for its own qualities, and they have produced many beautiful contemporary works.

Stained glass is being revived by mid-twentieth-century artists as a means of expression in both liturgical and secular art. Mosaic is gaining new respect and popularity as a medium for the enhancement of architecture.

opposite: 153. Lee Krasner and Ronald Stein. Mosaic mural, 2 Broadway, New York. Completed 1959.

above: 154. Joe Testa-Secca. Mosaic mural, Administration Building, University of South Florida, Tampa. Completed 1960.

Design in Fabrics

chapter 10

Nowhere is the handcrafted look more effective than in fabrics. Whether it is a block-printed textile or a work of distinctive weaving, fabric that is handcrafted has a quality that most people sensitive to color and texture find irresistible.

WEAVING AS AN ART

Weaving is the process of interlacing two sets of parallel threads to form a web, an operation that can be carried out in a variety of ways (see pp. 145–147). For centuries hand weaving was the only means of producing fabric, but hand methods almost disappeared when mechanized factory looms came into use in the nineteenth century. Originally, textiles were made solely of natural fibers. Variations of basic weaving patterns were introduced only by occasional changes in fashion. The revival of hand weaving derived from the same causes that prompted the renewal of pottery making. Mass industrial production had flooded the market with standardized products, but, at the same time, a newly affluent and discriminating public began, in reaction, to search for distinctive and individual crafts. Thus, people interested in the unusual patronized the handcraft cultures of underdeveloped communities and began to collect materials from the past. When American designers revitalized the use of the hand loom, they found a sympathetic and appreciative audience.

The horizons of the contemporary weaver stretch to realms never envisioned by the craftsmen of the past. Power looms and a world of new fibers offer unlimited challenge to the weaver, and the range of uses possible for textiles in modern living challenges the imagination. Interiors of rough brick, stone, and wood paneling require fabrics with weight and variety, and in designing for such environments, the artist-craftsman can explore all aspects of textural interest and creative treatment. Open-space architecture invites room dividers for which fabrics can be one of the most appropriate materials (Fig. 155); they modify the acoustics and supply a visual accent. Ecclesiastical needs include symbolic hangings, woven reredos, and altar cloths, all traditional accouterments subject to new expression. Because of the increasing demand for handwoven textiles, the weaver is enjoying new status. In addition to being a craftsman, he has become an artist who is expected not only to produce but to *design* unusual and original textiles. He has developed the viewpoint of the artist—experimenting, finding new fibers, and trying unexpected color combinations. Meanwhile, artists have turned to weaving as a medium for their designs. Textile making is no longer only a process but is an art as well.

The difficulty of supplying the demand for hand weaving has led once more to the collaboration between artist and industry. Textile engineers have constructed machinery of such versatility that almost any effect can be achieved with speed and skill, including designs the artist works out in advance on a hand loom. As a result, some of the large textile manufacturers employ top creative talents to develop new fabrics and designs, and they attain with quantity production a high level of quality and originality.

THE IMPORTANCE OF FIBERS

Any fabric is the expression of the fibers of which it is made. The world of fibers reaches into the far corners of the earth, and it is enriched continually by science and the imagination of the designer. Luster, softness, ruggedness or delicacy, opacity and sheerness, absorbency, and elasticity—all are characteristics found in fibers, and it is fibers and their characteristics that determine the appearance, "hand," and durability of finished fabrics. Such a textile as that reproduced in Figure 156 displays, for instance, the individual qualities of wild Haitian cotton that has been spun and woven by hand into a distinctive fabric, interesting for both its bulk and its texture.

For centuries the heavier fibers used for warmth have come from the fur or hair of animals: the wool of the sheep; angora, mohair, and cashmere from different varieties of goats; alpaca from the llama; and combinations of woolen fibers mixed with fur from rabbits and other animals. Among the natural fibers the lighter ones

left: 155. Alan and Dottie Fannin. *Plait.* c. 1968. Handspun rayon and bleached flax blend, height 5′8″. Collection the artists.

above: 156. Haitian cotton, handspun and handwoven for Jack Lenor Larsen, Inc.

originate with plants. Cotton, for example, comes from the bolls of the cotton plant, and flax has, for at least seven thousand years, been cultivated for linen. Hemp from Asia and jute from East India are used to make a fiber much like linen, but it is coarser and can serve for the construction of mats and rug backing. Jute fibers enjoy considerable popularity, especially when dyed in vivid colors and woven into a texture like that of burlap. Silk fibers are the result of interaction between plants and animals. The silkworm creates from either mulberry leaves or oak leaves. When it is the latter, the long silk fibers that are produced are of a tougher quality. Once grown and collected, natural fibers must be carded, spun, or twisted into yarns before they can be transformed into fabric. It is an age-old process.

Designers today exploit both natural fibers and synthetics, or man-made fibers, the latter having opened new doors in fabric design. Fibers can be made from chemicals, from glass, wood, feathers, and even from steel. Recently, an upholstery fabric was woven of mohair and stainless steel filaments that could be molded to furniture. Another textile, woven entirely of aluminum, is flexible, flameproof, and durable. Plastic mesh, yarns of Saran, Dacron, Lurex and Orlon are often combined with natural fibers to produce fabrics with the best qualities of both natural fibers and synthetics. Stretch fabrics are knit of elasticized yarns to fit chairs and sofas, often with unusual effects (Fig. 157).

METHODS OF MAKING FABRICS

The term *fabric* applies to any cloth that is manufactured. The process can be *felting,* which consists of rolling and pounding fibers together under heat and pressure to form a compact and even sheet. Another method is *lacing,* which is done with a single thread fastened onto itself, as in knitting, knotting, crocheting, tatting, or looping. *Sheeting* is also a technique for making fabric, and it consists of rolling various plastics into sheets. There is also *intertwining,* which involves two sets of threads interlocked with one another. The most usual form of intertwining is weaving, and the term *textile* specifies fabrics that are woven.

The *structural design* of any fabric includes weaving and any other process that can establish pattern by means of fabric structure. *Decorative design* refers to all the methods of printing on fabric and to appliqué, embroidery, hooking, and any other processes for decorating fabric after it has been constructed.

157. *Firebird* (1967) is an Art Nouveau stretch print of textured Caprolan nylon by Jack Lenor Larsen, Inc. Chair design by PIERRE PAULIN for Artifort.

WEAVING

Once spinning was developed, by 3000 B.C., the possibilities for unusual effects in weaving were much increased. Whereas variations in the earliest weaving had to be obtained with color, spinning made possible the addition of many other characteristics, which could be given to the combed or carded fibers as they were spun or twisted into yarns. With virtuosity and imagination the modern fabric designer has expanded these basic possibilities into an almost limitless range of effects. Some designers incorporate grasses, seed pods, or feathers into their fabrics, using their distinctive natural shapes as integral elements of the structural design (Fig. 158). The subtle, earthy colors of broom corn, cattails, thistles, goldenrod, and various barks can articulate warps of linen and wool and make exciting textiles with a harmonious, natural quality. Glycerin is used to prevent brittleness, and a coating of plastic preserves the forms indefinitely.

above left: 158. DOMINIC DIMARE. *Sculptural Form.* 1966. Linen, jute, and wool, with feathers; 5'10" × 1'10" × 7". Collection S. C. Johnson & Company, Racine, Wisc.

above right: 159. Native weaver at work on a simple loom.

Despite the invention of power equipment for weaving, nothing is yet possible in power weaving that cannot be done on a hand loom. Therefore, the basic requirement of the textile designer remains a knowledge of the loom. This is the organ upon which the weaver plays, pouring forth his harmonies of color and texture. His entire body moves in a simple rhythm, while the design flows from the loom as finished textile. Even when the weaver uses a simple form of loom (Fig. 159), his harmonious movements are clearly evident.

The simplest loom is a rectangular frame of wood with warp threads stretched parallel to each other across the length of the frame and secured at opposite ends. The weaver passes a needle carrying the filling thread, or weft, back and forth across the loom and places it alternately over and under the individual threads of the warp. Obviously, this type of loom is slow to operate and is therefore unsuitable for large pieces of fabric. To facilitate operation, the *hand loom* was developed. This machine, with only minor variations, was invented independently by every civilization that practiced the art of weaving. It still provides the standard method for creating handmade fabrics and for developing the new designs that are adapted to the power looms for the purpose of mass production.

The hand loom is mounted on a sturdy frame of wood or metal in order to give support to the moving parts (Fig. 160). The principal difference between the hand loom and the simple loom is that on the hand loom the warp threads are run alternately under and over a pair of flat wooden rods, while the two sets of warp threads are controlled separately by treadles. Thus, the weaver can raise one set of warp threads by pressing the treadle with his feet, which action forms a triangular space known as a *shed* between the two sets of alternate threads and the *beater* (a comblike device that separates the warp threads and keeps them in correct position). He throws the *shuttle* containing the weft thread through this space. Next, he brings the beater forward toward the cloth to place the weft thread in the cloth. He then

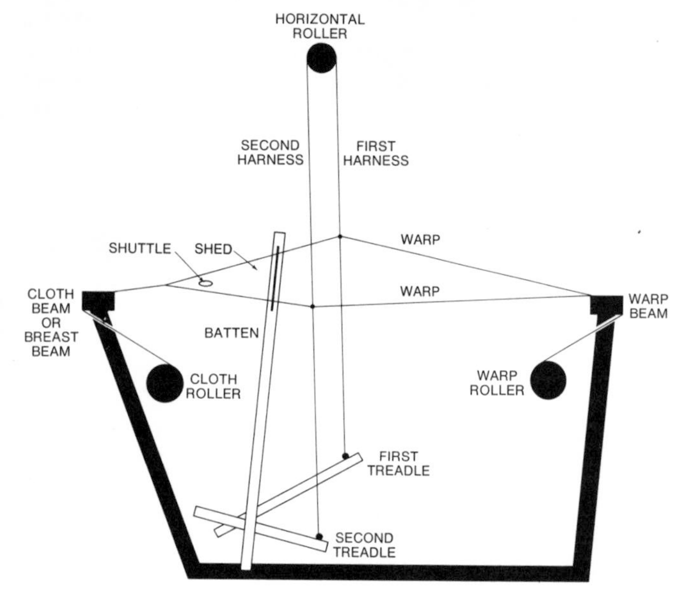

above left: 160. This cross section of a hand loom shows the basic parts and the principal steps in operation. The shuttle carries the weft back and forth through the shed, and the weaver reverses the warp threads by moving the treadles between each passing of the shuttle.

161–162. Threading a loom involves two basic steps.

above right: 161. The warp threads are separated and held apart by wires.

right: 162. The yarns are worked through the heddles—vertical wires with eyes that hold the yarns in position for raising and lowering.

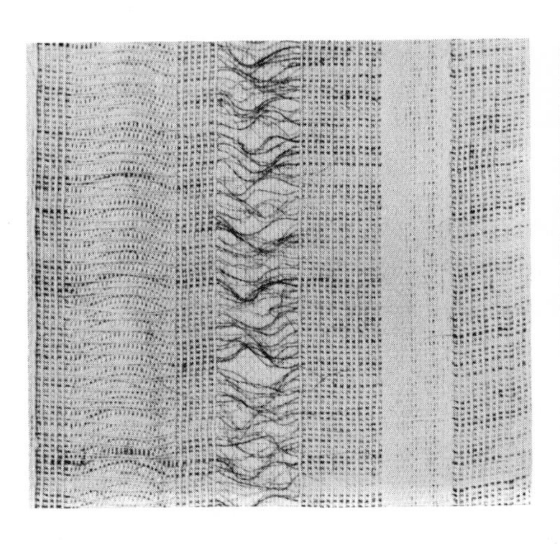

far left: 163. Natural fibers are combined in this textile by Jack Lenor Larsen and Win Anderson.

left: 164. Floating yarns provide texture and pattern in this textile by Boris Kroll Fabrics. Both the triangular sections and the rectangular areas between them are created with floats.

raises the alternate set of warp threads, automatically interlacing warp and weft. As a repeated operation, the motions become easy and rhythmic with the rows of fabric developing rapidly into a length of textile.

The threading of the loom plays an important part in design (Figs. 161–162). For special effects, varied arrangements are possible. Warp threads of different colors and weights can be used for stripes or blocks of pattern, while a number of shuttles containing threads of varying colors and textures can be interspersed in creating the weft.

STRUCTURAL DESIGN IN TEXTILES

Structural design depends upon two factors: the type of fiber used and the way in which it is woven. Even with all the synthetic fibers now in use, the most attractive weaves still have natural fibers either in combination with synthetics or blended in unusual combinations of their own. An interesting mixture is found in the fabric by Jack Lenor Larsen illustrated in Figure 163. Larsen is known for his imaginative combinations of fibers and for the fascinating textures he creates with them. Speaking of his work, he says: "The constant in my work is not intellect, but love. About the time I learned to weave I read the French poet Paul Eluard, who wrote, 'If you love the intense cloud, pour into every image its warm summer blood.' More than anything else, that is what I have tried to do, so that in a world with too little to delight the eye and please the hand, the color and texture of fabric might be something to love, and to remember."[1]

There are several ways in which fibers can be combined to create a textile. In *plain weave,* one warp thread is interlaced with one weft thread, to produce, for instance, linen, burlap, and percale. When two or more threads of each kind are interlaced, the result is *basket weave,* as in monk's cloth. When a thick warp thread is used with a medium or thin weft, the result is a *rib weave,* of which poplin is an example.

Floating yarn is a popular variation in which either the warp or weft yarns float over or under several opposing yarns (Fig. 164). Long floats can emphasize the texture as in piqué or twill, or they can, by minimizing it, produce the smoothness of satin.

In *leno* weaves, two or more parallel warp yarns are crossed, and the weft yarn is passed through the opening. This technique creates effects such as those found in openwork curtains.

right: 165. The texture of cut loops is clear in *Shetland*, a rya rug designed by Egetaepper.

far right: 166. *Ondine* is a white-on-white brocade by Boris Kroll Fabrics. The design is based on an 18th-century floral pattern.

below: 167. KAY SEKIMACHI. *Nagare III*. 1968. Handwoven monofilament, 7′4″ × 1′ × 1′. Courtesy Lee Nordness Galleries, New York.

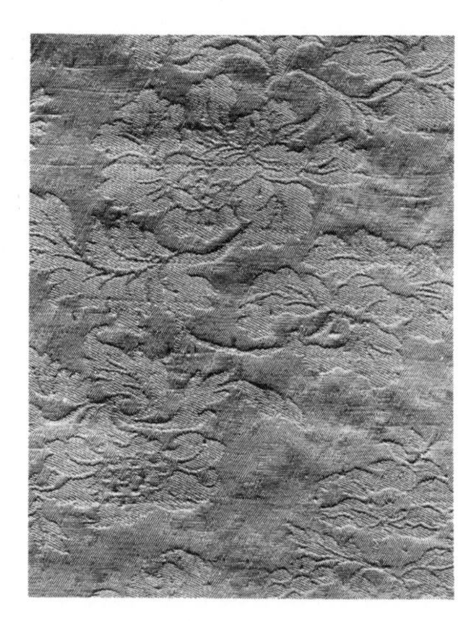

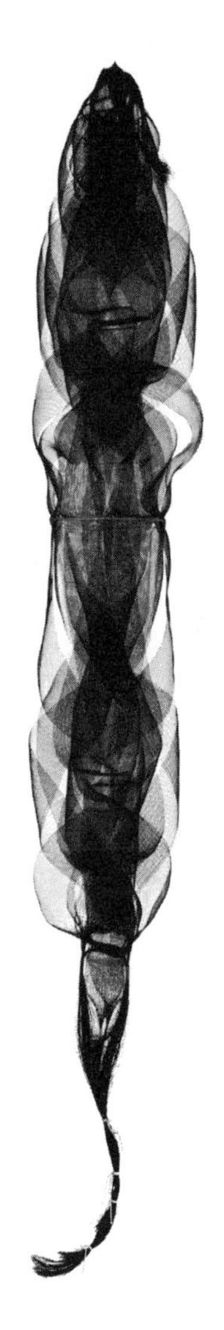

Pile weaves have two sets of weft threads, one of which creates the loops. These loops can be seen in terry cloth and in some novelty weaves. When the loops are cut, the result is cut pile, such as in velvet and in rya rugs (Fig. 165).

Figure weaves come in many complex variations. There are different ways of creating designs on the hand loom by working contrasting yarns into the background at intervals. However, the Jacquard loom is typically used for machine figures. This mechanism can have 1200 or more hooks and needles, and it is guided by a series of cards that are perforated to correspond with the pattern being worked. Such figure weaves include brocades and damasks (Fig. 166).

Another aspect of structural design lies in three-dimensional weaving. Contemporary designers show remarkable ingenuity in using various fibers and techniques to achieve a three-dimensional effect (Fig. 167).

TAPESTRY

Tapestry has been created since the fifteenth century B.C. in Egypt, principally on hand looms. The earliest examples of tapestry weaving are three linen textiles found in the tomb of Thutmose IV, now on exhibit in the Cairo Museum. The outstanding characteristic of tapestry weaving derives from the fact that no weft thread is carried entirely across the warp, except in rare instances when the design requires it. Each section of the design is woven with a weft of a certain color, which is inserted back and forth over the section where that color appears in the pattern. The weaver works from a *cartoon*—or drawing the actual size of the tapestry—which is placed under the warp threads; and since the weaving is done on the reverse side, he notes his progress in a mirror located on the other side of the tapestry.

Tapestry weaving was one of the major arts practiced in Europe during the Middle Ages, and it was carried to a high degree of perfection and complexity. The Flemish and French examples, such as the Rose Garden Tapestries (Pl. 15, opposite), are particularly well known. Many of them were commissioned to create a warm and quiet atmosphere in the stone halls of castles, and they were often maintained with the care appropriate for valued possessions. The tapestries produced in seventeenth-century Paris by the Gobelins Works were made by royal decree of Louis XIV. Persian and Chinese craftsmen also excelled in the art of tapestry weaving.

Plate 15. *Courtiers with Roses,* Franco-Flemish tapestry. c. 1435–40. Wool, 9′7″ × 10′11¾″. Metropolitan Museum of Art, New York (Rogers Fund, 1909).

Plate 16. English embroidered bed hanging (detail). Late 16th century. Silk and metal thread on satin. Metropolitan Museum of Art, New York (Rogers Fund, 1920).

Plate 17. Nik Krevitsky. *The Burning Bush.* 1964. Stitchery and appliqué, $26\frac{1}{2} \times 25''$.
Collection Mr. and Mrs. Morris A. Kaplan, Highland Park, Ill.

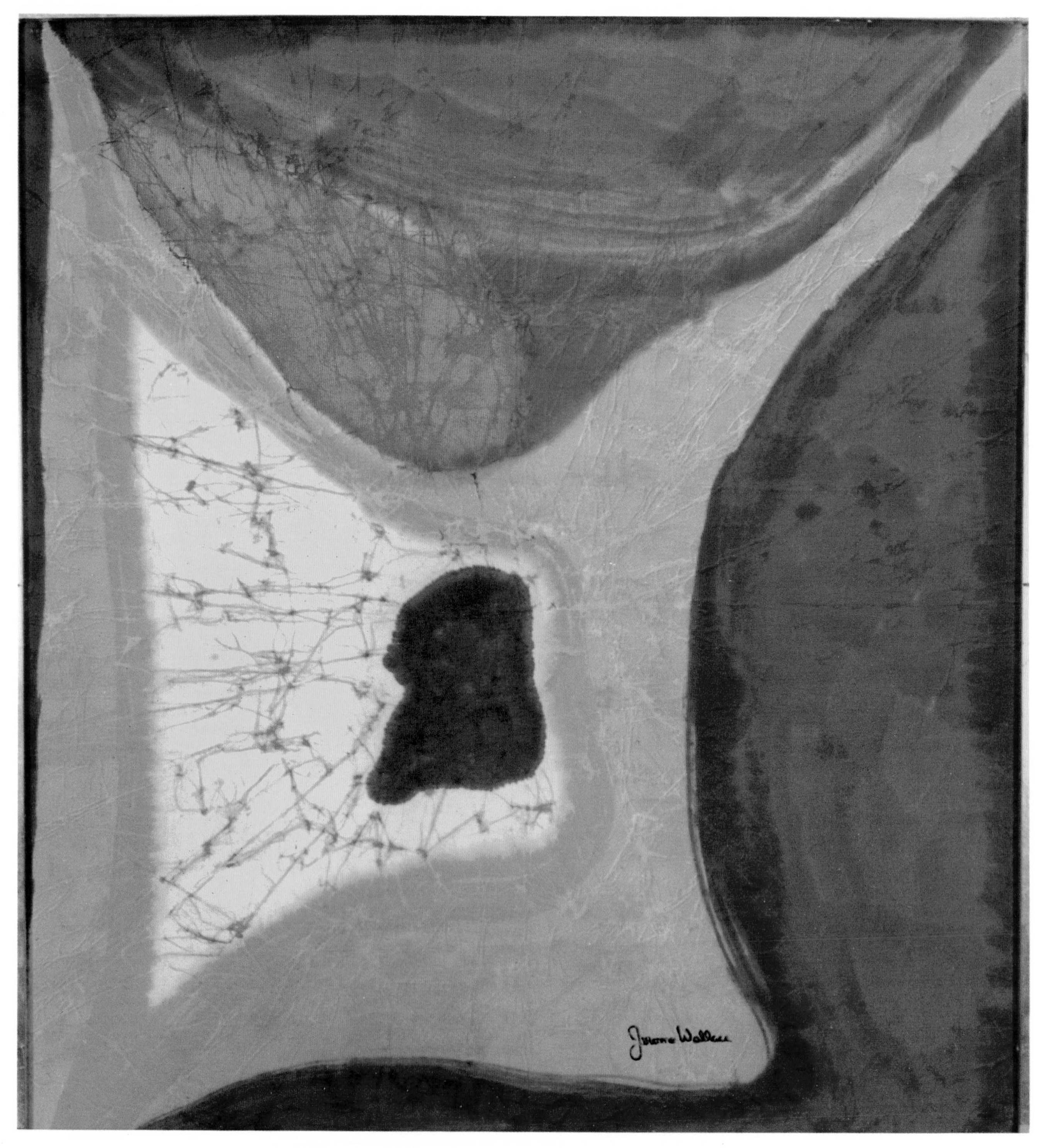

Plate 18. JEROME WALLACE. *Butterfly Tears.* 1968. Batik, $40\frac{1}{2} \times 37\frac{1}{2}$″.
Courtesy Lee Nordness Galleries, New York.

Like stained-glass making, tapestry weaving has been revived as an art form relevant to modern life. After 350 years of inaction, the Aubusson tapestry weaving tradition was revitalized in France following World War II. Such is the success of modern tapestries that over 500 international exhibitions have been held to show the work of twentieth-century craftsmen who weave by traditional methods in order to arrive at contemporary modes of expression.

American weavers, on the other hand, show complete freedom from tradition. Mildred Fischer develops her tapestries from a variety of sources. She is a painter as well as a weaver and often creates works in both arts simultaneously, while maintaining the integrity of each. She says: "Colors and patterns seen in city and country intrigue me: layers of light in ocean water at night; spaces and rhythms and lines associated with the sycamores, birches, or pines; people and festivity. There is a process of sifting and mulling until only what seems to be universal remains; then it, too, is simplified, sometimes to the degree of becoming an abstract symbol." Imbued with a love of travel, Miss Fischer confesses that "unspoiled Finland" is her favorite spot and was the inspiration for such works as *Elokuu* in Figure 168.[2]

The fabrication of tapestry by hooking is a method employed by many contemporary artists. Although this is not tapestry in its true sense, the term is used because the results have a similar texture and because they are put to comparable uses. In hooking, the yarn is pulled through a stiff backing from the underside, frequently by means of a hand-held hooking machine. Loops are left on the front to form a nubby texture. No loom is involved.

Another ancient art now lending itself to contemporary expression is *macramé,* in which structural design is achieved by the knotting of yarns into varied patterns. Based on the designs used by the ancient Babylonians, American whalers, and the makers of Turkish veils, this is an art that twentieth-century designers explore with increasing ingenuity, creating three-dimensional forms as well as two-dimensional fabriclike constructions.

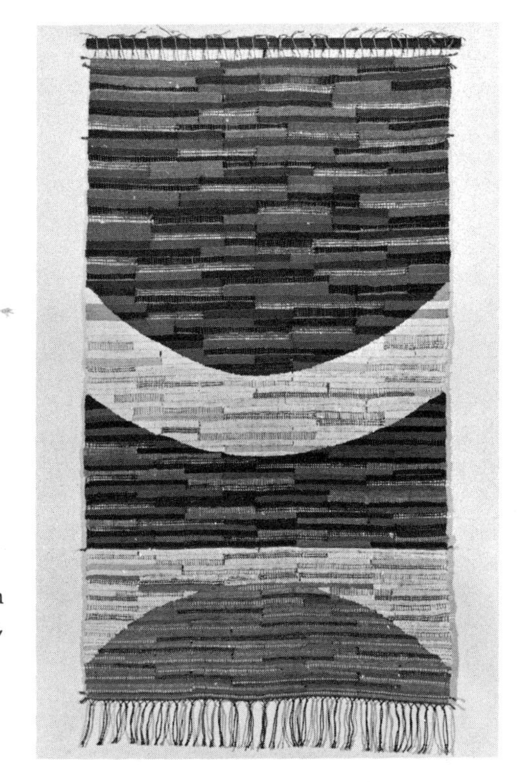

168. Mildred Fischer. *Elokuu.* 1967. Linen yarns and transparent celanese strips, 4′7″ × 2′6″. Collection the artist.

above: 169. Nik Krevitsky. *Forms.* 1965. Stitchery and appliqué on linen, 22 × 28″. Collection Betty Richards, Phoenix, Ariz.

right: 170. Two students collaborate in making a silk-screen print. Here the frame on which the silk is stretched is settled into place for the printing of the next section. The squeegee used for forcing ink through the open areas of the silk is visible between the hands of the student at left.

DECORATIVE DESIGN IN FABRICS

Design is applied to fabrics by one of two general processes: embroidery or appliqué, and printing.

Embroidery is an eloquent testimony to man's need for creative expression. From the time he took a sharp fishbone or pointed stick and invented the first needle, man has not been able to resist the lure of decorating fabrics by the application of bright-colored threads. Every kind of garment—from peasant costumes in cotton and wool to liturgical vestments made of silk and heavy satin—has been painstakingly decorated with intricate and colorful designs. Traditional motifs such as meadow flowers and woodland birds have appeared on costumes in all parts of the world, and have been variously interpreted according to the perceptions of individual cultures. Similarly, historical events have been recorded in detail on elaborately stitched royal mantles. Here, as in tapestry, the design predilections of a people find insistent expression. French medieval embroidery is characterized by sweetness and grace; early Spanish embroideries reflect the Moorish influence, while Persian embroidery is resplendent with the animals and arabesques that Moslems used in lieu of the human image, which their religion prohibits in art. The Elizabethan wall hanging reproduced in Plate 16 (p. 150) is embroidered with naturalistic flower, fruit, and vegetable motifs, and it offers poetic evidence of the English love of nature and gardening. The "strapwork" surrounding the natural forms is a design feature that was often used in European art of the sixteenth century, during the decades art historians term Mannerist.

In Colonial America every well-trained little girl had to make a sampler of various embroidery stitches as a part of her education. Household linens were embroidered as a matter of course, and although quilt making reached a high level of achievement, embroidery was considered an essential household craft rather than a fine art. Decorative designs were created also in *needlepoint,* a type of allover pattern worked on canvas in small, regular stitches, and in *crewel* as well, which is a similar technique that involves the use of woolen yarns loosely twisted. Even these styles of embroidery, however, were directed primarily at such utilitarian objects as cushion covers and footstools.

The contemporary approach to embroidery is marked by a bold use of color and by an honest regard for the stitches themselves, with the result that now one speaks more often of *stitchery* than of embroidery. The heavy structural character of thick threads and yarns makes modern stitchery more than mere surface adornment; it becomes significant and expressive form (Fig. 169). In many instances the decorative sewing is combined with appliqué. Here, pieces of fabric are sewn onto the surface of the material, and the embroidery is worked around and over them in much the same way that clay is inlaid and glazed in pottery. The total effect is highly imaginative, with colored fabrics and interesting yarns working together for the creation of a lively design.

Nik Krevitsky, a contemporary designer in stitchery, sometimes uses leather, metallic filaments, beads, feathers, straw, and raffia in combination with the more traditional elements of fabric and yarn, often with overlays of fabric or networks of thread. Being intrigued with the interaction of color and light, he often achieves a feeling of transparency in his work, as in some areas of *The Burning Bush* (Pl. 17, p. 151). Dr. Krevitsky says: "I try to say something personal about my world which someone else may share because he recognizes in it something of his world."[3]

PRINTING

The printing of design on fabric is traced back to 1000 B.C. in China. In the intervening ages there have been many variations in the process, but most methods can be classified in one of four ways: *direct printing, dyed method, discharge method,* or *resist printing.*

The direct method includes *block printing, intaglio,* and *stenciling.* All are used in advertising design, as well as in textiles and wallpapers. The use of linoleum and wood blocks on fabric is a particularly interesting technique, for the results can be a happy combination of fabric texture, individual design, and allover pattern.

In block printing the design is carved in relief on a block, often of wood, and the inked block is pressed onto cloth or paper, which receives the design from the raised and inked areas of the block's surface. A separate block must be prepared for each color, and each color is printed separately. The intaglio method is dependent upon a copper cylindrical plate that is incised with the lines of the intended design. When the plate is inked and its surface has been wiped clean, the incised lines hold the ink that transfers the design to the fabric. The copper cylinders of intaglio printing are driven by rotary presses. The press operation can print several colors at once, and it is a faster, easier, and more flexible—consequently a more widely used—process than block printing, although in intaglio as well each plate or cylinder carries a single color.

Principal among stenciling methods is *silk screen,* in which the design is supported by a sheet of silk stretched across a wooden frame (Fig. 170). The parts of the design

above left: 171. *Taormina,* a hand-screened fabric by Boris Kroll Fabrics, was printed from a Dacron screen on lightweight cotton.

above right: 172. Designs created by tie-and-dye methods are characterized by a natural quality reminiscent of mineral strata, growth rings in trees, or plant forms. *Bokashi,* by Boris Kroll Fabrics, is a tie-and-dye print on nylon velvet.

to be printed are left untouched, while the remainder of the silk is blocked off with a plastic coating. Ink is then pressed through the silk with a squeegee, or wide rubber-tipped wedge, imprinting the form of the design on the material underneath. Such a process was used in the handprinting of the fabric illustrated in Figure 171. The spacing in this design is not mechanical, but is instead repetitive in the casual, random, and subtle way of daisies scattered over a field or stars filling a summer sky. Unity is retained by balance of forms and space, by arrangement of motifs in groups, and by a delicate adjustment of horizontal, vertical, and diagonal patterns. The sense of movement created by repetition gives the fabric a rhythm that will increase when the material is hung in folds. The block or screen is just the beginning of the flowing, continuous, variable fabric that is printed from it.

Other printing procedures include the *dyed method,* which depends upon the preparation of the cloth by application of a *mordant* or fixative, a substance that combines with dye to form an insoluble compound or *lake.* The mordant is applied to the fabric, a process that is followed by aging and fixing, and then by dyeing. The mordant causes the dye to produce a design.

The discharge method utilizes the action of acids, alkalies, and oxidizing and reducing agents for the destruction of dyed color. The dye is applied and then removed in patterns to produce the desired design.

Resist printing prevents dyeing from taking effect by blocking out sections of the fabric. One of the oldest forms of resist is *batik,* a term applied to the process, as well as to the fabric (Pl. 18, p. 152; Fig. 172). Long practiced in China and Japan, it is now associated with Indonesia. To make batik, the artist applies wax to areas of cloth that are not to be dyed. He then dips the fabric into the dye. When the exposed areas of the fabric reach the desired color, he peels the wax from the fabric. A variation in this type of process is the "tied and dyed" method, by which the fabric is tied in knots and then submerged in the vat of dye. The result is an accidental quality that is itself an interesting design (Fig. 173).

Some artists experiment with "found" textures, using such materials as corrugated cardboard or wire screen for inking and printing on fabrics. Sponges, spools, wood, and erasers are other objects that can be used for this purpose. Textile paint, printing ink, and oil paint can be applied and "printed" onto the fabric, either as design or as accent for block prints. Grass and twigs may be inked directly and printed on fabric, lending their own characteristics to the finished design.

173. The fluid quality of tie-and-dye printing is beautifully suited to loose, flowing garments.

Fabrics in all their variations are a vital part of architectural decoration today. Just as medieval tapestries conserved heat and suppressed echoes, so contemporary textiles lend warmth and softness to the vast expanses of glass, steel, marble, and concrete of modern architecture. Their strong tactile quality appeals to the senses and lends interest to otherwise smooth surfaces. The uncluttered lines of modern furniture provide an ideal support for upholstery of printed or woven fabrics Movable screens covered with textiles make effective room dividers, and panels of fabric are frequently used in the cabinetwork of high-fidelity equipment. Textiles are easy to transport and are simple to install. They don't break, and most fabrics can be cleaned by standard processes. From every aspect, the collaboration of the architect with the textile designer offers intriguing possibilities for the future.

SUMMARY

Handcrafted fabrics have a quality that people sensitive to color and texture find irresistible. Contemporary weavers create remarkable designs for textiles that are adapted to modern interiors.

A fabric is the expression of the fibers that compose it. Designers today use not only natural fibers, but also synthetics, metal, and fibers made from glass, wood, or feathers.

The term fabric refers to materials made by a number of methods, including felting, lacing, sheeting, and intertwining. Weaving is a form of intertwining, and textiles are fabrics that are woven. Despite the invention of power looms, nothing can be done by machine that cannot be done on hand looms as well.

Structural design in textiles depends upon two factors: the fiber that is used and the way in which it is woven. There are many kinds of weave: plain, basket, rib, floating yarns, leno, pile, and figure weaves that include Jacquard, brocade, and damask. Three-dimensional weaving intrigues contemporary designers. In both France and the United States, tapestry weaving has been revived in recent years as a significant art form.

Decorative design in fabrics falls into one of two categories: embroidery or appliqué, and printing. Printing can be done by block printing, by the intaglio method, or by stenciling, which includes silk screen. Other variations of printing are the dyed method, the discharge method, and resist printing.

Design in Wood

chapter 11

Wood enters into every area of human existence. From weapons to ceremonial and religious objects, from the structure of the home and its contents to the fire on the hearth, wood has served man faithfully for thousands of years. He has used it to meet his needs, but he has also learned to see its beauty and to respect its integrity. An experienced craftsman knows, for example, that each piece of wood is an entity with its own peculiarities of growth and cut (Fig. 174), and he must consider these differences in working with the material. There are indeed such variations of grain that sections of wood taken from the same trunk may have quite different patterns, while retaining the essential qualities of grain belonging to the species.

above: 174. Wolf Strache. *Cross section of Yew Trunk.* 1956.

CHARACTERISTICS OF WOOD

The growth of annual rings in the outer or cambium layer of the trunk determines the grain structure. Each year, in temperate zones, trees produce two rings of growth. The early or spring wood is lighter in color than the later or summer wood, and the rings alternate between light and dark to form a definite grain pattern. Grains can be varied further by the manner in which the wood is cut (Fig. 175). The wood

below: 175. Most wood is cut in one of three ways, each presenting a distinctive grain pattern.

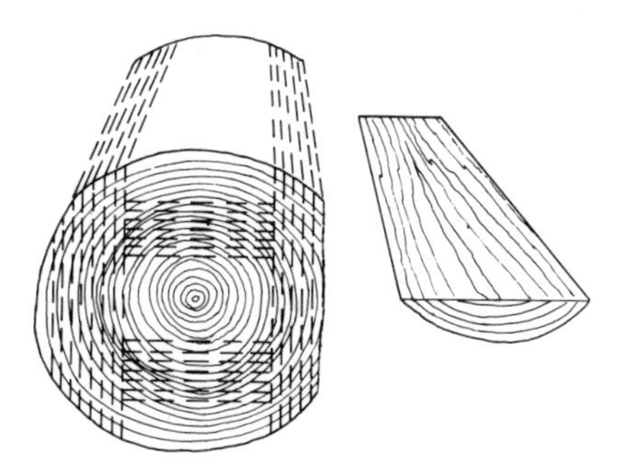

Plain (flat) sawed (cut tangent to annual rings)

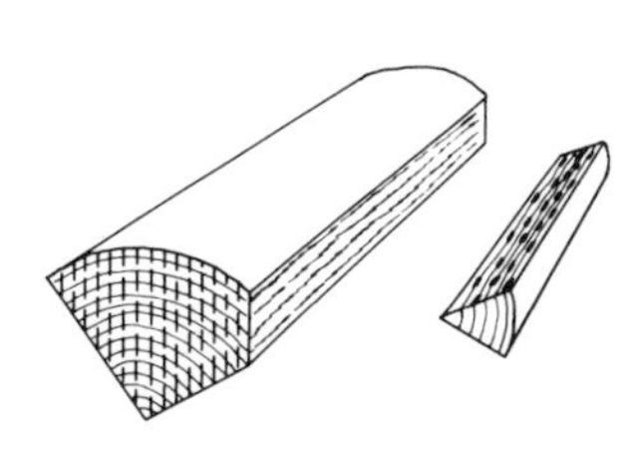

Quarter sawed (showing figure)

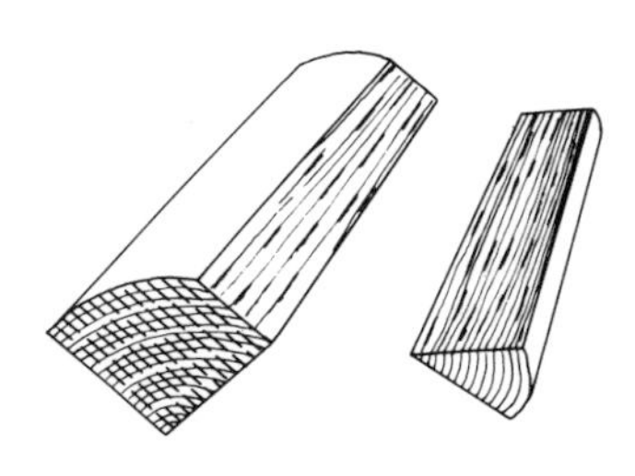

Rift sawed (showing a pencil line grain)

may be etched to emphasize the grain; it may be striated to create parallel ridges of different widths. When wood is cut at right angles to the axis of the trunk, the lumber is *straight-grained.* If, however, the fibers twist around the trunk, or if the wood is cut at an angle other than a right angle, the resulting lumber is *cross-grained.*

Wood is classified as either soft or hard depending on the type of tree it comes from. Wood from broad-leaved deciduous trees is called hardwood, that from coniferous trees is known as softwood. These terms refer to the cellular structure rather than to the actual hardness of the wood. Hardwood contains long ducts called wood fibers that extend vertically through the trunk and serve as a mechanical support only, while softwood is composed mostly of *tracheids,* which are primitive conducting cells.

Chestnut, rosewood, satinwood, tulip, amaranth, lemon, birch, holly, harewood—what a treasure of characteristics the names imply! Rich colors, intriguing grains,

above: 176. Raoul Hague. *Old King's Road Kyserike.* 1966. Walnut, 4′2″ × 4′10″ × 2′10″. Collection the artist.

left: 177. Furniture made of teak has great durability and takes a soft, lustrous finish. This chair was designed by France and Son for John Stuart Inc.

texture, consistency, and durability are all traits that vary with the individual woods and offer a vast range of possibilities for the craftsman-designer. A little stain and several coats of wax can reveal unsuspected beauty in almost any piece of wood. Many times the grain suggests a design, as if the form itself had been contained within a block awaiting the artist's chisel to set it free (Fig. 176).

SOME WIDELY USED VARIETIES

Walnut is one of the most serviceable and versatile of woods. An ideal cabinet wood, it is outstanding for its rich color, durability, and beauty. Walnut can be *turned* and made into bowls or other small objects, and it has long been a favorite material for carving. Much of the paneling in medieval cathedrals and castles, for example, was made from walnut.

Mahogany comes in many varieties from the jungles of Central and South America, the West Indies, and Africa. Philippine mahogany is an excellent material for paneling and for hollow-core doors; it is relatively inexpensive, and it has an attractive grain that takes a fine finish. Brazilian mahogany is particularly beautiful when used for decorative pieces in which the grain can be exploited and a high polish applied.

Oak has traditionally been a favorite wood for floors and furniture. Its resistance to wear made it popular for school and office furniture early in this century when white oak with the "golden oak" finish was in great demand. Although teak has replaced white oak for this purpose today, "limed oak" and "bleached oak," with their light finishes, are adaptable to contemporary surroundings.

While not suitable for carving, *maple* has a toughness and a warmth of color that make it a fine material for a good many other purposes. It is one of the two woods most frequently employed in Early American interiors. "Bird's eye maple," popular in the 1920s, is achieved by cutting across the grain to reveal a unique circular pattern in the wood. It is no longer in favor today because of the waste involved in its manufacture. Maple still appeals, however, to many people who prefer informal and hospitable room interiors with a traditional character.

Pine was used extensively during the Colonial period and is in demand today for paneling, for furniture, and for reproductions of Early American artifacts, such as spoon racks, spice cabinets, and canister sets. It is a wood that attains a soft *patina* when stained and waxed. Because of its low cost and light weight, and because it warps and shrinks little, lumber from both white and yellow pine is important in building construction. Furthermore, white pine is easily worked and is one of the woods employed by graphic artists for making woodcuts.

Teak, a tropical wood of marked strength and durability, has become one of the most desirable materials for contemporary artifacts and furniture. Teak is grown primarily in India, Thailand, and Burma, where for centuries it has provided substance for the construction of ships and temples. The wood has a somewhat lighter color than walnut and responds beautifully to oils, which bring out the grain and give a soft luster to the surface. Teak furniture needs little care and is extremely durable. Well-designed desks, tables, buffets, and chairs (Fig. 177) acquire further elegance and strength when made of this wood.

Fruitwood, including cherry, apple, pear, as well as certain rare varieties, takes a sumptuous finish and possesses a wide range of warm tones. Frequently employed in combination with leather and brass, it contributes opulence and richness to interiors of traditional design.

left: 178. *Thunderbird,* totem image in Stanley Park, Vancouver, B.C.

below left: 179. *Presentation of Christ in the Temple.* Franco-Flemish. Early 16th century. Oak panel, c. $35\frac{1}{2} \times 10\frac{1}{2}''$. Metropolitan Museum of Art, New York (Cloisters Collection, Purchase, 1950).

HISTORIC DESIGN IN WOOD

The imaginative treatment of wood is a characteristic of primitive cultures. Masks, totems (Fig. 178), and everyday utensils are often carved and painted with great simplicity and expressiveness, in forms that are both beautiful and grotesque.

The ancient Egyptians furnished the tombs of their dead with numerous wooden carvings whose lines and forms are remarkably clean and simple. The superb inlaid designs and gold embellishments of these pieces give them a place of distinction among the finest historical styles.

During the Gothic period, the cathedrals became veritable treasure houses of wood carving. An excellent example of medieval carving is the Franco-Flemish panel of the *Presentation in the Temple* (Fig. 179). In the castles as well, wood carving had an important decorative function. Elaborately carved panels graced walls, chests, coffers, and cupboards. Wood was so profusely decorated by the time of Louis XIII that in France the structure of the furniture was fairly smothered in ornamental shells, swags, flowers, fruits, and cupids.

The eighteenth century was the period of the great English cabinetmakers. Furniture by Sheraton, Hepplewhite, and Chippendale was generally restrained in its carving. It also revealed a genuine respect for the beauty of the wood. In much of this furniture contrasting grains and finishes were played against one another to form designs of light and dark and to establish plain and patterned areas. Thomas Sheraton achieved recognition for his satiny inlay and for the subtlety of his carving, a refinement of craftsmanship that can be seen in the delicate reeding of his chair legs (Fig. 180).

Inlay in furniture is an ancient art. Fifteenth-century Italian examples of inlay are extremely intricate (Fig. 181). Tiny pieces of wood were set to form arabesques, fruit, flowers, architectural scenes, and human figures. This kind of inlay is called *intarsia.* Another type is *marquetry,* which consists of veneers inlaid with wood or other materials, such as ivory and marble, and which possesses a flat surface suitable for floors and table tops. *Parquet* is the term used to characterize inlay that has predominately geometric patterns, such as herringbone or basketweave (Fig. 182).

above: 180. Sheraton-style armchair, from New York. 1790–1800. Mahogany. Museum of Fine Arts, Boston (M. and M. Karolik Collection).

above right: 181. Francesco di Giorgio and Baccio Pontelli (?). Room from the Ducal Palace at Gubbio, Italy. 15th century. Walnut, oak, beech, rosewood, and fruitwoods. Metropolitan Museum of Art, New York (Rogers Fund, 1939).

right: 182. The natural grain and texture of parquet flooring seems particularly appropriate to modern interiors.

above: 183. Charles Eames' plywood chair (1946) uses interesting grain as its only decorative element.

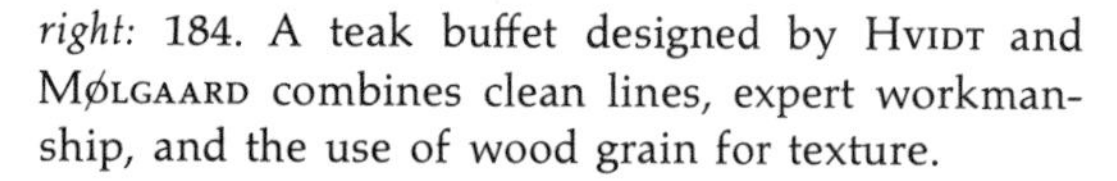

right: 184. A teak buffet designed by Hvidt and Mølgaard combines clean lines, expert workmanship, and the use of wood grain for texture.

The castles and churches of Spain reflect the Moorish presence in Iberia, and their heavy paneling and exotic forms are wonderfully enhanced by the beauty of wood and polychromed tiles. The study of historical furniture not only provides ideas for modern design but gives evidence of man's long appreciation of wood.

CONTEMPORARY DESIGN IN WOOD

Designers today employ techniques that effectively extend the possibilities of wood as a creative medium. *Plywood* is invaluable where lightness and strength are needed. It is made of thin layers of wood, usually three or five in number, which are glued together, with the grain of each layer at a right angle to the grain of the layer above it. Sometimes a layer of fine wood is glued to layers of cheaper wood, making the plywood a base for a decorative *veneer.* Charles Eames' chair (Fig. 183) demonstrates one way that walnut-veneered plywood can be molded to fit the human body.

Interesting forms can also be achieved with *laminated* wood, which, like plywood, consists of layers of wood glued together, but which differs from plywood in that the grain of each layer is parallel. The parallel structure makes it possible to bend and shape laminated wood in new and remarkably plastic ways. *Bentwood,* too, is very flexible. The craftsman makes it by first cutting pieces of wood to the desired size, then by employing steam to soften these pieces and machines to fashion them into shapes demanded by imaginative design. Almost unlimited uses can be found for *flexwood,* which is composed of paper-thin sheets glued to a flexible backing. It can be applied to objects in much the same fashion that wallpaper is.

Although the machine has taken over many of the craftsman's tasks in the making of furniture, it is human hands that must still glue and join the cut pieces together. The craftsman, therefore, maintains many of the same standards and demonstrates many of the same skills that he did in the past. The buffet illustrated in Figure 184 reveals no intricate carving or turning, yet it derives from careful workmanship. The *below:* 185. The grain of teak, oiled and rubbed, gives a design quality to this end table.

right: 186. The warmth of wood paneling is combined with other natural textures to provide a comfortable, secure environment. JOHN YEON, architect.

drawers are beautifully proportioned, and in their variety no two are exactly the same size. Furthermore, the skillful handling of the grain has become an important element of the design.

The beauty of the grain is also a factor in the design of the teak wedge table represented in Figure 185. With its slightly bowed and subtly tapered rectangular shape, the table is even simpler in its form than the buffet. There is no ornamentation of any kind, although the cane of the shelf possesses a texture that complements the grain pattern of the table top.

A velvety finish is one of the distinguishing characteristics of most contemporary furniture. Lacquer and varnish have been replaced by oil and wax. Even when certain woods require protective coatings, several thin applications of wax are preferred to heavy layers of varnish. To avoid a high gloss, the craftsman sands and rubs the wax with pumice after each application.

Wood paneling is manufactured in a variety of woods and finishes. Some paneling is finished by hand to produce a soft patina (Fig. 186). A driftwood effect may be created by the application of diluted white paint that, when rubbed, accentuates the grain. From dignified oak wainscoting to the rustic knotty pine of American recreation rooms, wood paneling has known a popularity that stems not only from its richness and warmth, but also from its ease of maintenance.

Wood is employed for purposes other than the paneling of walls or the making of furniture. Small artifacts such as bowls and trays, as well as works of sculpture, provide further challenges to woodworkers and to artists. The craftsman who made

far left: 187. These free-form bowls designed by ARPEA (1967) consist of contrasting bands of wood grain.

left: 188. LEO AMINO. *Jungle.* 1950. Mahogany, height 4′8″. Whitney Museum of American Art, New York.

below left: 189. EDVARD MUNCH. *The Kiss.* 1902. Woodcut, $18\frac{3}{8} \times 18\frac{5}{16}$″. Museum of Modern Art, New York (gift of Abby Aldrich Rockefeller).

the bowls illustrated in Figure 187 has stressed the natural beauty of the wood and has related the different grains to one another so as to create a textural harmony. Only in wood could such a design be realized.

The sculpture by Leo Amino reproduced in Figure 188 reveals a subtle handling that recalls the table in Figure 185. There is the same gentle tapering and the same refining of form. There is also a sensitive arrangement of negative and positive spaces that, when viewed from various angles, makes the work seem alive, as if it were growing and mutating.

Wood has played an important part in the communication of ideas through the written word. The medieval "block books" were printed from letters raised on a block of wood, from which the background has been cut away. First used in Europe during the thirteenth century, this method of printing with wooden blocks had been developed by the Chinese many centuries earlier. With the innovation of movable type cast in metal in the fifteenth century, wood lost its preeminence in the field of verbal communication. It retained, however, its importance in the realm of pictorial communication, for some of the most magnificent woodblock illustrations ever created were produced by Martin Schongauer and Albrecht Dürer in the late fifteenth and early sixteenth centuries. The pictorial images that originate in blocks of wood

190. Stanley Kaplan. *Sailboats and Fish.* 1966. Philippine mahogany, length 5′. Collection Mr. and Mrs. William Finkle, Wantagh, N.Y.

have a texture and a character that cannot be approximated in any other medium, for the grain makes the wood as much a part of the expression as the artist's own design (Fig. 189).

Stanley Kaplan is among the most imaginative of the contemporary artists working in wood. He writes: "Wood is an extremely flexible medium for artistic expression, and, in its plank form, the sculptural and painting possibilities are challenging for inventive spatial creations."[1] Kaplan started working with wood when printmaking was his medium of expression. He observed his wood blocks, both stained with ink and cleaned with turpentine, and admired them as forms in themselves. Soon he began to carve and stain planks of wood, and to create from them wooden murals. In the example illustrated in Figure 190, the texture of the wood establishes the background pattern. This pattern is amplified and complemented by the carving of the sections that make up the design. Staining is augmented by touches of paint, which give both light and dark accents.

What the artist achieves with wood depends upon his understanding of the individual pieces he works with and upon the imagination with which he releases their hidden beauty. He must adapt his methods to the material, rather than force the material to succumb to his methods. With the proper approach, wood yields effects that are both exciting and surprising, effects that indeed reward the artist with a beauty of tone and of texture that cannot be achieved in any other material.

SUMMARY

The uses of wood reach into every area of human existence, providing for man's needs in many ways. Some of the most popular varieties of wood are walnut, mahogany, oak, maple, pine, teak, and fruitwoods. Historically, wood has been an essential material for building construction and for furniture. Many kinds of wood inlay have been developed by furniture makers of the past. Intarsia, for example, is the creation of intricate designs with contrasting colors and grains of wood. Marquetry is formed by inlaying pieces of wood, ivory, or marble to achieve a flat surface. The design of parquet is geometric in appearance. Wood paneling lends both warmth and practicality to interiors.

Plywood, laminated wood, bentwood, and flexwood are all types of wood that are easily adapted to contemporary designs. Wood may be turned and carved to create bowls and accessories; it may be fashioned into woodcuts, into works of sculpture, and into murals.

Design in Metal

chapter 12

Wood makes a warm and attractive background for human activities, but metal sounds forth its uses to the world. Great bronze bells peal and toll the hours and crises in men's everyday lives. Metal dominates the highways in the ever-changing designs of automobiles. It rides the rails in trains, crosses the seas in ships, and explores outer space in rockets. Metal graces banquet tables the world over with elegant flatware and goblets, and it complements and adorns man himself with ornaments of silver and gold and with settings for jewels.

We often think of metal as being hard, cold, impersonal, and unyielding. These characteristics are not typical of all metals, however. Gold, silver, and tin are so soft they must be fortified with other metals before they can be used effectively. Silver and copper are excellent conductors and warm quickly to the touch. Far from being impersonal, metal has lured more men to their deaths than any other substance. It has called them into the dark recesses of the earth's surface to discover and extract ore for its intrinsic and commercial value. Although it may be rigid when it furnishes support for skyscrapers, metal yields willingly to the sensitive hands of the artist. Its expressive possibilities are particularly apparent in *Zig II* (Pl. 19, opposite), a painted steel sculpture by David Smith. Smith himself best explained his affinity for this metal when he wrote: "I work in most media, but my especial material is steel, that which has been longest in my experience, and which seems to me unique in sculptural media. . . . It is structure, movement, progress, suspension, cantilever and at times destruction and brutality. Its method of unity need not be evident. Yet its forms of geometry, planes, hard lines are all constant with the that of my time."[1]

An important difference between wood and metal is the sharp diversity in the methods of their handling. Wood is worked primarily by the *subtractive* process. The craftsman begins with a large piece of material, and then he cuts, chips, and chisels it until he attains the desired result. Metal, on the other hand, is treated by the *additive* method. The metalworker welds, rivets, and pours his material while it is in a molten state. Once it has cooled and set, he can change the form of his work by chipping, pounding, or forging, but he employs these steps only for the refinement of the shape rather than for its actual creation. A bowl of wood is carved from a

opposite: Plate 19. David Smith. *Zig II.* 1961. Painted steel, 8′4½″ × 4′5¼″ × 2′6″. Norton Simon, Inc., Museum of Art, Fullerton, Calif.

solid block with considerable material cut away; a metal bowl is formed from a flat sheet, and very little metal is discarded. Metal sculpture, too, is built up or cast rather than cut from a block (Fig. 191).

CHARACTERISTICS OF METAL

Metal possesses three important and unique characteristics: *tensile strength, malleability,* and *ductility.* The tensile strength of metal lies in its resistance to breakage or rupture by stress placed upon it. This quality of steel made possible the building of the Golden Gate Bridge (Fig. 192). Steel cables support the entire weight of the concrete roadbed and the traffic upon it, yet the cables are so small in diameter that from a distance they actually resemble fine spun wires.

The second characteristic, malleability, refers to the capacity of metal for being shaped or extended under great pressure. The term itself comes from the Latin word for mallet. No other material can be so thoroughly hammered and raised without cracking and breaking. The characteristic malleability of gold, for example, makes possible the creation of gold leaf and of such works as the German chalice represented in Plate 20 (opposite).

Ductility is the quality in metal that permits it to be drawn out into fine wires. Platinum has been reduced to wire that is 1/20,000 of a millimeter in thickness.

opposite: Plate 20. Chalice, from Germany. Early 17th century. Gold, enamel, and jewels; height 9″. Metropolitan Museum of Art, New York (gift of J. Pierpont Morgan, 1917).

left: 191. Seymour Lipton. *The Loom.* 1965. Nickel silver on monel metal, 5′10″ × 3′11″. Courtesy Marlborough-Gerson Gallery, New York.

below: 192. Joseph B. Strauss. Golden Gate Bridge, San Francisco. 1933–37.

far left: 193. HENNING KOPPEL's graceful sterling silver pitcher (1952) was raised from a single sheet of metal, with the handle added later.

left: 194. PHILIP NEGROLI. Parade helmet. Italian. 1543. Embossed and chiseled steel, width 13¾″. Metropolitan Museum of Art, New York (gift of J. Pierpont Morgan, 1917).

METHODS OF WORKING METAL

Raising is the most usual method of creating objects from a sheet of metal. The craftsman raises metal by hammering out the form in relief. The pitcher illustrated in Figure 193 was raised from a single sheet of silver. *Beating down* is the reverse of raising, for in this process the craftsman places the sheet of metal over a recessed area that is about as wide and as deep as the desired object, and he then hammers the metal into the recess with a mallet. *Spinning* is executed with machines. Pitchers, goblets, vases, and tumblers can be formed on a lathe from flat sheets of metal. *Casting* is the melting and reforming of metal into specific shapes. Molten metal is poured into molds to form either solid or hollow pieces. There are several methods for casting bronze artifacts (see Chap. 17).

DESIGN IN METAL

The individual characteristics of metals determine the purposes for which they will be used. Silver and copper are particularly beautiful and are easily worked. Both lend themselves to *chasing* and *repoussé,* as well as to various other techniques. Chasing is accomplished with tools of hardened steel that have smooth and somewhat rounded tips. Their function is to incise the metal to form a two-dimensional design. Repoussé, or embossing, is created by outlining the design with a tracing tool, and then by raising the surface of the metal from the reverse side to form the relief, as in the German helmet represented in Figure 194. A contemporary adaptation of repoussé is seen in Lynn Wolfe's copper doors for the Danforth Chapel (Fig. 195). By employing heat and certain chemicals and by the use of a variety of tools, the craftsman can add texture and design to the surface of metal and thereby arrive at an infinity of interesting effects.

The most highly prized metals are silver and gold. Since man's prehistory these prestigious metals have been basic materials in ceremonial objects and in human adornment. They have great beauty, weight, and solidity; furthermore, they are almost indestructible. They were the only metals considered precious until platinum was discovered in the sixteenth century.

Silver, although precious, is a relatively accessible material. The annual world production of silver is ten times that of gold. The United States and Mexico produce 80 percent of the world's supply of silver. Both silver and gold must be alloyed with copper to make them hard enough for use in plate or in coinage. Sterling silver, for example, is actually 92.5 percent silver and 7.5 percent copper.

Silver possesses four qualities that make it both desirable and costly: luster, permanence, scarcity, and pliability. Its one great disadvantage is a tendency to stain.

British plate is one of the most familiar uses of silver. (The name is taken from the Spanish *plata,* meaning silver.) Plate is usually solid silver that has been shaped into various articles and decorated with chasing. Sheffield plate, however, is composed of sheets of copper sandwiched between layers of silver. The term silver plating designates the practice of applying silver to a copper base.

Hallmarks were first employed by silversmiths in London and later in Colonial America to ensure a standard of purity and to prevent fraud. They are small impressions that are usually placed on the bottom of the silver articles to identify the date and place of its fabrication. The leopard's head, originally known as the king's mark, indicated that a silver object contained at least 92.5 percent silver. Later a *lion passant* (walking lion) was introduced as the standard mark, and the leopard's head was retained as the London town mark. Birmingham, on the other hand, used an anchor as its hallmark, while Sheffield utilized a crown and Edinburgh a castle. Some cities used the city arms, as in the case of Chester with three wheat sheaves and a sword. A statute in 1363 introduced the maker's mark, which was often a device such as a fish, key, or fleur-de-lis taken from the sign outside the goldsmith's shop, frequently combined with the initials of the maker. Letters of the alphabet were also incorporated into a marking system to indicate the year of assay. The hallmark is an invaluable guide for collectors of antique silver. Such Early American pieces as the sugar box by John Coney (Fig. 196) and the candlesticks by Edward Winslow (Fig. 197) are readily identified by their silversmiths' marks.

below left: 195. Sculptor LYNN WOLFE puts the finishing touches on the repoussé copper doors (1954) for the chapel at Colorado State University.

below: 196. JOHN CONEY. Sugar box. 1690–1710. Silver, height $4\frac{1}{2}$". Colonial Williamsburg Collection, Williamsburg, Va. The maker's mark "IC" can be seen in block letters on both the exterior of the cover and the interior of the box.

bottom: 197. EDWARD WINSLOW. Candlesticks. 1710–25. Silver, height $7\frac{1}{16}$". Colonial Williamsburg Collection, Williamsburg, Va. The maker's mark "EW" appears in block letters with a fleur-de-lis within a shield on the base of each.

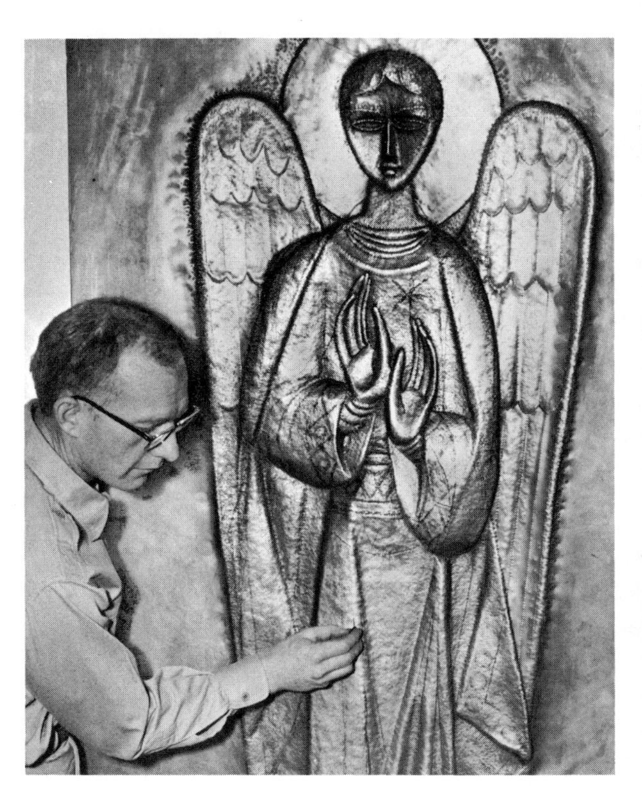

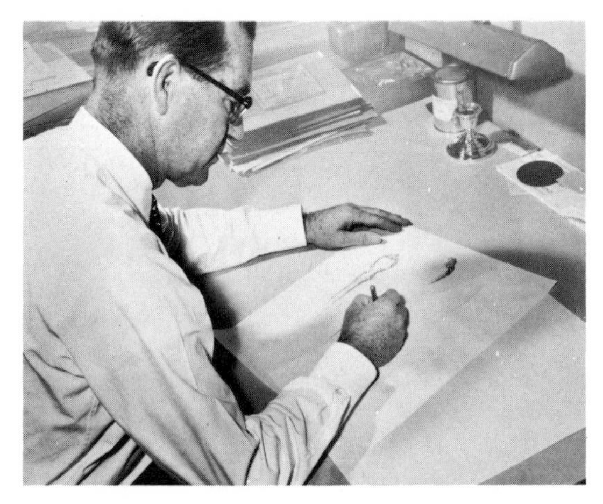

198. The first step in the creation of silver flatware is the design sketch.

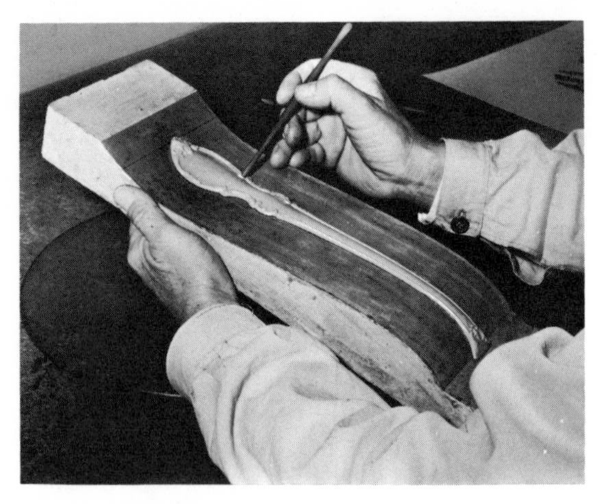

199. A large model is formed in red wax so that every detail can be perfected.

200. A blank is made in the required size and shape.

201. The blank is punched out in its final outline.

202. The blank is passed between heavy rollers to distribute the metal in correct proportions.

203. The bowl is stamped from a contour die.

204. The design is now stamped on the handle.

205. Hand chasing is done by a skilled craftsman.

Each of these marks consists of two block letters above a fleur-de-lis, the latter of which is inscribed within a shield or a heart.

Available in a wide range of designs, silver flatware is a valuable and cherished possession in many homes. The creation of a piece of flatware is a process that involves both artist and machine (Figs. 198–205).

The capacity of silver to be shaped into small decorative pieces has made it a favorite metal for jewelry. The intricate jewelry styles of the past are in striking contrast to the utter simplicity of contemporary jewelry design (Fig. 206).

Pewter originated as a substitute for silver. It is similar in color, and it is suitable for many of the same purposes. In Colonial America few families could afford silver, but most had a supply of pewter, which included such utensils as the tankard reproduced in Figure 207. Before 1700 the best pewter consisted of nine parts tin to one part copper. Cheaper grades contained lead as well. Today, antimony and bismuth have replaced copper, and lead is no longer used. Pewter is short-lived,

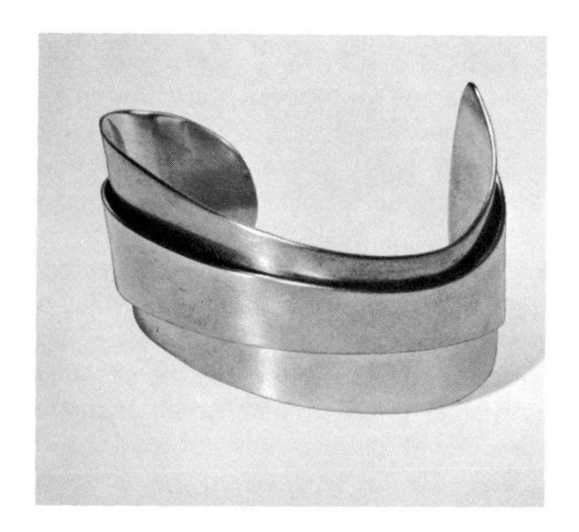

below left: 206. The workability of silver makes possible the creation of an unlimited range of forms, from delicate filigree to this contemporary bracelet by HELEN SCHEIER ADELMAN.

below: 207. JOHN WILL, SR. Tankard. 1752–66. Pewter, height $7\frac{1}{8}''$. Colonial Williamsburg Collection, Williamsburg, Va.

208. IRV BURKEE designed these sliding doors, in which large copper panels with reversible designs are recessed in heavy wooden frames.

but it can be recast. The metalworker melts down the worn pieces and pours the molten metal into molds. Many people collect old pewter for its attractive satiny appearance and for its sentimental value. Indeed, some people even prefer it to silver. Craftsmen in Holland have created remarkable pewter pitchers, teapots, and other pieces that are characterized by smoothly flowing lines. American craftsmen tend to be more conservative, however, and they continue to make copies of original Colonial pieces.

Copper was known to prehistoric man and was probably the first metal he learned to work with. It is an excellent conductor of heat, and it is highly resistant to corrosion, qualities that place it in great demand for electrical and plumbing equipment. The rich, reddish color of copper offers many possibilities to the designer. The sliding doors by Irv Burkee (Fig. 208) reveal an effective combination of copper and wood. In this work the craftsman has perforated the metal and accented it with heavy beaten wire that is riveted to the panels. He has emphasized the details of the designs by allowing the metal around the designs to become discolored by oxidation, and he has given a satiny glow to the background by rubbing it with pumice. Craftsmen in many countries today produce distinctive and beautiful copper pitchers and tea kettles. Innovations and developments in the past have often retained their importance to the present day. The French introduced copper bottoms for cooking pots perhaps as early as the seventeenth century. This is a technique that makes possible the rapid and even spread of heat over the cooking surface. Chinese and Egyptian craftsmen applied a wash of pewter over the surface of copper to achieve a combination of silvery and reddish tones. Such a technique is used to finish bowls, vases, plates, and pitchers.

Brass is about 60 percent copper and 40 percent zinc. It has many practical uses because it does not rust. When the metal worker desires greater hardness he adds tin. The resulting metal is then employed in mechanical parts that are subjected to concentrated wear. The use of brass in sculpture, vases, bowls, and similar objects has been an important industry in China and Persia for centuries, with the brass often inlaid or engraved with elaborate designs. Brass has a yellower cast than copper, and it takes a high polish. It is widely used for musical instruments, and it is a favorite material for decorative hardware, such as hinges, doorknobs, and locks.

Bronze is an alloy of copper, tin, and various other metals. It is darker, harder, and longer lasting than brass. Its rich, brownish-red color is found in desk accessories and medals, and bronze is the principal material from which bells are made, giving them fine tone as well as durability. Bronze is also one of the most important materials for sculpture that is cast from molten metal. The monumental doors and decorative panels cast in relief for important buildings, both religious and secular, are examples of an art form with a noble tradition.

Aluminum, one of the lightest and most plentiful of metals, can be treated in a variety of ways—chasing, etching, and hammering—to produce practical, inexpensive, and very attractive trays, bowls, and kitchen utensils. Aluminum may also be employed in such purely decorative works as the screen reproduced in Figure 53.

Tin is, surprisingly enough, one of the most expensive of all metals, and it has many applications in addition to that in the so-called tin can (which actually contains more zinc than tin). Mexican craftsmen have imaginatively adapted tin to such items as lighting fixtures, trays, and wastebaskets. Sometimes tin is supported with wood to give it solidity. In addition, Mexican craftsmen have given tin a whole gamut of fanciful forms, from whimsical roosters to ornamental frames (Fig. 209).

209. Mexican tinsmiths are skilled in adapting the metal to gay and whimsical designs, as seen in this contemporary mirror and candle holder.

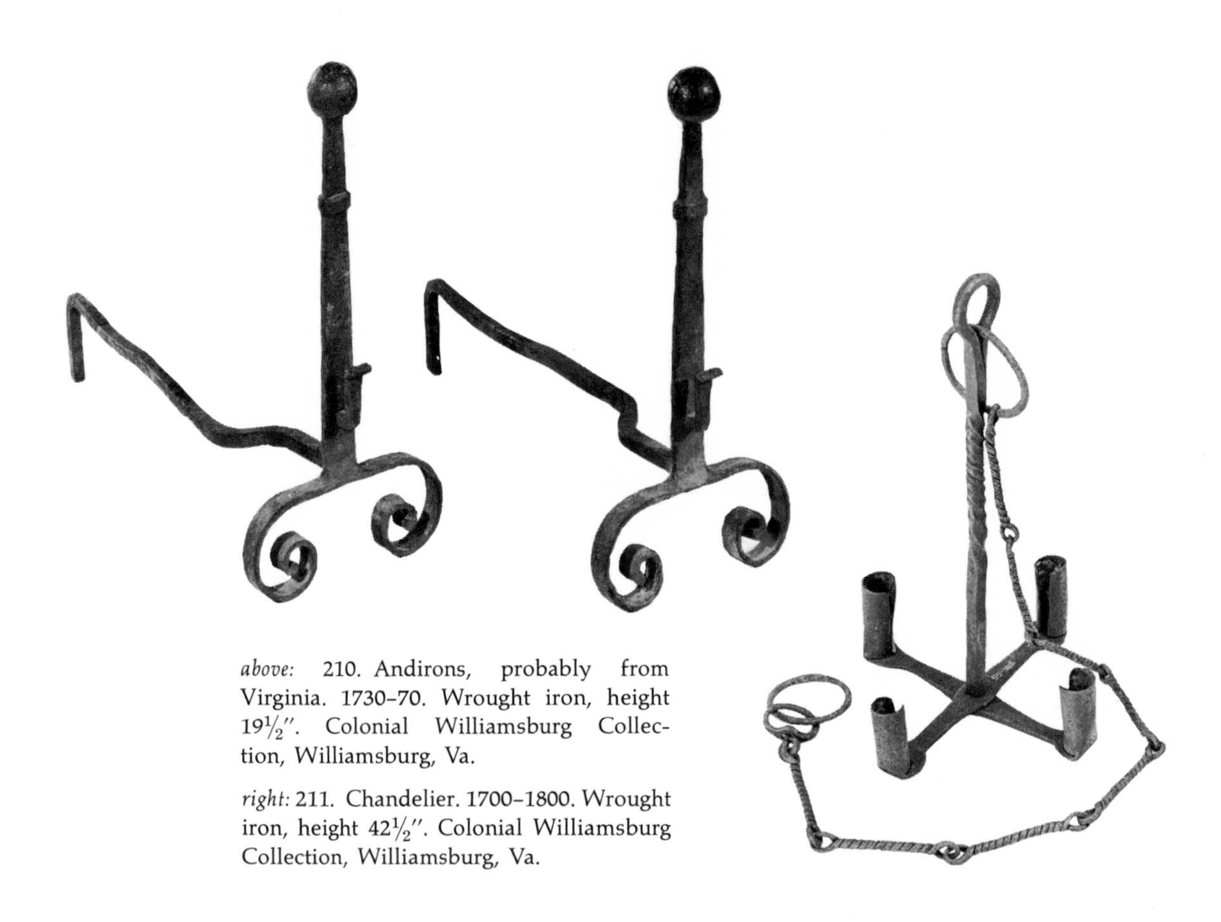

above: 210. Andirons, probably from Virginia. 1730–70. Wrought iron, height 19½″. Colonial Williamsburg Collection, Williamsburg, Va.

right: 211. Chandelier. 1700–1800. Wrought iron, height 42½″. Colonial Williamsburg Collection, Williamsburg, Va.

Iron is so successful as a structural material that we sometimes lose sight of its potential for decorative design. Wrought iron is quite popular in architectural embellishments and in fireplace implements, weathervanes, and modern candelabra. Elaborately designed wrought-iron gates, railings and grilles are especially characteristic of domestic architecture in the South and Southwest United States and in those regions of the world influenced by Spanish and Moorish styles. In Byzantine churches large-scale wrought-iron lighting fixtures were frequently dominant features. In Colonial America wrought iron had many practical and decorative uses (Figs. 210–211).

Steel is basically an alloy of iron and carbon with an admixture of other elements, but steel is manufactured in thousands of types from different compositions designed to serve specific purposes. Essential to an almost limitless range of products, from structural girders to carpet tacks and tools, steel is also a superb medium for the contemporary artist. The alloy for stainless steel contains about 12 percent chromium, and often a small percentage of nickel, to prevent corrosion. It makes an excellent and inexpensive tarnish-free tableware (Fig. 212) that is often similar in design to silver flatware. Some contemporary stainless steel pieces have lustrous finishes like that of old pewter. Indeed, stainless steel is a most satisfactory replacement for both pewter and silver in the manufacture of hollow ware objects, such as sugar bowls, pitchers, and decorative containers. It is also fashioned into attractive and highly serviceable oven-proof serving dishes. Its impermeability to stains and its hardness of surface give stainless steel a practical advantage over other metals.

CONTEMPORARY USES OF METAL

Our exploration of metal as a medium for design would be incomplete if it failed to include some of the more dramatic and less typical innovations of contemporary craftsmen.

The ductility of metal is the determining factor in the creation of the cross reproduced in Figure 213. Ruth Asawa has taken extremely fine galvanized wire and tied it into a form that is an intriguing combination of symbolic and natural imagery. It is both a cross and a suggestion of an organic growth, with a clear relationship to twigs, grass, and dried weeds. This visual simile generates certain philosophical speculations that emerge from the fact that the cross of the Crucifixion was cut from a tree. It connotes man's misapplication of nature to destructive purposes, but this is only one of many interpretations made possible by the originality of the design.

above: 212. Jette steel flatware was designed by JENS QUISTGAARD for Dansk Designs Ltd.

left: 213. RUTH ASAWA. *Cross.* 1968. Tied galvanized wire, diameter 4'6". Collection the artist.

214. JOHANNES PETER HÖLZINGER. Restaurant, castle gardens, Karlsruhe. 1967.

An entirely different use of metal is seen in the restaurant illustrated in Figure 214. This strikingly contemporary building is all the more unusual in contrast to its setting, for it is located in the ancient park of Karlsruhe Castle in Württemberg. The park itself has been redesigned and fitted for public use by the architect Johannes Peter Hölzinger in collaboration with the sculptor Hermann Goepfert. This restaurant is one of many architectural "islands" set in the wide green expanses of the park. It consists of a space roofed by a hanging "horizontal sculpture," whose configuration is reflected in the pool before it. Although the walls of the restaurant are formed of plastic, the roof is constructed of modular steel, whose strength and rigidity make possible the effect of suspension that gives the structure its distinction. Square "eternit" tubes bring graduated light inside by day and become reflectors of the sky at night.

ENAMELING ON METAL

One of the most fascinating applications of metal is as a base for enameling. Such metals as copper, steel, cast iron, silver, and aluminum can be employed for this purpose. The enamel, called vitreous, is a low-firing glass manufactured in a powdered state. Vitreous enamel is produced in transparent, opaque, and semiopaque forms. In the finished work the supporting metal either shows through or is concealed altogether, according to the degree of opacity in the enamel. Transparent enamels take on a luminous quality from the light that is reflected by the metal underneath.

above: 215. H. B. HELWIG. *Two Couples.* 1968. Grisaille mat enamel, diameter 11¼″. Courtesy Lee Nordness Galleries, New York.

right: 216. PAUL HULTBERG. *Luke Hot.* c. 1968. Enamel, 18″ square. Courtesy Lee Nordness Galleries, New York.

To form colors, metallic oxides are melted with the glass enamels. Colors can also be created by adding fine clay and chemical salts in prescribed proportions to the clear enamel *frit* or powder.

Each metal has its own special type of enamel with which it will fuse most successfully. Copper is probably the metal most frequently employed. Steel also serves as a base for enamel and is used in bowls, trays, panels, and murals by the skilled enamelist (Figs. 215–216). There are various methods of applying enamel, but the most satisfactory process is to coat the metal with a solution of gum tragacanth and then to shake the fine enamel powder onto the coated surface. The piece is then fired in a special kiln or—if the pieces are small—with a torch. The heat causes the enamel and the metal surface to fuse.

Many decorative techniques are possible with enamel. Silk screen and stenciling are graphic processes that may be used. Also suitable is *sgraffito,* in which a design is scratched through the enamel surface to reveal some of the metal underneath. Working with a small brush, the enamelist can use a painter's technique for creating effective designs. A ruling pen or compass will produce even lines and circles in enamel, just as they will on paper. Liquid gold, silver, platinum, and lusters can be added for rich and decorative surfaces. Craftsmen employ copper enameling to produce colorful and effective modern jewelry.

Enameling is a unique art that combines the characteristics of pottery glazes with the lustrous quality of metal, and it complements the best qualities of metal with imaginative color designs.

SUMMARY

Metal plays a varied role in man's life, offering many possibilities for the fulfillment of his needs. The artisan shapes metal into objects by means of the additive process; that is, he builds forms out of sheets and strips of metal.

Metal has three distinctive characteristics: tensile strength, malleability, and ductility. It can be worked by raising, by beating down, by spinning, and by casting. Designs in metal are created by chasing and by repoussé or embossing.

The applications of metal are varied according to the properties of the individual metal. Silver and pewter are often put to the same purposes, although silver is considerably more durable. Copper and brass are both used to achieve fine and distinctive works of art. They are also quite practical because of their durability. Bronze provides material for bells and medals, as well as for statues and decorative objects. Aluminum and tin are both practical and ornamental. Iron and steel are essential in building construction, and stainless steel is a popular substitute for silver and pewter in the manufacture of flatware, bowls, and other household utensils.

Enameling on metal is a decorative art that combines a glassy luster with the qualities of metal to achieve unique results.

Design in Apparel

chapter 13

Man's own adornment is one of the most capricious and imaginative fields open to the designer. Because most people utilize their apparel as a means of expressing or improving their status in society, clothing design is both challenging and creative.

We often assume that the first body coverings were worn for protection from the elements, but anthropologists assure us that this is not the case. Even man's earliest wardrobe of skins, headdresses, and jewelry was selected and worn primarily to enhance his appearance. When we realize that Greek athletes, whose bodies were the glory of Athens and Sparta, took part in competitive sports without clothing, we may suspect that adornment even in ancient times was perhaps promoted by individuals of less than heroic proportions in an effort to counteract the inequities of nature's endowments. Certainly the traditional function of clothing has been to identify and reinforce the status of the individual.

Judges, professors, and clergymen are associated with special garb that brings to them all the dignity and prestige of emblematic tradition. Academic attire dates back to the twelfth century and has been modified only superficially to distinguish different degrees and colleges. Ecclesiastical vestments have an even longer history. Both of these distinctive forms of apparel provide effective means of preserving the continuity and historicity that give man a sense of his own place in time.

Because the purpose of attire has been essentially social in nature, design has been subject to as many changes as society itself. Fashion moves in cycles and frequently swings from one extreme to another. In an effort to keep abreast of these changes, the fashion business has burgeoned into a $4 billion industry employing over a million people. The designer is at the very heart of this activity.

Psychologists tell us that clothing has a deep-seated effect on individual behavior. It affects one's carriage, emotions, and total personality to such an extent that dramatic character changes often result from different modes of dress. Variations in dress and in appearance frequently are striking evidence of the generation gap today. An entire generation has, for example, adopted the long hair and sideburns characteristic of a simpler era. Grooming, whatever its style, nevertheless carries

217. John J. Audubon. *Hooded Merganser.* 1827–38. Watercolor. New York Historical Society, New York.

over into other activities, and the social advantages of attractive and appropriate dress are far-reaching.

In the early twentieth century the fashion industry catered primarily to women, but, in the full context of history, the emphasis on female dress has been a relatively recent development. Nature has always been more lavish in her adornment of the male, and, traditionally, it has been the male who sought by his appearance and behavior to attract attention. This is apparent in the plumage of birds, as illustrated in Figure 217. The gay feathers of the male are fundamental to the ritual of mating, while the neutral coloring of the female is essential to the protective function she performs for her brood. Until the nineteenth century the human male took his cue from nature. The Georgian man spent at least five times more on clothing than he allowed his wife, and it is said that his predecessors spent far more on personal adornment than they did on their mistresses.[1] Fine laces, furs, brocades, satins, velvets, and ribbons were all part of masculine embellishment from the time of the sixteenth century. This elaborate style reached the pinnacle of elegance during the reign of Louis XIV in France. In the nineteenth and early twentieth century, however, society women concentrated much more on lavish dress than did men, who gained a reputation for conservatism in attire. Only recently have men reaffirmed their traditional interest in adornment. Within the past ten years they have begun to show interest in brilliant colors, in variety of styling, and in such materials as furs and decorative fabrics.

BASIC PRINCIPLES OF FASHION DESIGN

A good fashion design naturally consists of the same elements and principles as any other good design. Nevertheless, a basic consideration is that the design must meet the needs of the human body. It is necessary to define these needs according to the personality of the wearer. It is equally important to consider conditions in which a garment will be worn. A woman who stands in a receiving line, for instance, does not require the freedom of movement needed for dancing or walking. The hoop and panniers of the past lent themselves magnificently to court life, but they can be tolerated only for brief periods of time by active women today. From the medieval coat of arms to the space suit with its built-in air conditioner, clothing has had to fulfill the needs of the wearer.

The same honesty that permeates the designer's work in architecture and in the crafts has at last found its way into the design of contemporary clothing. The overemphasis on tiny waistlines and on little feet in past styles has given way to a desire for comfort. On the whole, contemporary clothing displays rather than conceals the human form. It expresses the natural grace of the body, and it is hygienically sound.

In clothing, as in music, *rhythm* is an important principle. The adaptation of a garment to the lines of the body results in a rhythmic interaction of line and form that changes with every movement. A successful garment must be attractive when the wearer stands, walks, and sits. Folds and gathers that fall from strategic structural points contribute to the flow of rhythm, while *repetition* of accents and trimming provides a rhythmic beat. The *emphasis* of the design is usually on the wearer's face, toward which all adornment directs attention. Even though the designer may be tempted by beautiful materials and colorful designs, he should remember that the purpose of clothing is to enhance a person, not to dominate him. The costume acts as a subtle conspirator. It emphasizes all that is noteworthy in one's appearance, but it must not supplant the individuality of the person it adorns.

Variety is essential in dress, but its success is dependent upon the effect sought. A striking costume can result from a dress with simple lines and solid color, accented by a vivid scarf or an unusual piece of jewelry. Variety can be carried to greater lengths in formal wear, where contrasting fabrics and materials are frequently woven into a skirt or draped over it in panels or overskirts. A colorful cummerbund and matching tie lend a certain amount of variety to men's informal evening wear.

Balance in fashion design can be either symmetrical or "informal." The human figure is never perfectly symmetrical, and clothing it in styles with symmetrical lines may correct certain inequalities. On the other hand, a dress with an informal balance in its lines may be much more interesting. A band of contrasting material that runs down one side of a garment, a pin on the shoulder or lapel, accenting pleats or stitching—all of these give informal balance when set off by mass or form or by eye-catching detail.

Form is implicit in the well-designed garment not only in the shape it clothes but in the nature of the design itself. A garment that looks nondescript while hanging on a rack may take on considerable distinction when it is filled out by a human form. Like sculpture, an item of apparel must be designed to be seen from all sides. To show its full potential, the dress or suit must be given substance. The pleats and folds of the ensemble, the way the fabric drapes and falls—these elements are effective only when the dress is actually worn. It is then also that the garment brings out the best features of the human form itself.

As in all design, *unity* is a guiding principle in a successful garment. In this sense, unity means the appropriateness of the materials that are used together, as well as the effectiveness of their color harmony and of their linear rhythms. Unity exists when every part is a pleasing and logical development of every other part. Unity determines the relationship of the garment to the wearer and to all accompanying accessories. It can even extend to the environment and background against which the dress or suit is worn.

ELEMENTS OF FASHION DESIGN

Line has already been mentioned in connection with rhythm in dress. The lines of a garment must be considered in relation to the wearer as well. The lines of apparel are determined by two factors: the style of the costume and the proportions of the figure. When a design is created for the ready-made market, each garment is fashioned according to standard measurements for all sizes. Obviously, any given design will look better in some sizes than in others. When a designer is commissioned to *custom design* a garment for an individual, however, he has the advantage of being able to adapt the lines to a specific build and size and to work toward a more carefully refined effect.

The fact that vertical lines are, on the whole, more flattering to the average figure is demonstrated by the exaggerated proportions of the fashion models in drawings that appear in advertisements. Such drawings emphasize a slim and elongated silhouette that has become accepted in the world of fashion as the ultimate in sophistication and elegance (Fig. 218). The fact that relatively few people are able to translate their own appearance into this fashionable vision seems to have little effect upon their aspirations. Most people hope for a miracle of design that will transform their ordinary selves into new and exciting personalities. In their endless search for such magic, they place implicit faith in the designer.

Just as vertical lines contribute height and slimness to the figure, so horizontal lines can shorten a long waist, give fullness to a thin neck, and widen too-narrow shoulders. A full or diamond-shaped female form often must be modified by the designer in an effort to slim the hipline and focus attention on the upper portion of the figure. This is accomplished by establishing diagonal lines in a yoke, by stitching or other detail around the neckline, and by vertical seams or stitching in the skirt. A tall thin figure, on the other hand, can be given greater fullness by the use of numerous devices, including horizontal stripes or gathers and pleats to provide softness of line.

Texture is provided by the fabric or by the trim, which could be tucks, ruffles, stitching, lace, or braid. When the fabric is inherently fascinating, the garment is usually left rather simple. Plain and less interesting materials lend themselves to more elaborate designs. The clean lines of the coat reproduced in Figure 219 complement the boldly patterned wool, which could never have been used effectively in a garment with intricate styling. Furs, silk blouses combined with wool suits, or men's poplin shirts worn with tweed are all basic attempts to create variety in texture.

Color changes with the cycles of fashion, providing one of the most exciting aspects of fashion design. Main Streets everywhere are brightly colored by the imaginative 'brushwork' of creative fashion designers. The effects of color on eyes, hair, skin tone, and figure make it of vital concern to all fashion-minded women, and their wardrobes reflect the increased interest in color characteristic of modern life. Their coats, for example, are no longer conservatively neutral in color, but have vibrant hues that extend to the entire spectrum.

Size is another element that must not be allowed to overwhelm the wearer. In this context we do not mean the actual size of the clothes but the proportions of the design. Bulky collars and sweeping cloaks are usually limited to figures with the height to carry them. Furthermore, the choice of materials must be made on the basis of size. Small people can become lost in heavy woolens, whereas oversized individuals may look ridiculous in flimsy fabrics designed to appear dainty. The

choice of the appropriate material has a great deal to do with the unity and coherence of the final design.

The *shape* of a garment can be surprisingly varied, considering that it is designed to cover a standard human figure. For example, the shape of a man's lounge suit is quite different from that of a business suit or dinner jacket. The difference lies not just in the shoulder width and in the fit at the waist, but in the draping of material from the shoulders, in the hang of the coat, and in the folds of the trousers as well. Variations in women's attire are even more apparent. A dress may hug the body, fall from the shoulder, or billow over layers of petticoats. There are two primary factors that determine the shape of a garment: first, the pattern itself, which establishes the shapes of the various parts and of the whole, and, second, the method of construction, which governs the amount and position of fullness and drape.

above: 218. Fashion drawings emphasize the tall, slim figure which will show garments to best advantage.

right: 219. The simple A silhouette in this Dior coat permits the use of a boldly patterned wool.

In the actual process of designing, the designer reverses the order of these two factors. He drapes a piece of muslin over the figure of a model and rearranges the material until it falls in a way that pleases him. He then cuts, pins, and bastes (a method of holding the pieces together with large stitches), shaping each section until he achieves the effect he has visualized. Only then are the pieces of muslin used as patterns, either for cutting the actual fabric or for preparing paper patterns that are sold to dressmakers.

above: 220. The Chanel jacket has been the basis for hundreds of variations, such as the three illustrated here.

left: 221. PIERRE CARDIN was a pioneer of the new interest in men's fashions. This blazer is a typical example. Drawing by PAUL SCHMITT.

THE EUROPEAN INFLUENCE

Since the seventeenth century, when all of Europe was dazzled by the brilliance of the French court, Paris has been the center of *haute couture,* or high fashion. Many of the world's leading designers have served apprenticeships in the Paris salons, and the semiannual showings of new Parisian designs continue to exert great influence upon the fashion world.

For many years there was a basic difference between the French and American fashion industries, a difference that prevented any real competition between them. Parisian designers considered their creations works of art and insisted that they be constructed with the finest workmanship. They catered to conservative and wealthy women who spent much of their time in the company of men and who made a habit of dressing for men. These women preferred gradual change to startling innovations. There was a tendency on their part to spend a great deal of money on each costume rather than to amass a vast wardrobe of inexpensive clothes. American women, on the other hand, were more easily influenced by the unusual, the novel, and the fad. They attempted to keep abreast of the latest developments and to compete with other women in their dress. Machine-made clothes met their demands with rapidly produced and inexpensive products, and facilitated constant change in their wardrobes.

With the advent of high-speed transportation and the new affluence of the American middle class, the differences between the French and American fashion industries have become less marked. French couturiers, as well as other European designers, cater to wealthy women the world over and have even entered the middle-class market with ready-made garments. American designers, on the other hand, have succeeded in emulating the French and have found a market for their own designs among fashion leaders both in the United States and abroad.

In spite of these changes, however, Paris continues to have an influence upon American taste. Copies of Paris originals are marketed in the United States in a wide range of prices, which brings them within the budget of most American women. The names of French designers are familiar to every fashion-minded American woman, who is generally well aware of what has occurred at the latest Paris showings. Courrèges and Yves St. Laurent have a strong influence on American fashion, and Hubert de Givenchy is known internationally for the elegant simplicity of his designs. Perhaps no one has had more influence both in America and in Europe than Madame Gabrielle "Coco" Chanel, who revolutionized fashion in the 1920s. Half a century of designing has scarcely dimmed her prestige in the world of fashion. She is credited with the adaptation of pants for women. She also originated such classics as skirts worn with sweaters, the collarless jacket, short, pastel gloves, the pillbox hat, and the entire concept of separates (skirts, blouses, pants, sweaters, and jackets) that can be combined into many different costumes. Her experiments with fabrics introduced many hitherto uncommon materials: cotton piqué, jersey, corduroy, lamé, and geometric and abstract prints. Chanel jewelry, Chanel perfume, and Chanel suits have become cornerstones of many fashionable wardrobes. In Figure 220 are reproduced a few of the classic designs based on the chic and simple Chanel neckline and short, straight jacket.

Paris has had an influence upon men's fashions as well. Pierre Cardin made the first real innovation in male attire in years when he introduced tight pants and high narrow shoulders and generally revived interest in colorful and distinctive apparel (Fig. 221).

By the middle of the twentieth century, Paris began to share the fashion limelight with other European centers. Rome and Madrid have both established themselves as forces in the fashion world and have exerted a strong influence on Western dress through the work of Valentino of Rome and the young Spanish designer Mitzou, who has popularized fashions made of leather. English designers of Chelsea and Carnaby Street, notably Mary Quant, flashed into the fashion scene with the "mod" look, which utilized plastic fabrics and interlocking elements, such as long body-covering stockings and short one-piece dresses, that set the swinging pace for youthful fashions the world over. The result is a cosmopolitan flavor in fashion that is quite consistent with the jet age, in which distances around the globe are measured in terms of hours.

FASHION IN AMERICA

While elegance is the keynote of Parisian fashion, American designers have come into their own as creators of clothes particularly suited to the active and informal life in the United States. Fashion houses have sprung up in Los Angeles, San Francisco, Phoenix, Chicago, Minneapolis, Dallas, St. Louis, and Denver. These houses create and sell clothes that reflect the life, both casual and formal, of their own regions. The corps of outstanding designers includes Norman Norell, Claire McCardell, Molly Parnis, James Galanos, and Pauline Trigère. Numerous younger designers are coming into prominence each year. Probably the most original of these is Rudi Gernreich, who first startled the fashion world with his topless bathing suit, and who has made dramatic use of the miniskirt. He has employed vinyl,

transparent panels, and jarring color combinations to create free-moving and bold designs that have particular appeal to young women. An impact on men's fashions was made by Oleg Cassini when he brought out his "Nehru" or "Mao" jacket based on the garments worn by Asian statesmen (see p. 193).

Western wear has become a distinctive category of American design. It features fashions inspired by traditional cowboy and Indian attire (Figs. 222–223). The growing popularity of skiing has created a demand for ski clothes, which form an important segment of the fashion market today. Ski outfits are derived from such sources as Scandinavian sweaters and Eskimo parkas (Fig. 224). Insulated garments developed for space flights are applicable to ski clothes as well. Processes for moistureproofing and for strong, flexible weaves adaptable to stretch pants make sports garments lighter and more comfortable than ever before. *Après-ski* clothes that are worn while relaxing by the fire add a touch of glamor to informal attire and include imported knits and velvet pants and jackets.

Fashion designers in America have three main outlets for their talents: creating models for ready-to-wear items, producing designs for companies that sell patterns to home seamstresses, and operating their own small shops, where they design and create originals for individual customers. Some designers devote their talents to specific items, such as hats, shoes, or other accessories. Some specialize in a type of apparel that until recently was unknown in the Paris salons: at-home attire, sports clothes, lounging clothes, and children's wear. American designers bring fashion into millions of homes on isolated farms or in small towns by designing for mail-order houses, large department stores, and clothing chains. These designers have made fashion consciousness an almost universal trait of American women.

222–223. Clothing styles associated with the Old West continue to influence women's fashions.

opposite left: 222. "Cowboy" suit, complete with pants, vest, boots, and ten-gallon hat.

opposite right: 223. "Indian" dress, designed by VIOLA SYLBERT for Albert Alfus.

right: 224. Enthusiasm for skiing has opened a new field of colorful designs for warmth and action. Design by LJUNGBERG of Norway.

above left: 225. *Charioteer,* from the Sanctuary of Apollo at Delphi. c. 470 B.C. Bronze, height 5′11″. Museum, Delphi.

above right: 226. An evening dress designed by CEIL CHAPMAN derives its ultimate inspiration from the clothing of ancient Greece.

right: 227. A modern variation of the dirndl. Drawing by PAUL SCHMITT.

far right: 228. The traditional peasant dirndl.

SOURCES OF INSPIRATION

A thorough knowledge of the history of costumes is of inestimable value to a fashion designer. This knowledge is an important source of inspiration, a source that is supplemented by travel and by the study of contemporary trends and fads.

Historical styles continue to provide ideas for twentieth-century dress. The ancient Greek chiton (Fig. 225) was the basis for the Empire waistline of Napoleon's day and has become a mainstay of contemporary fashion as well (Fig. 226). The hoopskirt of the antebellum South can still be seen in bridal or ball gowns.

Innumerable American fashions have sprung from the soil of foreign lands. Styles derived from a South Sea Island or a remote Italian countryside are created with a few deft strokes of the designer's pen. The dirndl (Fig. 227), with its full skirt and tightly laced bodice, comes directly from the peasant costumes of Austria (Fig. 228). Oriental influence is found in slit skirts, in frogged openings, and in mandarin collars, such as the one on the raincoat reproduced in Figure 229. The most recent adaptation of the mandarin design was the "Nehru" or "Mao" collar that appeared in men's clothing and which represented the first dramatic change in the styling of men's suits and formal wear for over fifty years. The enthusiasm for boots and for fur hats is in response to the Russian influence (Fig. 230). Fabric

right: 229. The classic mandarin collar is revived every few years in women's fashions. Drawing by NICOLE.

below: 230. The boots and furs so popular today were inspired by Russian styles. Coat (*left*) by BONNIE CASHIN; cape and pants (*center*) by VICTOR JORIS for Cuddlecoat; lambskin coat (*right*) by Beged-Or; Cossack hat by ADOLFO.

231. The romantic sweep of paisley in this dress shows the influence of Persian styles. Design by KASPER for Joan Leslie.

design has been affected by East Indian and Persian colors and designs (Fig. 231), by Polynesian tapa cloth and batiks, and by South American embroidery.

Sometimes designers turn to paintings for ideas. In 1965, Paris designer Yves St. Laurent launched his fall collection with prints based on the nonfigurative paintings of Piet Mondrian (Fig. 232). The Mondrian influence sprang up at once in dresses and in men's parkas, shirts, and ties. The blocky designs had particular appeal to young people because of their bold colors and smart, contemporary appearance (Fig. 233). The introduction of vinyl fabrics, metallic cloth, and paper dresses has brought the influence of Pop and Op Art into young fashion design and has given them a gloss and glow that are quite new (Fig. 234). Because of the new industries, the developments in science, the advances in communication, and the experiments in art, the entire world has become a treasure house of inspiration for the fashion designer.

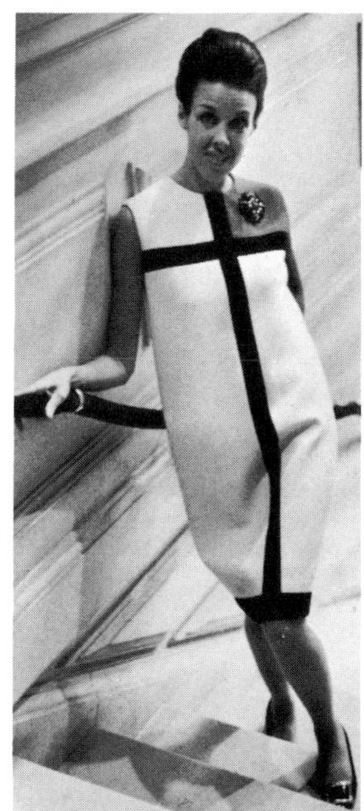

right: 232. Piet Mondrian. *Composition in White, Black, and Red.* 1936. Oil on canvas, $40\frac{1}{4} \times 41''$. Museum of Modern Art, New York (gift of the Advisory Committee).

far right: 233. The "Mondrian" dress was designed by Yves St. Laurent.

below: 234. Linked aluminum dress and hood by Jakobine Hobbs.

FASHION AND STYLE

There is a distinct difference between fashion and style. *Fashion* is usually defined as "the prevailing mode," and it depends largely upon what has been established by fashion designers. Changes are not only frequent but drastic, and the economic stability of the huge industry is maintained by intimidating most people into changing their wardrobes regularly. Fashion-minded individuals discard clothes far more often because they are outdated than because they are worn or faded.

Fashion is a sociological and cultural phenomenon. *Style,* on the other hand, is the expression of an individual's taste. Just as an artist has his own style in his work, so an individual may set his own distinctive style in dress. This style may be characterized by idiosyncrasies of apparel, or it may consist of such elegance and simplicity that it is copied by fashion designers who then popularize it. A woman in an eminent position may change her style of dress very little from year to year and retain the basic elegance or picturesque quality that has become a distinguishing attribute of her personality. Such people frequently have their clothes custom made to retain their individuality despite prevailing fashion.

COSTUME DESIGN

The design of costumes for the theater is closely related to fashion design in many ways. In both fields the designer must know how to adorn the individual in the most effective manner possible.

Like the set designer, the costume designer is instrumental in establishing the mood and character of a play. Before the first word is spoken or the initial gesture made, the audience gains an impression of the play as the result of these two artists' work. The set designer establishes the atmosphere and allocates the physical boundaries of the play. The costume designer creates specific characterizations with his designs. He plays a vital role in the production by making improvements and subtle adjustments to his costumes and thus to the characterizations right up to the final curtain. If his work is successful, it will have done much to reinforce the dramatic purpose of the playwright, producer, and actors.

Three Requisites of a Costume Designer

Historical Background A basic knowledge of past fashions is one of the costume designer's most important tools, but an awareness of tradition must be supplemented by thorough research. Basic knowledge is not enough when designing for the theater. Any inaccuracy, no matter how minute, is always picked up by someone in the audience, and the prestige of the play thus suffers. A successful designer will know where to find detailed information on the clothing of any given period, and he will assist the actors in the mechanics of wearing such clothing. Historical plays, therefore, require a knowledge of period and place, as well as of character (Fig. 235).

Familiarity with the Script Both the designer of the set and the costume designer must know the play's content thoroughly in order to give it the reinforcement and expansion it deserves. The lines tell much, but the personal habits and outlook of the characters can also be communicated by details of the costumes, which add another dimension to the development of the plot (Fig. 236).

A Practical Store of Sources and Possibilities The costume designer must know current prices of materials and accessories, because he is expected to work within a rigid budget. He will undoubtedly be subjected to last-minute changes in script and interpretation, and he may be asked to produce quite suddenly a pair of magenta gloves or alligator shoes, or an outdated and worn dress in a strange town where the play is having its tryout. A knowledge of shops, costume sources, and methods of creating effects is indispensable to the costume designer.

235. ERNST STERN costume design for Molière's *Le Bourgeois Gentilhomme.* 1912. Victoria and Albert Museum, London.

236. Zero Mostel as Tevye in *Fiddler on the Roof.*

Design and Theater Costume

The elements of design have an important function in theatrical production. Action is "blocked" to create balance and order on the stage, and costumes are designed to establish the cast members' varying degrees of importance. A supporting player must not be costumed in such a way that he will divert attention from the stars or from the featured players unless, of course, a dramatic purpose can be served by so doing. The costume designer uses the elements of color, texture, and line to preserve the proper relationships between actors and to relate each actor to his background. A character at odds with his environment may wear clothes that make him stand out, thus subtly emphasizing his struggle to the audience. An officious person may be dressed in elaborately figured clothing to create a feeling of restlessness. Thus, the costume designer must enable the actors to merge with or emerge from their background according to the needs of dramatic action.

The principles of design are equally important. Free and rhythmic movement is basic to an actor's performance, but it can be hindered by tight and uncomfortable clothing. It is the costume designer's task to provide garments that make possible the actor's graceful and unimpeded motions upon the stage. The costume designer must also ensure balance between costumes and stage set. He can repeat or contrast in his costumes the colors, lines, and textures of the set. A printed costume should not be used for a character who will sit upon a printed sofa. The colors of the apparel must contrast with the walls against which the actors move. Variety can be

237. Costumes for the Alwin Nikolais Dance Company.

achieved by the presentation of brilliant costumes against a subdued background, as in a medieval setting of dark corridors in cathedrals or castles. Unity results from the effective repetition of color, line, or texture in both the costumes and the setting.

An innovative use of form characterizes the work of a young dance group, whose leader visualizes the performers as a structural unit, costuming them accordingly (Fig. 237). Costume thus attains a sculptural quality which permeates the set, giving substance to the action.

Light is an important factor in the design of theatrical productions. The costume designer must work in close collaboration with the lighting expert if his efforts are to be successful. A costume designer should know, for example, that comedies are usually lit with pink and amber lights, while mysteries are shrouded in blues and greens. Furthermore, the costumes should always be tested in the actual light that is to be used.

Costume design for the theater and design for fashion are interdependent in many ways. The costume designer must know about current fashions. Indeed, if the play is successful, his costumes may exert an influence upon the fashion industry itself. In motion pictures as well, costumes frequently initiate nationwide fads. The film *Cleopatra,* for example, created interest in Egyptian jewelry, and *Flower Drum Song* briefly popularized Oriental fashions. Thea Van Runkle was paid only $3000 to design costumes for the movie *Bonnie and Clyde,* and yet she succeeded in bringing about a significant revival of the 1930s style (Fig. 238).

American women have a strong inclination to copy other women, particularly women who are beautifully groomed or who have glamorous roles in plays and movies. Therefore, the costume designer's efforts not only affect the character and success of theatrical productions but, in addition, provide a visual ideal for the women who attend plays and motion pictures.

SUMMARY

Fashion is an important area of design because of the relationship of clothing to behavior and to social status. In the world of nature and in human history the male has been more elegantly attired than the female. During the past 150 years male clothing became quite conservative. Lately, however, men's fashions have achieved greater elegance and elaboration.

A sound knowledge of the human form is the first requisite of a fashion designer. The principles of design are the most important factors to be considered in his work. The basic elements are line, texture, color, size, and shape.

Paris has been traditionally a strong influence on the world of fashion, although new centers of fashion have arisen elsewhere in Europe and in America. Inspiration for fashion design comes from historic sources, from travel, and from varied influences, including paintings or other works of art.

Fashion is the prevailing mode, whereas *style* is the distinctive expression of an individual's taste.

Costume design has much in common with fashion design and at times is the forerunner of fashion. A costume designer should possess these requisites: 1) historical awareness, 2) familiarity with the script, and 3) a knowledge of sources, materials, and garments. Design in the theater requires a close relationship between the set designer, the lighting expert, and the costume designer.

238. Faye Dunaway as Bonnie Parker.

Design in Bookmaking and Printmaking

chapter 14

The arts of bookmaking and printmaking both arose from man's need to find an efficient, economical, yet esthetically satisfying means of recording ideas for communication to large numbers of people. The two arts evolved separately, yet they supplemented one another early in their development. Medieval woodcuts and engravings were pasted onto the pages of hand-lettered manuscripts to illustrate the text. Then, with the invention of movable type in the mid-fifteenth century, the arts were united, for woodcut illustrations could be printed with the text in a single process.

The high point in the union of bookmaking and printmaking was reached at the beginning of the sixteenth century, when books illustrated with woodcuts were widely circulated. Later, prints were used to reproduce paintings, for propaganda, and for political satire, and they were a popular medium for reporting news events until the 1860s, when Winslow Homer produced his famous series of Civil War

239. *Rameses Offering Food and Flowers to the Goddess Isis,* sculptured bas-relief from the Temple of Rameses I. 19th Dynasty (c. 1305–1190 B.C.). Metropolitan Museum of Art, New York (gift of J. Pierpont Morgan, 1911).

scenes for *Harper's Weekly*. But Matthew Brady, with his camera, was also recording the tragedies of the war, and the public was increasingly interested in the "real" image, rather than the artist's interpretation. The development of photography marked the virtual end of printmaking as a method of conveying information.

The twentieth century has come to regard bookmaking and printmaking as separate crafts, each valued for its intrinsic characteristics. The production of books, particularly for the mass market, has become a highly mechanized process, and never before in history has such a fund of information been so readily accessible to the general public. The making of prints, on the other hand, is seen as a unique art form, quite distinct from painting, yet treasured for its "hand" quality. Original prints are indeed original works of art, often signed by the printmaker and commanding high prices from collectors. Still, however, bookmaking and printmaking involve the same basic methods—relief, intaglio, and planography. Both may be described as *graphic* arts, a term that historically has been used to embrace those arts that rely for their effect primarily on drawing, rather than on color. In current usage the word graphic includes all the arts and crafts that employ mechanical, or partially mechanical, methods for multiple reproduction.

BOOKMAKING

A fine book holds a unique place among man's treasures. Not only can it provide a record of great ideas and literary invention, but it can also be a work of art in itself. By combining beautiful papers, ink, type, illustrations, and binding it is possible to produce an esthetic expression worthy of the most noble content.

EVOLUTION OF THE BOOK

From the earliest symbols scratched on stone to the mass-produced books of the twentieth century, the thoughts of man have been preserved with respect and devotion. The ancient Egyptians threaded their hieroglyphics through their painting and sculpture as a running commentary (Fig. 239). They used not only stone but also scrolls made from the thick stems of the papyrus plant. This pictorial record evolved into Greek writing (Fig. 240) in which many of the most important works of literature

240. The famous Rosetta Stone is inscribed with Egyptian hieroglyphics at the top, demotic or commonly used Egyptian characters in the center, and Greek letters at the bottom. British Museum, London.

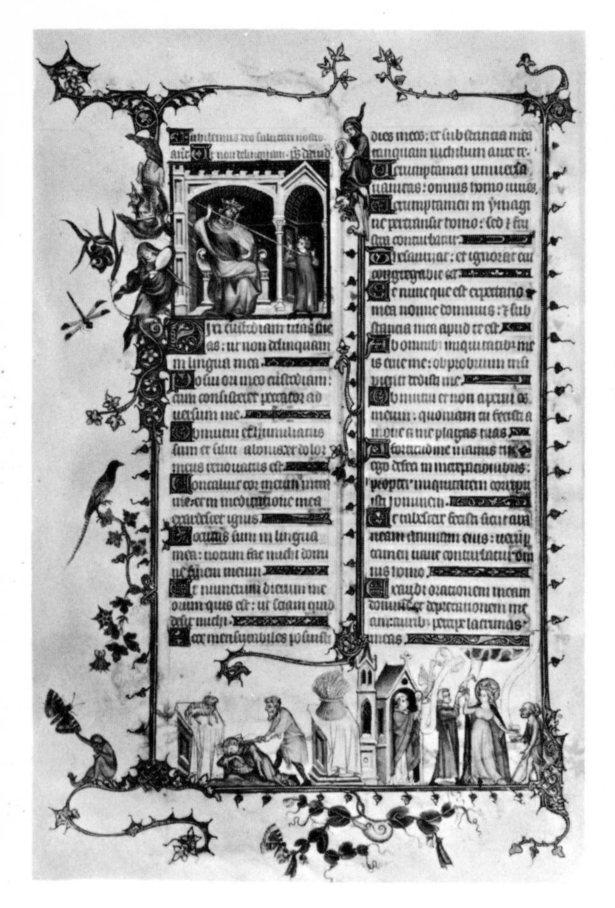

left: 241. JEAN PUCELLE. *Saul and David,* from the *Belleville Breviary.* c. 1323–26. Illuminated manuscript. Bibliothèque Nationale, Paris.

below: 242. SHEN CHOU. *Poet on a Mountain* from *Landscape with Poems.* 15th century. Ink and color on paper, height $15\frac{3}{4}''$. Nelson-Atkins Gallery, Kansas City, Mo. (Nelson Fund).

were preserved on parchment scrolls made from the skin of young sheep. In the Early Christian period, the scroll gave way to the parchment *codex,* the predecessor of the bound book. During the Middle Ages devoted monks kept Western culture alive by painstakingly copying and recopying the texts of Christianity as well as those of ancient Greece and Rome. These medieval manuscripts were often illuminated—or hand painted—with elaborate pictures and designs (Fig. 241). The custom of illuminating manuscripts existed in the Far East as well. Many extraordinarily beautiful books were executed in India, for example, in which the illustrations consisted of small painted scenes in vibrant oranges, yellows, blues, and delicately applied gold leaf. The Chinese and the Japanese, like the ancient Egyptians, inserted written commentary into their paintings (Fig. 242). This calligraphy often took the form of poetic statements that became an integral part of the painting itself. The Chinese are credited with the invention of paper, which was exported to Europe during the Middle Ages.

Effects of Printing

The invention of the printing press in the fifteenth century resulted in an immediate increase in the use of paper, for parchment was too stiff and too expensive for the new printing process. The appearance of the text, however, was not drastically changed. The characters that made up the typeface in the earliest printed books were copied from hand-lettered manuscripts, and initial letters were often drawn

Plate 21. ANDO HIROSHIGE. *Rain Shower on Ohashi Bridge.* 19th century. Color woodblock print, height $13\frac{7}{8}''$. Cleveland Museum of Art (gift of J. H. Wade).

Plate 22. Corita Kent. *The Beginning of Miracles.* Serigraph in 23 colors, $14\frac{1}{2} \times 19\frac{1}{4}''$. University Gallery, University of Minnesota, Minneapolis.

by hand (Fig. 243). The books, therefore, had much the same aspect as medieval manuscripts. Nevertheless, the advent of movable type had widespread repercussions. The printing of books lowered their cost to a fraction of what it had been and brought them within reach of many people for the first time. A new and widespread interest in literature spurred the attempt to preserve old manuscripts so that the heritage of the past would not be lost. This, in turn, led to the development of bookbinding for the safekeeping of documents and literary works. Handwritten manuscripts had been bound chiefly by monks, who used thick oak boards covered with tanned deerskin. These bindings were sometimes embellished by goldsmiths and jewelers with tooling, encrustations of gems, metal clasps, and mountings. The advent of printing led to the use of leather and such cheaper materials as cloth and paper. By the eighteenth century quarter- and half-leather bindings appeared. This paved the way for case bindings made of cloth-covered paper boards. Finally, in the twentieth century, the flexible cardboard and heavy paper covers of paperbacks were developed. Paperbacks are designed for wide and inexpensive dispersal, rather than for centuries of use.

TWENTIETH-CENTURY BOOK DESIGN

Man's desire to clothe the written manifestations of his knowledge in worthy form presents many challenging opportunities to the designer. The principles of design govern every aspect of a book's creation, from its content to its physical appearance. Book design today falls into two categories: the book produced in quantity for the large popular market, and the hand-bound volume created by a small number of artist-craftsmen for private collectors and museums.

THE POPULAR MARKET

By far the largest segment of the book industry finds its audience in the popular market—the general reader, schools, colleges, and public libraries. An increasingly discriminating public demands books that are attractive and well designed, and it is to this end that the graphic artist directs his efforts.

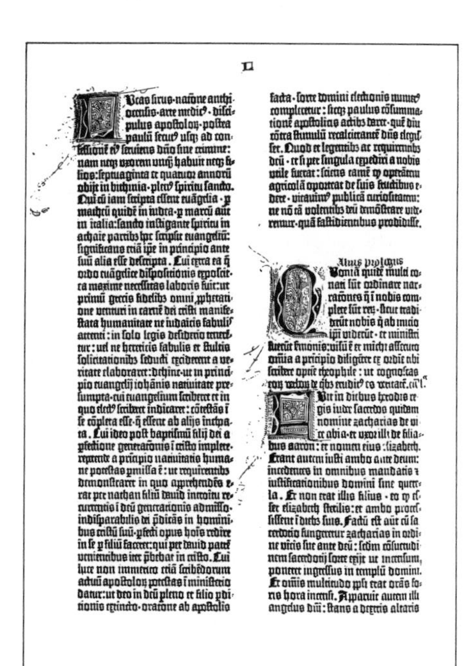

243. Page from the Gutenberg Bible. 1452–56. Rare Book Division, New York Public Library (Astor, Lenox, and Tilden Foundations).

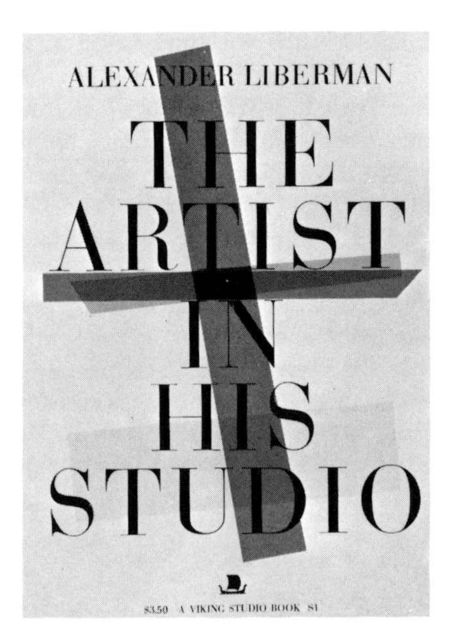

far left: 244. Jacket design for *The De-Romanization of the American Catholic Church,* by Edward Wakin and Father Joseph F. Scheuer. Design by HERB LUBALIN and FRAN ELFENBEIN.

left: 245. Jacket design for *The Artist in His Studio,* by Alexander Liberman. Design by ALEXANDER LIBERMAN.

below left: 246. Cover design for *AIA Guide to New York City,* by Norval White and Elliot Willensky. Design by JEROME KUHL for Herb Lubalin, Inc.

Cover Design

The first thing one notices about a book is its "package"—the dust jacket or paper cover that encloses the book. The main purpose of exterior design is to attract the attention of the potential buyer and to make the book's contents seem more interesting. In the highly competitive field of book merchandising, covers and jackets are planned to be as conspicuous as possible when placed on the crowded shelves of bookstores. This is especially important for books whose reputations have not yet been established.

The cover designer's primary task is to interpret the book's content in an effective manner, and he can accomplish this in several ways. He can combine striking color and form with a symbolic suggestion of the contents, as in the jacket reproduced in Figure 244. He may create an abstract design that alludes to the contents without becoming a literal representation (Fig. 245). Type alone, when it is used with taste and imagination, can produce a cover design that is remarkably attractive (Fig. 246). Expressive type is exploited particularly well in the cover for a biography of e. e. cummings (Fig. 247). The poet's famous lower-case signature has been combined with a simple drawing to create a design that is both whimsical and oddly disturbing—much like cummings' poetry.

Dust jackets of hardbound books often wear out very quickly, but the case bindings underneath must be made for years of use. Bindings are usually conservatively designed, with muted colors and simple forms. Durability is a primary concern, because the life of the book depends largely upon the strength of the binding. Special editions frequently have *endpapers* that reflect the character of the book and are consistent with the binding.

Paper, Type, and Layout

The concept of organic book design implies a close affinity of paper, type, binding, content, and illustrations. The choice of an appropriate paper is, therefore, an important factor in the book's total design.

The basic processes for making paper have not changed in over 1800 years. There are, however, many kinds of paper, and their different characteristics depend principally upon the raw materials from which they are made. The cheapest grade of newsprint is made from wood pulp, while the finest paper is created from the fibers of cotton or linen. The medium grades are mixtures of the two, combined with such fibrous materials as straw, leaves, and bark. Sometimes a synthetic substance is added for strength. Melamine, a plastic recently added to the formula for paper currency, is said to have increased the life expectancy of each dollar bill from 12 to 17 months.

Type styles have undergone many changes since the early "block books" printed from wooden type. (Today movable type is made from an alloy of lead, antimony, tin, and copper, a combination known as *type metal.*) Although designers have contributed many stylistic variations through the centuries, type faces can generally be classified according to four basic categories:

Black Letter   ROMAN   SANS SERIF   *Italic*

The type face used for most books today is a variation of the Roman type that was designed in the fifteenth century.

The layout of every page in a book must be carefully planned. The arrangement of text and illustrations, titles and subtitles, as well as the spacing of lines of text all play a part in the visual attractiveness of the book. A page on which the lines of text are set very close together will give the appearance of a darker tone than one on which there is a great deal of "air." As with any design, the layout of an attractive page of print is a matter of value, proportion, balance, and unity. The title page of a book is crucial, for it is usually the reader's first impression. The example reproduced in Figure 248 demonstrates how an attractive title page, integrated with cover design and page layout, creates a unity of design.

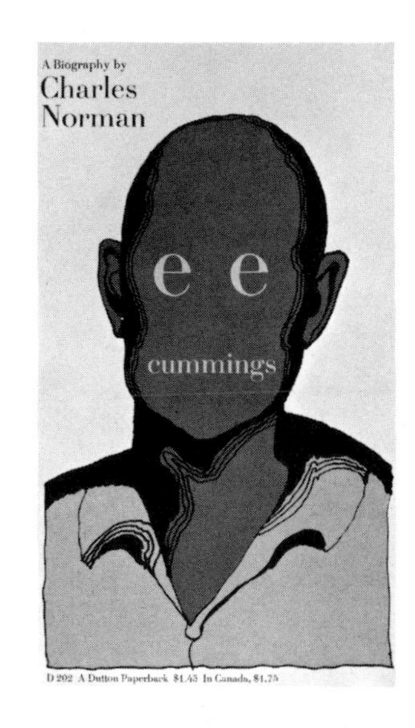

above: 247. Cover design for *e. e. cummings: A Biography,* by Charles Norman. Design by MILTON GLASER.

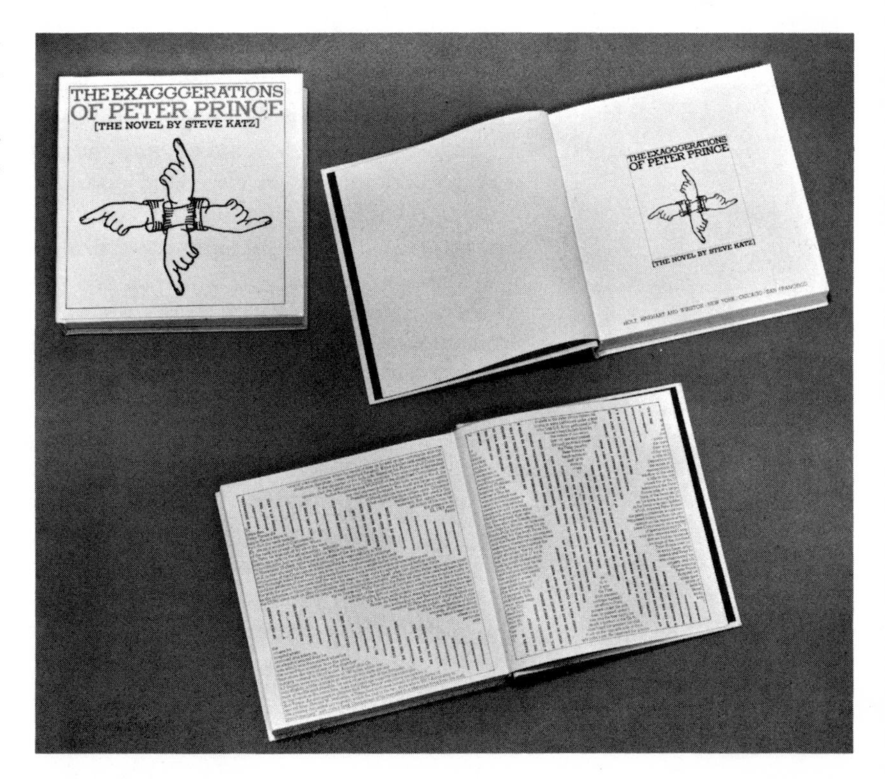

right: 248. Jacket, title page, and interior design for *The Exagggerations of Peter Prince,* by Steve Katz.

PRINTING PROCESSES

Writing has always been closely associated with pictorial images and, in fact, ultimately derives from pictorial representations. The drawings that unfold before the reader's eyes on a papyrus or parchment scroll, the illuminations of a carefully rendered manuscript, and the meticulous diagrams in a scientific text have all contributed to the effectiveness of "thoughts frozen on paper." Illustrations are particularly important in children's books, where they enhance and explain the printed word; in some works of poetry and fiction they are used for decorative effect.

For centuries illustrations were hand drawn or hand painted; later they were printed from wood blocks and copper engravings. Recent technical developments have greatly increased the possibilities for book production. New photomechanical methods can reproduce an unlimited variety of pictorial representations, but, in general, illustrations are classified in two basic types—*line cut* and *halftone.* A line cut is an image that consists of lines or solid masses of undifferentiated black and white, with no shaded areas. Examples are pen-and-ink drawings, woodcuts, and wood engravings. Halftone illustrations are characterized by intermediate values of gray that range from solid black to pure white. Photographs, wash drawings, and paintings are examples of halftone copy. The processes used for the reproduction of illustrations, as well as for the printing of text, fall into three broad categories: *relief, intaglio,* and *planography.*

Relief

Relief refers to any process in which the image to be printed is raised from the printing plate and takes the ink directly. The ink is then transferred to the paper by pressure. In photomechanical reproduction the relief process is called *letterpress.* The procedures for reproducing various types of copy are described below:

Line Cut To reproduce a line cut by the letterpress method, the copy is photographed onto a photosensitized glass plate that serves as a negative. The negative is printed on a zinc plate that has been coated so as to sensitize the surface and cause the parts exposed to light to become hard and insoluble in water. Washing removes the unexposed coating, and the plate is inked and dusted with a fine *ground.* The ground adheres to the inked portions of the plate and is brushed off the remainder. The plate is then immersed in an acid bath, and the portions not coated are eaten away. The remaining plate is the relief from which the print is made.

Halftone Halftone reproduction requires one additional step beyond those used in making a line cut. The original copy is photographed onto a photosensitive plate through two sheets of glass that have been etched with parallel diagonal lines placed at right angles to form a grid, or *screen,* effect. The picture is thus broken up into a series of dots, and the variation in the size of the dots is determined by the amount of light that strikes the plate. These dots create the illusion of shading. In newspaper photographs the dots are visible to the eye, but in finer printing they are not discernible. The subsequent steps are identical to those in making a line cut: the ground is applied, and the plate is etched and then printed.

Four Color The preparation of color material for printing is an extension of the halftone process. It begins with transparent color positive film, such as Ektachrome and Kodachrome. From the "transparency" the three primary colors—yellow, red, and blue—plus black are separated into four independent negative films by rephotographing the original color positive through a series of filters—a blue filter for yellow, a green one for red, and red-orange for blue. The black film is the residue of values left on a fourth negative film after the primary hues have been separated from the original color positive. The separation films are then exposed against another film to provide screened halftone negatives that can be used to make the plates appropriate to the process selected for printing the color reproduction.

Since it is by recombining into a single reproduction colors printed from several different plates superimposed on top of each other, the impressions made by the four plates must be accurately aligned—be printed "in register." Otherwise, the image would appear blurred and out of focus.

The number of colors used in color printing is not invariable. Sometimes only the primary colors are separated and plated, while black is omitted altogether. It is also possible to separate, plate, and print more than four colors, and the result of such multiple-color printing can be rich and subtle indeed. But four is the typical number of colors used in "full" color reproduction, and with skillful preparation and presswork they can be made to reproduce almost any color effect.

Intaglio

The word *intaglio* comes from the Italian word meaning "to incise." It is used to describe a printing process that is, in essence, just the reverse of relief, in that the parts to be printed are etched *into* the plate and are lower than the ground. The resultant depressions are filled with ink, and the ink is transferred to paper by pressure and suction. In photomechanical reproduction, the intaglio process is called *gravure.*

Gravure In gravure reproduction a screen similar to that employed in letterpress is placed over the plate to be used for printing. The plate is then etched to duplicate the copy. The screen creates square areas on the plate that are etched to form cups, which are all the same in diameter but differ in depth. The deeper cups hold more ink and print a darker image. Because the squares in the gravure screen system are all the same size and vary only in the amount of ink they hold and deposit on the paper, gravure is a genuine halftone process, whereas the dots of letterpress and offset (see below) merely simulate tonal gradations by their varying sizes. In gravure it is possible to achieve a deep, velvety black, sparkling white, and an infinite range of detail and tonal distinctions in both monochrome and full-color printing.

Planography

Planographic printing employs a flat surface, with neither depressions nor raised areas. Instead, the parts that are meant to print are treated to accept a greasy ink which other areas repel. The process thus is based on the antipathy of grease and water. Ink is transferred to paper by direct contact.

Lithography The commercial lithographic process is called offset lithography or simply *offset.* In offset printing a thin metal plate is created through steps similar to those used in making letterpress plates. The result is a smooth plate whose surface has varying degrees of hardness and softness. The hard areas are ink-receptive, or printing parts; the soft areas are water-receptive and are nonprinting. The offset plate is wrapped around a rapidly turning cylinder which comes in contact, first, with a set of water rollers, then with a set of ink rollers, and finally with a cylinder wrapped in a rubber blanket. An impression cylinder carries the paper and presses it against the rubber blanket, from which the inked image, picked up from the metal plate, is printed.

Offset printing has several advantages. The plates last longer because they do not print directly but through the intervention of the rubber cylinder. The latter also permits greater speed and the printing of fine images on mat paper. It is by offset that the text and illustrations—both black and white and color—of this book have been printed.

Collotype Collotype differs from offset lithography in that no screen is involved. The printed image, therefore, gives the effect of continuous tone, or smooth gradations of dark and light, rather than a series of dots. Collotype plates are covered with a photosensitive gelatine sheet onto which the image to be printed is projected through a film negative. The gelatine becomes impervious to water in varying degrees, according to the amount of light that strikes it. The plate is then soaked in water. Areas exposed to the greatest intensity of light hold less water and therefore accept more ink, so that they print darker. The reverse is true for the lighter tones.

Collotype is rarely used, because the plates wear out very quickly, and its success depends upon the most rigidly controlled atmospheric conditions. Both of these factors make it a very expensive process. However, for limited editions it is capable of very high-quality reproduction.

Printing and methods of reproduction have become increasingly varied because of extensive experimentation in the field. Often two or more of the methods described above can be combined in a single book to produce the highest quality in text and illustration. The selection of the most appropriate process for a particular book plays an important part in its overall design.

THE COLLECTOR'S MARKET

The collector's market, while comprising only a tiny portion of the book industry, is nonetheless an important segment of the field. Books produced for this audience—mainly museums and a select group of private collectors—are generally issued in limited editions and are necessarily quite expensive. Every element of such books—paper, type, layout, binding—is given the meticulous attention that an artist might devote to a painting or a sculpture. This is the "fine art" of bookmaking.

Paper

The paper in a leather-bound collector's edition is quite different from that in a popularly priced novel. Expensive books may have a heavy linen paper or, as in religious works, an extremely thin but strong onionskin. The choice of paper depends upon the intended thickness of the volume and upon the appropriateness of a particular kind of paper to the total design. A special grade of paper may even be chosen for its "feel"—the tactile sensation one has in turning the pages. An important factor is durability, for leather-bound volumes are meant to last for centuries, not merely for a few readings.

Hand Bookbinding

The final step in the creation of a fine book is achieved by the few dedicated craftsmen who restore, design, and bind books by hand. Free from the contingencies of the competitive market, these artists turn their efforts toward producing volumes for discriminating collectors and private libraries. Such an audience appreciates the best in materials, design, and workmanship. Collectors are sympathetic to the idea that books, like any other works of art, are not meant to be owned by any one person but are to be preserved in the best manner possible until they can be passed on to others. The art of bookbinding is a very old one, and standards of craftsmanship today are maintained at much the same high level that prevailed in the medieval guilds. This does not mean, however, that hand binders are limited to traditional designs. Many contemporary craftsmen have shown, through their adaptation of old techniques to innovative designs, that hand bookbinding can indeed be an exciting and imaginative field.

Binding materials are expensive, and the labor involved is painstaking, yet there is room for considerable ingenuity in the application of both. Some volumes cost thousands of dollars, and it is estimated that a minimum of twenty hours of labor is required for each book. The time and expense result not so much from the actual binding as from the decorative design that is applied.

The bookbinder of today has a long and honorable tradition behind him, a tradition that began in Ireland and spread to England and the Italian monasteries during the Middle Ages. One of the most influential figures in the United States was Hazel Dreis, who for many years maintained a studio in California, and who trained a group of hand-picked students in the methods she learned from Lawrence Decoverly in London. Mrs. Dreis organized her studio in the manner of a European workshop and insisted that her students acquire a rich background in papermaking, music, drama, painting, sculpture, and archaeology. This diverse knowledge formed the basis for intelligent and sensitive design for all types of books.

The main purpose of a binding is to preserve the text. Whatever decorative design is applied thus becomes a function of the basic structure. Although the earliest bindings were usually composed of wooden panels hinged and clasped in metal, leather was for centuries considered to be the most practical binding material for achieving permanence. Many different leathers have been used. Nigerian goatskin is a favorite because of its durability and smooth grain. Occasionally the skins are bleached to ensure a more uniform color, but in the finest bindings this is not done, because bleaching threatens the longevity of the material and thus of the volume. Calfskin bindings are beautifully textured; however, since they derive from an immature animal, they do not have the permanence of goatskin. The most durable material for very large volumes is pigskin, but it is a thick leather and is apt to be rather stiff. In recent years a wide variety of new materials have been introduced. In addition to leathers, fabrics, papers, and plastics of every conceivable texture are combined with new binding processes to create effects never before possible.

Books are bound in sections called *signatures,* a term left over from the Middle Ages. Medieval bookbinders were often illiterate, and in order to avoid confusion, each section was labeled with an initial letter. The signatures were bound in alphabetical order, then glued to a cloth and enclosed in leather. The finest bindings were also laced along the spine to increase their strength and to provide greater security for individual pages. These painstaking methods are still used today by hand bookbinders all over the world.

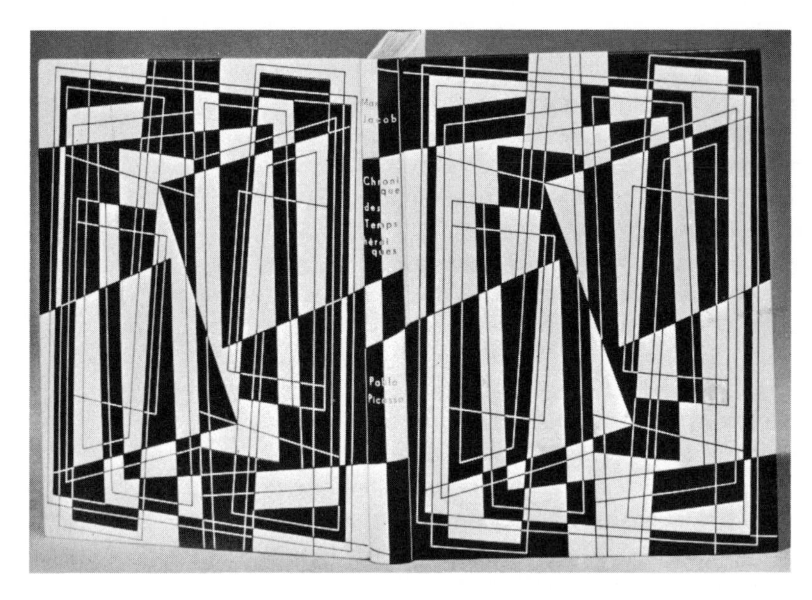

249. This binding for Max Jacob's *Chronique des temps héroiques* was designed and executed by Pierre Martin.

The design of a hand binding is a personal achievement that results from the craftsman's intimate knowledge of all the factors that make up a book: the subject matter, the type, and the paper on which it is printed. The craftsman must consider the book's purpose before deciding upon the decoration. Gold tooling, inlay, and overlay, for example, would not be practical for a frequently used reference book. The hand binder also appraises the type face, the paper, the illustrations, and the text in order to create a binding that can best express the very essence of the book.

Among the most creative of contemporary bookbinders are Pierre Martin in Paris and Edward McLean in Durham, North Carolina. Although they are thousands of miles apart, the two men have a generally similar approach, a consuming interest in the interpretation of a text, and the highest standards of craftsmanship.

Pierre Martin has his own atelier in which he creates original designs primarily for the work of contemporary French authors whom he admires. A master binder, Martin experiments with unusual designs, notably a series of mosaiclike effects in leather. These are extremely difficult to execute and are striking in appearance. Figure 249 shows one such design in calfskin, which indicates a preoccupation with space and form that is almost cubic. Martin refers to some of his bindings as *trompe l'oeil* (fool the eye), because they have such a three-dimensional quality. A fascinating aspect of his style is his exploration of geometrical forms. Like many other contemporary artists, he feels that such forms are fitting symbols of our age, and he uses them to create designs for a variety of books. He contracts or stretches shapes to produce what he calls "twisted geometry" (Fig. 250). The narrow strips of leather representing these forms are chosen with great care and are meticulously integrated into a unified design.

Edward McLean, who was trained under Hazel Dreis, is currently bookbinder-in-residence at Duke University. He has designed bindings for a wide variety of books, from Latin treatises to the United States Constitution, and he did much restoration work on volumes for the Folger Shakespearean Library in Washington, D.C. Two of McLean's bindings for old manuscripts are illustrated in Figure 251. Each has a rich and distinctive quality that gives eloquent testimony that the manuscript within is worthy of the finest care.

McLean proves with his bindings that an interesting book design is no more difficult to create than a dull one. Each binding tells its own story, whether it contains a tale of the Old West or selections from the English theater. In his western bindings McLean frequently uses bandana fabrics combined with the hide of unborn calves to give an unusual and authentic appearance.

Both of these artist-craftsmen exemplify in their work the highest standards to be found in the design and creation of books today. They represent a small group of artists who supplement the efforts of that larger company of men who work with major publishing houses in the production of books for wide distribution. With the tremendous number of inexpensive books on the market, one sometimes forgets that much knowledge is available only because devoted craftsmen through the centuries have taken the trouble to preserve it in usable forms. If it were not for the art of bookbinding, each new generation would have had to repeat much of the basic research and exploration that had already been accomplished. Viewed in this light, the design of books becomes not only a fascinating field for the designer but a serious responsibility for succeeding generations.

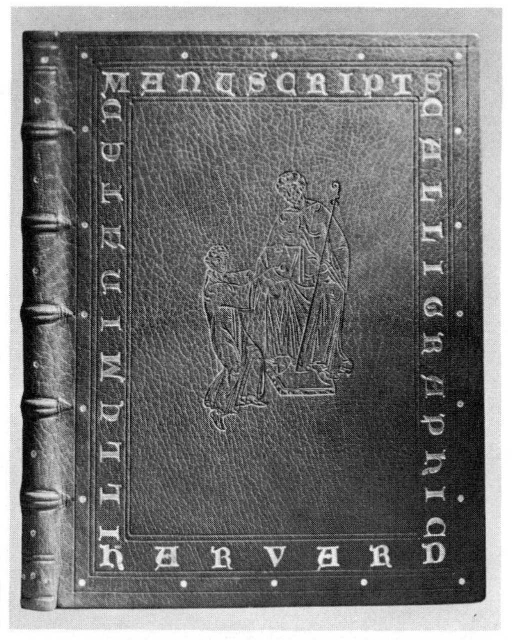

above: 250. Pierre Martin's "twisted geometry" provides a distinctive binding for *Août,* by Saint-Pol-Roux.

right: 251. Edward McLean designed classic bindings for two old manuscripts.

PRINTMAKING

The art of printmaking has a very long history. Its origins, like those of bookmaking, may be traced to the ancient Egyptians, who used wooden blocks as stamps. The earliest known woodcut reproductions were made in China in the ninth century A.D., and by the thirteenth century the technique had been introduced in the Western world. Printmaking reached its apogee in sixteenth-century Europe, with the work of such men as Albrecht Dürer (Fig. 252), Lucas Cranach, and Hans Baldung Grien. Later artists used their printmaking skills for the reproduction of paintings, for propaganda, for social satire, for political commentary, and for the reporting of current events. Only in the twentieth century has printmaking been accepted as an artistic expression in itself, valued for the unique effects it is capable of producing—the fine grain of woodcut, the subtle textures of aquatint, or the meticulous line of engraving.

The techniques of printmaking are very much the same today as they were several centuries ago. As with photomechanical reproduction, they may be grouped into three general categories—relief, intaglio, and planography—with the addition of a fourth, serigraphy, technically a variation of the planographic process.

Relief

The oldest printmaking processes are the relief methods. In their most typical form they preserve the qualities of the material from which they are made, translating these qualities into an artistic expression. The most common methods are woodcut, linocut, and wood engraving.

Woodcut Woodcuts have a charm that has never been surpassed by more recent innovations in printmaking. The basic technique is simple: the image to be printed is projected or sketched on the *side grain* of a block of wood, then the areas that are not to be printed are cut out with knives or gouges. The block is inked, and

far left: 252. ALBRECHT DÜRER. *Melancholia.* 1514. Copper engraving, $9\frac{3}{8} \times 6\frac{5}{8}''$. California Palace of the Legion of Honor, San Francisco (Achenbach Foundation for Graphic Arts).

left: 253. WILHELM LEHMBRUCK. *Prodigal Son.* c. 1912. Drypoint, $11\frac{1}{4} \times 7\frac{7}{8}''$. Fogg Art Museum, Harvard University, Cambridge, Mass.

the image is transferred to paper by pressing or rubbing. Because they are cut with the grain of the material, woodcuts have a hand-hewn look, and the feeling of the wood itself is apparent. A woodcut such as the one reproduced in Figure 189 possesses characteristics that cannot be imitated in any other medium. In *The Kiss,* Edvard Munch has used a very fine tool to produce an image that seems to blend into the firm grain of the wood. Even the knots are left to complete the design. The result is rough and solid, but with a feeling of sound craftsmanship.

Many artists use heavy linoleum blocks as a substitute for wood, and in this case the result is called a *linocut.* The technique for cutting and printing is exactly the same.

The woodcut technique is easily adapted for making color prints, and in this art the Japanese artists are particularly renowned. An excellent example is reproduced in Plate 21 (p. 203).

Wood Engraving Wood engravings differ from woodcuts in that they are cut from the *end grain* of the wood. A very fine tool called a *burin* is used, and this results in finer lines and greater detail than are usual in woodcut. The typical wood engraving shows slender white lines against a dark background.

Intaglio

As the term implies, images to be printed by the intaglio processes are cut *into* the ground, rather than having excess material cut from around them. Ink is thus retained in the incised areas, rather than on a raised surface. Intaglio processes include metal engravings, drypoints, etchings, aquatints, and mezzotints.

Engraving Metal engravings are executed with burins or gravers on sheets of copper, zinc, or steel. The artist pushes the V-shaped burin tip into the surface of the metal to gouge out the lines of the design. He then heats the plate, rubs ink into the grooves, and wipes the surface clean.

To print the plate, the artist carefully places it face up on the bed of a press. He then lays dampened paper on the inked plate, covers the paper with a blanket of felt, and applies pressure with a heavy roller. The roller forces the paper into the grooves, and the ink is thus transferred to the paper.

Before the development of photomechanical processes, this method was used for making reproductions of paintings and for printing book illustrations. It reached a high point artistically with the work of the German artist Albrecht Dürer (Fig. 252). Copper engraving is still employed for seals on official documents, postage stamps, paper money, and fine stationery.

Drypoint The printing process for drypoints is much the same as that for engravings, but the method of preparing the plate is quite different. Drypoints are usually executed on copper plates with needlelike instruments that have steel or diamond points. The resulting lines are much finer than those made by the burin. Instead of being pushed into the surface, the tool is drawn across the plate, and a *burr* or tiny curl of metal is left along the edges of the lines. When the plate is inked, this burr retains the ink, so that the printed image has a velvety appearance that recalls the darker accents in a fine pencil drawing. In Wilhelm Lehmbruck's *Prodigal Son* (Fig. 253) the line is both varied and expressive, giving the picture a quality not to be found in other types of printmaking.

left: 254. James Abbott McNeill Whistler. *Black Lion Wharf.* 1859. Etching, $6 \times 8\frac{13}{16}$". Fogg Art Museum, Harvard University, Cambridge, Mass.

right: 255. Mary Cassatt. *La Toilette.* 1891. Aquatint accented with drypoint, $14\frac{15}{16} \times 10\frac{1}{2}$". Metropolitan Museum of Art, New York (gift of Paul J. Sachs, 1916).

Etching The term etching comes from the German word meaning "to eat." In this process the lines of the image are eaten into the metal plate, rather than being gouged out with tools. The etching technique was used originally for decorating coats of armor, and in the sixteenth century it came into use as a method of illustrating books.

To create an etching the artist coats a polished metal plate (usually copper) with a protective film of waxlike substance called the *ground.* The lines of the drawing are then scratched into the ground with a blunt needle, thus exposing the metal in the areas that are meant to print. The plate is immersed in an acid bath, and the acid eats into the exposed lines, etching them permanently. Finally the plate is inked and printed in the same manner as engravings. Whistler's *Black Lion Wharf* (Fig. 254) shows how a skilled artist can achieve effective and intricately detailed imagery by means of the etching technique.

Aquatint Aquatint is a variation of the etching process. The artist covers a metal plate with a powdered resinous substance and then heats the plate, causing the resin particles to harden and adhere to the metal. He then immerses the plate in an acid bath, and the acid eats into the metal around the resin particles to create an allover effect of tone. This process may be repeated several times, and some areas may be stopped-out with varnish, which resists the acid, to produce gradations of light and dark. The print that results has a soft and beautiful tonal quality that can be compared with an ink wash (Fig. 255).

Mezzotint An even darker tone is the characteristic of mezzotint, another variation on the etching technique. The artist first goes over the entire plate with a *rocker,* a tool with many sharp cutting teeth. He holds the tool at a right angle to the plate and digs up the surface, producing a covering of burrs. When the plate is printed, these burrs create a very dark tone. In areas that are meant to print lighter the artist partially removes the burrs with a *scraper,* while the lightest areas are produced by smoothing the burrs completely with a *burnisher.* The print reproduced in Figure 256 illustrates the dark, brooding quality that is typical of mezzotint.

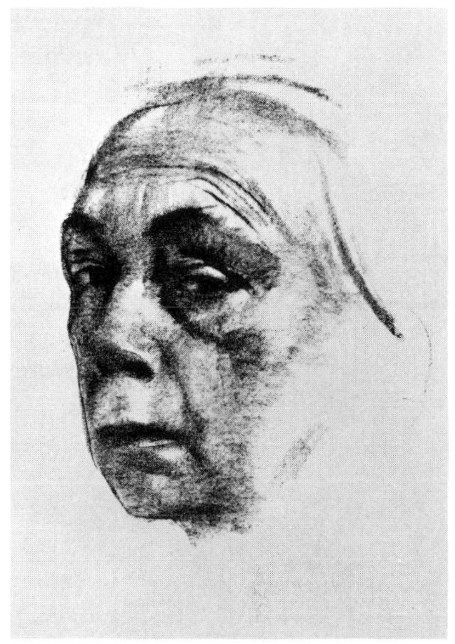

left: 256. MARIO AVATI. *Nature Morte aux Trois Pepins.* c. 1953. Mezzotint, $10\frac{1}{4} \times 11\frac{3}{4}''$. Courtesy FAR Gallery, New York.

right: 257. KÄTHE KOLLWITZ. *Self-portrait.* 1924. Lithograph, $17 \times 12''$. Fogg Art Museum, Harvard University, Cambridge, Mass.

Planography

The hand process of planographic printing—that is, printing from a flat surface—had its origins in England and Germany in the late eighteenth century. The only major technique is called lithography.

Lithography The art of lithography is unique among the printmaking processes in that, traditionally, it incorporates the qualities of stone. In recent years lithographers have used zinc plates to make their prints, but for centuries the image to be reproduced was drawn on a special Bavarian limestone, and it is with this technique that the process is usually associated. To create a lithograph, the artist first draws on the stone with a grease pencil or with a brush or pen dipped in a greasy paintlike substance. He then treats the stone with a solution of gum arabic to make the drawn image insoluble in water and applies nitric acid, which makes the undrawn areas repellent to ink. The stone is then moistened with water. The drawn areas treated with gum arabic do not accept the water, but the undrawn areas remain moist. Thus, when ink is rolled over the surface of the stone it is retained by the drawn areas but does not adhere to the wet surfaces. The artist places damp paper onto the stone and applies pressure, thereby transfering the image to paper. The distinguishing characteristic of lithographs is a texture reminiscent of the stone itself, as evidenced by Käthe Kollwitz' *Self-portrait* (Fig. 257).

Serigraphy

Silk Screen The terms serigraphy and silk screen are interchangeable. The basic technique is described in Chapter 10 (see pp. 155–156), where it is applied to the printing of fabrics. The identical process may also be employed in making prints and posters, and several screens may be used to produce many colors. The silk-screen print reproduced in Plate 22 (p. 204) has a rich baroque quality made possible by the use of 23 separate screens. The possibilities of silk screen have been explored by contemporary artists who often combine silk screen with other media, including oil paint, to produce unique and effective results.

Printmaking and methods of reproduction have become increasingly varied with the invention of new tools and machines and the combination of two or more techniques. Plastics and slate may be carved in the same manner as wood blocks, and dentists' drills have been used as burins. Relief blocks are built up with textures of cloth and wire. No limits are prescribed as long as the artist achieves the effect he wants. All of these possibilities have their influence on book illustration, for printmaking of all kinds continues to be associated with mechanical reproduction, and new developments in one field inevitably affect the other.

SUMMARY

Through the centuries the thoughts of man have been preserved in various ways, culminating in the related arts of bookmaking and printmaking. There are two types of book design: the book that has wide distribution in the popular market and the hand-bound book created by master craftsmen.

The cover or jacket design of a popular book serves the function of packaging and attracts potential buyers. It should be integrated with the choice of paper, type, and layout to create a total design that is both attractive and appropriate to the contents.

Mechanical methods of illustration and printing are divided into three general categories: relief, intaglio, and planography. The relief method is called letterpress, intaglio printing is known as gravure, and planography includes offset lithography and collotype. Any of these may be used to reproduce line cut, halftone, or four-color illustrations.

Hand bookbinding is the work of a few devoted craftsmen who are thoroughly trained in a long tradition of binding and leatherwork. The basic purpose of this type of binding is the preservation of the text, yet bookbinders through the centuries have taken great pride in creating beautiful works of art.

The art of printmaking has a very long history, and contemporary printmakers still employ techniques that have been in use for centuries. Printmaking techniques are classified in the same categories as are mechanical processes. Relief methods include woodcut, linocut, and wood engraving; intaglio prints may be made by engraving, drypoint, etching, aquatint, or mezzotint techniques; and the major planographic process is lithography. A fourth category, serigraphy or silk screen, is also used for the multiple production of images. Contemporary artists often combine methods to produce new and exciting effects.

New developments—tools, materials, and machines—affect both bookmaking and printmaking, for the two arts continue to be associated.

Design for Selling

chapter 15

Advertising art is an expression of its time. It depicts modern life in all its ramifications, and, in addition, it clearly indicates by its very nature that it is a form of communication designed to be viewed by people in a hurry, people with many things on their minds, people whose attention must be caught and held a moment in spite of themselves.

Advertising art has existed at least since 3000 B.C., when the ancient Sumerians employed pictures to advertise their wares, and rather elaborate pictorial signs have been known ever since the Middle Ages in Western Europe, but never before has the consumer been so rushed and harried and advertising so competitive as in the twentieth century. Although the red-and-white-striped barber pole and the three balls of the pawnbroker's shop were once sufficient to announce the existence of a service, today's businessman feels the need to prove not only that his store or service is there, but that it is better than others available. To do this he depends upon brighter colors, bigger lettering, and flashier signs than those of his competitors. Fortunately, he has also come to depend upon the services of the artist.

THE ARTIST AND ADVERTISING

The question often arises: Is advertising design really art? No matter how one answers this question, it is nevertheless true that advertising requires the talents of people who have a sound and thorough art training. The role of the artist is indeed essential for the achievement and maintenance of high standards in advertising design.

The earliest known advertising agency opened its doors in England in 1812. Since then advertising has become a multimillion dollar industry. Because of the tremendous economic power it wields, the advertising industry virtually controls the destinies of the mass communications media, and through them it exerts great influence upon the public.

Advertising agencies are directed by men who know the psychology of selling and have on their staffs experienced and knowledgeable art directors. It is the job of the art director to put the advertising *campaigns* into forms suitable for magazines,

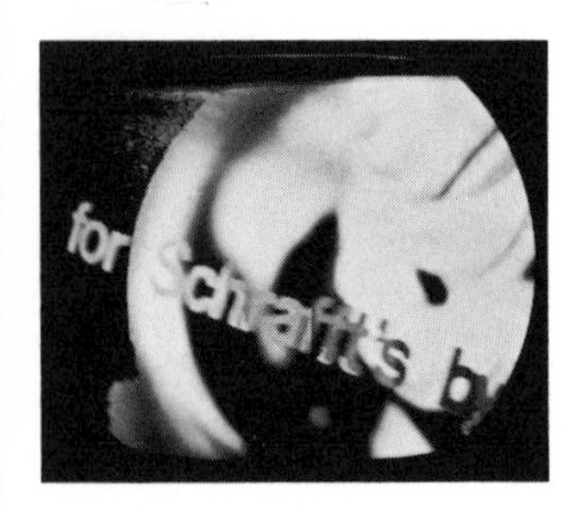

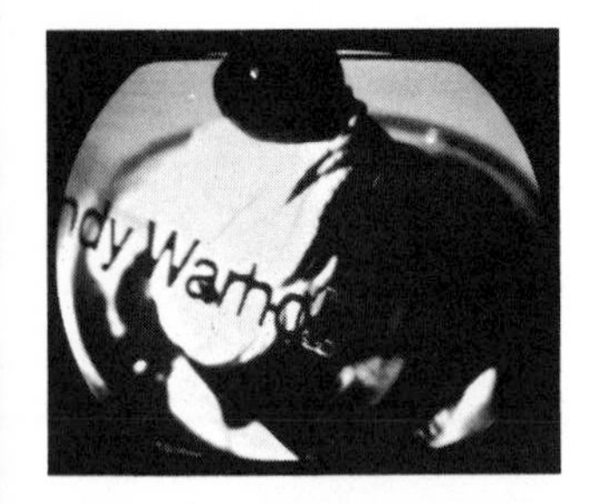

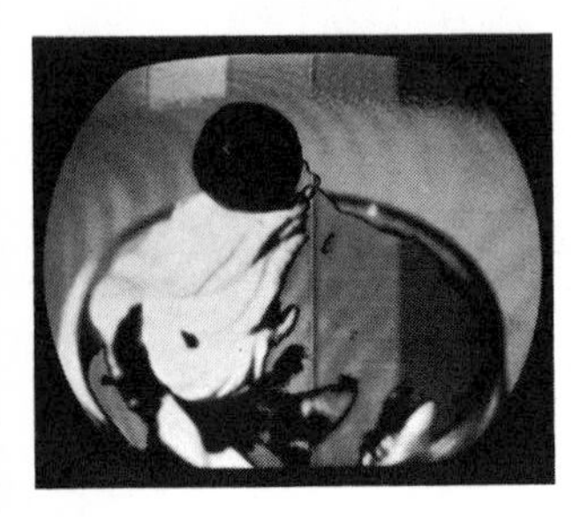

newspapers, and television. When an art director reaches an understanding with a client, he turns to the graphic artists and copywriters on the agency's staff to create the proposed designs and the text, or *copy*. This procedure is often reversed, however. The copywriter first decides on the text for the advertisement and then submits this to the art director, whose staff artists design the *layout* and provide the *illustration*. Some agencies also employ free-lance artists who have achieved recognition outside the field of advertising. Such artists as Andy Warhol, who created the award-winning Schrafft's commercial (Fig. 258), and the American painter James Hill, who painted the head of Edgar Allan Poe reproduced in Figure 259, bring originality and a high level of excellence to the advertisements they design. In recent years it has become fashionable for an advertiser to commission a "name" designer who will then demand of the client carte blanche to do whatever kind of ad he wishes. This has resulted in some extremely creative—and successful—advertising campaigns.

ADVERTISEMENT AS ART

Answers to the philosophical question of what constitutes a work of art have filled many volumes. There is, however, no clear dividing line between what is art and what is not. An advertisement can and at times does fulfill the requisites of a work of art. First of all, however, it must satisfy the requirements of good advertising: it must create a demand for the client's product. To accomplish this, the advertisement embodies some of the same principles of design that have been discussed throughout the book. Only in this way can the ad attract attention, hold interest, and put forward a clear, precise, and succinct idea.

The first of these principles is balance. The elements in the advertising layout should be arranged to achieve the harmony and balance that can ensure the viewer's immediate and favorable reaction. The balance might be symmetrical, as in the Volkswagen ad in Figure 260. The copy and headline are centered below the illustration to create a classically symmetrical composition. This simple, forthright style is carried through in Volkswagen's entire advertising campaign, and the public has learned to associate it with Volkswagen. Once this kind of identification is established, it is possible to create an ad such as the one reproduced in Figure 261, in which only the monogram "VW" provides a clue to the product.

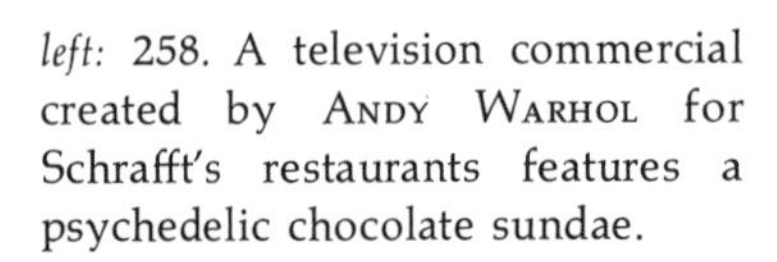
left: 258. A television commercial created by Andy Warhol for Schrafft's restaurants features a psychedelic chocolate sundae.

right: 259. Painter James Hill created a distinctive institutional advertisement for John Hancock Mutual Life Insurance Company.

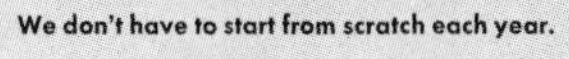

A second principle is emphasis. In a complex layout there must be a hierarchy of elements that present a logical development from the dominant element to the least important. The Dansk ad reproduced in Figure 262 ably demonstrates how the illustration and the copy in *boldface* immediately attract the eye, giving emphasis to the essentials in the layout and, by contrast, creating interest in the information contained in the smaller and lighter type. The boldface copy and the illustration are the most important elements in this hierarchy and serve the client's purpose by putting across his message quickly and clearly.

The third principle is unity. The layout must be planned and executed as a whole, with all the elements working together to express a single idea. This idea may be strengthened by emotional overtones, as in the advertisement for sneakers seen

above left: 260. Clear, uncluttered photographs and forthright copy with low-key humor have become the trademark of the advertisements for Volkswagen of America.

above right: 261. So readily identifiable is the Volkswagen style of advertising that the name of the product is not even mentioned in this ad.

right: 262. This award-winning advertisement for Dansk Designs Ltd. juxtaposes the clean lines of flatware against the pure form of fruit.

left: 263. Highly expressive of the product is this advertisement showing old and new sneakers.

below: 264–265. Two advertisements for Coca-Cola emphasize a spirit of conviviality.

in Figure 263. A photograph of a new pair of sneakers alone might well have conveyed information about the appearance of the shoes, but it would not in any way have expressed their comfortable familiarity. Even the position of the old pair with the overlapping toes suggests the casual manner in which they are worn and recalls those times, perhaps, when one is most completely at ease. There is no need here to advertise in an urgent manner or to employ the "hard sell," for people do not have to be convinced. Sneakers, the copy explains, are "as classic as a string of pearls, as basic as a black dress." The advertisement is simply telling us that the old familiar style has survived and is still available. All the elements in its format work together as a unified whole to express effectively and simply this one idea.

The Coca Cola advertisements in Figures 264 and 265 offer superb examples of unity. The Coke bottle is placed conspicuously in the illustration and is surrounded by the ingredients of a picnic lunch or a summer snack. Again the viewer is confronted with a single idea, an idea that likewise evokes an emotional response, memories of past picnics and snacks on hot summer afternoons.

If the advertisement achieves its goal by means of one of these three principles and makes the viewer conscious of the product involved, it has fulfilled its function. In this way it also meets a criterion of good design. Strong design, of course, is not necessarily fine art. Yet, occasionally, an advertisement does indeed qualify as a work of art. The "Portfolios of Great Ideas" sponsored by the Container Corporation of America include some very remarkable and beautiful advertisements (Figs. 266–268). In them are illustrated the work of painters, sculptors, and designers whose commission was to interpret the great ideas of man in an associative relationship between the visual arts and literature and philosophy. Designed originally as a series of advertisements for *Time,* the portfolios contain a separate plate for each "idea," and each is composed of a commissioned painting or sculpture and the related quotation. The name of the sponsor is discreetly placed at the bottom of the layout.

266–268. An admirable collaboration between art and industry has been achieved in the portfolios by Container Corporation of America.

above left: 266. Lines from Dylan Thomas are expressed visually by JOHN MASSEY.

above right: 267. A quotation from Alfred North Whitehead is interpreted with a painting by HERBERT BAYER.

right: 268. Fyodor Dostoievski's words are expressed in a painting by REGINALD POLLACK.

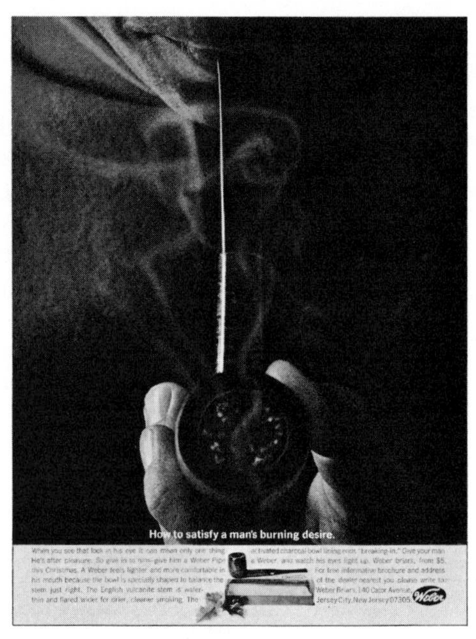

left: 269. Guerlain projects the spirit of a perfume with this classic photograph.

above: 270. Onofrio Paccione designed and photographed this ad for Weber Briars.

Equally remarkable is the ad for Guerlain perfume illustrated in Figure 269. The reader's eye is caught and held by the stark beauty of a classic Oriental profile and masses of gleaming hair. Thus, the name of Guerlain is quietly associated with an image of dramatic elegance. This is surely one of the finest recent examples of advertising art.

KINDS OF ADVERTISING

The public is exposed daily to at least two specific kinds of advertising. Magazines, newspapers, and television screens are filled with designs and pictures publicizing specific products. They also carry a second kind of advertising, one that is concerned with services. The latter promotes the services offered by such enterprises as insurance companies (Fig. 259), car rental agencies, and airlines. One might add a third kind of advertisement—that providing information of public interest and concern. This includes the antismoking campaign, announcements of charity drives, and statements in behalf of the United Nations. Most large agencies handle at least one such campaign as a public service without remuneration.

A second method of categorizing advertisements is by the result the advertiser hopes to achieve, and in this context the ad may be either direct or indirect. *Direct advertising* is called for when immediate results are expected. Department stores, for example, usually prefer this approach. They list telephone numbers in their ads so that customers can call in their orders, or else they provide coupons that customers can fill in and mail. Grocery and department stores often announce special sales, striking a note of urgency by suggesting that prices will soon be higher. Direct advertising may also fill an immediate need. Overshoes advertised in a newspaper on the day of a bad storm usually sell very well.

Holiday advertising makes the most of the direct approach, showing every kind of commodity as an adjunct to festivity or as a possible gift. In Figure 270, the deftly held pipe bowl, the polished wood of the stem, and the subtle wisps of smoke curling in the background all imply a relaxed atmosphere that is underlined by the copy. The catch line makes use of a *double-entendre,* followed by the words, "When you see that look in his eye it can mean only one thing. He's after pleasure. So give it to him—give him a Weber pipe this Christmas." The sprig of holly suggests the forthcoming holiday and brings to mind an image of a family gathered before the hearth and Christmas tree. The viewer is led to believe that the pipe is indeed an essential part of this picture.

Indirect advertising, on the other hand, is effective for building a reputation and establishing the desirability of a product or a service, with an emphasis on future as well as immediate results. Much magazine advertising is of this type. Consumers may become interested in the merchandise promoted and, later, when shopping, remember the brand name and ask for it. The Dansk advertisement (Fig. 262) is an excellent example of this type of advertising. Each ad in the series presents a different product, carefully arranged and beautifully photographed, so that the name Dansk gradually becomes linked in the public's mind with simplicity and good taste. Similarly, the catch phrase in the copy for the Coca Cola advertisements—"things go better with Coke after Coke after Coke"—acts as a theme that runs through the ads of an entire campaign, giving unity to a comprehensive promotional scheme.

Many organizations employ both direct and indirect advertising to achieve different goals. This is seen particularly in the advertising campaigns of the various airlines. The Federal Government controls air routes, and in order to avoid giving unfair advantage to one airline or another, it assigns at least two carriers to every major route. The Government also regulates fares, which are identical between any two points for each line serving those cities. The airlines, therefore, must use other devices to attract customers. Direct advertising is aimed at the traveler who has already made up his mind to go on a trip and who has two or three airlines to choose from. It stresses greater comfort, better food, more exciting entertainment, or ingenious methods for keeping children occupied. This type of advertising flourishes in peak tourist seasons and is concentrated in the cities from which people do much traveling. Indirect advertising, however, attempts to build a favorable image of a particular airline in the minds of the general public. It is aimed at people who have no immediate plans to travel or who, if compelled to travel, might be more disposed toward train, bus, or automobile. When these people do plan a trip, they will remember that a particular airline is "friendly" (Fig. 274) or "safe," and they will choose that one over the others. Indirect advertising can create a general sense of confidence in air travel and cause travelers to decide in favor of a trip by air instead of one by sea or rail.

A special category of indirect advertising is the *institutional* advertisement which has as its aim the creation of goodwill for a particular firm or organization. The Bell Telephone Company, admittedly a monopoly, built such a campaign around the slogan, "We may be the only phone company in town . . . but we try not to show it!" The Container Corporation's "Great Ideas" series (Figs. 266–268) says virtually nothing about that company's product. It does, however, create an enduring effect upon the viewer by means of the original art and understated quotations, an effect consonant with the public image that the corporation wishes to maintain.

ADVERTISING MEDIA

Advertising has come a long way since the days when a journeyman painter visited the farmer whose barn had the proper exposure and painted "Carter's Little Liver Pills" on the roof or wall in letters high enough to be seen by people driving nearby in their Model T's. The barn advertisement evolved into the billboard, a medium so popular for advertising that highways approaching cities soon became veritable corridors, whose walls of signs concealed most of the adjacent scenery. However, as man's clutter has extended farther and farther beyond the cities, a new respect for the natural countryside has arisen, and it is to be hoped that eventually the billboards will be completely removed. Always banned from national highways and many local turnpikes, the billboard has now been voted out of existence in more than half the states, and other states may legislate against it in the near future. The billboard, with its quick message directed at motorists, is relinquishing its position to the car radio. Meanwhile, the same sort of advertising will continue in posters, which are more adaptable than billboards to frequent change.

The travel poster is a kind of classic, having long been a decorative fixture in classrooms, playrooms, and in the private collections of inveterate daydreamers. The examples in Figures 271–272 show two approaches, one whimsical and the other realistic. The merry-go-round atmosphere of the poster for India (Fig. 271) is as colorful as a bazaar, suggesting the exotic qualities of the East and stressing the gaity and excitement of a country characterized by tremendous cultural contrasts. This is make-believe imagery, of course, for it is probable that nowhere in India would the traveler find anything quite like the scene depicted here. Flying into San Francisco, however, the visitor would see something very much like the panoramic view reproduced in the poster in Figure 272, and he is likely to retain forever thereafter a similar image of the Bay City. The poster depicts the spirit of the city as well as its physical appearance—the harbor, the Golden Gate Bridge, the tower on Telegraph Hill, and the clusters of white buildings spread over sides of the city's hills. Above these landmarks the seagulls convey the feeling of the open sea and far places, from which so much of San Francisco's color is derived. In both of these posters there is a feeling that attracts the viewer and emphasizes the lure of travel.

An important advantage of magazine advertising is that it reaches a national audience and is effective for nationally distributed products or services. It can also

271–272. Travel posters offer colorful opportunities for design, ranging from the whimsical to the nostalgic.

serve the interests of a limited number of large stores that solicit mail orders or the patronage of people who visit metropolitan centers frequently. The necessity of having to prepare copy months in advance limits magazine ads to products of reasonable stability. The need for a quick and catchy message is not so urgent here, since it is assumed that anyone with time to look through a magazine will stop occasionally to read an interesting advertisement. The principal need is for a provocative headline or a design that will arouse curiosity or make a strong impression.

The newspaper remains the primary means of advertising for retail stores, for persons and firms offering services, for such institutions as banks and insurance companies, and for local tradesmen. Because the newspaper carries the current news, it is read more avidly than other advertising media by what its advertisers can assume to be a receptive audience. Advertising design for newspapers varies from involved layouts to single fashion illustrations. Department stores spend 70 to 90 percent of their total advertising budget for newspaper ads.

Handbills and package enclosures are less widely used but still require the skills of a layout designer and, occasionally, an artist. Package enclosures in particular are likely to need drawings or designs to provide instructional information.

Television is the chief contender for primacy in American advertising. Its effectiveness as an advertising medium is dependent on the elements and principles of design, which themselves acquire a new dynamic quality once they have been applied to the time, space, and movement characteristics of television. The television screen brings information to the viewer with little effort on his part, and this basic facility makes possible a tremendous impact. Size, shape, color, line, texture, and mass are directed to make an immediate impression on the eye and mind, and the principles of form, rhythm, unity, and variety can be seen in action in a wide range of commercials, from the simple spot announcement to the restrained and tasteful advertisements for Hallmark, Xerox, and other similar sponsors.

The field of television advertising is both broad and challenging. With young people spending an average of 1200 hours a year before the television screen, the responsibility of the television designer becomes a vital one. Much television advertising employs exaggerations that may mislead the young. Commercials handled with taste and integrity, on the other hand, can have a far-reaching effect, stimulating favorable responses because their claims seem reasonable. The use of humor provides a subtle and often charming way of presenting the sponsor's message (Fig. 273).

273. The cartoon technique is used with subtlety and wit in this commercial for Alka-Seltzer. Here a man is seen in heated argument with his much-abused stomach.

274. A specific type face may become identified with a particular advertiser, as in the case of United Air Lines.

The positive aspects of the television potential are so challenging that the negative possibilities must be fully realized in order to redirect their adverse effect into proper channels. Originality and ingenuity are essential to counteract the boredom inevitably generated by continued repetition or the overuse of the trite and obvious. Designing for television is one of the most promising opportunities available to the graphic designer, an area in which a simple catchword or slogan can be caught up overnight in the national life and a new product impressed upon the general consciousness in a matter of minutes.

TYPE AND LAYOUT

Because of the growth of advertising, the twentieth century has seen the development of type design in a seemingly infinite variety. Type created especially to express a specific product or feeling is not unusual. The type reproduced in Figure 274 was not designed especially for United Air Lines, but it is still quite distinctive. The flowing script suggests flight and at the same time enhances the feeling of "friendliness" that United hopes to induce. Since type is the medium through which the message is articulated, its importance to the advertisement cannot be overestimated. This importance carries over into the body of the copy that supplements the drawing or design. The copy is the substance of the advertisement, giving relevant information to enable the viewer to know what is being advertised and why. Not only must the copy be legible, but it must be placed in such a way that it can be read quickly and without effort. Although the illustration or design is usually the dominant factor in attracting interest, the copy serves to reinforce or explain it.

PACKAGING

Even after a product is skillfully advertised, it may yet gain or lose a sale because of its packaging. In these days of self-service markets, it is quite possible for a customer to go shopping for one product and substitute another because its package looks more appealing. Attractive packaging performs several functions: (1) it helps to sell the merchandise by identifying and distinguishing it from competing articles; (2) it facilitates a better display, thus making it easier for the merchant to put the article before the public; (3) it frequently improves the appearance of the merchandise itself; (4) it helps to keep the product clean and attractive; and (5) it reduces selling time, effort, and cost.[1]

left: 275–276. A feeling of feminine elegance is imparted to products in the "Ultima" series.

below: 277. Men's toiletries require a more rugged, masculine format.

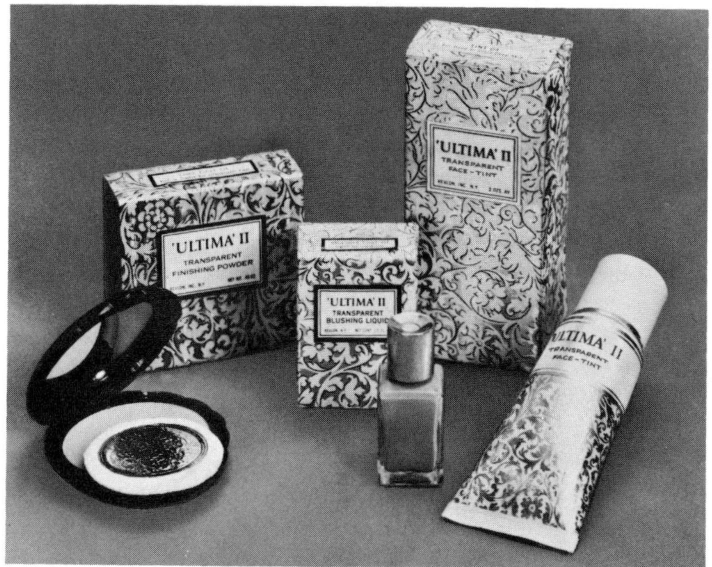

The role of the artist in package design can have a marked effect on sales, and it involves a knowledge of the principles of design as well as an active imagination. An example of ingenuity in packaging women's toiletries is the Ultima series by Revlon (Figs. 275–276), in which a floral pattern is carried as a theme throughout the promotion of a line of related products. The design used on boxes, tubes, and bottles gives a feeling of elegance and femininity. The same floral pattern is applied to posters and other display materials, which the firm provides for merchants who sell the products. The packaging of men's toiletries, on the other hand, tends toward leather or wood textures (Fig. 277), and it frequently carries a sporting theme. Coats of arms or medallions used as labels lend an air of nobility, and touches of brasslike ornament provide the masculine version of elegance comparable to that achieved in the floral design for women's cosmetics.

278–280. Packaging for household items is most effective when a convenient, efficient container is combined with simple design and clear type.

Although the packaging of products for personal use stresses elegance or status, that of foodstuffs or household necessities requires a different approach. The emphasis is usually on health and cleanliness and on the ease with which household tasks can be accomplished. The beauty of polished surfaces, which denote fastidious housekeeping, is the primary concern of the Johnson Company (Figs. 278–280). Clean lines, simple shapes, and clear lettering are the keynotes of their packaging, which makes use of one or two bright colors for accent.

Chapter 14 noted that book jackets are essentially a matter of packaging. The same thing can be said for record albums. Photography plays a part in the design of many album covers, but there is also an opportunity in the packaging of records for the graphic designer to create something quite imaginative. The examples in Figures 281 and 282 are not only interesting compositions in themselves, but they successfully direct the viewer's interest to the music the albums contain.

ETHICS IN ADVERTISING

The designer should at all times be aware of the need for ethics in advertising. We all hear regularly about the lack of integrity in advertising, about the attempts of advertisers to manipulate the public with false or misleading information and to cause it thereby to purchase products it neither needs nor wants. Advertising on television seems to be especially subject to suspicion, perhaps because television is the medium with access to the largest national audience, therefore the medium with the maximum power to influence, for good or for bad, the decisions of the consumer public. It must be admitted, however, that whatever the medium used, there is in advertising the instrument of enormous economic gain, and concomitant with this is the temptation to distort absolute truth for the sake of material profit. The designer who takes good and accurate substantive material and creates from it an attractive package or effective ad has a grateful public to greet him; he does not need to promise results that are impossible. The ads of the John Hancock Insurance Company and the Container Corporation of America arouse far more appreciation from a discriminating public than inane or insistent ads that offend the general intelligence.

281–282. The visual interpretation of music is one of the most difficult and intriguing of design problems.

right: 281. Music at MIT. Art director JACQUELINE S. CASEY.

below: 282. Violin Music of Schubert. Art director JOHN BERG.

Advertising in itself is a catalyst that brings together producer and consumer. It has been an economic necessity throughout the world for many centuries, and the questionable practices of a few have never overshadowed its importance for the many. For the artist who enjoys being in the midst of a high-pressured, vital business, advertising design can be both an adventure and a challenge.

SUMMARY

Advertising is an expression of its time. Today's advertising depicts modern life in its various aspects and caters to its hurried pace. An advertisement usually consists of two parts: the illustration and the copy, or written matter. An advertisement must create a demand for the client's product. To accomplish this effectively it employs three principles of design: (1) balance, (2) emphasis, and (3) unity. By means of these principles, the ad can (1) attract attention, (2) hold interest, and (3) put forward a clear and precise idea. There are two main kinds of ads: those that publicize specific products and those that are concerned with services. Both kinds may be either direct, urging the immediate purchase of a particular product, or indirect, planting the value of a product in the viewer's mind for future purchase.

Advertising media include billboards, posters, magazines, newspapers, coupons, catalogues, handbills, package enclosures, radio, and television. Television is a medium with unlimited possibilities. A knowledge of its possibilities for both constructive and detrimental influences is necessary before the television designer can direct his efforts effectively.

Type is an important element in advertising design and can be adapted to express almost any idea. Packaging can effect the gain or loss of a sale and is thus a vital consideration for the designer. An effective design serves several purposes: (1) it helps to sell the merchandise; (2) it facilitates a better display; (3) it frequently improves the appearance of the merchandise itself; (4) it helps keep the product clean and attractive; and (5) it reduces selling time, effort, and cost.

Advertising is an exciting field for the designer and one that is vital to the economy, for it plays a major role in bringing producer and consumer together. The ethics of advertising are of primary importance and should be the basis for any effort in the field, aiming at attracting the customer but not deceiving him.

Painting as Design

chapter 16

In the long history of painting, the subtle relationship between this art form and design has been reinterpreted many times. There has always been a design element in painting, especially in such large-scale works as the wall decorations of Egyptian tombs and Cretan palaces and in the great fresco cycles of medieval, Renaissance, and Baroque cathedrals. In easel paintings as well, design has remained a basic characteristic—the framework or composition within which the subject is developed. Generations of painters would agree with Washington Allston's remark to a student: "A painter may be blessed with every gift of nature, but unless he has acquired the art of design he can never express himself."[1]

The tumultuous evolution of twentieth-century painting—with its experimentation, its revolutionary developments, and its world-wide search for ideas—has produced many works which have been condescendingly labeled "design" rather than painting, even though they have been applied to canvas and have been hung upon a wall. The question of labels is not particularly relevant, for the definition of painting accepted one hundred years ago is now inadequate. Art critics complain that if they turn their backs for a moment, a new development appears, and works of art no longer fit the convenient pigeonholes they formerly occupied. Whether a work is a painting, a sculpture, a construction, a relief painting, or a Happening is not important; what matters here is that all of these works are fundamentally involved with some consideration of design.

PAINTING MEDIA

Before exploring design in various types of painting, it would be helpful to understand the materials artists use. The material used for a work of art is called the *medium.* In painting, the medium is determined by the *binder,* the vehicle that holds the particles of pigment in suspension and makes it possible to spread pigment as paint onto a support ground. It is the medium, therefore, that enables the painter to use pigment plastically, whether he paints with a brush or a knife. It is also possible to refine the elements further and say that the vehicle turns powder into liquid and the medium is the agent that determines the viscosity of the vehicle, its thickness or thinness. In the oil technique, linseed oil is the vehicle, and turpentine the medium.

The oldest type of painting medium appears to have been *encaustic,* a mixture of hot beeswax and pigment that was perfected by the ancient Greeks. This challenging technique has been revived by contemporary artists in their search for new effects (see Pl. 25, p. 239). The material is applied to wood with a brush or a metal instrument known as a *cauterium.* As the wax cools the cauterium is heated, and successive layers are applied, making possible considerable plasticity and intricate modeling. Heat lamps and torches may be employed to fuse wax and pigment, thereby producing unusual effects. In encaustic, the beeswax is the vehicle and heat the medium.

Tempera generally has egg as a binder, although animal and vegetable glues may also be used. It is most often applied to a *gesso* ground built up on wood panels with a mixture of white pigment, gypsum, and glue. *Casein,* with a binder of milk curd, is water soluble and may be applied to gesso panels, cardboard, paper, and other surfaces. Since ancient times wall paintings have been executed on lime plaster. If the plaster is dry, the technique is called *secco;* painting on wet plaster is known as *fresco* (see Fig. 285). For tempera, casein, and fresco, the thinning agent is water.

Oil paint came into general use in the fifteenth century. The pigment is ground and mixed with a binder of linseed oil, which dries slowly but permits precise manipulation. The artist must wait for each layer of paint to dry thoroughly so as to prevent the paint film from cracking. However, the flexibility of oil paint allows the creation of either an opaque or a translucent film, and also permits overpainting in areas the artist wants to change. Oil paint may be applied *alla prima,* that is, in one direct operation, or it may be built up in successive thin layers or *glazes.* The latter method accounts for much of the soft modeling of the Old Masters. It may also be applied *impasto,* which is paint applied so thickly, often with a palette knife, that its texture assumes an expressive role all its own. Impasto reveals something of the quality of paint as a plastic medium. The *supports* for oil paint are, typically, canvas, Masonite, or wood.

Watercolor is bound by gum arabic, while *gouache,* an opaque watercolor, contains, in addition, a paste of zinc oxide. Both are soluble in water and lend themselves to rapid painting. Used on specially prepared paper, transparent watercolor has a clarity and a sparkle that sets it apart as a medium of freshness and spontaneity.

Among recently developed media, pigments bound with *acrylic* polymer emulsion have gained wide popularity. The ingredients of this binder are produced entirely by scientific means. The small molecules of plastic are united into a single larger molecule or *monomer.* When many monomers are joined in a chemical union, they form a tough, durable *polymer.* The enduring quality of polymer makes it an important discovery for the preservation of paintings.

Because the medium of acrylics can be either water or more powerful solvents, the artist can paint them both "thick" and "thin." In acrylics, he can add glaze upon glaze, like layers of bright, transparent cellophane, and create a paint film of extraordinary inner brilliance. On the other hand, it is possible to build up thick layers of paint at once without danger of peeling. The film created is porous and allows moisture to pass through the film without cracking it. Thick white acrylic paste combined with traditional paints and applied to canvas can provide a surface for creating a *collage.* Artists today press paper, fabric, wood, wire netting, and any number of other materials into this sort of paint, to make the most of its adhesive qualities and to achieve unique effects. Some painters even work with ordinary house paints, enhancing their surface texture with plaster, sand, and gravel. Gold leaf may be applied for accent. Experimentation leads to new uses for established materials, as well as to exciting and unusual combinations of the old and the new.

ATTRIBUTES OF PAINTING

In order to understand where design leaves off and painting begins, and how a design becomes a painting, it is helpful to consider the three attributes that are traditionally associated with a painting: *subject, form,* and *content.* Form and content are actually inseparable, but for clarity they will be explored independently in their relationship to design.

Design and Subject

Giorgione's *The Holy Family* (Fig. 283) has an obvious subject, and one can see that the picture has form, not only in the individual figures and the architectural background, but in the underlying structural design, or composition, that is the basis of the whole painting. The content is the tenderness, quietude, and intimacy of a small family grouped in a humble setting. There are in the Giorgione no wise men, shepherds, or animals that often appear in representations of the Nativity, but there are dignity and warmth in the artist's portrayal of the simple family group. The Christ Child seems to be pointing, and the adults are watching him with reverence, making it clear this is no ordinary child. In spite of the everyday surroundings, it is evident that something remarkable is involved. Content, then, is the implicit feeling that the artist brings to the forms of his work, and it is this feeling or experience that one attempts to share when he approaches a work of art.

In addition to these qualities, *The Holy Family* has a strong sense of design. The structural design can be seen in the diagram in Figure 284. The composition is based

left: 283. GIORGIONE. *The Holy Family.* c. 1478–1510. Panel, $14\frac{11}{16} \times 17\frac{15}{16}''$. National Gallery of Art, Washington, D.C. (Samuel H. Kress Collection, 1952).

below: 284. Structural diagram for Fig. 283, *The Holy Family.*

on a balance between two dominant archways and the block forms of the architecture. The circular element is repeated in the arrangement of heads, spaced in such a way as to form an inverted arch in opposition to the larger arch formed by both heads and bodies. The rectangular shapes are echoed in the distance through the open archway. Here, too, is a small curve that carries the circular form through the composition, and this motif is found as well in the rocks at both sides of the painting, and in the knees of the adult figures. The painting, therefore, is composed of a series of arcs and rectangles sensitively distributed throughout the composition and tied together by the two principal arches.

The decorative design of the painting depends on the lines and shapes of the composition as well as on its color and texture. The leafy texture of the trees is balanced by the solid surfaces of the wall and floor, and the small folds in the Virgin's sleeve echo the vertical grain of the boards at the extreme left. The color is a similar study in balance, not only in hue but in value, for the light area that directs attention to the child is contrasted with a band of dark around it, then repeated at the edges of the composition where dark passages complete the balance.

This is only one example of the attention to design that is characteristic of great paintings. It is a most enlightening experience to trace the reproduction of a painting on a sheet of paper and to consider thereby the main structural lines without concern for subject. Areas of texture can be added in an abstract way, and light and dark values can be indicated. When the tracing paper is removed and examined as a design in itself, a great deal can be learned about the compositional methods of the artist and about his attitude toward structure and design.

One of the greatest design achievements of all time is the ceiling fresco of the Sistine Chapel in Rome, planned and executed by Michelangelo in the sixteenth century (Fig. 285). The problems that faced the artist stagger the imagination. Over 5000 square feet of space was to be decorated, and Michelangelo had to compensate for the arch of the vault by constructing his figures in such a way that they could be viewed without distortion from the floor of the chapel 68 feet below. The artist's task was further complicated by the architecture of the building, with its lunettes (crescent-shaped areas above the arched windows) and its spandrels (triangular shapes at the corners of the room linking the walls with the vault of the ceiling). Michelangelo's masterful accomplishment is even more impressive when we realize that he completed the entire ceiling—with a total of 343 monumental figures—in just four years.

285. Michelangelo. *Creation of Adam,* detail of Sistine Ceiling. 1511. Fresco. Vatican, Rome.

Plate 23. PAUL CÉZANNE. *Chestnut Trees at the Jas de Bouffan.* 1885–87. Oil on canvas, 28¾ × 36″. Minneapolis Institute of Arts.

Plate 24. Paul Gauguin. *Mahana No Atua* (*Day of the God*). 1894. Oil on canvas, 26 × 34½″. Art Institute of Chicago.

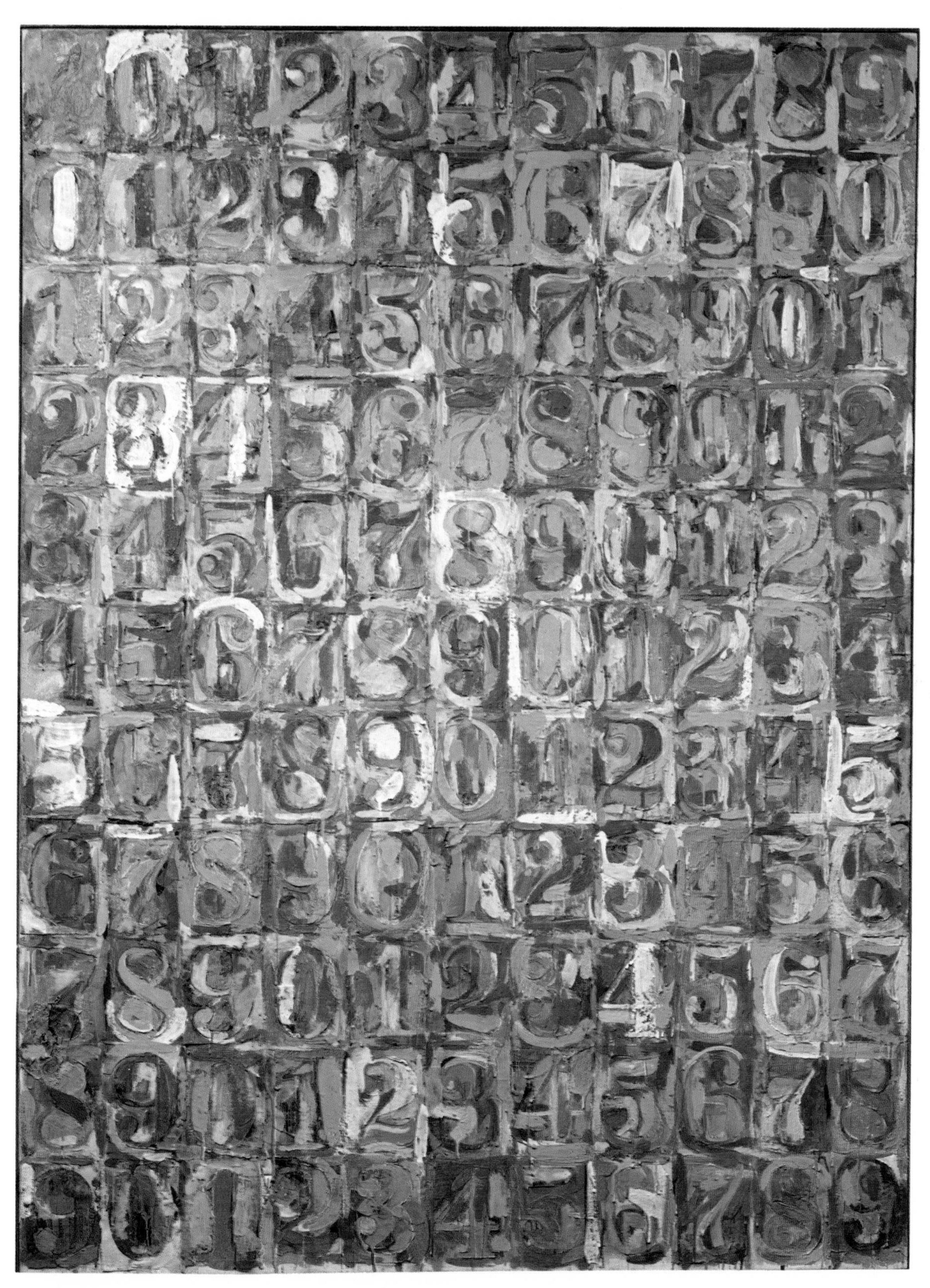

Plate 25. Jasper Johns. *Numbers in Color.* 1958–59. Encaustic and collage on canvas, 5′7″ × 4′1½″. Albright-Knox Art Gallery, Buffalo, N.Y.

Plate 26. Frank Stella. *Protractor Variation I.* 1968. Fluorescent acrylic on canvas, 5 × 10′. Courtesy Leo Castelli Gallery, New York.

The main narrative is organized into nine sections depicting three central themes—the creation of the world, the creation of man, and the origin of sin, the last of these including scenes from the life of Noah. Twenty youths, or *Ignudi* (nudes), are grouped around the nine central compartments, and these in turn are flanked by a chorus of prophets and sibyls who foretell the coming of the Redeemer. Episodes from the Bible fill the spandrels, and the lunettes contain figures representing the ancestors of Christ who further anticipate His coming.

The problems of design preceded but did not surpass the physical difficulties involved in the fresco technique in which color is applied directly to a wet layer of lime plaster. If the plaster were allowed to remain unpainted for more than a day, a film of lime would form that later would cause the painting to look patchy; and if the plaster were not properly mixed, a scum of mold would accumulate. Michelangelo had to execute the work from a high scaffolding, from which it was impossible to view the total effect. Consequently, it was imperative that he work out a meticulous design in detail on full-sized drawings called *cartoons.*

No reproduction can do justice to a composition of such size and scope. It must be seen to appreciate the intricacy of the design. Yet even a detail, such as *The Creation of Man* (Fig. 285), gives a sense of the dynamism, balance, and structure of the entire work. The *contrapposto,* or counterpoise of body motion, as in the figure of God, is a dominant Michelangelesque characteristic. This movement contributes tremendously to the impact of the work, providing strong rhythmic patterns in which forms and values are balanced one against the other. The white frescoed background, contrasted with the darker values of the painting, creates an interplay of negative and positive forms. The content is revealed in the powerful figure of God as He reaches to touch life into the quiescent figure of Adam, shown at the moment before he receives a will and personality of his own. Michelangelo has thus suggested that the creative act of God was a spiritual act as well. These two figures are the nucleus from which radiates the story of mankind in all its aspirations and follies.

Design and Form

Paul Cézanne devoted a lifetime to the study of form and its relationship to color. Like the Impressionists before him, he moved from the studio into the open air to capture natural sunlight on his subjects. However, he felt that the Impressionists, in their preoccupation with the fleeting effects of light on color, had lost the sense of structural solidity. Such artists as Claude Monet (Pl. 2, p. 40) and Camille Pissarro (Fig. 286) captured the sparkle of sunlight in a way that had not been achieved before,

286. CAMILLE PISSARRO. *La Place du Havre.* 1893. Oil on canvas, 23 × 28″. Art Institute of Chicago.

287. Nicolas Poussin. *Landscape with the Burial of Phocion.* 1648. Oil on canvas, 3′11″ × 5′10½″. Louvre, Paris.

yet their shimmering color, applied in small dotlike strokes, gave the surfaces of their canvases the allover quality of a tapestry in which solid forms were subservient to light and texture. Cézanne's objective was to paint "Poussin from nature." Nicholas Poussin (Fig. 287) was a seventeenth-century classical painter who carefully constructed his landscapes and figures according to the principles of ancient Roman architecture and sculpture. Like most traditional painters, he used somewhat restrained color. It was this classical heritage, this structural integrity, that Cézanne was to restate for the twentieth century.

Cézanne painted many still lifes, portraits, and landscapes, striving always to combine form with color, whether the form was an apple, a figure, or a stone building. Many of his landscapes were executed in his native Provence, a territory in southeastern France. In Plate 23 (p. 237) one senses the solidity of the wall and buildings and knows that they are anchored securely in the ground. The hills are firm and heavy, and the trees have a strong feeling of weight as well as of pattern. The design is lyrical and rhythmic, with an *architectonic* quality, a term used to describe a sense of structure as though the painting were actually built of solid forms. The rhythm flows through the branches of the trees and is echoed in the smaller trees in the background, with a strong counterpoint provided by the horizontal forms of the wall. The repetition of the solid buildings in the hills and the rhythm of the trees provide two motifs woven together into a unity.

Cézanne's contemporary, Paul Gauguin, interpreted form as a series of musical harmonies bound together in rich colors. Gauguin had been a successful stockbroker, an art collector, and an amateur painter when, quite consciously, he determined to change his life and devote it entirely to art—painting, sculpture, and ceramics. After working in Paris, Brittany, and Arles, as well as in Martinique, he left France in 1891 for Tahiti, where he hoped to develop a new art based on the pure, primitive, natural life of Polynesia—to realize an art and a life yet unpolluted by European industrialization. *The Day of the God* (Pl. 24, p. 238) is strong in both color and design

far left: 288. Georges Braque. *Violin.* 1910. Oil on canvas, 46 × 29″. Kunstmuseum, Basel.

left: 289. Marc Chagall. *I and the Village.* 1911. Oil on canvas, 6′3⅝″ × 4′11⅝″. Museum of Modern Art, New York (Mrs. Simon Guggenheim Fund).

and in the simple rhythms basic to nature. It is a triangular composition rising to an apex in the figure of the god, whose shape is repeated in reflections in the water. The balance is almost symmetrical: a central figure flanked by recumbent forms, and the trees in the left background measured against the bulk of the mountains on the right. The pattern of light and dark is fluid and rhythmic, and it is related to the floral designs in the garments of the native women. These colorful native rhythms, as well as the flat, abstract forms that express them, had a pronounced influence on later painters. Cézanne's sense of structure and Gauguin's warmth and poetry represent two elements that have appeared repeatedly in contemporary painting.

When subject matter is as important as it is in the works of Giorgione, Michelangelo, Cézanne, and Gauguin, careful analysis of a painting is necessary to appreciate fully the qualities of design that make it a masterpiece. However, when form and color overshadow subject matter, the design is readily apparent. Among the first painters to move from an emphasis on subject matter to a concentration on form were the Cubists. In the early part of the twentieth century this group, spearheaded by Georges Braque and Pablo Picasso, translated Cézanne's interest in form into an abstract development in which people and objects were depicted in terms of geometric planes (Fig. 288). In Braque's *Violin,* as in all abstract paintings, there is a point of departure from an actual model, yet in his preoccupation with overlapping forms, the artist has deemphasized both subject matter and color. The painting is a harmony of lines, shapes, and planes, simplified to their most essential structures. The curves of the violin are echoed at intervals throughout the painting to create a rhythm of repetition. Patterns of light and dark also lend rhythm and balance in their flowing distribution, and unity is created by the interplay of lines and angles.

A conscious subordination of subject matter to design is obvious in Marc Chagall's *I and the Village* (Fig. 289). Drawing on his childhood memories of a small village in the Ukraine, Chagall has worked out a dreamlike scene in which the images are recognizable, but are combined in unexpected relationships. This device is also used in *Surrealism,* an art based on the activities of the subconscious. In *I and the Village* a circle dominates the canvas, drawing together the heads of a man and a cow, who regard each other amicably. A village street in the background balances the triangle formed by the man's hand and the leaves he holds, while a peasant and his wife duplicate the scale of the small figures of the cow and milkmaid. The wife is turned upside down, partially as a concession to design, for in this position her arms continue the diagonal of the peasant's scythe. The colors of this painting are soft and ethereal, and the values carry through in a rhythmic pattern. The overlapping planes are reminiscent of Cubism, but they do not completely obscure the subject matter.

Design and Content

All of these paintings have content, a quality related to subject matter but with more far-reaching implications. Content cannot always be put into words any more than the harmonies of music can be fully understood from a printed score; yet one is just as conscious of its presence as one is of the mellow tone of a violin. In a painting with an explicit subject matter, the content usually is not difficult to grasp. It is the peacefulness of a landscape, the heroic quality of a battle scene, the serenity of an old woman. It is the weatherbeaten aspect of an ancient barn that tells of howling winds and glaring sun, or the gnarled resistance of a tree that stands alone in spite of mountain gales. One does not always *see* the content; one sees the form, and the content is transmitted because of the way the form is handled.

This statement also holds true in a painting without subject matter. In this case, however, the content is part of the design, and it can be more elusive. One must learn to sense it as he learns to appreciate the nonobjective form. This requires an emotional or intuitive response that goes beyond intellectual appreciation of the artist's genius. Just as one comes to accept the existence of a microscopic world that has never been seen, and of the infinite cosmos whose immensity cannot be fathomed, so one must be willing to unlock the doors opening from the conscious world to that of the spirit, as it is explored in modern painting, sculpture, music, poetry, and theater. In the seventeenth century, the French philosopher Blaise Pascal speculated that human knowledge is like a sphere continually increasing, so that the larger its volume, the greater the number of points of contact with the unknown. Three centuries later this idea applies not only to the expanding fields of science, but also to the new intuitive expressions of art. It has been said that Einstein's theory of relativity seems strange only when one refuses to rearrange traditional patterns of thinking. The same thing can be said of modern painting.

DIRECTIONS IN CONTEMPORARY PAINTING

Abstraction

Development of contemporary painting has followed several trends, many of international scope, relating the work of painters in several countries by their common preoccupation with interpretations of space, form, and content. A large body of this work can be categorized as abstraction, which in varying degrees is independent of its original model. Abstract painting made its first tentative appearance in the

290. WASSILY KANDINSKY. *Composition #2*. 1910. Oil on canvas, 3′2¼″ × 4′3¾″. Solomon R. Guggenheim Museum, New York.

years preceding World War I and soon became a dynamic expression of the twentieth century, with its chaos, experimentation, and restlessness. Out of this development a variety of approaches have evolved, many of them completely removed from the realm of the objective.

Wassily Kandinsky, founder, following the Revolution, of the Russian Academy of Arts and Sciences, used rhythmic lines and exotic colors to achieve a high degree of abstraction. In Figure 290 one can see that he has started with recognizable subject matter and refined it drastically to create a painting in which forms and colors, values and lines are more important than the original objects. Kandinsky, who later became a teacher at the Bauhaus, turned to nonobjective painting as early as 1910. He was determined to free his work from all reference to known objects in order to express pure sensations and moods much as music evokes the same responses without the need for words.

Expressionism

Expressionism was a movement that developed in Germany before World War I. It drew its influence from Vincent van Gogh, Edvard Munch, and the Fauves, or "wild beasts," who were active in France in the first decade of the twentieth century. The aim of the Expressionist artist has been either to express the emotions aroused in him by his subject or to depict the inner nature of that subject. A similar effect can be seen in the earlier work of certain Gothic sculptors and in the paintings of El Greco (Pl. 1, p. 39), whose style projects a strong and expressive quality.

above: 291. Jackson Pollock. *Number I.* 1948. Oil on canvas, 5′8″ × 8′8″. Museum of Modern Art, New York.

left: 292. Microscopic view of areolar tissue.

Abstract Expressionism is a style that became indigenous to the New York scene in the decade just following World War II. The work of Jackson Pollock (Fig. 291) is representative of its most radical form. Trained by Thomas Hart Benton to paint with meticulous realism, Pollock gradually developed a more personal expression. His large canvases were often spread on the floor, while he jabbed color at them or strode violently back and forth dribbling paint, layer upon layer, in intricate allover patterns. The longer one studies the work the more one sees planes of color and activity vibrating, changing, developing. As in all paintings, Pollock's work requires continued observation if it is to convey its message. In seeking this message, one might find it interesting to note the similarity between the form of *Number I* and a microscopic view of tissue of a leaf (Fig. 292). It is possible that the artist in his striding and flinging of paint unconsciously touched on a rhythm basic to nature. In any case, Pollock's revolutionary canvases were among the influences that made American painting for the first time a respected force in world art.

Abstract Expressionism took many forms, embracing both works of art built up in swaths of color and those composed of free-form color patches and dribbles. A common characteristic was the new monumental size. Franz Kline's *Mahoning* (Fig. 293) is typical of this school of art. Its dimensions are nearly 7 feet by 9 feet. Kline painted in broad energetic brush strokes, usually black on white, suggesting the conflict of opposing forces. His giant forms seem to collide in mid-air like falling girders, and yet they appear to be held in suspension by the impact. It is possible to see in Kline's work the clash of basic forces everywhere—in the stresses and strains of construction and reconstruction, in the essential conflict between good and evil, and in the myriad facets of interpersonal relationships. His often violent physical expression is a coming to terms with the conflicts inherent in everyday life, and these conflicts provide his content.

The physical activity involved in the work of painters like Pollock and Kline gave rise to the term "action painting." Such a term acknowledges both the dynamic, painterly quality evident in *Number 1* and *Mahoning* and the spectator's *kinesthetic* response to works of this character. Implicit in action painting (and not all Abstract Expressionist painters worked in the "action" mode) is the sensation of movement and tension that it causes the viewer to experience, more or less throughout his being. Artists concerned for kinesthesia seek to evoke in the viewer the same kind of sensory response that the spectator might feel in watching ice skaters and ballet dancers, or the same sense of physical and emotional involvement that the painter experienced in working his canvas.

In such works as *Number I* and *Mahoning,* the question of design moves to an intuitive plane rather than an intellectual one. It is not possible to dissect these paintings and come up with clear statements that prove they have a traditional design quality; but as the viewer develops his sensitivity, he can realize that they are satisfying both as design and as works of art. Pollock and Kline were both artists of high purpose and seriousness, and the viewer may be certain that these painters, new and innovationary as their esthetic was, were fully aware of the weight and value of line, form, texture, rhythm, and balance.

Abstract Expressionism was a powerful style that polarized the interests and forces of modern art for almost a decade, but like all such movements, this one was confronted by ideas that have been in reaction against both its abstraction and its subjective, expressionistic character.

Dadaism

In the years following World War II the directions that had been charted in the first half of the twentieth century led to an explosion of hitherto unimagined expressions. During and after World War I a group of young artists, sensing the futility of a world ravaged by war, created the Dada movement. The very name adopted by the Dadaists demonstrates the whimsical contempt these avant-gardists had for

293. FRANZ KLINE. *Mahoning.* 1956. Oil on canvas, 6′8″ × 8′4″. Whitney Museum of American Art, New York (gift of the Friends of the Whitney Museum).

the established institutions of Western culture. It derives from a French word—really a nonsense sound—meaning hobbyhorse. The Dadaists sought to reveal the stupidity and senselessness of a world that would indulge in mechanized killing and to prove that European society had lost all sense of moral and esthetic value. Dada exhibitions consisted of such ready-made objects as shovels labeled as works of art, a reproduction of *Mona Lisa* embellished with a moustache, a toy monkey in a frame with the label *Portrait of Cézanne* (the point of which was to label painters of representational art the "apes of nature"), and any other device that could be contrived to shock the public. The use of the atom bomb revived the distaste and rebellion that had given rise to Dada. Dadaist influence can be seen in some of the new styles that developed after World War II—from Pop Art to Minimal Art—and Dada was certainly a factor in the invention of the Happening.

Pop Art

Pop is the opposite of abstract and subjective art, for it consists of the most palpable and visible public images and artifacts in modern experience. The practice of painting objects from the world of the mass consumer had origins in England, but it was the American artist R. B. Kitaj who in 1956 gave the title Pop to a painting. The label was picked up by a critic who applied it to a burgeoning art form, and Pop Art was on its way. The movement did not attract wide attention until 1962, when five American painters exhibited works in which the commercial and mechanical aspects of twentieth-century life were exploited. Objects that had become stereotyped through constant exposure were carefully and precisely rendered as works of art. Yet even in this prescribed treatment, each man chose a different aspect of commercial vulgarity for his personal attention. Jasper Johns focused new interest on old clichés with his paintings of numbers (Pl. 25, p. 239) and the American flag. Roy Lichtenstein found his inspiration in the comic strip, which he blew up into monumental proportions. James Rosenquist chose the billboard for his subject; Robert Indiana painted traffic and commercial signs, which he reproduced with almost mechanical exactitude. Andy Warhol, in particular, raised the collective eyebrows of the public with his Campbell's soup cans. He began simply with tomato, then worked his way through the entire Campbell line, often repeating the images in grocery-shelf manner until they formed an allover pattern on the canvas. Tom Wesselman specialized in soft drink bottles and food products, such as giant hamburgers and Cokes. Television and other forms of mass communication were now fair game for serious painters.

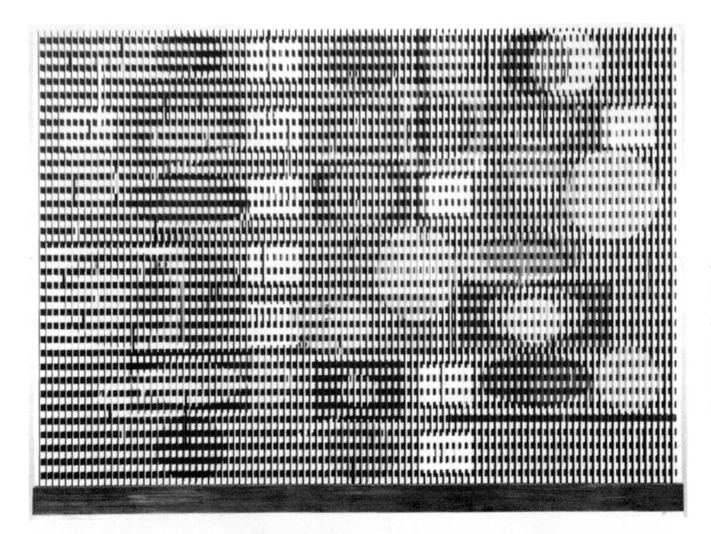

294. AGAM (YAACOV GIPSTEIN). *Double Metamorphosis II.* 1964. Oil on aluminum, in 11 sections; 8′10″ × 12′2¼″. Museum of Modern Art, New York (gift of Mr. and Mrs. George M. Jaffin).

Once the initial shock of such paintings had been sustained, quantities of critical commentary were published in an attempt to explain the new phenomenon. Marshall McLuhan, who has taken as his field the interpretation of the impact of mass communications on human perception, calls Pop Art "low-grade" imagery, in which there is little content or information, thus forcing the viewer to supply his own meaning through personal experience and associations. It has been suggested that the widespread reproduction of paintings has eliminated the value of uniqueness in a work of art, and that the Pop artists are simply reacting to this situation. Still another opinion holds that the contemporary artist is trying to develop an awareness of a stereotyped, mass-produced society by flaunting the banality of its products. In other words, he is giving modern man the "art" he has chosen to live with.

Op Art

Op Art attracted widespread notice in 1965 at the time of the Museum of Modern Art's exhibition, "The Responsive Eye." *Time* magazine takes credit for the label Op, referring to the optical illusions involved in the paintings and constructions, illusions that have long been studied by the science of optics. Painters through the centuries, notably Leonardo da Vinci and the Impressionists, have explored optical effects. Contemporary painters, however, have new luminous and fluorescent paints with which to pursue their experiments, and they can reproduce infinite numbers of tiny squares, dots, circles, and lines in vibrating and often dizzying combinations. The availability of plastics, especially Plexiglas, has encouraged artists into three-dimensional exploration as well, producing a body of work that dissolves the dividing line between painting and sculpture.

The artists themselves have various ways of expressing what they do in optical painting. Yaacov Agam calls Op Art "an adventure of the eyes" (Fig. 294), while Victor Vasarely describes his Op paintings as the integration of linear forms that produce a reaction. Richard Anuszkiewicz seeks to control the reactions of the viewer by his use of shapes and colors, thus establishing a firm contact between artist and audience. Op Art can be considered a reaction to both Abstract Expressionism and Pop Art, since it forswears both emotional expression and social commentary.

Minimal Painting

Like Op Art, Minimal Art is part of the "post-painterly abstraction" that has characterized American painting since the general departure from Abstract Expressionism in the late 1950s. It is not only abstract but aggressively nonrepresentational in its conscious avoidance of all references to figuration and to spatial illusion of the rational, Renaissance sort (see Fig. 44). Unlike the rich, impasto, painterly surfaces of the Abstract Expressionist pictures, Minimal painting usually offers immaculately smooth, unarticulated surfaces, and neat, even "hard" edges between planes of pure color. It has a linear clarity and a high-key color range that produce designs of great openness and lucidity. A "cool" art, Minimal is quite distinct from both Abstract Expressionism and Pop.

In 1960 Frank Stella began painting canvases stretched in circles, triangles, and other geometric shapes. Stella's work (Pl. 26, p. 240) has had a strong influence on other young painters, who feel that art should be completely removed from any concern with society, reality, or human interest. Stella designs his canvases with protractor and compass, and even though the colors are filled in by hand they appear to

left: 295. Zoltan Kemeny. *Vitesses Involontaires.* 1962. Copper relief, $39\frac{3}{8}$" square. Rijksmuseum Kröller-Müller, Otterlo.

below: 296. Cross section of human bone.

have been stamped out on a machine. Stella writes: "Whatever interest I have in people I have in daily contact with them. I don't want them walking around in my paintings."[2] A reviewer has described Stella's work as lacking form and content together, so that the viewer sees a painting as a unique object without human association. It is this reduction, dehumanization, and mechanization of art that have resulted in the label "minimal art," that is, art with a minimum of involvement on the part of the artist. The human element has been so diminished that entire compositions are produced by machines or drawing instruments, much as drafting or commercial art has been done in the past.

Such painting also becomes minimal by the number of traditional problems the artist has eliminated from his work. Stella makes no attempt to reproduce recognizable images of people and nature, nor does he require that his painting simulate space and movement through it. By casting out figuration and rational perspective as the legitimate interests of his art, Stella has taken upon himself a still greater responsibility than did the Old Masters. This is to create significant art out of the barest means—pure color, flat surface, and the shape of the canvas at its edges.

Relief Painting

In "relief painting"—so called because it bridges the division between painting and sculpture—the artist creates a three-dimensional effect by gluing pieces of wood, metal, plastic, or other materials to his background, and painting over or around them to create a unified design. A formal design executed in this manner can be seen in Figure 295. Zoltan Kemeny, a Roumanian artist, has created a circular design from blocks of brass in varying sizes. Kemeny's design is surprisingly similar to a microscopic view of human bone (Fig. 296). However, this comparison in no way suggests that the artist derived his inspiration from microscopic material. It simply points out that even when an artist deliberately moves away from specific reference, his work may still be very close to designs that already exist in nature.

RECENT TRENDS

In a field that changes so rapidly, it is necessary to be aware of new trends set by individual artists—trends that may, in ten years, develop into important movements for the art of the future.

The minimalization in Stella's work and that of his colleagues set the stage for introducing into art mechanical technology even more radical than that provided by drafting instruments. Recently, artists have employed motors, electric lights, and other technical equipment to provide the viewer with an art experience that goes beyond the visual. In the purely visual realm, the magazine *Computers and Automation* sponsors an annual contest in computer art, in which the entries are executed entirely by a machine programmed by an operator-artist. These works range from geometric compositions to delicate constructions that resemble natural forms (Fig. 297).

An increasingly frequent approach is the creation of polyvisual paintings, in which the aspect changes every time the viewer moves. This point of departure leads to many varieties of construction, some built in superimposed layers, others composed of planes of Plexiglas in which reflections and transparency play an active part. This new field has limitless possibilities, as can be seen in Julio Le Parc's *Continuel Lumière Mobile* (Fig. 298). The motor and lights cause the image to change

above: 297. HARUKI TSUCHIYA. *Tragedy of Seven.* 1968. Computer painting.

right: 298. JULIO LE PARC. *Continuel Lumière Mobile.* 1963. Aluminum and wood, 15′ square. Courtesy Howard Wise Gallery, New York.

continually before the viewer's eyes. Other works have accompanying sounds or smells, so that several senses increase the observer's involvement.

The new trends fall into many categories, yet one characteristic unites them—their unfettered spirit. This makes any attempt to pigeonhole and label completely futile. The fact that contemporary painting seems to express modern man's preoccupation with technology emphasizes the tendency to dissolve the wall between life, art, and science. Just as the division between painting and sculpture is being weakened, so science, technology, and art are becoming compatible. There has been a tendency to compare contemporary art unfavorably with that of past eras. But to appreciate the art of the twentieth century one must realize that this period is, inevitably, quite different from any that has gone before, and art forms naturally express the general evolution of human experience.

All the paintings discussed in this chapter have one trait in common: an attention to the principles of design. The work may be subtle or vibrant, filled with powerful form or lyrical mood. Yet with all the revolutionary aspects of twentieth-century painting, there remains one constant, a basis in design that relates it to all the manifestations of art since the beginning of time.

SUMMARY

Painting has always been associated with design. A successful painting considers the elements and principles of design.

The material used for a work of art is called the medium. Media in paintings include encaustic, tempera, oil, watercolor, gouache, and acrylic. Some painters combine paint and other materials to form a collage. The three traditional attributes of a painting are subject, form, and content.

Contemporary painting has taken several directions. By the time of World War I, abstract art had already been developed. A second major current in contemporary painting is Expressionism, a modern tradition that was continued and enriched after World War II by the New York school known as Abstract Expressionism. Pop Art is an attempt to create esthetic objects out of the commercial and mass-produced trivia of the twentieth century, while Op and Minimal Art are concerned for the purity of visual experience. Current trends are toward a fusion of art, life, science, and technology, the result of which often obscures the distinctions between painting and sculpture. Motorized paintings or constructions may demand from the viewer the response of several senses rather than that of sight alone. Even the computer is now programmed to produce works of considerable beauty, works consistent with the view of some artists that Minimal Art—art made with minimal means and without human involvement—is most appropriate for twentieth-century man. Yet even the most revolutionary developments in art have one characteristic in common with the art of the past—a basis in design.

Sculpture as Design

chapter 17

During a talk at the University of Colorado in 1956, sculptor Alexander Archipenko, was asked to discuss his work. He replied: "Creativeness is not a human endeavor. Nature does the creating but endows certain human beings with spiritual power and facility for expressing nature's creativeness. When the spiritual power reaches a peak, the result is a masterpiece."

The sculptor is perhaps better qualified than anyone else to appreciate fully the discoveries to be made from natural design. The sculpture created by man is an extension of natural forms, compounded into the forms of the human body or into some other expression of his creative instinct. Just as nature's three-dimensional designs range from smooth pebbles to rugged mountains, so man's work encompasses a broad span from tiny amulets to monolithic buildings that have all the attributes of sculpture. This is a field that combines the adventures of plastic expression with the satisfactions of structural design, for the sculptor may bring forth miracles from blocks of stone, chunks of wood, and strips of metal.

KINDS OF SCULPTURE

Sculpture traditionally is divided into two categories. It can be *freestanding* (sculpture in the round), or it can be *relief* sculpture (attached to a background). Relief can vary in depth. Sometimes the relief is merely incised in stone and becomes, in effect, a drawing rather than a carving. The Egyptian sculpture in Figure 239 is slightly raised from the background, however, and is thus an example of *bas-relief* (or low relief). When the figures project to the extent of half their thickness or more, the sculpture is called *haut-relief* (high relief).

From the standpoint of design, each type of sculpture presents distinct problems. A renowned freestanding statue is Michelangelo's *Moses,* (Fig. 299). The sculpture was commissioned as part of the tomb of Pope Julius II, and it was to have been one of forty figures planned for the original design. The tomb was a monumental, almost sublime conception that, after many vicissitudes, Michelangelo was forced to reduce to the relatively unambitious wall tomb it now is. The *Moses* survives as

299. MICHELANGELO. *Moses.* c. 1513–15. Marble, height 8′4″. San Pietro in Vincoli, Rome.

the central figure in the wall complex. Through the centuries it has remained a symbol of awesome dignity. This is the work of a man who had great empathy with the substance of marble, who knew every crystal and vein within the block of stone he worked, and who never selected a section of marble without first seeing it in the rays of early dawn, when light would reveal the purity of its texture.

The sixteenth-century painter and critic Giorgio Vasari wrote of the *Moses:* "No modern work will ever approach it in beauty, no, nor ancient either." He praised especially the treatment of the hair. "His flowing beard descends so softly, hair by separate hair, as though the chisel had become a pencil." The explicit detail with which Michelangelo treated the facial contours, the musculature, and even the veins of the hands testifies to the arduous hours he spent dissecting human bodies for the intimate knowledge his work required. The *Moses* is compact and self-contained, and it exemplifies Michelangelo's belief that one should be able to roll a piece of sculpture downhill without any part of it breaking away. There is a solidity and a tension in the figure, especially in the position of the arms and in the carriage of the head. The angry expression is suggestive of the *terribilità,* or awesome force, that Michelangelo himself is said to have possessed. When the contours of a statue had been shaped to his satisfaction, Michelangelo had assistants polish the stone carefully in order to bring out the translucent glow of the marble. As a result, draperies seem pliable, and flesh appears capable of movement and response. Beyond this, the subject and the less tangible content provide elements that make the *Moses* almost overwhelmingly powerful.

A century earlier Lorenzo Ghiberti had created one of the great masterpieces of bronze relief sculpture in his doors for the Baptistry of the Cathedral of Florence (Fig. 300). This was a difficult design problem in both subject matter and form. The late medieval style of representing Old Testament subject matter demanded that Ghiberti include more than one incident in some of the panels. Furthermore, the problem of condensing the Bible into ten panels, yet separating one episode from another, required considerable planning and technical skill. Ghiberti adapted his background to his needs by sloping it so that the foreground figures are partly in the round, while the background figures, which may form another scene, are flattened out to give the illusion of depth. Some of the panels contain more than a hundred figures, as well as architecture, ships, and details of landscape, and it is obvious that great skill was involved in their execution. Critics have complained that Ghiberti treated each panel as an easel painting rather than as a piece of sculpture. This criticism, combined with Vasari's comment about *Moses'* hair, demonstrates that sculpture and painting may not have been far apart even in the fifteenth century. The mastery of design in Ghiberti's panels is clear when one views the two doors and their borders of large figures interspersed with the natural plant and animal forms of Renaissance naturalism. The Baptistry doors were so admired by Ghiberti's contemporaries that it was said their beauty was sufficient to serve for the Gates of Paradise.

TWO SCULPTURAL METHODS

Not only do Michelangelo's *Moses* and Ghiberti's bronze doors represent the two *types* of sculpture, but they also exemplify the two basic sculptural *methods:* the *subtractive* and the *additive.* These two methods are directly related to the materials involved. When working with wood or stone, the sculptor uses the subtractive method. He starts with a large mass and visualizes the form within it; then he gradually cuts away the material until this form emerges. He tries to achieve a

300. LORENZO GHIBERTI. *Gates of Paradise,* east doors of the Baptistry, Florence. 1425–52. Gilt bronze, height 18′6″.

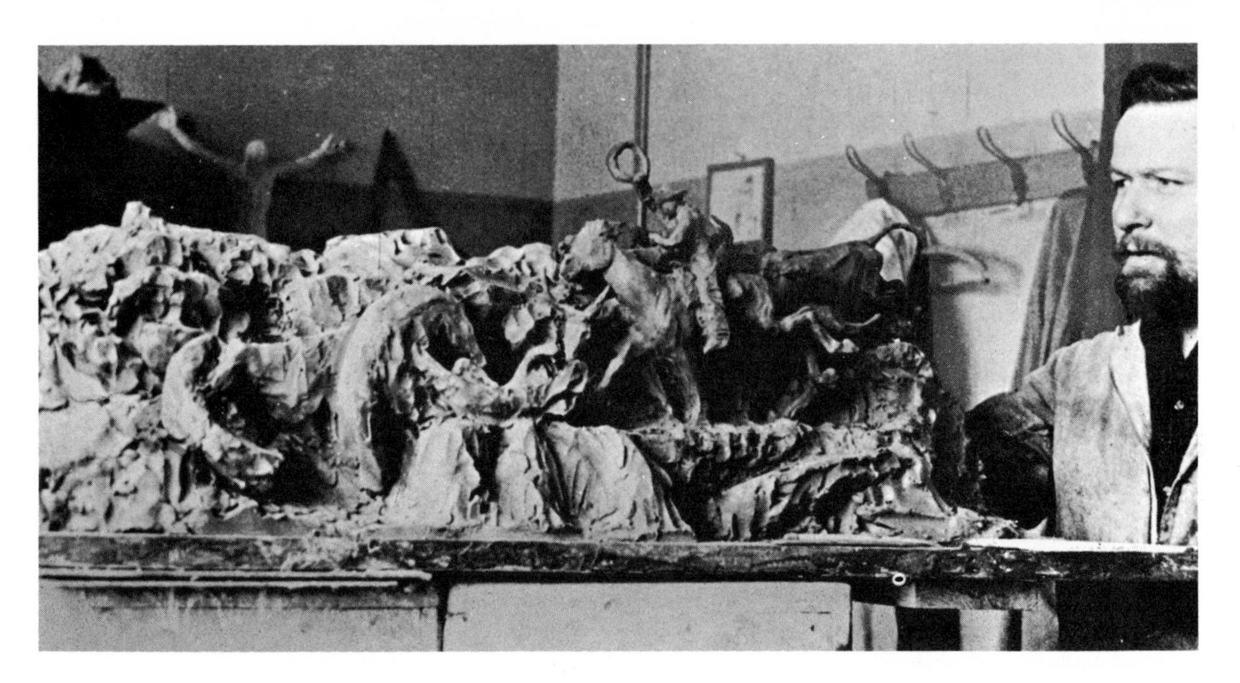

top: 301. HARRY JACKSON. Wax model for *Stampede,* Figure 302.

above: 302. HARRY JACKSON. *Stampede.* 1958–59. Bronze, $60\frac{1}{4} \times 25 \times 16''$. Courtesy Kennedy Galleries, New York.

left: 303. HARRY JACKSON. *Stampede* (detail).

structural design that balances gravity, weight, volume, and spatial composition. Thus the figure of *Moses* sits solidly on its base with no feeling of imbalance that might disturb the viewer. It is executed in such a way that its proportions are convincing from any viewpoint. There is a depth of carving that gives it sculptural power; yet it retains the strength of the original mass. The figure conveys a feeling of dynamic movement through the vigor of its pose.

In the subtractive method, the sculptor begins by making preliminary sketches on paper. He may then work out his design in a small model of wood or clay, for one mistake in the full-scale work could be catastrophic. Usually in this first conception he thinks only in terms of large abstract masses and leaves details to be developed after the form has been blocked out. In this way the sculptor can establish the rhythms among the masses, as well as the overall proportion and line. After the basic relationships have emerged, the artist can devote himself to textures and details.

The additive method is more flexible. Clay, wax, and metal are the materials most often used, and with all three it is possible to build up, tear down, change, and modify without danger of ruining the finished work. Frequently a metal *armature* is used with clay; it is a skeleton of heavy wire that forms the basic lines and holds the clay together so that it will not crack of its own weight.

Clay and wax are used principally as a basis for the *casting* of metal. Metalcasting is a complex process, and an understanding of its difficulties fosters new respect for the bronze statues in parks and city squares. The sculpture is first modeled in wax or clay, which allows for minute detail and careful manipulation of forms. Figure 301 shows sculptor Harry Jackson at work on the wax model of *Stampede.* The forms are built up around an inner core of nonmelting waste material, such as clay. When the wax model has been completed, the sculptor sends it to a foundry to be cast, usually by the *cire-perdue* (lost wax) method. In this process, a mold, usually of ceramic material, is built around the model. The mold is smooth on the outside, but conforms to the wax model in every detail on its interior surface. The mold is then fired in a kiln. In the firing process the wax melts and runs out through openings provided for the purpose, thus leaving a space between the mold and the inner core of the model. Into this space the molten metal is poured and then allowed to solidify. Figure 302 illustrates the finished bronze of *Stampede,* and a detail of the cattle is reproduced in Figure 303. The *cire-perdue* process has a definite advantage over the subtractive method in that several sculptures can be produced from the same mold. Furthermore, the sculptor is not confined to the compact form preferred by Michelangelo. The additive process lends itself to such extensions into space as the horns of cattle, which would not be as appropriate to the nature of stone or to the methods of working in it.

Another casting process is *sand casting,* which can be done in a variety of ways. One method works as follows: the original model of wax or clay is placed in a mold that can be taken apart in halves, and damp sand is packed around the model firmly enough to hold its shape. The model is then removed, the two halves of the mold are placed together, and the liquid metal is poured into the mold. *Relief casting* is done in a flat bed of wet sand into which the design has been modeled in reverse. Bronze, plaster, or cement is poured into the design and allowed to harden. Concrete panels for exterior walls can be done in this manner, after which they are cemented into place.

New materials are sometimes particularly useful in sculpture. In a variation of sand casting, styrofoam takes the place of the wax used in traditional casting

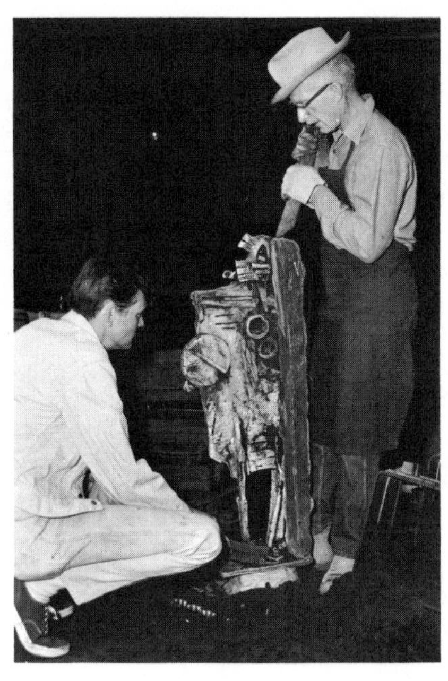

304–305. LYNN WOLFE. *Cloak of Honor.* 1966. Aluminum, height 38″. Collection the artist.

far left: 304. Molten metal has been poured into a styrofoam model causing the latter to vaporize. The fumes cast sand from the mold into the metal, thus creating texture.

left: 305. The finished sculpture is cleaned and polished.

methods. In the new *cavityless mold system,* the sculptor makes a model of styrofoam, which is then enclosed in a conventional wet sand mold. Molten metal is poured into the styrofoam causing it to vaporize, and the fragile styrofoam is replaced with durable metal in a single step (Fig. 304). As the styrofoam vaporizes, the fumes cast sand into the surface of the metal and add interest to the texture already supplied by the sand of the mold (Fig. 305).

Other additive processes involve arc and acetylene welding, riveting, and bolting metal together into compositions of varying complexity. Some artists create sculpture from "found" objects—parts retrieved from junkyards, complete with rust and broken edges. These pieces are considered as new forms without reference to their original purpose.

CONSIDERATIONS IN SCULPTURAL DESIGN

For many centuries sculpture has been associated with buildings, and it therefore has certain characteristics that seem more closely related to architecture than to any of the other arts. The earliest large sculptures were designed as embellishments for tombs and temples, and they were meant to preserve the souls of the dead or to pay homage to the gods. Portable sculpture consisted mainly of charms or idols, which were treasured for their beneficent effect on the gods, either as amulets to ensure fertility or as charms to oversee the general well-being of the possessor. Large statues were so closely related to architecture that much of the Egyptian sculpture in the round was firmly attached to the wall, and could therefore be considered very high relief. Even Greek statues, which were otherwise so superbly finished, were frequently left rough at the back when they were intended to be placed against a wall.

This association with architecture affected sculptural design in several ways. First, it emphasized large forms that could be viewed from afar with no loss of detail and that were in keeping with the larger scale of the building of which they were a part.

306. EDGAR BRITTON. *Genesis.* 1967. Cast bronze, height 14′. Holly Sugar Plaza, Colorado Springs, Colo.

Second, it necessitated certain refinements to accommodate the lower eye level of the viewer. In the sculptured friezes on ancient Greek temples, for example, the upper portions projected farther from the background than did the lower sections, so that the forms would catch the most favorable effects of light and shade. Unlike the painter, the sculptor whose work is commissioned to fill a certain spot can, to a great extent, control the conditions under which it will be viewed. Ideally, he can make a thorough study of changing light throughout the day, and even throughout the year, and he can attempt to choose the material or the surface treatment that will utilize these conditions to best advantage.

Since the Renaissance, sculpture has been freed of the restrictions imposed by the decorative needs of architecture. But sculpture in the round has long played a part in city planning, and it is becoming once more an important element in the design of buildings. The Bauhaus esthetic of simplified forms in building design created a gap between architecture and the tradition of realistic or classical-academic sculpture. Contemporary sculptors have consciously worked to close the gap by creating sculptural forms consonant with twentieth-century architecture. A good example is Edgar Britton's *Genesis* (Fig. 306). Designed for the plaza of the Antlers Hotel in Colorado Springs, the sculpture is effectively placed against the rugged silhouette of the Rockies. This Old Testament subject derives new meaning from the architectural forms and the natural beauty of its surroundings. Here Genesis means not only a beginning, but a continuation of growth, always reaching toward new expression and unattained goals.

THREE ATTRIBUTES OF SCULPTURE

While sculpture is involved with the same elements and principles of design as the other arts, there are certain aspects of design that are particularly relevant to this plastic art. The attributes of sculpture can be grouped under three principal headings. First, the work must have *form.* Form in its purest sense suggests a three-dimensional mass of structural material that has been given artistic significance. Second, there must be *organization,* which refers to the coherence of the form, and to the use of line, texture, light, and shadow, and, in some cases, even color. Organization, therefore, involves the arrangement of structural components into an integrated design. Third, the sculpture must have *content,* or significance for the observer. It may be representational or symbolic, or, like nonobjective painting, it may speak a language of its own through form.

Form

In all the arts form is of primary importance, but in sculpture it is a physical, tangible presence. One cannot truly appreciate sculpture from a distance. To achieve its fullest expression, sculptural form should be felt with the fingers, the arms, the entire being. The individual thus satisfies a need to become a part of something outside his own body, to associate himself with something that can be absorbed into his total experience. The great nineteenth-century sculptor Rodin recorded the advice he received from his teacher: "When you carve, never see the form in length, but always in thickness. Never consider a surface except as the extremity of a volume, as the point, more or less large, which it directs toward you."[1] This feeling of bulk and volume, of something tangible that can be embraced, is an intrinsic quality of a piece of sculpture. It leads to an entirely different conception of form than that found in painting, where the third dimension, however effective visually, remains an illusion on a two-dimensional surface. Looking at and touching a piece of sculpture should give the same sense of satisfaction that comes from fingering a smooth pebble or stroking the stock of a rifle to give it a hand-rubbed finish. Sculptors undoubtedly are the artists who have this sense of tactile quality developed to the highest degree. The viewer should try to develop a similar sense in himself when he "experiences" a piece of sculpture.

The *kinesthetic,* or *kinetic,* element enters into sculpture even more than into action painting. This technique is not new. The ancient Greeks often exaggerated the action of their sculptured figures. The frieze of the Parthenon, for example, presents a swirling, vital pageant of rearing horses and human forms in varying aspects of muscular activity. Myron's *Discobolus,* seen in the Roman copy in Figure 307, trans-

307. MYRON. *Discobolus (Discus Thrower).* Roman copy after bronze original of c. 460 B.C. Marble, lifesize. National Museum, Rome.

mits the tension of imminent action throughout the figure, although present-day athletes have demonstrated that a discus thrower does not necessarily take this pose—that it could, in fact, very well throw him off balance. The sculptor's intent obviously was to impart to the viewer a sense of the muscular stress necessary for an athletic feat, in a manner that involves feeling more than diagrammatical accuracy. This supposition is reinforced by the fact that Myron depicted another discobolus in the same stage of action but in quite a different position.

Twentieth-century sculptors have extended the kinetic element from muscular interpretation into more abstract areas that relate to movement in general. Many of these expressions have been made possible by new materials, as seen, for example, in the work of Domenico Mortellito (Fig. 308). This graceful flock of birds could have been done only in urethane, a lightweight polymer used widely in industry as insulation for boats, surfboards, and buoys. It presents to the sculptor an entirely new range of possibilities in texture, lightness, rigidity, and speed of execution. The delicate interplay of negative and positive space in *Birds* would be virtually impossible in wood or stone, and casting in metal would be wholly unfeasible. Urethane is a highly practical material; its light weight permits a sculpture to be suspended in space where it can revolve freely with changing air currents. This element of movement is perhaps most important, for it makes of the sculpture a continually changing interpretation of flight as it is viewed from different angles and in every variation of light. Thus, action becomes fused with form, one of the most effective results to be achieved in sculpture.

Painting and sculpture have undergone a similar metamorphosis insofar as manner of expression is concerned. For many centuries, sculpture was concerned primarily with the portrayal of the human figure, but in the twentieth century there is new interest in form as an entity unto itself. No longer does the appreciation of a sculpture hinge on the sort of feeling that Pygmalion is said to have had toward his statue of Galatea, which, because of his love for it, was transformed by Aphrodite into a living woman. The merits of a sculptural form do not necessarily depend upon accuracy of representation. Rather, the form should be worthy of appreciation for itself alone, on a purely esthetic level. Such is the case with Barbara Hepworth's *Sphere with Inner Form* (Fig. 309). There is an abstract beauty in this work that needs no translation. The balance of positive and negative space provides the only variation

left: 308. Domenico Mortellito. *Birds.* 1965. Artfoam, diameter 32″. Collection University of Delaware, Newark, Del.

below: 309. Barbara Hepworth. *Sphere with Inner Form.* 1963. Bronze, height 38″. Courtesy Marlborough-Gerson Gallery, New York.

left: 310. Henry Moore. *Reclining Figure.* 1938. Cast lead, length 13″. Museum of Modern Art, New York (purchase).

below: 311. Lynn Wolfe. *Young Woman Combing Her Hair.* 1958. Clay and plastic, height 27″. Collection the artist.

in the smooth surface, resulting in a purity of form that makes the viewer want to run his hands over the marble, to stroke it until he has absorbed all the subtleties of the surface and all the fullness of form that it encompasses.

Organization

The second attribute of sculpture concerns the way forms are put together. Frequently this is a matter of materials, as in the case of Mortellito's *Birds.* Sculptors sometimes will interpret the same subject both in stone and in bronze, but they will treat the two pieces quite differently, even though the design is basically the same. A head in stone may be smoothly rounded, while the same head in bronze would be broken into planes to exploit the effects of reflected light. Organization may be modified to emphasize or minimize shadows, depending upon where the work will be placed. Textures and colors must be organized for balance and interest. Arrangement of forms into positive and negative space is an important factor, as was seen in Barbara Hepworth's *Pierced Form.*

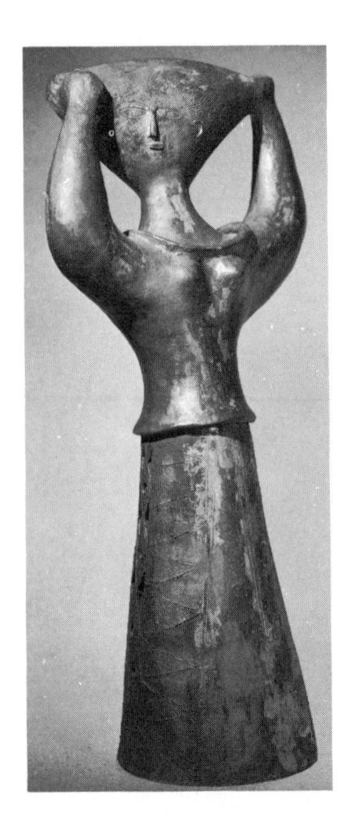

An effective analysis of the artist's approach to sculptural form can be made by comparing different interpretations of the human body. Henry Moore's *Reclining Figure* (Fig. 310) is abstracted to a high degree. The primary concern is not with anatomical accuracy, but with a design composed of positive and negative spaces. These spaces are organized in such a way that a sense of rhythm and balance overrides the preoccupation with human anatomy. Moore has definite feelings about the negative spaces or holes in his work:

> A hole can itself have as much shape-meaning as a solid mass. . . . The mystery of the hole—the mysterious fascination of caves in hillsides and cliffs. . . . The first hole made through a piece of stone is a revelation. The hole connects one side to the other, making it immediately more three-dimensional.[2]

Two other versions of the human figure are illustrated in Figures 311 and 312. In Figure 311 the sturdy figure of a young girl in clay and plastic combines massive solidity of form with a certain youthful buoyancy. *The Last Trumpet* (Fig. 312) is a sandcast bronze with a strong linear quality and an interesting texture that exists not only as surface treatment but as an inherent quality of the form itself. The organization in each case is highly individual: the same general subject matter, differently interpreted, produces two strikingly unique works of art.

right: 312. LYNN WOLFE. *The Last Trumpet.* 1964. Bronze, height 20″. Collection the artist.

far right: 313. ISAMU NOGUCHI. *Integral.* 1959. Greek marble, height 4′1¼″. Whitney Museum of American Art, New York (gift of the Friends of the Whitney Museum).

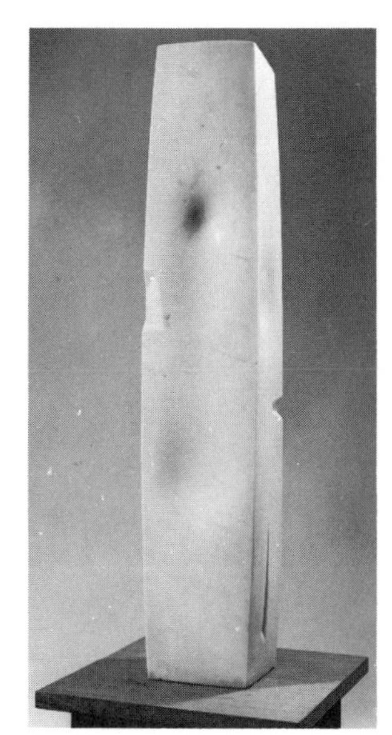

Content

All sculpture has content that lends significance or meaning to the work. As in painting, the content of sculpture is often more obvious when it is embodied in recognizable subject matter. Yet the content of nonobjective works may be more purely esthetic, for it requires a greater sensitivity to the subtle implications of form. Isamu Noguchi's *Integral* (Fig. 313) is so simple that one might pass by without noticing it, yet it is the kind of form that becomes more significant as one studies it. The subtlety of the upward curve is reminiscent of *entasis*—the almost indiscernible curve of columns on Greek temples that provides a sense of living form. The indentations suggest grave *steles*—carved upright markers used by the Greeks. There is a kind of magic in the quality of the form itself, a magic closely related to the content. This relationship of form to content often has a symbolic connotation, as Henry Moore pointed out in connection with his own work in 1937:

> The meaning and significance of form itself probably depends on the countless associations of man's history. For example, rounded forms convey an idea of fruitfulness, maturity, probably because the earth, women's breasts, and most fruits are rounded, and these shapes are important because they have this background in our habits of perception.[3]

Content may be associated with movement, which again involves the kinetic element. In 1932, Alexander Calder, an American sculptor, first exhibited a group of moving constructions, which, at the suggestion of his friend Marcel Duchamp, he called "mobiles." In discussing his work nineteen years later, Calder said:

> . . . . the underlying form in my work has been the system of the Universe. . . . the idea of detached bodies floating in space, of different sizes and densities, perhaps of different colors and temperatures. . . . and some at rest, while others move in peculiar manners, seems to me the ideal source of form. . . . Then there is the idea of an object floating—not supported. The use of a very long thread. . . . seems to best approximate this freedom from the earth.[4]

Calder explained that it is not essential for others to grasp what *he* has in mind—as long as they have something else in *their* minds. In *Red Petals* (Fig. 314) Calder has created from sheet metal a combination of fixed and mobile forms that change their relationships according to the air currents and lights playing upon them. The solid shapes of metal are balanced against the linear forms that support them, and their movement might remind the viewer of petals, as the title suggests, or of fluttering leaves, swirling snowflakes, or the rippling of wind across a field of grain. As Calder has intimated, the content lies in the mind of the viewer and derives from his own experience.

CONTEMPORARY TRENDS

In sculpture, contemporary work tends toward a synthesis of art and technology, of art and science, and of sculpture and painting. Twentieth-century sculpture is an international art form, which has been made possible by the ease of transportation and communication. Form, organization, and content are directed by a space-age environment and by new materials that make possible forms suggestive of this age. Color and light have achieved new importance as elements of design. In addition to these general trends, certain identifiable movements have emerged.

Constructivism

Constructivism originated shortly after World War I, and its influence is still important for contemporary artists. The Constructivists accepted the emergence of an industrial and technological society and placed their emphasis on structure rather

314. Alexander Calder. *Red Petals.* 1942. Aluminum, height 9′2″. Arts Club of Chicago.

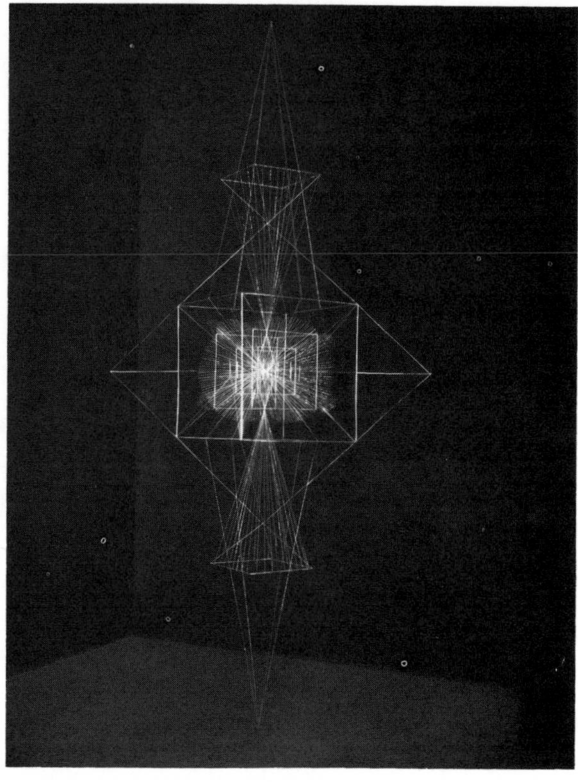

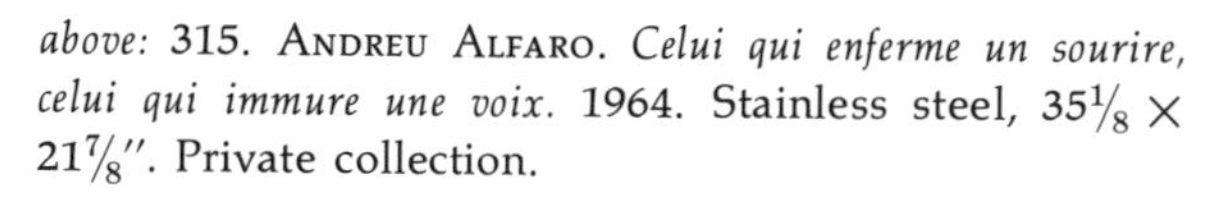

above: 315. ANDREU ALFARO. *Celui qui enferme un sourire, celui qui immure une voix.* 1964. Stainless steel, $35\frac{1}{8} \times 21\frac{7}{8}''$. Private collection.

right: 316. RICHARD LIPPOLD. *Variation Number 7: Full Moon.* 1949–50. Brass rods, nickel-chromium, and stainless-steel wire; height 10′. Museum of Modern Art, New York (Mrs. Simon Guggenheim Fund).

than on surface appearance. They rebelled against modeled or carved forms in favor of constructions that created dynamic relationships in space. Time and space were considered the elements of life, and the Constructivists tried to interpret them as the essentials of their sculpture. Alexander Calder was associated with this group in his invention of the "stabile," the inert counterpart of the mobile. A recent example of Constructivism is a sculpture by the Spanish artist Andreu Alfaro (Fig. 315). The construction is composed of two simple iron forms, yet they are only a part of the design. Just as important is the way in which the metal carves the air into dynamic negative space flowing in and around the positive shapes of the metal.

Constructivism includes sculpture from found materials (sometimes called "junk art") and many forms of welded steel sculpture. It also encompasses constructions of wire, string, brass rods, and similar materials, as in *Variation Number 7: Full Moon* by Richard Lippold (Fig. 316). Lippold described this work as follows: "We can hope—even prove—that our wisdom is stronger than our weapons . . . Patience and love are the elements which gave [this work] life, and patience and love must be used in all dealings with it; its hanging and its seeing." Lippold considers his art to be a delicately calculated manifestation of his ideas, as opposed to the impulsive gestures of Expressionism. He works with space, captured by "the most seductive other materials I can arrange."[5]

Happenings

Although the exact origins of the *Happening* are disputed, the new art form came into public prominence in 1960 when Jean Tinguely built an enormous machine named

317. Jean Tinguely. *Homage to New York: A Self-constructing and Self-destroying Work of Art.* 1960. Assemblage of piano, machine parts, bicycle parts, weather balloon, fireworks, etc.

"Lucifer" in the garden of the Museum of Modern Art (Fig. 317). Its official title was *Homage to New York: A Self-constructing and Self-destroying Work of Art,* and five and a half weeks and $1500 were required to assemble it. In 28 minutes it had reduced itself to dust in the museum garden. This took place during the dark days of France's Algerian crisis, and Tinguely built the elaborate self-destroying machine as a symbol of political terrorism. It served as a warning of the dangers inherent in twentieth-century civilization: a self-destructive homage consummated in a single, unrepeatable act. Happenings often were laboriously "improvised" in an effort to convey a symbolic message related to the times. The first event that might truly be called a Happening took place in 1952 at Black Mountain College in North Carolina, when Robert Rauschenberg and John Cage created a mixed-media production that was later repeated at the New School in New York. Allen Kaprow, one of the leading advocates of the Happening as an art form, held the first of a series of Happenings in 1959 at New York's Reuben Gallery. Unrehearsed, and at times presented without an audience, the Happening was an attempt to integrate the arts with life—a combination of visual and auditory effects with the spontaneous reactions of the participants in a specially selected and prepared environment. This environment could be a New York gallery or a museum garden, a college classroom or auditorium, a supermarket, the kitchen of a private home, and so on. Happenings invariably exist in three dimensions, so they may be related to sculpture. At the same time a certain amount of painting may be involved, and there is clearly an element of the drama. A Happening, then, may be considered to be a compendium of all these art forms and yet distinct from each of them.

Environmental Sculpture

A relationship to the Dadaists, who exhibited found objects as works of art, can be seen in the "environmental sculpture" of certain contemporary artists. George Segal expresses an acute feeling of alienation in his dehumanized figures reconstructed from plaster casts of his friends (Fig. 318). These stolid figures appear to move in a dreamlike state; they offer no message, unless it is the lack of communication in a mass-produced world. Other examples of environmental sculpture are the soft plastic typewriters, washbasins, and telephones created by Claes Oldenburg. Oldenburg has attempted to separate these objects from their usual functions, theoretically giving them a poetic connotation because they have been rendered useless. Louise Nevelson assembles walls of commonplace objects, which she arranges in stacked boxes and crates—objects such as bowling pins, finials, and rough-cut wood blocks sprayed in uniform colors (Fig. 319). The underlying theory in these arrangements is that objects removed from everyday use create a new awareness of form and design that is independent of personal identification. These artists, by taking elements of man's environment out of context, try to make their audience view this environment in a different light.

Minimal Sculpture

Like Minimal painting, Minimal sculpture utilizes geometric forms devoid of any identifiable human association. One of the leaders in this area is Tony Smith. In 1965 Smith began making blueprints and models of large structures with pure form

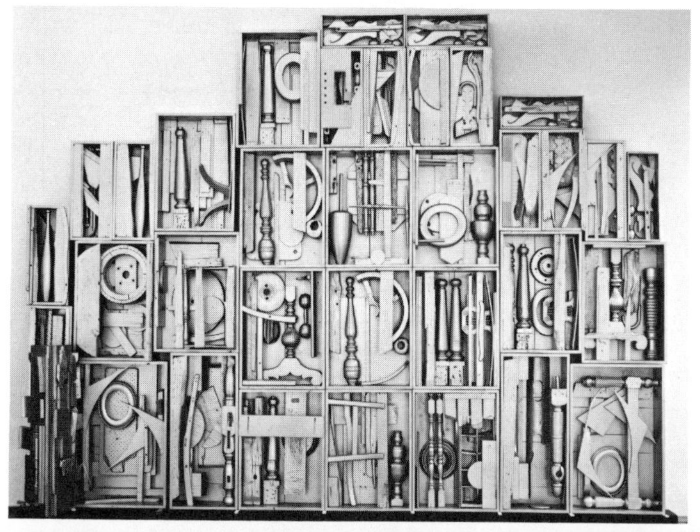

above right: 318. George Segal. *The Diner.* 1964–66. Plaster, wood, chrome, formica, and Masonite; 8′6″ × 9′ × 7′3″. Walker Art Center, Minneapolis.

right: 319. Louise Nevelson. *Royal Tide IV.* 1960. Painted wood, 11 × 14′. Courtesy Galerie Rudolf Zwerner, Cologne.

320. TONY SMITH. *Die.* 1962. Steel, 6′ cube. Courtesy M. Knoedler & Co., Inc., New York.

and taking them to a sheet metal fabrication shop to be constructed. Two years later his work was in such demand that he had to switch to black-painted plywood to save time. His works are geometric, yet they are anthropomorphic—related to human characteristics in an abstract way—and through their monumental size Smith feels he is scaling them to twentieth-century architecture (Fig. 320). He believes that present-day art has had no landmark, that it needs something like his sculpture to relate it to contemporary life.

Minimal sculpture may have an open construction—built of pipes and girders painted bright colors to create forms suggestive of playground equipment. It may take the form of spires or columns, or other shapes more closely related to geometry and machines than to human beings.

Luminal Sculpture

The use of light as an element of design has resulted in Luminal sculpture. This broad category includes such things as beams of light moving in ever-changing patterns, as well as more permanent compositions made of Lucite and Plexiglas, painted metal, or batteries of colored lights. Lights may be placed under or behind a sculptural form for subtle illumination, or they may occupy a conspicuous spot where they themselves become a part of the design. These lights may change constantly or they may remain fixed (Fig. 321).

Neon, Plexiglas, and flat metal fragments are the materials preferred by Chryssa, a Greek-American artist who stresses "the cool mind" in her interpretations. Chryssa had long been interested in signs, newspapers, lists of names in office hallways, and types of letters. Ultimately she came to the conclusion that real truth is fragmented and repetitive, and it is these characteristics of modern life that she tries to express in her constructions. Consequently, in her studies of *The Gates to Times Square* she

left: 321. Howard Jones. *Skylight Series.* 1969. Brushed aluminum and light bulbs, 5′ × 5′ × 3″. Courtesy Howard Wise Gallery, New York.

above: 322. Chryssa. *Study for the Gates #5.* 1967. Neon and Plexiglas, 43 × 34½ × 27½″. Courtesy Pace Gallery, New York.

calls each work a fragment (Fig. 322). The cool mind, according to Chryssa, avoids even its own patterns of thinking because they will become trite. She writes: "I am afraid that all these human patterns and habits, all this garbage, interferes with the creative process, so I try to leave as much of it out as I can. The less I am in love with 'nature' and 'people,' the clearer my work becomes."[6] The artist times the lighting on her constructions at intervals of a second or a second and a half and controls the intensity so that no one color will dominate. In this way she seeks "complete equalization" as the most perfect form of balance. Though light is of paramount importance in Chryssa's work, each of her sculptures has an artistic integrity in its structure alone, so that even if a transformer burns out, the work remains valid.

The newest materials for sculpture are electronic devices—cathode tubes, transistors, and photoelectric cells. From these are fashioned strange and intriguing constructions that speak eloquently of a technological age. Often the results have little to do with traditional ideas of design; they look rather like a cartoon for a weird machine, whose sole function is to express its involvement with man's inventions. Lights flash, noises rumble, and electronic music issues forth as the viewer's hand reaches in to break an I-beam, or his body sets up an interaction with radar.

When John Baur took over as director of New York's Whitney Museum, he said:

> There's a bubbling over of creative energy in every direction today, and the injection of new talent and new movements gets more frenetic all the time. However, new movements tend to overshadow artists doing good work in older styles, and that's why it is important to maintain a catholic point of view. It isn't the movement that counts as much as the individual [artist].[7]

This viewpoint is necessary to an understanding of sculpture and painting today, for this is a time of experimentation, and new materials make the work of inventive artists bewilderingly versatile. If one has a knowledge of design, it can help him to make sound judgments concerning individual artists and their work, even though the work does not follow traditional ideas. There may be only form, or only light, or only linear space delineated by wires and rods. Much of what is seen today is pure experimentation that will lead eventually to more acceptable art forms. In fact, many critics feel that the world of art is on the verge of a great breakthrough. A developed sensitivity to basic design concepts—as well as an open mind—will help to evaluate these new and startling innovations.

SUMMARY

Traditionally, there are two kinds of sculpture: freestanding and relief. There are two sculptural methods: subtractive, involving wood or stone that is carved from a block; and additive, in which metal or some other material is built up into a sculptured form. The usual procedure for working metal is by casting. This is often done by the *cire-perdue* method, involving wax and molten bronze or other metal. Sand casting is a related process, and this has been expanded by contemporary sculptors into the cavityless mold technique built around styrofoam.

In the past the basic consideration in sculptural design has been its relationship to architecture. Placement and lighting effects must also be considered in designing a piece of sculpture for a specific location.

There are three attributes of sculpture: form, organization, and content. Particularly important in sculpture is the *kinetic* element. This may mean anything from the viewer's feeling of muscular action in seeing a sculptured human figure to actual movement in the sculpture itself.

Contemporary sculpture has followed several trends. Among them are Constructivism, Happenings, environmental sculpture, Minimal sculpture, and Luminal sculpture. The newest materials are electronic devices that are combined in fantastic ways to include the viewer in an experience with lights and sounds. Such constructions are examples of the inventiveness of artists in an electronic age, and they must be assessed by an audience with a strong background in design and an open mind, before their contribution to the field of art can be established.

Design in Photography

chapter 18

The Camera enters the field of art with a heavy responsibility. Many people credit it with having triggered nonobjective painting by taking the field of realistic representation out of the painter's hands. Why should the painter spend years developing his skill in reproducing nature, the argument goes, when the camera can do the same thing in $\frac{1}{50}$ of a second?

Much that the camera does in a split second is, of course, not art. The purpose of photography in science, industry, and communication is more often to record facts than to achieve artistic effects. When the professional photographer uses his camera as an artistic medium, moreover, his work involves much more than the fractional second in which the shutter is open. Each photograph is the culmination of long experience, innate sensitivity, and often of deep psychological insight.

NATURALISM AND REALISM

The problem of accurate representation involves a question of semantics, in which present-day critics and art philosophers make a distinction between *naturalism* and *realism.* Naturalism has to do with the visual or "natural" appearance of things, while realism delves further, beneath the surface, into actual reality. This may appear to be a very subtle nuance of meaning, but it is nonetheless a valid one. A similar distinction is made between the various ways in which an actor may approach a new role. He may make up his face to resemble that of the character he is to portray; he will study the character's walk, the inflections of his voice, his little gestures and mannerisms—in sum, he will discipline himself to resemble the *natural* appearance of the person he is portraying. On the other hand, an actor may decide to *become* that person, to allow the character's personality to so dominate his entire being that the actor's own identity is threatened. The character's problems, his neuroses, his fears, his personal crises become those of the actor, who, for the duration of the film or play, eats, sleeps, thinks, and even dreams the role he is playing. He has thus captured the *reality* of the part. In art this distinction is a matter of content. The understanding and sensitivity the artist puts into his work determines the difference between naturalism and realism.

A truly great work will go beyond representation and seek eternal values. A portrait of a child may show one small individual dressed up and posing, or it may show the enduring restlessness of childhood restrained for a moment but bursting with energy. Such differences are just as clear-cut in photography as they are in painting. The photograph in Figure 323 exemplifies the characteristics of great portraiture in the study of an old man reading his Bible. This man has specific personality traits, yet he is not just one old man. He represents all old men everywhere, workworn and weary, resting for a few minutes at the end of the day, seeking assurance from his religion that his struggle is not futile. Photographic results such as these do not come merely from the choice of an interesting subject. They involve the development of confidence and interest, a rapport between photographer and subject, which allows the camera to bring out to the fullest the characteristics that the photographer wishes to emphasize. They depend on technical skill, on lighting for accentuation, and on focus that catches a clear image of the face while slightly blurring the lamp and the Bible.

The camera is the instrument of the photographer, just as brushes and paints are the tools of the painter, but the creative effort lies with the photographer himself. It is he who (1) *sees the possibilities of the subject,* (2) *has the ability to bring out the significance of those possibilities,* and (3) *possesses the technical knowledge to obtain the effect he is after.*

TECHNICAL ASPECTS OF PHOTOGRAPHY

Since the first two qualities are useless to the photographer without the third, it would be well for us to look into the technical side of photography before we consider its artistic aspects. The idea behind the camera was formulated by Leonardo da Vinci, who wrote that rays of light entering through a small hole in the wall of a darkened room transmit to the wall beyond "all the traits of their original both as to colors and form, except that everything will be inverted." In 1568 Danielo Barbara substituted a lens for the pinhole to achieve a clearer image, and in 1727 a German physicist moved toward the invention of film when he discovered that sunlight affects salts of silver, and when he made experiments with nitric acid, silver, and chalk to preserve images made by sunlight.

323. Bruce Roberts. *Old Man With Bible.* 1960.

Plate 27. Charles Steinhacker. *Autumn Sky, Allagash.* 1968.

Plate 28. David Vine. *Greenwich Village Snowscape.* 1969.

Photography as it is known today is generally traced to the discoveries made in 1829 at Chalon-sur-Saône, France, when Louis Daguerre and Nicéphore Niepce developed a process for obtaining permanent pictures from the action of sunlight. Ten years later Daguerre perfected the "daguerrotype," a permanent image created by the exposure to light of a plate sensitized with a coating of iodide of silver and then subjected to the action of mercury vapor and hyposulphite of soda.

As a result of many complex developments in the following years by George Eastman and others, the modern camera has emerged—a marvel of precision. Yet the basic principle is still the same as the one Leonardo jotted down in his notes. The darkened room (in Latin, *camera*) is the first requisite, fulfilled by the interior of the camera itself. The film is the surface upon which the image is recorded, and the process of recording is effected by the admission of light through a lens.

THE LENS

Without light there can be no picture, and the quality of the light that is admitted depends largely upon the lens. Light rays are bent or refracted when they pass from air to glass or glass to air, and this is the principle governing the manufacture of lenses. The curving of the lens to control this refraction is what makes the lens the most important and most costly part of the camera. The finest lenses are manufactured from optical glass with a high refractive index—that is, glass that has great light-bending power.

Differences in lenses are based on two factors: the *focal length* and the *f-rating.* Focal length is the distance from the lens to the focal plane where parallel rays of light are brought to a point by the lens (Fig. 324). In other words, it is *the distance from the lens to the plane where the film is located.* The f-rating determines the "speed" of the lens and is found by *dividing the diameter of the lens into its focal length.* For instance, an f/8 lens has a diameter of $\frac{1}{8}$ of its focal length; an f/3.5 lens is 1/3.5 of its focal length. The smaller the f-rating, the greater the speed of the lens. Just as $\frac{1}{2}$ is larger than $\frac{1}{8}$, so an f/2 lens requires a faster shutter than one whose f-rating is f/8.

There are many types of lenses, and the differences between them are determined by their focal lengths. Lenses with longer focal lengths shorten distances and dimensions and are known as telephoto lenses. They are especially useful in photographing wild animals and birds that cannot be approached at close range. The shorter focal length lenses exaggerate distances at the sides of the field of vision and make it possible to squeeze more into a picture that is taken in cramped quarters. These are called wide-angle lenses.

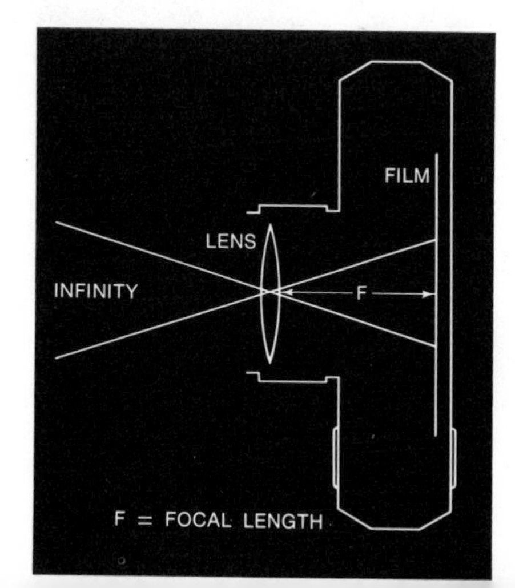

324. The focal length is the distance from the image to the lens.

325. The amount of exposure of film to light determines the relative lightness or darkness of the image. Of these three examples, the photograph at top is overexposed, the bottom photo is underexposed, and the one at center is normal.

THE DIAPHRAGM

The best cameras have a diaphragm built on the same principle as the iris of the eye. This consists of overlapping metal leaves which control the opening of the lens. The f-numbers indicated on cameras actually control the size of the diaphragm opening, and the relationship of this diameter to the focal length is designated by the f-numbers by which the photographer can set his camera. Because these numbers give an accurate relationship between lens and focal length, they come out in varying ratios, such as 5.6, 8, 11, 16, and 32.

These relationships can become highly technical. There is a large body of literature available to explain the physics of light refraction and its effects upon various lenses. The main reason for changing the f-rating of a lens is that a wider diameter permits faster pictures (such as action shots), while a smaller one increases the sharpness of objects in the background. The latter is called *depth of field.*

THE SHUTTER

Although the lens and the diaphragm control the relationship of light to the film, the shutter has the final word. While the shutter is closed, the film remains in darkness, but when the shutter is opened for a split second, the picture is "snapped." The diaphragm is regulated according to size, but the shutter is controlled as to length of time. The speed of the lens must be correlated with the amount of time the shutter is open, that is, with the shutter speed. Box cameras usually have a shutter speed of $^1/_{30}$ of a second, whereas more complicated cameras can be set for any speed from one second to $^1/_{1250}$ of a second. In the early days of the camera indoor group portraits often had a stiff, posed appearance. The lack of sufficient lighting made it necessary for the subjects to remain motionless for several seconds while the shutter was open. The refinement of photoflash equipment, however, has made it possible to augment indoor light with a bright flash that is simultaneous with the opening of the shutter, thus cutting down on the exposure time.

The proper relationship between the amount of light, or diaphragm opening, and the shutter speed is basic to successful photography. If a race horse is to be photographed at $^1/_{1000}$ of a second, the time of exposure for the film is so infinitesimal that the diaphragm must be wide open in order to admit enough light for the image to register. On the other hand, a landscape with no action can be photographed at a shutter speed of $^1/_{25}$ of a second with a smaller diaphragm opening. This provides sharper focus for objects in the distance, and greater depth of field.

The effects of three light-time relationships can be seen in Figure 325. Underexposure could be caused by either too small a diaphragm opening or too short a time of exposure, while overexposure would result from too large an opening or too long a time of exposure. Similar difficulties can arise from the misuse of light in developing and printing. Photographers sometimes deliberately overexpose for special effects, particularly when they want to evoke a certain mood.

THE FILM

Today there are many types of film on the market—color and black and white, indoor and outdoor, still and motion picture. They are designed not only for different purposes, but also for varying conditions of light and color sensitivity. However, any film consists of two basic parts: the *support* and the *emulsion.*

326. Remarkably different effects can be achieved by photographing the same subject with different filters. In the first photo (*right*) no filter was used. The sky is very pale and washed out, and the clouds are barely discernible. The second photo (*opposite left*) used a K2 (yellow) filter to darken the sky and provide greater contrast, while in the third (*opposite center*) an X1 (green) filter was employed to achieve still greater contrast and to present the natural colors of the foliage. The final photo (*opposite right*) was made with an A (red) filter, which creates very dramatic effects of dark sky against white cloud forms.

The Support

The purpose of the support is to provide a base for the light-sensitive emulsion. The support itself is insensitive to light, but it is transparent, so that the light can reach the emulsion. Originally all supports were heavy glass plates, and such plates are still used in some large professional cameras. George Eastman's invention of flexible film in the early 1880s made possible the design of simple cameras that could be used by amateurs. Most supports today are made of triacetate plastic, which is coated with the emulsion.

The Emulsion

The emulsion starts as bar silver, which is dissolved in nitric acid to form silver nitrate. This, with potassium bromide, is added to a chemically superior variety of gelatin warmed to a syrupy consistency. Since the silver and bromide combine to form light-sensitive crystals, the work is done in darkness, and the residual potassium nitrate is removed from the gelatin by washing. The remaining silver bromide is caught in the gelatin and becomes the emulsion with which the support is coated. The earliest emulsions were sensitive only to light in the ultraviolet and blue-violet portions of the spectrum, but later discoveries revealed that adding various dyes would provide greater sensitivity to objects of other colors. Panchromatic film contains dyes that give it substantially the same color sensitivity that is found in the human eye.

Color film contains three separate emulsions. Kodacolor, for example, has a red-sensitive emulsion next to the support with a gelatin-filter layer over it, then a green-sensitive emulsion and another filter layer, and finally a blue-sensitive emulsion on top of all the others. Each layer of the film forms an image in one of the additive primary colors. Processing this type of film is extremely complicated. A dye image is produced in the complementary colors of magenta, yellow, and turquoise (or cyan) in each emulsion layer. When the developing is complete, the

original film appears as a negative from which positive images can be made in the form of slides or color prints.

Films have four characteristics that distinguish them from one another: color sensitivity, speed, graininess, and contrast. Color sensitivity is largely a matter of the dyes used in the emulsion, making some film more sensitive to green or red or blue than to other colors. The speed of film is its general sensitivity to light, and this comes from the manufacturing process. The longer the emulsion is "cooked," the larger the grains of silver bromide will be and the greater the sensitivity, thus requiring less light in exposure. Graininess depends upon the size of the grains in the emulsion, and it usually does not become a factor except in enlarging. Contrast is a question of values; it involves the ability of the film to show distinctions between closely related tones in the brightness scale.[1]

FILTERS

Although different types of film can be purchased for various situations, it is sometimes more effective to use filters that fit over the lens. A filter is a piece of dyed gelatin or glass that either absorbs or transmits rays of light, depending upon their color relationship to the filter. The object is to use a filter that will absorb the colors the photographer wants to subdue, and that will transmit the colors he wants heightened. There are over a hundred light filters available, and they can do everything from providing contrast in portraits to dramatizing cloud effects. In the example reproduced in Figure 326, four different filter conditions were used, causing variations in both sky and branches.

DEVELOPING THE FILM

Developing is a process by which chemicals turn the silver particles on a film to black in exactly the same proportion as their exposure to light. Three trays of solution are used for the process, which is carried out in a darkroom lighted only by a special safety light. The paper backing is peeled off the film, and the film is put into a roll tank containing developer. The developer changes the latent image on the emulsion into a visible image composed of grains of metallic silver. The density in each area of the film depends upon the amount of light that fell on the area during exposure.

The image is developed completely within four minutes, and the film is then rinsed in cool water. It is next immersed in a fixative, which clears away the developer, and finally it is washed under running water for 15 minutes. The result of this procedure is a strip of negatives that may be cut apart and used for making prints or, in the case of color transparencies, may be cut and mounted for projection.

MAKING THE PRINTS

The printing process is again related to the effects of light. The negative is placed against a piece of glass in a printing frame, with the emulsion side held by clips against a piece of special printing paper. There are many types of printing paper, all coated with special emulsions of one kind or another. As in the case of film, the photographer must experiment with various types of paper to find the one that best suits his needs. With the emulsion on the paper in contact with the emulsion on the negative, the frame is held near a white light bulb for a matter of seconds. Here again, the length of exposure will affect the result. The paper is removed and put through a second series of three trays. The first contains developer, which brings out the image very quickly. The relative darkness in the print can be controlled during this step as well as through the original exposure to light. When the print is dark enough, it is plunged for a few seconds into the stop solution in the second tray, and finally it is submerged in a fixative, which terminates all chemical action. After this step, the print can be exposed to light and left to dry.

The process described above results in a *contact print,* which is the same size as the negative. Enlargements are made with a special machine that works on the same principle as the slide projector. Suspended above the photographic paper, the enlarger projects the image from the negative onto the paper from a distance, thus making the picture larger. This projected image is the enlargement.

left: 327. BRUCE ROBERTS. *Pump.* 1960.

right: 328. TODD WEBB. *The El.* 1947.

PHOTOGRAPHY AS ART

Familiarity with films, developing, and printing processes falls into the realm of mechanical or scientific knowledge. The fine line between good technical photography and artistry is crossed only by the photographer with the eye and soul of an artist. The creative photographer understands that light—the essential of any photograph—can be his most valuable ally in design. It has been said, in fact, that in photography light *is* the great designer.

The photograph reproduced in Figure 327, for example, has the sort of subject that might be ignored by anyone without a creative imagination, yet the proper lighting and an interesting angle have resulted in a composition of great charm. The diagonal lines of the pump and the wood in the background focus attention on a cluster of leaves bathed in sunlight on the surface of the dark water. The light-struck rim of a bucket encircles the leaves like a frame and continues around the pump, bringing out the highlights of its form. Textural interest is provided by the rough grain of the wood juxtaposed with the smoothness of water and metal; and unity is achieved by the arrangement of scattered leaves echoing the center of interest, and by the repetition of curved forms. Thus, elements of line, form, texture, rhythm, and balance have been carefully combined to create a dramatic photograph from an utterly simple subject. Beyond these principles of design, however, there is an emotional quality, a nostalgia that recalls a quiet place close to trees and cool water and a simple fulfillment of simple needs. A typical response to this photograph might begin: "That reminds me of a place I knew as a child. . . ." This, then, is the content, the realism that makes the composition far more than just a technically competent picture.

Todd Webb's *The El* (Fig. 328) has a drastically different subject matter, yet the same principles of design are present. The rumble of the El as it sways along its tracks is anything but quiet, and the piles of stone mounting upward are the epitome of noisy progress. Yet here again, light has added a creative touch. The opposing faces of the buildings, seized just at the moment of greatest contrast, form a pattern of light and dark broken by the smaller lights and darks of windows. The gloomy bulk of a low building in the left foreground balances the darker portions of the skyscrapers. Webb has chosen his angle with painstaking care to balance the lighted mass of the center building with the light-bathed wall at the right. These panels of light carry the eye downward to the train itself, still drenched in sunshine as if at the bottom of a canyon. Here is all the wonder, the soaring and plunging, and, above all, the limitless contrast that is the essence of the city.

Color, of course, provides tremendous possibilities for photographic artistry. The photo by Charles Steinhacker in Plate 27 (p. 273), although a fascinating composition, is primarily a study in color. The variety in both texture and color so characteristic of autumn is vividly portrayed in the spray of green foliage dramatized by a burst of gold and accented by the linear quality of trunks and branches. Texture, color, and line all contribute to the strong compositional movement, a rhythm that soars upward with much the same sense of grandeur that is associated with the lofty vault of a Gothic cathedral. The color of the foliage is given added impact by the vivid blue sky that forms the background, presenting the viewer with the essence of an October day in the forest.

In contrast to the glowing sunshine in the Steinhacker photograph, the work by David Vine in Plate 28 (p. 274) expresses the loneliness of a winter night. Here again color is eloquent in creating a mood. The scene is not extraordinary; it is simply

above: 329. PHILIP HYDE. *Aspens, Sierra Nevada.* c. 1956.

right: 330. BRUCE ROBERTS. *Wall and Steeple.* 1959.

a series of Greenwich Village backyards separated by trees and fences. Yet the photographer has captured the bleak, purplish aura cast by the new snow and contrasted it with the glow of anticipated warmth from a single lighted window. This dramatic juxtaposition of cold and warm complementary colors suggests the emotions and sensations that are aroused by a winter night in the city.

LIGHT AS THE DESIGNER

The study of lighting effects is a never-ending experiment. With floodlights and reflectors the photographer can manipulate his lighting to achieve dramatic effects or a specific mood for any given subject, and it is only through experimentation that he can obtain the most striking results.

Light plays a particularly important role in the effectiveness of Philip Hyde's photograph in Figure 329. The composition is an interplay of light and dark diagonals, which are produced by strong sun caught at the most dramatic moment. Each lighted area is emphasized—the aspens become soft and billowing, the rocks become sharp and jagged, and the snow heightens the contrast between the two. Softness and sharpness create a balanced rhythm: the rocks are echoed in the gravel in the foreground and the aspen is repeated in miniature in the tufts of grass. The procession of vertical trunks marching up the hillside cuts across the diagonals and lifts the eye toward the mountain beyond. The mammoth size of the mountain is implied by the strong masses of stone and the fields of snow that drift down into the range of the photograph, but it exists in its entirety outside the field of vision. This is one of the most effective devices in any art form—the suggestion of realms beyond what can actually be seen.

Light is important to the composition in Figure 330 as well. The lighting is carefully calculated to lend drama to a simple subject; moreover, an effective design is created by patterns of light and dark. The shadow cast upon the wall falls in exactly the right place to frame the steeple, giving it an increased brilliance. The rough texture of the wall contrasts with the dark smoothness of the sky and with the light that seems to radiate from the steeple. Furthermore, the brilliance of the spire evokes a spiritual quality that contradicts the gloominess of the foreground. As in the photograph of the aspen, this setting had to be studied and the picture snapped at precisely the moment of maximum effectiveness.

Atmosphere becomes the ally of light in *Stump and Mist* (Fig. 331). Light is diffused by a mist that has settled over the forest. A chilly dampness moistens the stump in the foreground to bring out all the beauty of its structure, while the light striking the glistening surfaces highlights the wood and reveals new growth—moss, plants, and tiny trees—springing from the disintegrating wood. The mist helps to establish different planes: trees seem increasingly hazy as they recede into the distance. Most of all, the mist creates a mood—a dramatic contrast of blurred outlines and sharp bright forms, of death and regeneration.

The photographer with an artist's eye can inject a sense of drama into everyday scenes. For the contemporary photographer, however, there is art to be found beyond the obvious aspects of his environment. Art and nature are perhaps more closely allied in photography than in any other medium, for the photographer cannot take pictures of what is not there. On the other hand, through the modern equipment at his disposal, he can discover esthetic qualities in materials seldom noticed by the casual observer. With proper lighting and enlargement, many unlikely objects make fascinating photographs. Aaron Siskind, who has made a specialty of this type of subject, finds interest and beauty in old billboards, worn wood, and peeling paint (Fig. 69). In Figure 332 he has revealed the beauty of oil stains on crumpled paper and has created a photograph with many of the qualities of nonobjective painting. The possibilities for expression in photography are virtually endless.

For pure expressiveness it would be difficult to find a more effective study than Alfred Stieglitz' composition of the hands of his wife, the painter Georgia O'Keeffe

left: 331. Ansel Adams. *Stump and Mist, Northern Cascades, Washington.* 1958.

below: 332. Aaron Siskind. *Oil Stains on Paper.* 1950.

333. Alfred Stieglitz. *Georgia O'Keeffe's Hands.* 1918. George Eastman House, Rochester, N.Y.

(Fig. 333). In this photograph Stieglitz managed to embody everything that people have ever felt about hands: their grace and power, their artistry and expressiveness, their effectiveness as instruments of creation. The hands posed against a solid dark backdrop offer an effective contrast of light and shadow. Light models the forms of the fingers and lends power to the entire composition. This is photography at its best. It is not merely a picture of something, it is the essence of life itself.

THE PHOTOGRAM

In spite of the technical excellence of photographic equipment today, one of the most fascinating approaches to photography as an artistic medium eliminates the camera altogether. László Moholy-Nagy revived and developed the photogram on the basis of experiments made by early pioneers in the field who discovered the effects of light on chemically treated paper.

The photogram is created in the darkroom by placing various objects on photographic paper and turning a white light on them for a second or two. The paper is then run through a photographic developer solution, immersed in a fixing bath or "hypo," and finally washed with clear water. Both opaque and translucent objects may be used to create interesting effects, and the addition of three-dimensional forms that cast shadows increases the range of possibilities. A photogram can also be made by placing two panes of glass on the photographic paper with drops of water and oil between them, setting objects nearby and holding the light so that they cast shadows on the glass.

The photogram suggests a great many opportunities for artistic expression, for it combines the creativity of the artist with the spontaneity of the controlled accident.

MOTION PICTURES

Motion pictures consist of small frames of still pictures, each slightly different, projected at a speed that makes the images seem to move. Each picture is held in the projector for a split second and then moved on rapidly enough so that the persistence of vision is able to bridge the gap between frames. The viewer thus has the impression of a smoothly moving image.

On sound film a continuous narrow band that registers sound runs along the length of the film. After the film has passed through the picture-head on the projector, it runs through the sound-head, where a thin beam of light is projected through the sound track onto a photoelectric cell. The variations in density in the track caused by the recording of sound produce oscillations of intensity in the light beam, which are converted into electrical impulses. These impulses are amplified and carried to loudspeakers behind the screen.

Motion Picture Genre

The *genres* (or kinds) of motion pictures fall into four broad categories. *Fictional* motion pictures present a dramatic work for entertainment. This group includes fantasies and animated cartoons. An *educational* film may be a photographic essay on the life cycle of a South American moth or the correct method of mouth-to-mouth resuscitation. *Documentary* films present facts and events with a specific point of view or argument. The fourth category is the *experimental* film. Such men as Conrad Richter and Jean Cocteau have done considerable work in this field, as have other artists who find such devices as multiple screens, undulating screens, and the simultaneous projection of slides and moving images the exciting means of creating effects never before experienced by a motion picture audience. Dramatic steps were taken in this area at Expo 67 in Montreal. The visitor was completely surrounded by wide screen cyclorama film, which enveloped him in a way that produced a total experience that transcended mere visual sensation.

One experimental device is the Dynamic Frame, invented by the young American, Glenn Alvey, Jr., and developed by the British Film Institute in 1956. With this technique the director is freed from the rigidity of the film frame; he can choose any size playing area he wishes, changing it at will even within a specific shot. Alterations of shape as well as size are possible—from a narrow slit or small square to a huge rectangle—and even nongeometric shapes can be used.

Contrary to popular belief, the motion picture is related less closely to the stage play than to the novel. The camera provides the continuity, the variety of viewpoints, and the enveloping scenic and atmospheric effects that are possible in the novel but are limited in their application to the stage. In essence the film can make full creative use of its possibilities as a complex visual medium, whereas the stage depends for its effects largely upon dialogue and gesture.

The Motion Picture as an Art Form

Every principle of design employed by artists in other media is used in making a motion picture. As an art form, the film is a corporate effort involving a large staff of technicians, but its creative force is provided by the director, who is responsible for formulating the basic concept and for establishing the form, rhythm, variety, and, above all, the unity that make it a successful work of art. It is through editing that the director achieves the synthesis that he desires, and guides the thoughts and associations of his audience toward an understanding of his ideas. The most personal expression of his art begins when, with the help of a skillful editor, he starts to cut and join together the pieces of film.

334. An extreme closeup heightens the drama in *Last Year at Marienbad* (1962).

The texture of the film depends upon the *cutting* and the way the cuts are edited. Slow cutting calls for extended shots that create atmosphere, a sense of deep emotion, or any number of other effects involved with building or sustaining suspense. Quick cutting results in short shots that follow rapidly on one another. It is used to convey a sense of action or of an agitated mental or emotional state. *Montage* is a term used to describe an impressionistic assembly of quick shots that bridge a lapse of time in a film narrative by briefly indicating the passage of events. A *mix* or *dissolve* is the gradual merging of the end of one shot into the beginning of the next. It is produced by superimposing a fade-out onto a fade-in of equal length.

The art of the cameraman combines with that of the director to produce special effects. The composition of a scene depends upon three general factors: the form or movement of the subject, the position or movement of the camera as it relates to the subject, and the way in which the subject is lighted. One of the most important factors in determining the quality of a scene is the distance between the camera and the subject. *Full shots* or closeups are used to reveal the expression of a character, thus injecting emotion into a scene (Fig. 334). The *angle* from which a shot is taken can mold the reactions of the audience by distorting relationships of size or distance or otherwise dramatizing a situation (Fig. 335). The *speed* of the camera can achieve special effects by accelerating action or by slowing it down.

The motion picture was invented to settle an argument. Governor Leland Stanford of California, a lover of race horses, bet $25,000 that all four hooves of a galloping horse left the ground at the same time. In an attempt to prove the governor correct, Eadweard Muybridge set up a battery of 24 cameras to take pictures of the action in various stages. The French painter Meissonier saw the significance of the resulting photographs and arranged for Muybridge to go to France to exhibit them.

A special support for the film was needed to allow a quantity of photographs to be taken in succession at sufficient speed to make them appear to move. In 1889 Thomas Edison patented the Edison Kinetoscope, which used a thin flexible ribbon of transparent celluloid coated with photographic emulsion. This machine showed moving pictures to one viewer at a time on a 50-foot band of perforated film. Thus began commercial cinematography.

The great pioneer in motion pictures was David Wark Griffith, born in Kentucky in 1875. Griffith began his career with one-reel movies, and went on to make many of the most significant advances in the development of movie-making techniques. His innovations include the flashback; the full shot to show a character's expression; the simultaneous development of two parallel situations building toward the same climax; the use of a mounted camera on a moving car to film action shots; and the fragmentation of a single scene into a variety of shots from different angles to give a more intimate glimpse of the action. Russian filmmakers began to contribute to the artistic concept of editing after Lenin declared in 1918 that "for us, the most important of all the arts is the cinema." (Lenin, of course, was mainly interested in the motion picture as a medium for mass propaganda and for the molding of social attitudes.) Outstanding among the Russian directors was Sergei Eisenstein, who understood that the filmmaker may also be a poet, and who sought the underlying rhythm beneath the everyday dullness or apparent disorder of life.

Music and pictures have gone together since the days of silent films, when a pianist at one side of the screen trilled gentle love themes or pounded out ominous chords to enhance the action taking place on the screen above. As films grew in number and importance, a violinist and cellist were added to the piano, and finally, in the palatial movie theaters built during the 1920s, small orchestras often played selections suggested in musical cue sheets that accompanied the film. Eventually music was composed especially for important films. The advent of sound films changed the position of music radically, although it took directors a long time to realize it. Background music soon became a nuisance, often distracting the audience from the conversation of the characters. Music today is used primarily to advance the action of a film, to establish a mood, or to herald a change of locale or of pace.

The contemporary film as an art form has developed largely from the artistry of individual directors in various countries. Ingmar Bergman of Sweden and Antonio Antonioni of Italy are only two of a continually enlarging group of talented directors known for their use of symbolism, imaginative photography, or unique imagery.

335. Orson Wells' *Citizen Kane* (1941) was among the first films to experiment with distorted perspective and unusual camera angles.

A number of men, notably Norman McLaren of the Canadian Film Board, are experimenting with painting directly on film, striving toward a synthesis of time and space that has not as yet been perfected. It appears that more young people are turning to motion pictures as an art form than to any other artistic medium. If this is true, then it is clear that the film will be a most important art form—perhaps *the* most important—in the coming decades.

TELEVISION

Television consists of the instantaneous transmission of images, either fixed or moving, by electronic means over electrical transmission lines or by radio broadcasting stations. In its fundamental principles it resembles the method used to send news pictures, but in television the picture can be continuously changing.

In its early days television was considered chiefly to be a means of relaying events developed for other media. The game in the ball park, the horse race, and the concert or vaudeville show were brought into the home by means of television. As techniques developed, television came to be viewed as a medium in its own right, and its unique characteristics and advantages began to be exploited. Instead of pressing into crowds, craning for a view, the observer could now sit in his living room and enjoy an event from many angles, seeing the participants at close range and hearing their reactions. No other medium could make possible the intimate sharing, by an entire nation or even by the whole world, of the maneuvers of a political campaign, the suspense of an astronaut's flight (Fig. 336), or the poignancy of a national tragedy (Fig. 337).

The possibilities of television as an art form are just beginning to be realized, and its extraordinary potential for spontaneity, immediacy, and intimacy has barely been tapped. The performer is brought directly into the viewer's home; there is no stage or platform, no footlights, no orchestra or audience to separate performer and viewer. Such events as those indicated in Figures 336 and 337 take on new meaning when presented on the television screen. Individuals from other countries bring their music and customs into the viewer's experience; historical material becomes urgent and compelling; and works of drama acquire an immediacy that envelops the viewer totally in the action. The impact of television on education can scarcely be gauged, and its use as a direct educational device will undoubtedly be developed.

As in any art form, the elements of design are the materials with which the television producer works. The line, size, shape, and mass of a dramatic presentation may vary with the content and may be quite different from the same elements in a documentary. These elements will change in the approach to any given event, and they will determine the number of transitional shots, the emphasis on action, and the music. Texture and color are variables as well, depending upon the extent and spacing of commentary and action and the use of shots that set the mood.

The principles of design, of course, come into full play. A kind of rhythm is established in the telecast of a public event, which is presented in different ways by different directors who emphasize different aspects of the event. These same variations may determine as well the rhythm of other types of programs. Form and balance are basic concepts in a television show, for they determine the approach, the amount of background material, and the manner in which a climax is reached. Variety is of vital importance in holding the attention of the viewer and in presenting a subject in all its aspects, whether it involves revealing the varied talents of an individual or the many facets of a situation. Unity, as always, rises from the total conception of the director and his philosophy of what the program should accomplish.

336. Millions of Americans—and people in many parts of the world—watched as the crew of Apollo 11 stepped upon the surface of the moon.

337. An entire nation participated, through television, in the funeral rites for President John F. Kennedy.

Television is a field requiring the time and talents of a great many people. One channel devours vast quantities of material in the space of a week, and in order to avoid repetition (which weakens impact) a large staff must be constantly alert. There is far to go in designing for television, in creating more sophisticated and thought-provoking programs, and in fulfilling the tremendous potential for influencing taste, education, and values. In television, entertainment and communication can reach their highest peak—a synthesis of all the elements and principles of design with sight, sound, and immediacy—bringing about a reorientation of all the arts.

SUMMARY

Photography as an art requires long experience, innate sensitivity, and often deep psychological insight. Naturalism is the reproduction of the surface aspects of a subject, but realism delves beneath the surface into actual reality. It is realism that concerns the photographer. He must (1) see the possibilities of the subject, (2) have the ability to bring out the significance of those possibilities, and (3) possess the technical knowledge to achieve the effect he is after.

The lens is the most important part of a camera, for it is through the lens that light rays are bent or refracted to register the image on the film. Focal length refers to the distance from the lens to the film, and f-rating expresses the "speed" of a lens by comparing its diameter to its focal length. The diaphragm is a series of overlapping metal leaves that control the opening of the lens. The shutter controls the length of time the film is exposed to the light. Depth of field refers to the clarity of focus on objects at a distance from the principal subject in a picture. The film itself consists of a support and an emulsion. The emulsion is composed basically of silver bromide combined with various dyes to give color sensitivity. A filter is a piece of dyed gelatin or glass that either absorbs or transmits rays of light to give heightened effects or contrast. Developing and printing are done by careful control of light and the action of chemicals in solution. A contact print is a print the actual size of the negative, without enlargement.

The difference between good photography and a work of art depends on the photographer. The photographer who is an artist will find significance in ordinary scenes or objects and will use light as his ally in design. He will create moods by his choice of angles or his use of filters to diffuse the light.

Motion pictures as an art form make use of all the elements and principles of design. There are four basic kinds of motion picture: *fictional,* including fantasies, animation, and dramatic presentations; *educational; documentary,* which colors facts with an opinion or a point of view; and *experimental.* A motion picture is a corporate effort by many technicians, but its motivating force is provided by the director, who may use the medium as a personal expression. Joining the cameraman and actors, he can achieve great artistic merit and emotional impact. Two important pioneer directors were D. W. Griffith and Sergei Eisenstein.

Television is a unique art form because of its spontaneity, immediacy, and intimacy. The elements and principles of design play a vital part in the structure of any television program, varying with the concept of the director and with his intention as to what any given program should accomplish. The field of television is a vast and challenging one. It requires the time and talents of many people and possesses a tremendous potential for influencing taste, education, and values. Television at its best becomes a kind of synthesis of all the arts, directing them toward a new and vital art form.

Design and Environment

IV

Design in Architecture

chapter 19

Architectural design is intimately connected with the problem of *space,* and in this era of pioneering beyond the limits of the earth, the use of the word space has far-reaching implications.

THE MEANING OF SPACE

Space as a limitless expanse stretching to infinity is an awesome concept that defies imagination. Yet it is the same space that circulates freely about the earth, making it possible for man to move and breathe and develop as an individual. Some people when confined in a small space suffer what is known as claustrophobia; others, when confronted with vast reaches of desert or water, become victims of an opposite fear, which psychologists label *agoraphobia.* Both are terrifying psychological handicaps caused by one aspect or another of man's relationship to space.

The understanding of space and its effective use has a great deal to do with successful design. Positive and negative space are combined to create a piece of sculpture—the positive space forms the mass and the negative space flows around and through it. It is the space that remains within a ceramic pot or a silver bowl that determines its capacity and its use. The importance of space in architecture becomes clear if one conceives of space as being unlimited until the architect circumscribes it by erecting walls. The quality of the designed space determines the success of a building. It is only *after* the space is determined that the material, surface color, and texture of the walls are considered. One might even say that the demarcation of space is the *structural design* of a building, and the walls are merely the decorative design that enhances it.

The consideration of space leads to another characteristic of architecture, sometimes called the "fourth dimension." In music or literature *time* is an important part of experience, carrying the theme to a climax. Similarly, true understanding of a painting or sculpture requires of the viewer a certain expenditure of time. In architecture, however, the element of time is absolutely essential. To know a building thoroughly one must take time to walk through it, allowing his spirit to flow through

far left: 338. Ventral view of a starfish.

left: 339. Skeleton of a non-poisonous snake.

the space, over and around the divisions or walls, and out through the doors and windows. Anyone who has learned to "feel" a building in all its possibilities can sense almost endless dimensions in its relationship to the human spirit.

From the standpoint of space, buildings can be divided into two categories—*closed* and *open*. The same categories are found in nature. Mollusks have a protective shell that they carry with them wherever they go. This defensive coating is often remarkable in its structural development, as with the snail and the starfish (Fig. 338). The fundamental concern here is for protection. Although the animal cannot move quickly, the shield assures his safety under most conditions. The same principle applies to such temporary shelters as birds' nests, beaver dams, and honeycombs, —a simple outer covering that serves primarily for protection. The structure is built *around* the bird or animal resulting in a closed space. As prehistoric man outgrew his cave and began to build freestanding shelters, he followed this design. The adobe pueblo is of this type, as is the tepee of animal skins or the log cabin of the frontier.

Vertebrate animals, on the other hand, have an inner structure upon which the body is built, not so much for protection as for support (Fig. 339). The skeletal structure permits greater freedom, because the animal has no excess weight to carry, and also because of the increased versatility of movement—the ability to reach out, to grasp, and to run rapidly if necessary. His lack of a built-in shelter is compensated by his greater ability to attack or to escape. The open construction of buildings follows this principle. Stresses and strains are directed toward a basic inner structure, rather than concentrated on the outer walls.

Dynamic use of space is an outstanding characteristic of the Parthenon (Fig. 340), one of the great examples of open structure. This ancient Greek temple centers around the cella, or inner sanctum, where the statue of the goddess Athena was housed. This room, combined with a small treasury for offerings, once formed the inner core of the building, but now it has been largely destroyed. An open row of columns still extends around the building. The columns are an integral part of the structure, yet the spaces between them are large enough to permit small crowds to gather. Standing proudly on the Acropolis, the sacred hill rising above the city, the Parthenon appears as a series of columns drenched in sunlight and patterned by moving shadow, embracing space and shaping it. Vertical and horizontal lines throughout the building are slightly curved to give a sense of soaring upward and to suggest an organic quality relating the structure to its site.

STRUCTURAL CLASSIFICATIONS OF ARCHITECTURE

The Parthenon exemplifies the *post-and-lintel* system of architecture, in which two posts (in this case, columns) are erected, and the intervening space is bridged by a beam, or lintel, which is thrown across it. This is one of four structural classifications

by which works of architecture can be identified (Fig. 341). Each type of structure delineates space in a different way. The post-and-lintel construction creates angular space within two walls and a flat roof (or a variation of the peaked roof) above the horizontal beams.

The development of the *arch* provided architects with a new concept: curved and circular space. First used by the Mesopotamians, the arch became a truly creative element in the hands of the Romans. They repeated it in *arcades* for villas or for aqueducts; they placed arches in right angles to one another to form the *vaults* of their basilicas and law courts; and they rotated the arch on its axis to create the *dome,* as in the Pantheon. The principle of the dome was refined by later generations and ultimately emerged in such magnificent buildings as St. Peter's Basilica in Rome and St. Paul's Cathedral in London.

Three refinements of the arch resulted in the creation of the Gothic style: the flying buttress, the pointed arch, and ribbed vaulting. The *flying buttress* made it possible for Gothic cathedrals to soar higher than ever before, by carrying the extra

above: 340. ICTINUS and CALLICRATES. Parthenon, Athens. 447–32 B.C.

below: 341. Most traditional structures follow one of four basic types of architecture.

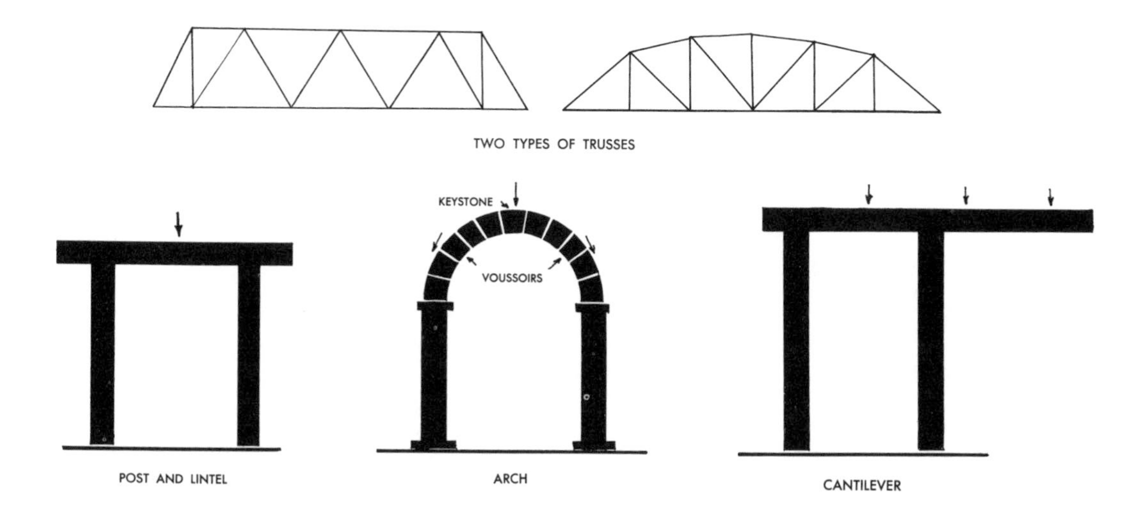

weight of the high walls and the raised vault through an exterior support to the ground (Fig. 342). A round arch must be set upon thick, heavy walls to support its weight and counteract the outward thrust of the arch; a *pointed arch,* however, because it is narrower, focuses the thrust of the arch at a lower point, thus permitting higher and lighter walls. The narrowing of the arch can be seen in Figure 343, as can the effects of *ribbed vaulting.* By breaking a vault into sections outlined by stone ribs, it was possible to fill these sections with a lighter weight material and to support the ribs with piers, to which *colonnettes* (or thin columns) were attached for a graceful appearance. When support was thrust on these piers, it became practical to open up the walls with stained glass windows, galleries, and arcades, which contribute to the spacious, airy quality of many Gothic cathedrals. The arch thus became not only a structural element but an esthetic and philosophical one as well, achieving an openness indoors and out, in which light and space flowed in and the inner spirit of the building emanated outward, into its gardens, the city, and the surrounding countryside. The cathedral was a dominant cultural force during the Middle Ages.

The *cantilever* system came into prominence with the development of reinforced concrete—concrete poured over steel rods or mesh that give it support and stability. With immense tensile strength, steel beams can span greater distances than either stone or wood. When this strength is combined with the strength of concrete under compression, a new and versatile material evolves. Beams embedded in walls of concrete and riveted or welded into place can support tremendous weights even when they are extended into space. This extension provides a new concept of open space, an approach in which space is articulated rather than circumscribed. One of the best-known cantilever constructions is "Falling Water," the house at Bear Run, Pennsylvania, that Frank Lloyd Wright designed for the department store owner Edgar Kaufmann (Fig. 344). The house is built on pylons, or piers, anchored in a foundation of natural stone, with cantilevers of tawny-colored concrete projecting dramatically over the waterfall. The cantilevers, which also serve as terraces, have no support at one end. They form layers of solid structure counterbalanced by open space. Glass walls carry the feeling of space indoors and contrast in texture with the stone of the chimney and the rugged quality of the surrounding wilderness.

below: 342. Cathedral of Notre Dame, Paris (detail of south side with flying buttresses). 1163-c.1200.

below right: 343. Choir vault, Amiens Cathedral. Begun 1220.

344. Frank Lloyd Wright. Kaufmann house ("Falling Water"), Bear Run, Pa. 1936–39.

The fourth system of architecture involves the use of *trusses.* Trusses are employed whenever it is necessary to span longer distances than can be bridged by post-and-lintel construction. The truss consists of a rigid framework of bars, beams, or other material that is so strong that it cannot be pushed out of shape. Trusses have long been used for steel bridges, as well as for large pavilions and for aircraft fuselages. The relationship of the truss to space is similar to that of constructivist sculpture, in which the inside and outside form part of the same space that circulates freely through the framework (Fig. 345). Similar structure is found in the skeletons of birds: light bones permit buoyancy yet retain strength through rigidity (Fig. 346).

above: 345. Trusses are the main structural element in the Rio Vista Bridge across the Sacramento River in California.

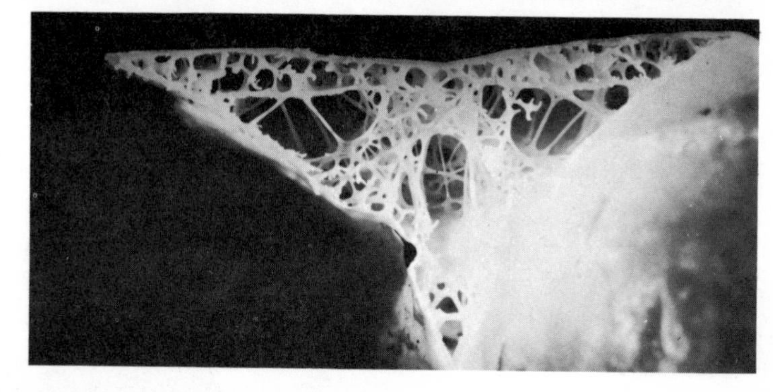

right: 346. Magnified cross section of a crow's skull.

left: 347. Pier Luigi Nervi and Annibale Vitellozzi. Palazzo dello Sport, Rome. 1957.

below left: 348. Pier Luigi Nervi. Interior of dome, Baths at Chianciano. 1952.

below right: 349. Chrysanthemum.

CONTEMPORARY ARCHITECTURE

Although the four structural classifications apply to much historic architecture, the work of contemporary architects does not readily fit the traditional molds. Even when basic structure depends upon the post and lintel or the arch, there is so much innovation and individuality in twentieth-century building that rigid classifications are no longer adequate.

Typical of twentieth-century architects, Pier Luigi Nervi of Rome places the primary creativity of the architect above and beyond the mechanics of structural systems. The architect must have complete control of these systems, of course, but mathematics and drawing are only tools that should be subordinate to the inspiration of the artist. Nervi's own work is eloquent testimony to these ideas. One of his most significant accomplishments has been the development of a revolutionary new kind of reinforced concrete called *ferrocement.* Ferrocement is very strong, but it is also thin, flexible, and elastic. It is composed of layers of steel mesh sprayed with cement mortar so that the total thickness of the material is only slightly greater than that of the mesh itself. Because of its superior strength and elasticity, ferrocement can stand great strains without cracking and can be used in incredibly thin slabs and shells. Often there is no need for the wooden molds ordinarily used for pouring concrete; instead the cement mortar can be applied directly to the shaped mesh.

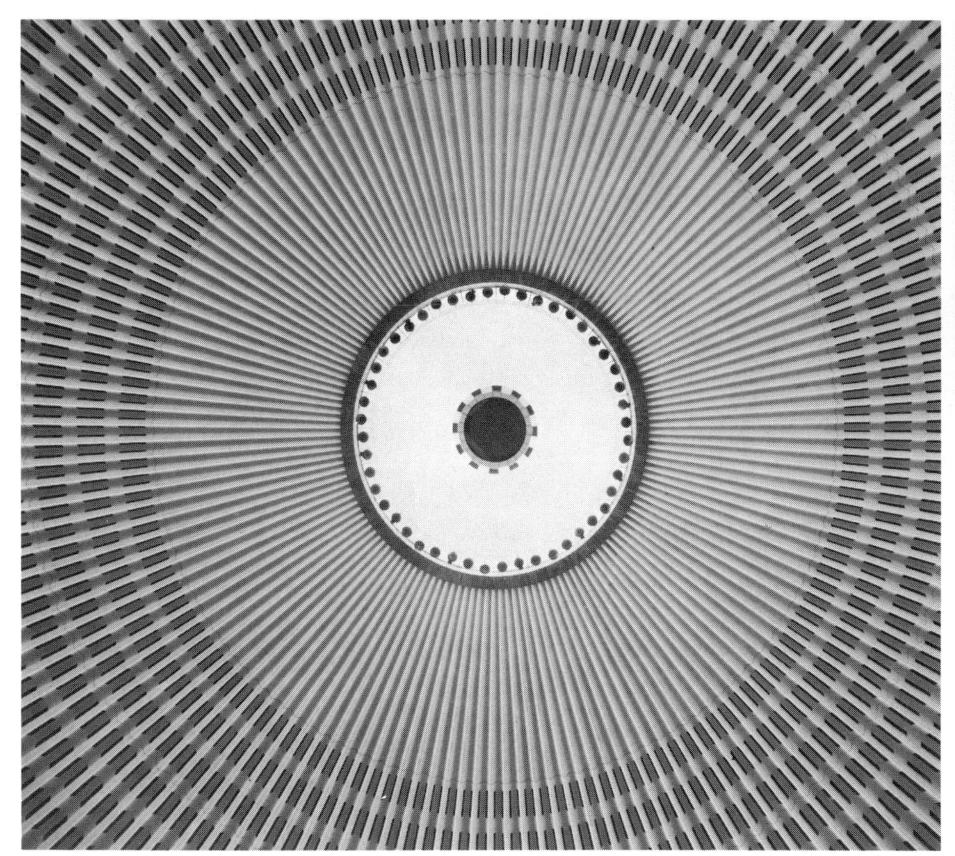

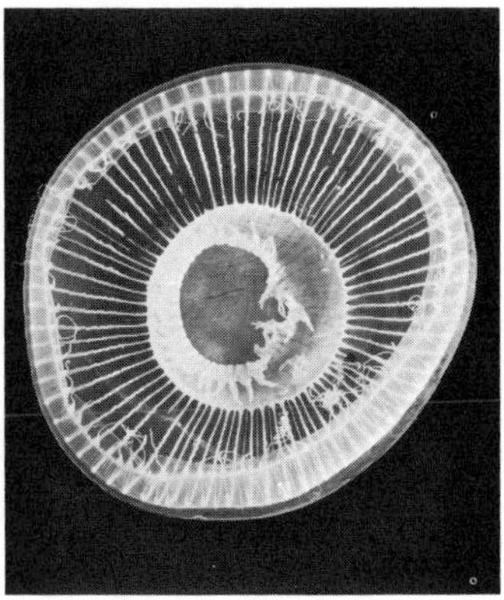

above: 350. Pier Luigi Nervi and Annibale Vitellozzi. Cupola and dome, Palazzo dello Sport, Rome. 1957.

above right: 351. Aequorea, a species of marine life.

The elimination of wooden frames, in fact, constitutes Nervi's second revolutionary contribution to architecture. Nervi substituted plaster molds to create smooth-flowing surfaces and also to allow for prefabrication. All kinds of shapes can be pre-molded from ferrocement and then lifted into place to form the kind of organic structure that is Nervi's specialty (Fig. 347). Conventional reinforced concrete presents many problems, but ferrocement has made possible the creation of structures with a natural organic grace unprecedented in architecture. The domed ceiling of the hall for the Baths at Chianciano (Fig. 348) bears a remarkable resemblance to the blossom of a chrysanthemum (Fig. 349). The intricate fretwork pattern of the ferrocement imitates the organization of the petals of the flower. Organic derivation can also be sensed in the cupola and prefabricated roof sections of the Palazzo dello Sport in Rome (Fig. 350) when it is compared, for example, with the aequorea, a form of marine life (Fig. 351).

The potential for organic form in concrete has had worldwide repercussions in architecture, leading to soaring, flowing shapes that seem newly relevant to the space age. Eero Saarinen, trained in the Finnish tradition of bold, clean architectural forms, designed many concrete buildings with a strong flowing and sweeping quality. Among them are terminal buildings at Kennedy International Airport in New

above: 352. Eero Saarinen. David S. Ingalls Hockey Rink, Yale University, New Haven, Conn. 1959.

left: 353. R. Buckminster Fuller. Kaiser Dome, Hawaii. 1957.

York and at Dulles International Airport in Washington, D. C., as well as the Yale University Hockey Rink (Fig. 352). All of these buildings relate both to nature in form and to the space age in concept, for they evoke the image of a huge bird about to lift off into the air.

A quite different but equally revolutionary approach to architecture is that of R. Buckminster Fuller who invented the geodesic dome (Fig. 353). Just as a flat sheet of paper can be made into a dome by crumpling its surface into a series of small planes, so Fuller has created domes based on small triangles combined into tetrahedrons. This system of building, which he calls "energetic-synergetic geometry," expands the possibilities of the dome to cover much larger areas than had ever before been enclosed by a circular construction. The triangular modules can be made of lightweight metal, and the resulting structure can be covered with any suitable material, such as plastic or cloth. Since 1947 Fuller has built more than 3000 geodesic domes, the largest housing the United States pavilion at Expo 67 in Montreal.

Twentieth-Century Religious Architecture

Religion has always been closely associated with architecture. It has inspired some of the greatest buildings in the world: Egyptian temples, Moslem mosques, the temples of Greece and China, and Gothic cathedrals. Even though the traditional concept of religion is no longer the dominant force in civilization, twentieth-century architects are discovering that one of their great challenges is to create church architecture that will express its own age. In the Gothic cathedral space was used in a symbolic way, flowing in and out of the architectural forms and reaching ever upward toward Heaven. Medieval man thought of space as the means by which all questions would be answered after death, when the soul soared off toward Heaven and complete understanding. Twentieth-century man sails physically out into space, and he finds in it the answers not only to philosophical questions, but also to his eternal curiosity about the universe.

The difference in these concepts of space is fundamental, yet in erecting religious architecture modern man still seems to feel the affinity of space with the striving of the human soul toward perfection. Nervi's model for a cathedral (Fig. 354) exemplifies this need to reach upward. The size of the trees at the base gives an idea of the tremendous scope of Nervi's design, soaring far above man's earthbound capabilities. Oscar Neimeyer's cathedral in Brasilia reaches upward in quite another way: its spidery frame is funneled into a cone 108 feet high (Fig. 355). Glass forms

right: 354. PIER LUIGI NERVI and CARLO VANNONI. Project for a cathedral in New Norcia, Australia. 1959.

below: 355. OSCAR NIEMEYER. Cathedral, Brasilia. 1960.

the walls between the spines, which lift up beyond the roof to give a feeling of reaching toward infinity. Still another interpretation is illustrated in the chapel (Fig. 356) by the Swiss architect and designer Charles Edouard Jeanneret, better known as Le Corbusier. This building, constructed for the small town of Ronchamp in France, has double symbolism. In addition to rising upward like the prow of a ship, it has a form suggestive of the headdress of French nuns in Brittany. The walls were made especially thick to provide insulation from the heat. They are built of steel and rock and concrete sprayed with a cement gun to give a rough and granular skin. Small rectangular openings, placed at irregular intervals, have been cut into the side walls only, so that the interior is spared from the hot rays of the sun. But a masterpiece of lighting is achieved in the separation of walls and roof by a narrow space through which light filters inside. Le Corbusier's definition of architecture stresses light rather than space: "Architecture is the masterly, correct, and magnificent play of the forms of light."

The fantastic organic forms of the Spanish architect Antoni Gaudí are particularly responsive to the play of light, as seen in the Church of La Sagrada Familia in Barcelona (Pl. 29, p. 307). Gaudí interpreted the twentieth-century emphasis on plasticity in a unique way, with curving, biological forms in cut stone.

ARCHITECTURE FOR LIVING

As important as civic and ecclesiastical architecture may be, nothing is more expressive of a civilization than its domestic structures. Here the individual spirit of man is nurtured, and here he most truly manifests himself. Dr. Carl Jung, the eminent psychologist, believed that the only real life is the individual life. Any group is the sum of the individuals who compose it, and a civilization is creative only to the extent that the individual man resists the pressures of the mob.[1] The interaction of a man with his environment is a phenomenon that has not yet been fully explained. It is known that a man, when he is placed in congenial surroundings, is quite a different person from the same man confronted with a hostile situation. The inspired home is not so much a matter of matching period furniture or blending certain colors; rather, it is the creation of an atmosphere in which the inhabitants can reach their fullest potential—socially, professionally, spiritually, and, of course, physically.

In designing any building, the architect is bound by at least four considerations: *function, site, climate,* and *environment.* These aspects are particularly important in a home, where people turn for relaxation and for respite from the outside world.

Function

Function, of course, is the primary factor in any design. In a home, function seems obvious: shelter from weather and protection from intruders. However, function can also be a highly personal matter. Some people use their homes as centers for entertaining; others require a quiet retreat to escape from the noise and frustration of the outside world. For some the home serves as a studio for painting or writing or making pottery. A doctor or dentist may have his home attached to his office, where he will expect to serve the public at any hour. Each of these aspects of the home suggests a different treatment from a design standpoint. Architecture, furnishings, and colors must be adapted to the specific requirements of the individual.

Function also takes into consideration the size and type of the family involved. The United States Public Health Association recommends minimum sizes for houses

356. Le Corbusier (Charles-Edouard Jeanneret). Notre-Dame-du-Haut, Ronchamp, France. 1950–55.

according to the number of people who live in them. One person requires at least 400 square feet of living space, two need 740, and three, 1000. A family of four should have a minimum of 1150 square feet, and a family of five, 1400.[2] In addition to the requirements for physical space, a well-designed house reflects the natural rhythms of life. The rhythm of the seasons dictates placement and landscaping. The daily rhythms of waking and sleeping must be considered in the arrangement of rooms and the provision for light and air. The rhythm of family growth and development must enter into the overall design. Through all of the stages of family life, consideration must be given to the requirements of activity and rest, entertainment and solitude, youth and maturity. Man's physiological and psychological needs must be fulfilled by both material conveniences and general atmosphere.

Site

In an ideal situation the *site* will be determined by the function of the building, but this is not always possible. Frequently the client possesses the land long before he decides to build on it, and the architect will have to adapt his design to the particular characteristics of the site. Such situations present a challenge and frequently result in unique designs. A group of young architects in California fought crowded land conditions by specializing in houses built on slopes of fifty degrees or more. Land that had been considered uninhabitable thus became the site of highly individual homes which made the most of decks and cantilevers and offered superb views.

Once the site has been established, orientation should be planned. Orientation may be described as *an interactive adaptation between the building, its purpose, and its environment.* This means opening a "picture window" in a wall that faces a natural landscape or a garden, rather than an alley or the living room of the house across the street. It means placing bedrooms in a quiet corner of the house, and not on a busy thoroughfare, or locating the kitchen in the rear so that children playing in the back yard can be supervised from the kitchen window. Orientation involves the exploitation of ready-made assets, such as large trees, a stream or pond, or interesting rock formations. The use of an existing boulder to accent the entrance to a house

357. JAMES M. HUNTER. Kenneth Norton house, Boulder, Colo. 1956.

in the mountains can be seen in Figure 357. The boulder establishes the spirit of the setting and also serves to separate the house from the carport.

Climate

Both function and orientation will be influenced by *climate.* The degree to which indoors and outdoors are integrated in a building will depend upon the weather that can be expected throughout the year. Warmer climates are conducive to truly open architecture, with patios and *atria,* or roofless garden rooms; colder regions will make more use of glass and brick to shut out the elements and create an environment within the house. Climate control is an important aspect of any building, and it involves many factors. Of primary consideration is the relationship of the sun to indoor living. In some climates the sun streaming through a window is an asset; in others, it turns the interior into an oven. These possibilities must be considered in advance, and provision must be made to catch the sun or to control it by vines, trees, or overhangs. Light-colored materials will reflect the sun, a fact that will determine roof and wall color. In any climate, air circulation is necessary to eliminate odors and to keep the atmosphere healthful. This can be done with cross-ventilation through windows, fans, or air ducts. Openings in the ceiling or at the tops of walls provide still more light and air, and air-cooling systems are essential in hot climates. The ultimate flexibility in orientation and climate control has been investigated by architects who have experimented with circular buildings that rotate gradually on an axis by the force of the sun's rays, which also provide solar heating throughout the day.

Environment

Although *environment* could be extended to include site and climate, it is usually considered in terms of the immediate neighborhood in which a building is located. This is one of the most vital aspects of housing design—and one that should be thoroughly studied before construction begins. There is little joy in a beautiful home if the owner of the adjoining property is allowed to operate a junk car lot. The arrival of a factory in a residential district can create havoc, lowering property values and destroying the pleasure of living in even the most attractive house. Cities have zoning laws to cover many of these contingencies, to keep industrial and commercial installations at a distance from established residential blocks. There are, however, many unfortunate situations that can arise, and the prospective home builder and his architect should be fully informed about the local laws and the intentions of people owning nearby property. Although standardization in housing is to be deplored, a certain consistency is necessary for comfortable living. A small house built in an area of imposing mansions would lose itself and detract from the neighborhood, whereas an impressive home built among more modest structures looks out of place and prevents the smaller buildings from showing to best advantage.

ORGANIC ARCHITECTURE

The relationship between a house and its physical environment was fully appreciated by Frank Lloyd Wright, an American architect who spent a long lifetime working to relate architecture to its surroundings (Fig. 344). The two most eloquent expressions of his ideas are his own homes, Taliesin North (Fig. 358) in Spring Green, Wisconsin, and Taliesin West (Fig. 359) near Scottsdale, Arizona. Wright was of Welsh descent, and when his mother presented him with some land on a hill in Wisconsin, he gave it the Welsh name Tal-i-é-sin, which means "shining brow." Later, when he built his winter home in Arizona, he set it in the clear sunlight of the desert where the name was equally appropriate.

The contrast between the two settings is striking, yet the basic concept is the same. Local materials are used to create a sense of unity with nature, and the lines of the design in each case complement the neighboring terrain to make an organic structure, in harmony with its surroundings. Wright spoke of the rolling green hills of Wisconsin as intimate friends, describing how they cradled Taliesin lovingly;

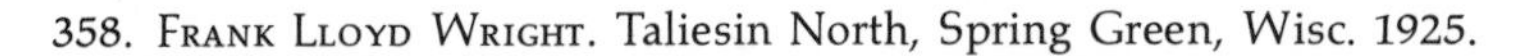

358. Frank Lloyd Wright. Taliesin North, Spring Green, Wisc. 1925.

left: 359. Frank Lloyd Wright. Taliesin West, Scottsdale, Ariz. 1938.

opposite: Plate 29. Antoni Gaudí. Church of La Sagrada Familia, Barcelona. 1833–1926.

he expressed the human scale of the landscape, with its slow winding stream and pastoral beauty:

> The buildings became a brow for the hill itself. . . . Then stone, stratified, went into the lower house walls and up from the ground itself into the broad chimneys. This native stone prepared the way for the lighter plastered construction of the upper wooden walls. Taliesin was to be an abstract combination of stone and wood as they naturally met in the aspect of the hills around about. And the lines of the hills were the lines of the roofs, the slopes of the hills their slopes, the plastered surfaces of the light wooden walls, set back into shade beneath broad eaves, were like the flat stretches of sand in the river below and the same in color, for that is where the material that covered them came from.[3]

Built in 1925, Taliesin North still embodies many features of the finest houses being designed today.

Taliesin West (Fig. 359), built 13 years after the Wisconsin house, has a more rugged setting that presented a greater challenge to the architect. Any building set in desert country must establish, in the beginning, its relationship to the sun. The first impulse is to counteract nature by constructing a protective shelter into which man can withdraw from the dazzling brightness and relentless heat. In this approach man builds in defiance of nature; he sets himself against it as a force to be resisted. In Taliesin West, however, nature is welcomed as an ally. Surfaces are broken into patterns that catch the sun, transforming it into endlessly changing lights and shadows and rendering it harmless. Here again, the contours of the landscape are continued in the lines of the house, and natural materials are used: stone from the desert outcroppings and wood from the nearby mountains. Interior comfort is assured by deep overhangs and thick insulating walls, yet the feeling of openness persists, thus creating a rhythmic interplay of light and space with coolness and protection

Plate 30. Frank Lloyd Wright. The Lloyd Lewis House, Libertyville, Ill. 1940.

(Fig. 360). Light balances shadow, wood balances stone, and variety within unity is achieved by the imaginative use of materials relating to the setting. The sense of unity is fostered by planning space to circulate around and through the structure, making the desert and the building interactive.

As in most of Wright's architecture, the emphasis is not on physical comfort alone. The importance of his designs lies, rather, in the creation of an atmosphere that nurtures both body and spirit. The soul of man is at ease with the materials of nature. It is free to soar out the windows and into the trees or over the desert with the clouds and birds. There is no sense of retreat from life; instead, one has a feeling of growth and development where a man can contemplate life's deepest meanings and reach out to find his own place in the universe.

This organic relationship of architecture to setting has been explored in other settings as well. Figure 361 shows a house built on a promontory overlooking Puget Sound and the Olympic Mountains west of Seattle. Here the problem is one of catching a breathtaking view without succumbing to the glare of sun and water, of blocking wind and rain from the southwest without destroying the feeling of kinship with the outdoors. Glass areas with deep overhangs face the sound, while vertical cedar walls protect the southwest side from the onslaught of the elements. The architect has used native woods, and he has made no attempt to affect a modern formula by using stone where the design does not require it. The simplicity of the walls and foliage reflects an interest in Japanese forms quite in keeping with this area, where Japanese fishing floats wash up on the beaches and Japanese ships dock regularly in the ports.

right: 360. FRANK LLOYD WRIGHT. Interior, Taliesin West.

below: 361. PAUL THIRY. David Stimson house, Seattle. 1949.

The floor plan shows an abstract design as well as a working drawing (Fig. 362). One can look at the division of space without thinking of rooms and imagine the various areas filled with color and texture. The design could stand alone with no relationship to utility. This is true of any good floor plan, for sound design on a two-dimensional surface is readily translatable into three-dimensional projection. In this house emphasis is placed on the large area forming the living room and on the surrounding terrace, which lends an accent. Balance is achieved by the extension forming the kitchen, breezeway, and garage, which counteracts the heavier, more intricate area containing the bedrooms. The predominant feeling is one of variety, with larger areas progressing in transition to smaller ones. Rhythm and unity are created by openings in the walls that provide a feeling of circulating space.

The floor plan is also workable from the standpoint of utility. The living room is at the back of the house and can be entered from the front only through the entry hall. This location protects it from unwanted callers, from the driveway, and from outside activity, while the hall lends a touch of suspense for anyone entering from the front. In the living room interest is centered on the view over sweeping lawns stretching to the sound and to the mountains. Any room can be entered without crossing the living room. The adjoining den forms a buffer between the living area and the isolated bedroom wing, where privacy and quiet are assured. At the opposite side of the living room, the dining room, kitchen, laundry, and garage extend one beyond the other. The dining room is easily served from the kitchen, and activities in the laundry, separated from the house by a covered breezeway, can be supervised while work is being done in the kitchen. There is easy access to the service yard, and the location of the downstairs recreation room keeps all of the areas of possible noise in one end of the house. All the rooms take advantage of the view, except for two smaller bedrooms designed for children. Considered strictly as a floor plan, the design is as successful as it is when viewed as an abstraction, and one feels that the opportunity to move and live in such a house in all its dimensions would be an exceedingly satisfying experience.

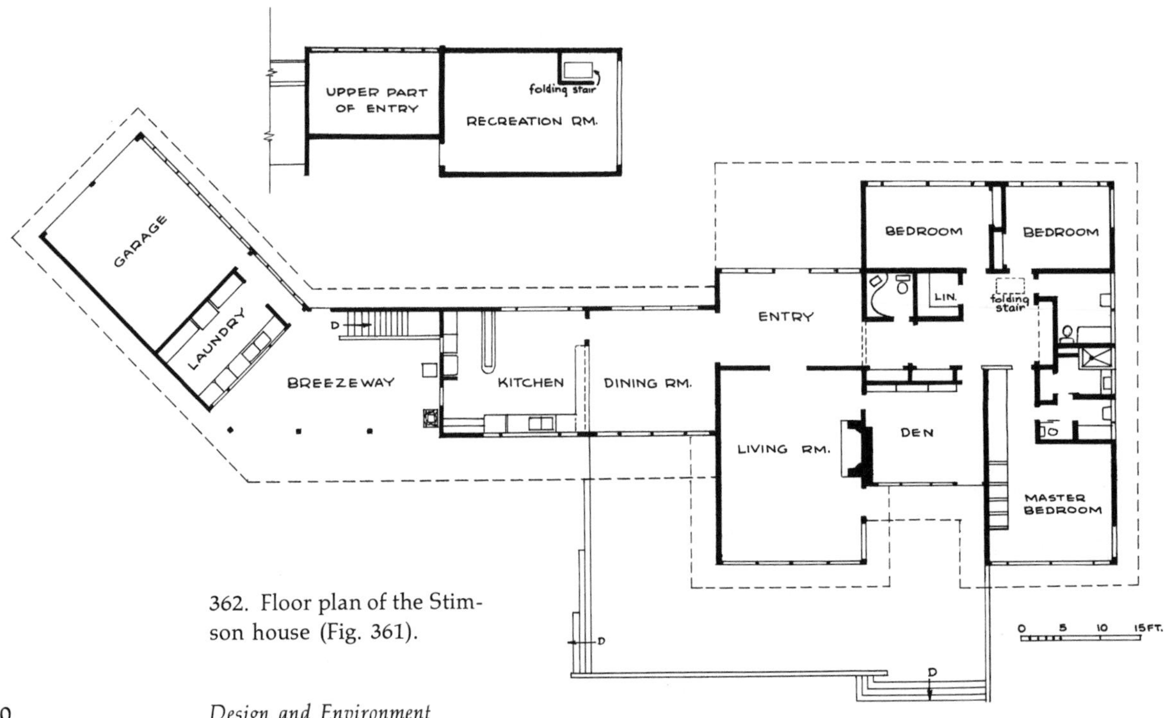

362. Floor plan of the Stimson house (Fig. 361).

363. Bruce Bicknell. Condominium, Aspen, Colo. 1967.

ARCHITECTURE FOR THE FUTURE

The use of ferrocement and the geodesic dome points the way toward new forms in architecture not yet imagined. Fifty years ago the Bauhaus influence was considered revolutionary because of its stern geometry. This trend gave way to an interest in soaring organic forms or geometric curves and domes. The space age will bring still more unprecedented shapes and patterns, and it can be assumed that many of them will reach upward to take man farther and farther from the ground.

The trends in design for homes already have fallen into patterns characteristic of a new era, an era in which people move about a great deal. Possession is no longer as important as it was in the days when the family mansion with all its treasures was handed down from generation to generation. Statistically, American families now average one move every five years, and the type of house that accommodates them has shown drastic changes. The *condominium* is one solution (Fig. 363). This is a type of apartment that can be purchased but that will be cared for by a permanent overseer whenever the owner is away. Such an arrangement is ideal for families who live in several locations, because of business or the change in season, or who must travel a good part of the time. High property taxes discourage home ownership in many areas, and the traditional rented apartment is finding new enthusiasts, with the construction of high-rise buildings in the hearts of many cities. These buildings, often landscaped and close to business and shopping centers, eliminate the strain of commuting, as well as the care of a lawn and the upkeep a house requires. Frequently apartment houses are organized as clubs, with an adjacent golf course and a shopping center on the premises. Supermarkets, drug stores, dry cleaning establishments, beauty shops, restaurants, and movie theaters are all within walking distance. Such homes are ideal for older people, who appreciate freedom from the tasks of homemaking and the convenience of having all their everyday needs fulfilled in one place.

For those who prefer separate units, mobile homes have become very popular. These can be temporarily installed in any city and moved from town to town at will. Many are roomy and well-designed, with compact furniture and ingenious use of space. Still another innovation is the prefabricated house, which can be purchased in modules and erected within a matter of days. Prefabrication is used for other types of buildings as well. One small college was built almost overnight. Trucks brought the buildings and furniture to the site, unloaded them into place on prepoured foundations, and departed, leaving the campus ready for occupation (Figs. 364–367).

THE IMPORTANCE OF THE ARCHITECT

The creation of an architectural design is a tremendous responsibility. Human development is dependent upon its surroundings, and the surroundings become a matter of buildings: schools and churches, libraries and museums, office buildings and hotels, and especially homes. The town is the sum of its buildings, and the

364–367. Prefabrication made possible the very rapid construction of Colorado Mountain College in Glenwood Springs, Colo.

right: 364. A prefab module is delivered to the site.

above: 365. The module is hoisted onto the previously poured foundation.

right: 366. Foundations for more modules are prepared two weeks after the first module was put in place.

367. Ten months after the delivery of the first module the completed classrooms and dormitories are furnished and ready for occupancy.

distant cityscape is a silhouette of its dominant structures. The intellectual climate of a community can be judged almost immediately by the relative importance of its factories or its museums and the predominance of beautiful parks or of extensive slum areas. The architectural designer has the opportunity to put his mark upon an entire area, to make a contribution that can change the lives of vast numbers of people. As Eero Saarinen expressed it: "Architecture should fulfill man's need for shelter, but it should also fulfill his belief in the nobility of his existence on earth."

SUMMARY

Architecture is primarily a matter of space that has been enclosed for effective use. In this context, buildings can be classified as closed or open. From a structural standpoint, there are four traditional classifications of architecture: post and lintel, the arch, cantilever, and the truss.

Contemporary architecture depends more upon the originality of the designer than upon traditional methods. Ferrocement is a material that makes possible an entirely new concept of architecture consistent through its flowing forms with the activities of the space age. The geodesic dome is another innovation, making possible the extension of a dome roof over a larger area than ever before.

Religion has always been a dominant factor in architecture. Twentieth-century cathedrals show a new concept of space and new ways of achieving a soaring effect.

Domestic architecture is one of the most important fields of design, inasmuch as man's personal life is centered in his home. The architect who designs a house must consider four aspects: function, site, climate, and environment.

The organic concept of architecture relates building and site in such a way that they seem visually interactive. Frank Lloyd Wright was the great proponent of organic architecture, creating an entirely new approach to home design.

New trends reflect the needs of a mobile population, which no longer feels it necessary to possess a family home. Such trends include condominiums, high-rise apartment buildings, mobile homes, and prefabrication. Whatever direction architecture takes, the architectural designer wields a vital influence, shaping whole communities with his designs.

Interior Design

chapter 20

The interior of the home provides an intimate environment for all who live there; it both expresses and influences their outlooks and personalities. Everything that the architect strives to accomplish in creating a setting for the individual comes to a climax in a well-designed interior. Architecture and interior design are not only closely related; they actually perform the same function. Together they represent the culmination of the creative effort that attempts to compose a beautiful space.

THE ORGANIC APPROACH

The organic concept of the interior involves a growing, changing environment consistent with the total personality of the people who live in it at any given time. Although the principles of design are applied in any attractive home, there is one basic precept that becomes the keynote: *a successful home is an expression of its*

368. JOHN LAUTNER. Living room, the Fisher house, Hollywood, Calif. 1955.

occupants—of their taste, their interests, and their aspirations. Such expression develops through a series of choices regarding color, form, texture, line, size, and a myriad of details that combine to form a unified whole compatible with the personality of the particular family or individual. A home will reflect current preferences, as well as past experiences, associations, travels, and personal relationships. A family heirloom may be the focal point around which a room develops. The homes of people who have led full and interesting lives often exhibit a warmth and richness that goes beyond a certain period or style. *Interior decoration* is concerned with arrangement of furnishings, as a period room is decorated in a museum; but *interior design* involves not only the furnishings but the structure, the environment, the experiences, and the personalities of the people within.

FOUR KINDS OF INTEGRATION

Integration of Structure with Interior Design

Perhaps the most obvious characteristic of organic architecture is the honest treatment of structural elements, particularly through the use of natural materials. In Figure 368, for example, the redwood ceiling joists embellish the interior, while at the same time they carry the eye outward to the overhang sheltering the patio where the redwood is continued. This use of wood is repeated in the wall paneling and the bookshelves. A forthright regard for structure is carried through in the fireplace, where no attempt has been made to disguise the roughness of the concrete blocks. The skeleton of this house is not something to be sheathed or veneered. Instead, it contributes character, warmth, and attractiveness to the whole interior.

Integration of Interior with Landscape

Another aspect of organic design concerns the integration of indoor and outdoor living areas. This is important today for two reasons. First, with the population increasing and the available space decreasing, it is essential that the best possible use of space be made. Second, the enjoyment of a home can be multiplied many times by expanding the activities of living into a natural outdoor environment. Even a relaxing view from a window can add to the pleasures of living and contribute to a family's well-being. Figure 369 shows the correlation that is possible between a

369. WARD THOMAS. Living room, the Thomas house, San Francisco. 1958.

modest home and a small plot of land. The chief factor in the indoor-outdoor relationship is the use of glass for walls separating interior and patio. With the dividing wall thus almost invisible, every foot of outdoor space is developed for the specific purpose of extending the living area. Textures of rug and plantings harmonize, with accents of greenery brought inside. The forms of the garden beds and the coffee table follow the same biomorphic lines, lines based on organic forms. The wood of floors and walls continues outward to form the deck and garden screens that divide the property from adjoining yards. No great amount of space is used here, either indoors or out, but nothing is wasted. Man is related to nature rather than being closed within his shelter, and his experience is extended into space, to the enjoyment of earth and sky and the changing seasons.

In Figure 370 the viewpoint is reversed and the integration is seen from the outside looking in. Here the outdoor space flows into the house and is carried by the continuous metal roof decking and the unbroken line between outside paving and inside flooring. Similar textures and forms of foliage extend through both indoor and outdoor areas, while the cement-block wall provides an effective transition, but does not completely separate the two areas. The use of louvered skylights inside as well as out unifies still further the whole architectural scheme. There is an overall unity composed of two motifs—the metal and the forms of nature. This is an example of the kind of harmony that can result when man finds a way to live compatibly with nature.

The integration of indoors and out can be carried into a further dimension by creative use of lighting. In recent years many inventive lighting devices have been developed, all of them far removed from the traditional overhead chandelier. Indirect lighting concealed behind window valances bathes the interior in a soft glow, which heightens the effect of the furnishings and causes intriguing changes in the colors of walls and fabrics. Diffused lighting from recessed fixtures in the ceiling dramatizes furniture groupings. The effect of light can be carried outdoors by placing lights under the soffits outside the windows. Spotlights hidden in the shrubbery may play over the whole garden or dramatize certain details. Shadows change continually with the movement of breezes, and when there is a pond or waterfall, the combination of light, shadow, and reflection becomes a fascinating interplay that opens the mind to new horizons of contemplation and relaxation.

Integration of Periods and Interests

The Importance of Discernment Discernment, or taste, is a quality that affects every choice one makes, but nowhere is it more apparent than in the decoration of a home, where it involves selectivity in gathering the materials to build a personal environment. Discernment is an acquired trait, developed and refined through years of observing, comparing, and analyzing the beautiful things of the world. There are four specific ways in which it can be developed:

1. By searching constantly for beauty; by exposure whenever possible to beautiful surroundings; by studying the contents of museums, books, and magazines.
2. By delving into other cultures to widen experience and appreciation.
3. By gaining an understanding of history and philosophy, so that artistic expression will have more meaning and depth.
4. By constant awareness of, and sensitivity to, one's own environment with a continuing desire to improve it.

above: 370. In this house, designed by A. Quincy Jones, there is an almost unbroken continuum between the interior and the garden.

right: 371. Architect Eliot Noyes designed this weekend house to blend with the ruggedness of the Vermont countryside.

Integration of Sensory Responses

The organic approach to interior design creates an atmosphere that involves all the senses. The eyes respond to colors, shapes, forms, and textures, as well as to the principles of balance, emphasis, rhythm, and unity. The ears are affected by the acoustics, which may either magnify or deaden noise. The furnishings can control the way ordinary sounds are transmitted, just as the placement of electronic components affects the reception of stereophonic sound. The smells of building materials, fabrics, rugs, and the woods of furniture have a potent effect on one's reaction to an environment. These elusive scents are heightened or overpowered by the odors from cooking, from wood burning in the fireplace, from waxes and polishes, or from cigarette or pipe smoke hanging in the air. The textures of walls and furnishings become tactile as well as visual experiences for the people living with them—the feel of the fabric of a chair, the roughness of the stone fireplace, the smooth finish of wood paneling or of a table (Fig. 371). Even the sense of taste is affected by the

above: 372. A kitchen can be as streamlined and modern as a laboratory, as in this example designed by Charles Moore.

right: 373. Some families prefer the warmth and color of a more traditional kitchen.

atmosphere in a house. Foods taste better in a congenial, relaxed environment where the sights, sounds, and smells contribute to the anticipation and enjoyment of eating. Beyond all of these there is a sense of well-being that comes from living in surroundings where the spirit moves freely in space, both inside and outside the house.

A SENSE OF TIMELESSNESS

When a home is integrated in these four ways, it achieves a sense of timelessness that makes it impervious to change. This does not mean that it is static. Any successful room adapts to expanding tastes, and occasional changes in color or a piece of furniture are refreshing. Nevertheless, a skilled handling of the elements and principles of design can transcend the boundaries of fashion to create a lasting and individual style.

This quality is exemplified in Plate 30 (p. 308). Frank Lloyd Wright designed this house in 1940, but no detail marks it as having been built in any particular decade. Much of the furniture is built in, and it thus becomes a part of the architecture. Wright believed in the unity of building and furnishings, and to this end he even created a line of tableware, linens, and accessories specifically coordinated with the houses that he designed. In fact, he sometimes refused a commission for a house unless he could specify the furnishings, since only in this way could he be sure to achieve the flexible, timeless quality that characterizes his architecture.

In the house reproduced in Plate 30 there is a strong sense of balance. The textures of carpeting and old brick balance the smooth, polished surfaces of the built-in shelves and tables. A feeling of serenity is created by the dominant horizontal lines of ceiling, bricks, and furniture, broken only by the occasional vertical accent of doors, windows, and fireplace wall. Rhythm is achieved by the repetition of brick and natural wood textures and by the emphasis upon the fireplace as the center of interest. Variety comes from the three basic textures combined with plants and art objects. There is nothing superfluous or meaningless. Unity of design derives from the coordination of natural materials throughout, as well as from the repetition of specific textures. This is a room where one could read, listen to music, talk with friends, or doze by the fire with an equal feeling of enjoyment and relaxation. It is a room not dependent upon fashionable colors or current trends in furniture—one that will remain contemporary through innumerable cycles of fashion.

FUNCTIONAL PLANNING

Just as in architecture, function is a primary consideration of interior design; the interior of a house must be designed to serve the needs of those who live in it. Whether the home is a one-room apartment or a vast estate, there are six phases that contribute to the creation of a successful design.

Deciding Upon the Spirit of the Home

The spirit of a home depends largely upon whether the home is to be used as a center for entertaining or as a retreat from a busy world. This decision will affect the choice of colors, textures, and furniture, as well as the way in which these elements are used. A room for entertaining will have warmer, livelier colors and a more ornamental decor than a retreat that is meant to be restful. The textures may be coarse for hard wear or smooth in more formal furnishings, depending upon the type of entertainment the family prefers. Furniture should be adaptable to varied use—sectional sofas that can be used as chairs, tables that will serve many purposes—and it should be flexible enough to accommodate groups of people for conversation, watching television, listening to music, or playing cards. Each room should have its individual spirit as well. Bedrooms may be used strictly for sleeping, or they may double as studios or sitting rooms. A kitchen, too, can play various roles. Figure 372 illustrates a room that proclaims its efficiency in clean lines, simple forms, and an atmosphere that suggests a laboratory, where cleanliness and order are the primary requisites. The kitchen reproduced in Figure 373, while just as clean and orderly, has a warmth and interest that make it more than just a room for preparing meals. It is a spot that could be the center of life in the home, where children gather to discuss their activities, or where visitors sit for a cup of coffee. Cooking would not be a concentrated effort that precludes distraction but an enjoyable occupation that is enhanced by the view from the windows and the conversation nearby. The display of spices and utensils gives the kitchen an old world flavor, so that cooking is seen as an art, visual as well as culinary. Each of these kitchens serves its purpose well; the difference in effectiveness lies in the personality of the cook.

Pinpointing the Needs and Wishes of the Occupants

Frank Lloyd Wright did not design attics or basements for his homes. He deplored wasted space, which he said inevitably became a catchall. Wright's contention was that storage space should be designed specifically for certain objects, for only in this way is all space used most effectively. Built-in cupboard and closet space is an American idea, evolving from the simple furnishings of the Shakers, a religious sect that came to New York from England. Emphasizing the dignity of working with the hands, they developed such utilitarian innovations as round barns, clothespins, and built-in storage. American builders have tended to allow for more storage space in houses built in recent years, but when an architect or interior designer is planning for a specific client, the client should be given the advantage of storage that is custom-designed. He must make a careful inventory of his interests and possessions.

left: 374. Wrapping packages can be a pleasure rather than a chore when all the materials are assembled in a convenient center.

below: 375–377. A basic floor plan may be adapted to the needs of different families.

375. Family (a) has three small children.

376. Family (b) has one school-age child.

377. Family (c) has children who have grown and moved away.

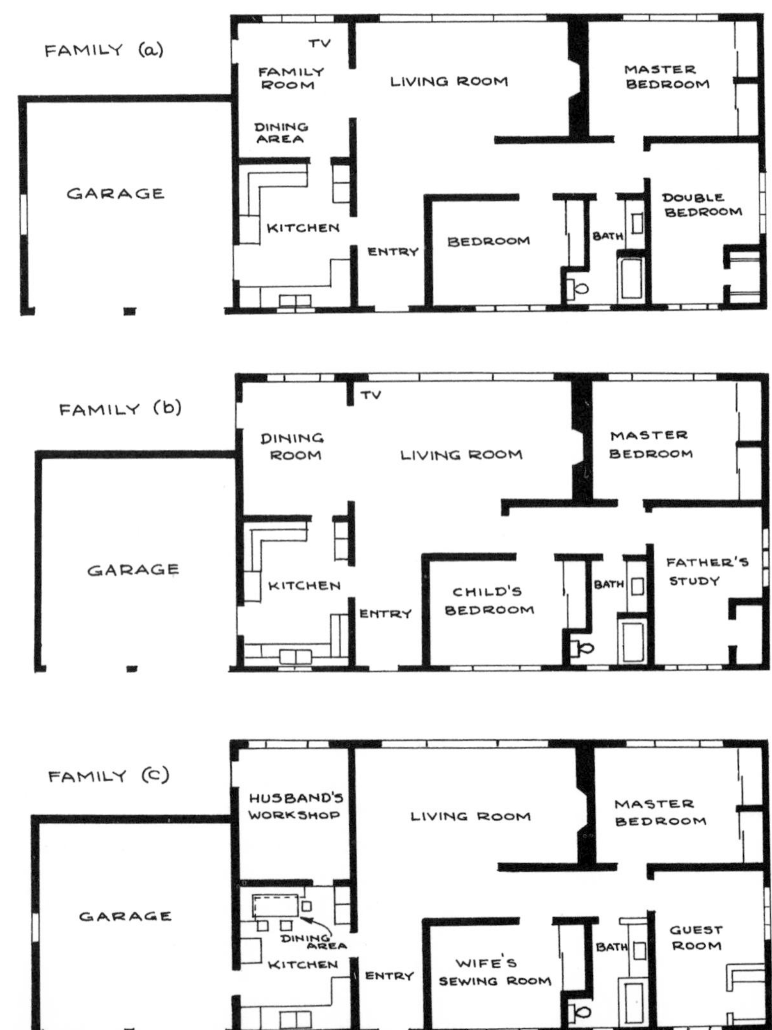

Special cupboards must be provided for bulky items, such as projectors and picnic baskets; shallow drawers should be designed for prints or drawings, place mats, and the like; and display areas should be planned for special collections, such as coins, pewter, or jade. Figure 374 shows a center for wrapping packages—a useful and convenient provision for a family that enjoys extensive gift giving. The efficient assembling of materials in an attractive spot with ample work space could transform a chore into an enjoyable art. These are the touches that give everyday tasks a special meaning, affecting the entire outlook and personalities of the people involved.

Organizing Allotted Space According to Specific Needs

When an architect designs a house, he can plan its space specifically to meet individual needs. However, when a family moves into an existing house the space is already distributed, but the use of it is not necessarily specified. In Figures 375 to 377 is shown a basic floor plan that has been adapted for three different families, demonstrating the flexibility that can be exercised by an imaginative interior designer. Family (a) has three children who use the smaller rooms as bedrooms. The room between the kitchen and the living room becomes a family room with a dining area at one end. There is space for other activities, such as watching television, and the mother can keep an eye on her family from the kitchen. In Family (b) there is one child of school age. The family room is used as a dining room, and the farthest bedroom is converted into a study. With this retreat available, the television set can be moved into the living room, which then becomes a center for family activity. Family (c) consists of a couple with grown children. The family room-dining room now becomes a workshop, where the husband can pursue his hobby of woodworking without creating disorder in the rest of the house. The study is used as a guest room for the children when they visit, and the small bedroom is a sewing room for the wife. A dining area is built into the kitchen. These are just three possible arrangements. If a family has special needs, such as a darkroom or an office for a dentist or a doctor, these could be fitted into this basic plan. Furthermore, the dining room could be blocked off from the living room and used as a utility room, or it could be closed off from the kitchen and converted into a library. With the exception of the kitchen and bathroom with their permanent fixtures, the adaptability of given space is limited only by imagination and the family's needs.

Figure 378 shows an excellent example of a room designed to meet a variety of needs within a small space. An area for sleeping, reading, studying, or writing

378. All the requirements for comfortable living are found in this attractive one-room apartment.

is combined with a fireplace and a cooking area just out of sight to the left to provide all the necessities for a student, a writer, or a businessman. There is even an extra bed for a guest. The design is handled with a creative touch that makes the attractiveness of the room even more obvious than its versatility. This is an area that could be furnished in a variety of ways, for the basic structure is relatively simple. Even the fireplace is not unalterably permanent. The solution chosen offers a complete one-room home with considerable charm.

Selecting Colors, Fabrics, and Furnishings on the Basis of Use, Appropriateness, and Beauty

Shopping for furniture and materials can be one of the most satisfying (and also one of the most trying) phases of interior design, for choices are the expression of the individual, and they determine to a large extent the entire character of the interior. The use of light colors can make a large room seem more intimate. Rough textures may suggest the feeling of bricks or fieldstone, while printed fabrics can serve as accents for wide expanses of smooth walls. The scale of pattern in fabrics can do much to regulate the size of the room and to establish its sense of liveliness or tranquility. The skillful use of an interesting pattern—both as a wall covering and as an accent—can lend elegance, as in the living room in Figure 379.

The combination of several compatible patterns in the same room is found in some period styles. In a contemporary interior, on the other hand, the trend is toward variety in textures rather than an array of patterns. Shag carpets, rough, open weaves in fabrics, stone, and wood provide stimulating surfaces, while retaining a simplicity consistent with twentieth-century architecture.

In the selection of furnishings for a home, the dramatic possibilities of lighting should be appreciated and explored. No longer is interior illumination merely a matter of scattered lamps and overhead fixtures; soft diffusion of light can imbue a room with a serenity not otherwise possible. Treasured pieces or interesting architectural features can be dramatized by spotlighting; fluorescent tubes mounted behind window valances can bathe a wall in a warm glow; and lights installed in planters create interesting shadow patterns. If an overhead light is desired above a desk or table, it can be incorporated into a fixture that is an important design

379. A brilliant blue wallpaper is used to unify this room. The same pattern that covers the walls has been used for accents against the stark white furniture and rugs. Design by W. & J. Sloane.

element in itself. Textiles and wall colors should be seen both in daylight and under artificial light to ensure the most effective coordination of all elements.

Choosing Furniture to Fulfill the Expressed Needs and Wishes of the Owner

The choice of furniture can be complicated by many factors. Furniture cannot be selected independently of the textures within the room or of the fabrics and materials used on walls or at windows. One may have to adapt furnishings to cherished possessions that hold an important place in the decor. In the living room of a city apartment (Fig. 380) two pieces of period-style furniture—a graceful end table and an upholstered chair—have been skillfully combined with contemporary pieces to create a warm and comfortable environment. The heirloom pieces blend easily with the clean lines of the modern sofa, while a fur rug pulls the whole room together.

Many interior designers are men who create their own designs for furniture and adapt the other elements of the room to complement this style. Men such as Miës van der Rohe, Le Corbusier, and Frank Lloyd Wright extended their creative talents from architecture to decorative and useful objects for the home. Hans Wegner and Finn Juhl have been strong influences in Scandinavian design for home furnishings. This is a field full of innovations and interesting ideas, introducing new materials and twentieth-century creativity into everyday living through furnishings.

Arranging Furniture for Comfort, Attractiveness, and Ease of Circulation

In the arrangement of furniture function determines the decisions, for placement depends upon different types of activity. A room planned for entertainment requires small groupings for conversation. Position of chairs in relation to tables and lamps must be considered. Lanes for walking are essential—space through which people can pass easily without the feeling of having to go around the furniture. Overall circulation refers to the ease of entry into the house and the passage from room to room. Although the furniture should be attractive, no single piece should be allowed to dominate a room, but should take its place in the total arrangement

380. Heirloom pieces blend easily with modern furniture in this room designed by Graziella Lobo.

in relation to the purpose that it serves. In Figure 380 it is evident that the heirloom pieces, while displayed prominently, do not require special consideration from the occupants. The contemporary furniture is grouped for conversation before the fire, and there is room for easy movement.

IMPORTANCE OF INTERIOR DESIGN

A beautiful interior affects everyone who comes in contact with it, adding to his pleasure and to his consciousness of the dignity of living in a well-designed environment. A sense of integrity is basic to interior design, for people are exposed daily to the materials and forms that furnish a home. Genuine materials such as real wood, brick, or stone should be used, and designs should be forthright and expressive of their own era. Copying historic styles is an accepted practice, yet this is a little like wearing a period costume in an effort to capture the elegance of the past. A knowledge of historic styles is a prerequisite for every interior designer, but the most satisfactory home is the one that blends the interests, possessions, and choices of its occupants into a unified whole that is expressive of their own time, as well as of their own personalities. Honesty in the choice of furnishings instills a sense of integrity in their owners. Cheerful colors and an inspiring view or a collection of well-loved books, paintings, or records offer refreshment and help to build the reserves of strength needed for the problems that lie beyond the limits of the home. Appreciation of other cultures broadens one's understanding and fosters an interested and tolerant outlook. More important, personality growth is encouraged where things that stimulate the mind are considered important. The interior of a home not only reflects the individuals who live there; it also—more than any other influence—molds and shapes them, determining their relationships with the world beyond their walls.

SUMMARY

The interior of a house sums up many of the things that the architect and the designer try to accomplish. The basic precept of any home is that it must express its occupants. The organic concept as applied to the interior means a growing, changing atmosphere consistent with the changing personality of the family that lives there.

Four kinds of integration are essential in a well-designed home: integration of structure with interior design, integration of interior with landscape, integration of periods and interests, and integration of sensory responses. A home integrated in these ways achieves a sense of timelessness that makes it impervious to changes in fashion.

Planning a home depends primarily on the function that it will serve—whether it is to be a retreat, a center for entertaining, a studio, or a combination home and office. Such planning can be done in six stages: (1) deciding upon the spirit of the home, (2) pinpointing the needs and wishes of the occupants, (3) organizing allotted space according to specific needs, (4) selecting colors, fabrics, and furnishings on the basis of use, appropriateness, and beauty, (5) choosing furniture to fulfill the expressed needs and wishes of the owner, and (6) arranging furniture for comfort, attractiveness, and ease of circulation.

Interior design is one of the most important design fields, since it affects people in their intimate daily lives. Not only does it influence people, but it also molds them by the values that it stresses through honest use of materials, appropriate colors, and furnishings that develop the intellect and the spirit.

Landscape Design

chapter 21

The development of natural surroundings for relaxation and beauty is an ancient art. Since man first planted seeds to raise food, a bit of land has been a basic need. The garden planned strictly for enjoyment is nearly as well rooted in history. The Old Testament establishes man's first habitat as a garden, and this symbolism of paradise has persisted. In a garden, man creates his personal dream world, his patch of perfection, where he can find the beauty and serenity that will shelter him from the pressures of living.

THE HISTORIC GARDEN

In some civilizations this "patch" has been an impressive one. Persian and Assyrian gardens formed the hunting grounds that prefigured the concept of the public park. Although no trace of them is left today, the Hanging Gardens of Babylon were considered one of the seven wonders of the ancient world. The gardens of Renaissance Italy, which were designed by architects, were often built on terraced slopes with marble balustrades and adorned with sculptures by the artists of the time. Painters, poets, and philosophers gathered there to discuss philosophy or to enjoy the extravagant fountains (Fig. 381). Cascades of water were sometimes poured forth to flood

381. Fountain of the Organ, Villa d'Este, Tivoli. c. 1550.

382. André Le Nôtre. Palace Gardens, Versailles. 1662–88.

out the guests in "water jests," a form of amusement considered wonderfully entertaining. It was not unusual to have a menagerie, with peacocks, ostriches, and strange beasts, wandering through the gardens.

French gardens were no less elaborate. The French adapted the Italian idea of gardening and created their own style of landscape. Instead of erecting a high garden wall, they used the moat as a boundary around their chateaux, thus expanding the area of their carefully planned vistas. Terraces were not popular with the French, who preferred labyrinths of hedges, forming long narrow areas hemmed in by woods. The culmination of French gardening was achieved by the architect André Le Nôtre who designed the gardens of the Palace of Versailles for King Louis XIV. The gardens stretched for miles and became an extension of the palace, a series of outdoor rooms that formed a fitting place for royalty to entertain. Magnificent fountains, waterways, and sculpture accentuated the elaborate plantings, which included the *parterre,* or designed flower bed (Fig. 382). The term *landscape architecture,* which originated in such masterpieces as the gardens at Versailles, was an accurate one, for buildings, foliage, sculpture, and waterworks were coordinated into a structural unity. Even the trees and shrubbery had an architectural quality because the art of *topiary*—the pruning of plants to take on geometric or other formal shapes—was very popular.

The Englishman, with his love of nature, freed his garden from the rigor of architecture. There were many examples of structural gardens built to complement British palaces, with topiary, sculpture, and even formal pools (Fig. 383), but in the eighteenth century an entirely different approach was developed. The English countryside was loved for itself rather than for what man could do to it. Instead of outdoor living rooms, the garden was apt to include groves and meadows that crept up to the windows of the manor house. Statuary gave way to bridle paths and walks, while the vistas of the garden broadened into untamed meadows or stretches of woodland (Fig. 384). The belief that there are no straight lines in nature gave rise to meandering streams, curving paths, and a naturalness in landscaping, based on the landscape style of Claude Lorraine. A scene was said to be "picturesque" if it resembled the paintings of Claude (Fig. 385). Green turf was more important than flower beds, and mirrors of still water were accented by a well-placed tree or a clump of trees.

above: 383. Blenheim Palace Gardens, Oxfordshire, England.

left: 384. Compton Wynyates, Warwickshire, England.

below: 385. CLAUDE LORRAINE. *Landscape with Dancing Figures.* c. 1648. Oil on canvas, 4′10½″ × 6′6″. Doria Palace, Rome.

left: 386. Knott Garden, Stratford-on-Avon, Warwickshire, England.

right: 387. Deane House Garden, Williamsburg, Va.

It was in the village garden, however, that the Englishman established himself as a true lover of nature. He was not interested in designing a spectacle; rather, he cultivated a small corner for the sheer love of digging in the soil and seeing what it would produce. The beneficence of a damp climate more than repaid the effort, and the little gardens of the English countryside have become renowned. Even geometrically shaped beds are softened by the exuberance of the growth within them, so that the resultant charm is a mixture of restraint and gaiety (Fig. 386).

Early American gardens had a strong British flavor mingled with Dutch influence. Only in the Middle Atlantic and Southern colonies was there enough leisure time to allow cultivation of the land for beauty alone. Mount Vernon and Williamsburg offer two excellent examples of Colonial gardens, and they may be seen today much as they grew two hundred years ago (Fig. 387). Topiary was a sign of elegance, and hedges and shrubs were trimmed into fanciful shapes that were echoed in formal flower beds. American gardens were never established on the elaborate scale of their European prototypes—probably because of factors relating to soil, climate, and the shortage of skilled gardeners—yet they attained a blend of formality and provincial grace that made them an effective expression of their time.

GARDENS TODAY

The contemporary garden derives from all the sources previously discussed and others as well. The atrium around which some modern homes are centered (Fig. 388) was introduced by the ancient Romans. They surrounded their gardens with columns, and roofed them to provide verdant spots for private enjoyment within the confines of a house. The outdoor *patio* had its source in southern countries, where even small areas are enclosed by walls or hedges and developed as a kind of outdoor living room away from the bustle of the world. The popularity of pools could well have been influenced by the Moorish garden, where the contingencies of a hot, dry land have caused water to be afforded a respect bordering on reverence.

Gardens in the late twentieth century have a unique importance. The world has become a crowded place in which three out of four people live in cities and spend many of their waking hours surrounded by glass and concrete. Public parks and gardens have been flattened by the bulldozer to become parking lots and mass housing projects. Washington, D.C., long noted for its landscaping, has already lost nearly 600 acres of parks to urban development, and even citizens' groups who recognized the threat are unable to retain parks and public squares when civic needs crowd in. As long as the population continues to grow, this trend will not be reversed, so it is clear that the best way to assure access to a place of beauty is to create it at home, where serenity can be combined with privacy.

Another factor in the modern appreciation of landscape design is the increase in leisure time brought about by computers and mechanized industry. Most people prefer to spend as many of their free hours as possible out of doors. Because of this preference, skiing, fishing, and camping have become billion dollar industries, and new interest has developed in outdoor living—such niceties as breakfast on the patio, a barbecue on the terrace, or an afternoon lying by the pool. As ski slopes and campgrounds become increasingly crowded, the value of a private retreat becomes more apparent, a place in which the individual can control his environment through his own design and choice of companions.

ESTHETIC CONSIDERATIONS

Elements of Landscape Design

Relatively few people paint their own pictures, write their own books, or design their own homes, but most people both design and plant their gardens, making landscape design an intensely personal form of art. The difference between a yard and a garden is a matter of the elements and principles of design. These elements are easily recognized and readily applied in landscape planning. Basic, of course, is the orientation of the garden to the site and to existing buildings. In a private

388. Irv Burkee. Atrium fountain. 1962. Chased copper mounted on old wood. Collection E. F. Armstrong, Aspen, Colo.

garden the size of the house and its location on the site will determine the scale and shape of the landscaped areas. The amount of space available will, of course, dictate the nature of the landscaping—whether there will be a small patio or an extensive terrace, a lily pond or a swimming pool (Fig. 389). The ground plan will also determine the type of individual plantings: large masses of evergreen, stretches of hedge, impressive flower gardens, or a single tree surrounded by ground cover. The larger the area the more possibilities there are for variety in shape. *Line* and shape will establish the degree of formality, so that the overall effect can be flowing and natural, or it can mimic the geometric treatment of historic formal gardens. Vertical line is created by the use of trees, whose trunks form strong, dark accents contrasting with the colors of the garden. In winter the stark bare branches become dramatic accents against the sky. Such trunks and branches contribute much to *color* as well, for even bark tone often changes from season to season. A landscape designer must consider winter color as well as summer. He should include evergreens and plants whose bare branches have interesting reds or yellows to replace the more spectacular colors of summer flowers. There are many attractive shades of green: the yellow-green of willow can be an intriguing contrast with the dark blue-green

left: 389. Large elements such as swimming pools require a sufficient amount of land around them to be effective as design.

below left: 390. This Japanese garden stresses the interplay of textures—rocks, gravel, pebbles, and concrete—softened by plantings.

below right: 391. Stone garden of the Tofuku-ji Temple at Kyoto.

of spruce. Beautiful gardens have been designed using greens alone, with lawns, evergreens, and border plants requiring little upkeep but offering almost unlimited variety. Fences and walls can contribute color, and colored gravel for walks, drives, and small areas of ground cover is often effective. Redwood bark and shavings, tanbark, or chips of pine bark add enrichment around shrubs, providing a carpet that will keep out weeds and will require little care beyond an occasional raking. Where grass requires too much care, low-growing *ground covers* afford a glossy deep green, or dwarf juniper can be used to provide a blanket of feathery texture.

The Japanese interest in *texture* has had a great influence on western ideas (Fig. 390). In Oriental gardens, an area of stream-washed pebbles is often used to form a "dry stream," and disks are cut from a log to create stepping stones with fascinating color and texture. Sand is raked into patterns with the same care that a formal flower bed requires in Western gardens (Fig. 391). The Japanese adapt the natural environment, accentuating its charm with a few plants carefully selected for the lines of their branches and the textures of their leaves. Trees and shrubs may be radically pruned to create dramatic lines, or they may be trained to provide orderly masses of texture.

Mass is used in many ways in landscape design—from background expanse of trees to clusters of small hedges or border plants. A clump of trees or a single large shrub can provide a stabilizing element in a corner or can act as a focal point in a wide stretch of lawn. Single plants may be used as accents, but for overall effect, plantings should be massed according to height, texture, and color. Even roses, exquisite singly, assume more importance in the total landscape when arranged in well-defined beds contrasted with lawn or edging plants.

Principles of Landscape Design

One of the most fascinating aspects of landscape gardening is the immense *variety* of plants. There are over 300,000 different kinds of plants in the world, and anyone who has studied a garden catalog knows that the difficulty lies in limiting oneself to plants that will grow successfully in a given place. If there is one principle of design that comes naturally to a garden, it is variety—variety in color, texture, size, and shape.

Rhythm is achieved by the controlled use of space for plantings or for walkways. Sweeping lawns possess a kind of rhythm, as do flower beds with curving edges. The biomorphic shape of a pond is rhythmic, and there is rhythm in curved walks or in the shape of a patio. *Repetition* comes from patterns of similar shapes or from a fence or wall that reappears at intervals under the growth of vines or climbing bushes. *Emphasis* may be focused on a pond, a furniture grouping, a patio, or a single beautiful plant or tree.

Form in a garden is determined by the basic layout and by the type of planting: the form of a garden heavy with evergreen will be quite different from that of a rose garden. Ponds, patios, and terraces play an important part in establishing form.

Balance comes from color, texture, and mass played against one another in satisfying proportions. Evergreens spaced to appear on both sides of a patio, colors repeated in various areas along a wall—these are typical of the manner in which balance transforms scattered flower beds into a total *unity,* the overriding design principle. Unity thus involves the relationship of all the elements to each other. It is achieved by adherence to a basic plan that remains consistent through the various seasons and through the changes made from year to year.

PHYSICAL CONSIDERATIONS

Topography

The character of the terrain may be the factor that determines the form landscaping will take. A flat area permits a variety of choices, but a steep slope or rolling hills require specific adaptations to ensure the success of growing plants. The device most frequently used to control an incline is terracing, in which retaining walls are constructed and soil is brought in to build a series of flat, step-like levels that can be cultivated. Slopes are sometimes blanketed with a low-growing ground cover that not only prevents the soil from washing downhill but is attractive in itself. Topography can be altered to create streams or waterfalls (Fig. 392).

Soil

A garden should be *of* the earth not *on* it; that is, plants should be adapted to the soil in which they grow. This may necessitate improvement of the texture or organic content of the soil by the addition of new materials. Sand will break up clay soil, and loam or compost from decayed vegetable matter, manure, or commercial fertilizer will enrich soil that is too sandy. The ideal texture is one that crumbles easily in the hand. Such soil is said to be *friable.* The relative acidity or alkalinity of the soil has to do with locale and climate, and this will influence the types of plants that can be grown successfully. Azaleas, rhododendrons, and other broad-leaved evergreens thrive in the acid soil of wet climates, whereas the plants of the desert and plain grow best in alkaline soil. Choosing plants that grow naturally in a given location and soil will eliminate frustration and disappointment. Proper drainage is necessary in any soil. Fast drainage can be controlled by adding organic matter to the soil to retain moisture. Slow drainage, which causes plants to stand in water too long, can be prevented by adding sand or gravel, which makes the soil more porous and allows water to run through more rapidly.

Climate

Climate is the fundamental consideration in the choice of plants. Some plants cannot stand cold winters; others will not grow above a certain altitude. Many flowers wither

left: 392. A pond and waterfall such as this can be built in a small area, providing beauty of sight and sound.

right: 393. A bit of wall and attractive plantings can impart privacy and charm to even a small corner.

and fade under the impact of intense sunlight. Flowering bulbs need a moist soil, and different species of trees have varying climatic needs. To a certain extent climate can be controlled: cool shady spots can be created with trees and fences, and pockets of warmth can be provided for sun-loving plants. Here again, however, it is safest to use only those plants that are readily adapted to the climate.

ENCLOSURES

Among the earliest examples of enclosed landscaping were the walled gardens of medieval monasteries. These gardens were entirely functional: they provided herbs for medicine, fruit for the table, and flowers for the altar, and the central fountain served as a source of irrigation. The wall was essential to keep the monks in and the dogs and poultry out. While enclosures today also serve to regulate the movement of people and animals, they are more often used for control of sun, wind, heat, and view. Instead of blocking out the view entirely, the enclosure most often will act as a screen, affording a degree of privacy without isolation. Even a small area can be effectively landscaped in this manner, thus giving it an integrity that would be impossible without the demarkation of a wall (Fig. 393).

The degree of privacy desired will determine the height, thickness, weight, transparency, and texture of the enclosure. Hedges may be planted, or *berms*—mounds of soil built to form a "natural" hill—may be used to ward off the sights and sounds of traffic. Water in the form of a moat can create an enclosure if the view beyond is attractive, and fences provide imaginative designs (Fig. 394).

EMBELLISHMENTS

Since gardening is a personal art, man often is impelled to add something individual to the natural setting. The addition may take the form of a pool, a statue, a bench, a sundial, or some other object created especially for the garden. When such embellishments are blended with natural growth, the effect can be one of great charm (Fig. 395).

The creative use of artificial light is particularly suited to a garden. Japanese lanterns for garden parties were used long before electric light was introduced, for the magic of shadows in a garden is irresistible. Today there are many types of subtle

left: 394. The design of an enclosure often establishes the character of a garden. Here circular segments of clay pipe are held tightly in a painted wood frame to provide a lacy effect for a series of outdoor dividers.

right: 395. In this garden designed by EVERSON and BIGLER, a circular fountain and two round redwood platforms are softened by the growth of plants, providing a poolside terrace in a natural setting.

396. A garden becomes an enchanted spot at night when lighting is designed for dramatic effect.

lighting that may be used to spotlight a plant or decorative corner or to illuminate a patio; a landscape is transformed when shapes and textures are brought into dramatic focus by concealed lights that silhouette tree trunks and branches or highlight the rough pattern of bark. All the elements that are combined in a garden are articulated by the play of light, thus creating greater contrasts or softer effects and casting an aura of enchantment over the entire setting (Fig. 396).

It has been said that the earth's surface is a habitat uneasily shared by man and nature, and shared at present to the detriment of both.[1] The garden is one of the few remaining environments where man and nature may live in harmony. Even the skyscraper often has its roof garden, relating the building to the earth from which it rises and softening the view of the glass and steel cityscape. On the ground, a small area of natural landscape can be the answer to a world in which conflict and confusion make more precious the serenity of a quiet retreat.

SUMMARY

From early times the garden has represented man's dream world, a spot where he can find peace and beauty. Historic gardens have often been elaborate, even architectural, although the spontaneous charm of the English village garden has had a long tradition.

The contemporary garden derives from many sources. It enjoys a unique importance because of the stress of twentieth-century living, which heightens the need for escape from tension. The increase in leisure time has also had its effect on gardening, for it allows more time for the enjoyment of the out-of-doors.

The elements of design apply quite clearly to landscape gardening, in which textures, lines, shapes, and colors play a natural and important part. The principles of design are vital also, transforming a collection of plants into an organized and balanced unity. Physical considerations in landscape design include topography, soil, and climate.

Enclosures and structural embellishments are two devices by which man can add a special touch to his landscape. Enclosures can be imaginative as well as practical. Embellishments combine the works of man with natural growth, producing a harmony between man and nature that has become increasingly rare.

Design for Cities

chapter 22

The city represents the sum of all man's arts. From the towering buildings that form its skyline to the smallest piece of jewelry, the results of man's creative efforts find a place in the vibrant organism that is the city. Art forms from the most remote areas make their way inevitably to the cities of the world, and crafted objects are gathered from the farthest outposts to be dispersed in city markets. The aggregate of man's knowledge is gathered in the libraries and universities, dramas are performed in the theaters, music is presented in concert halls and opera houses. In particular, works of visual art are threaded through the tapestry of city life, enriching it and helping to counteract the problems that inevitably arise wherever vast crowds of people gather. It is in the solution of these problems that the designer of today finds his greatest challenge.

EVOLUTION OF A PROBLEM

The modern city began as a solution to a problem. Through the medieval period cities consisted of clusters of people gathered together for mutual protection. Strong walls encircled the houses, and when the population grew, outer walls were erected to allow for expansion. The advantages of city living gradually increased, as improved facilities for health, cleanliness, and cultural endeavors became available. The advent of the machine brought dramatic changes—new developments in transportation that revolutionized commerce and the beginnings of industry that would eventually transform the world. Unfortunately, the machine brought with it an unmeasured potential for social and economic upheaval. The metropolitan slum and the industrial factory district emerged and rapidly became breeding places for civic turmoil.

The problems originating with the machine might not have become monumental if they had not been combined with a burgeoning population. In 1880 there was not a city in the Western world with a population of more than 1,000,000, but by 1967 80 metropolises boasted that number, and in the United States alone there were 192 cities with over 100,000 people. It is predicted that the American population will have doubled to more than 400 million before the year 2010, and four out of

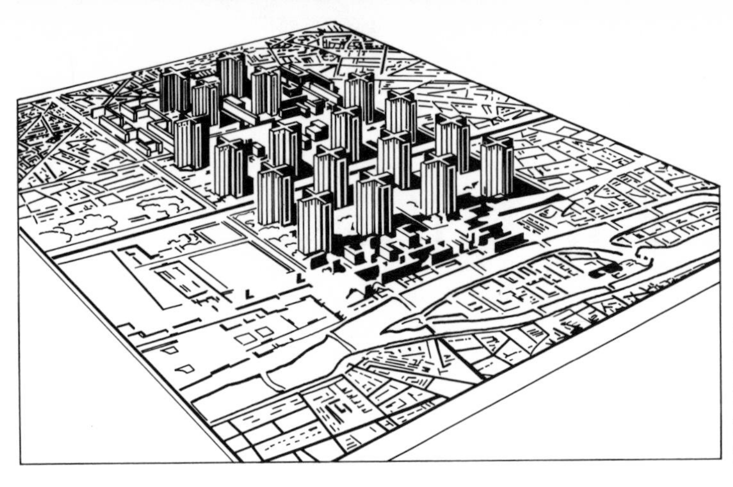

397. Le Corbusier's Voisin Plan (1925) would have redesigned the center of Paris to provide attractive housing and effective transportation for four times as many people as were actually living there.

five people will live in cities. There is now an automobile for every three persons in the United States. Thus the problem comes into focus: crowded urban areas overflow into jammed streets and highways, and the situation grows steadily worse.

THE PROBLEM OF THE CITY

The problem of the city is essentially a problem of balance: balance between man-made structures and natural areas, between large buildings and small ones, between sections for business and spaces for relaxation and refreshment. It has been said that if urban parks were to expand concurrently with city buildings, most of the problems of the city would not arise. Practically all the difficulties that have arisen—overcrowding, air and water pollution, inadequate facilities for recreation, insufficient means of waste disposal, and the ever-increasing encroachment of parking areas—are the result of an imbalance between the number of people and cars to be provided for and the amount of land available for their use. Racial tensions, while deeply rooted in historical injustice, have been brought to a crisis point, at least partially, by overcrowding and by an imbalance in economic and social opportunity.

The challenge is twofold: how to rebuild and improve existing cities, and how to design new ones to avoid repeating present problems. Of the two, the first is more complex because it involves undoing the errors of the past.

URBAN RENEWAL

Urban renewal is the term applied to rebuilding existing cities. So urgent is the need that the Federal Government has set up an agency for this purpose, the United States Department of Housing and Urban Development. This agency makes studies, analyzes problems, and gives awards to communities that have successfully solved an urban problem. However, the Federal Government can give incentive only; real solutions must come from the people who live in a community and who care enough to make the sacrifices necessary to carry them through.

Among the first to take an interest in rebuilding twentieth-century cities was Le Corbusier. In 1925 Le Corbusier designed a model for the reconstruction of Paris. This model, known as the Voisin (neighbor) Plan, embodied his theory that most cities need sweeping renovation rather than small and often uncoordinated reforms (Fig. 397). In the Voisin Plan housing was to be centralized in 16 glass-walled skyscrapers in the heart of the city, thus stacking houses vertically instead of allowing them to sprawl out horizontally. In this system, the people would be lifted above the fumes and noises of the city. The keynote of the plan was balance. Each building was to be designed in such a way that the negative space surrounding it was at least equal to the positive area of the building, providing each of the four wings with air, sunlight, and a view of the city. Landscaped areas were to surround the buildings, balancing the man-made structures with the soft textures and colors of nature. This revolutionary plan remains a model for the ideal modern city. Le Corbusier also designed city plans for Barcelona, Algiers, Stockholm, and Antwerp.

It is not often that such fundamental renovation as Le Corbusier's can be undertaken. Much redevelopment has to do with the razing of slum areas and the building of new high-rise buildings that provide more efficient and possibly more attractive housing. However, urban renewal can take many forms. Sometimes it has nothing to do with housing.

St. James, Missouri, is a small town in the Ozarks that faced an unusual problem. It became apparent several years ago that all the trees in town, mainly soft maples, were diseased or dying. The James Foundation, a fund bequeathed to the town for civic improvement, took the responsibility for having experts appraise the situation and make suggestions. As a result, bulldozers moved in and removed all the trees (Fig. 398). Subsequently, more than 27,000 sweet gum and holly trees were planted, varieties selected by botanists as most appropriate for that region. Ten years later St. James was known as the "forest city of the Ozarks" and was hailed as a place where citizens had worked together to beautify their community (Fig. 399).

398–399. The citizens of St. James, Mo., worked together to provide attractive landscaping for their community.

right: 398. In 1957 bulldozers and trucks removed the diseased soft maple trees that could not survive in the area.

below: 399. Thriving sweet gum and holly trees now line the streets of St. James.

400–402. A remarkable transformation has been made in the downtown area of San Antonio, Tex.

above left: 400. The river front area as it appeared before the renewal project.

above right: 401. The Paseo del Rio, or River Walk, is now one of the most attractive areas of the city.

left: 402. Trees, stone bridges, and pleasant walkways provide a tranquil counterpoint to the nearby office buildings.

An even more dramatic example of creating an asset from a handicap is the River Walk in San Antonio, Texas. For years the San Antonio River was a sluggish stream threading its way through the heart of the city. It brought periodic devastation by flooding, but for the most part it was ignored. Buildings were erected with their backs to it, and it was used intermittently as a dumping ground for waste (Fig. 400). Some city planners even suggested covering the river with concrete and using it as a sewer, but farsighted citizens took action. After 23 years of study they set up a River Walk Commission to prepare a master plan for the development of the river as a scenic attraction. Today the Paseo del Rio is a thriving business area, lined with fascinating shops and exotic restaurants, and featuring beautifully landscaped vistas that serve as a center of attraction for visitors and residents alike (Figs. 401–402). Striking variety has been created by this colorful yet peaceful oasis in the middle of a city—variety accentuated by the contrast of river and trees against tall buildings.

The balance between landscape and urban environment contributes to the sense of well-being of thousands of citizens.

One of the most urgent and difficult problems of the city is, of course, the removal of the slum and ghetto. This is not merely a matter of cleaning and rebuilding, but of upgrading an environment without displacing its inhabitants. I. M. Pei, a leading American architect concerned with the problem, feels that community involvement is an important factor in the solution. The residents must contribute to the planning and work to bring about the necessary changes. In Bedford-Stuyvesant, a black ghetto in Brooklyn that Pei helped to redesign, streets formerly used merely for parking were closed and converted into playgrounds. The young people of the neighborhood planted trees and laid bricks for the sidewalks. In a speech given in Portland, Oregon in June, 1968, Pei declared: "The youths won't destroy the trees they planted and they won't dig up the bricks they laid to throw in a riot. . . . They may not be the best parks in the world and the brick sidewalks may not be even and smooth, but they will be the result of the people's work."

The environment of the community and the quality of life in it are the responsibility of everyone. The application of democratic principles in making decisions and carrying them out is important to the success of any urban renewal program. Here, in fact, lies the crux of the entire problem of redesigning environment: Those involved must be concerned to the point that the design becomes their own problem, not something imposed from without but a goal for which they work with their own hands and energies. Only in this way is physical improvement likely to foster the social changes that will lead to constructive lives and the improved status of groups condemned by circumstance to exist in dilapidated and moribund environments. The architect and city planner may give esthetic guidance and direction, but the problem must remain a human one, and it can only be fully solved when human considerations are given first priority.

THE DOWNTOWN PROBLEM

One of the difficult aspects of city design is that efforts to solve one problem often create others. Quite different from Le Corbusier's *centralized* city design is the *decentralized* plan, which concentrates activity in the suburbs. The suburban shopping center was one of the phenomenal developments of the mid-twentieth century. It provided housewives with ample parking space, attractive surroundings, and large landscaped areas where they were free from traffic while they shopped. As the population moved steadily out of the cities downtown merchants and banks had no choice but to build branches in the suburbs. Centers became increasingly elaborate, with restaurants, flower beds, fountains, statuary, and architectural embellishments, and shopping assumed the character of an informal pastime that the housewife could undertake in the most casual clothes. The whole concept of the suburban center was an inspired solution for the shopper, but it left the downtown merchant with a nearly deserted store. The reaction was a movement to reinstate the center of town as an attraction. This movement has taken two directions.

The obvious solution was to bring to the heart of the city the same attractions that had lured the shopper to the suburbs. Victor Gruen and Associates, a firm of architects and city planners, has designed shopping areas for many cities, based on the closing of main thoroughfares to all but pedestrians. A typical plan centers around a mall, landscaped for color and texture, supplied with benches, play equipment, and sidewalk cafés, and provided with art exhibits and other events to attract interest.

403–404. The architectural firm of Victor Gruen Associates formulated a plan for the renewal of Fulton Way in Fresno, Calif.

above left: 403. Before the renewal project, Fulton Way was a rather drab, ordinary thoroughfare.

above right: 404. Now free of traffic and attractively landscaped, Fulton Way is a pleasant shopping mall.

opposite: Plate 31. GIUSEPPE MENGONI. Galleria Vittorio Emanuele, Milan. Completed 1867.

One such design was created for Fulton Way in Fresno, California (Figs. 403–404). Like the shopping center, however, this solution creates another problem. Traffic has to be routed around the shopping area, and fewer arteries are available to cars. The resultant traffic congestion can undo all the attractions provided by the mall. In each case this problem has to be solved before the shopping area is opened, if there is to be hope for sustained success.

The idea of a traffic-free shopping area is not new. In 1860 the city of Milan, Italy, staged a competition, inviting all citizens to submit designs for a covered *galleria,* to be built in the center of the city. The winning plan was that of Giuseppe Mengoni, and in 1867 the Galleria Vittorio Emanuele was officially opened to the public. The Galleria (Pl. 31, opposite) consists of two covered streets, 643 feet and 344 feet long, respectively, intersecting in the form of a Latin cross. The glass roof soars to a height of 88 feet and culminates in a central cupola 160 feet above the ground. Within this spectacular enclosure are nearly 100 smart shops, plus elegant restaurants and cafés. Since its inception the Galleria has been a meeting place for artists, writers, and musicians, as well as a gathering point for the entire population of Milan. In summer the airy coolness of the Galleria attracts throngs of tourists. The structure was heavily damaged in World War II, but it was completely rebuilt within 12 years, and today it stands as a monument to intelligence and foresight in city planning.

A striking example of urban reconstruction can be seen in Rotterdam. The core of the city was heavily bombed during World War II and had to be entirely rebuilt. The intelligence and foresight of the planners has converted a disaster area into a

BIFFI

Plate 32. Jason Crum. *East 29th Street Mural.* 1969.

right: 405. The Lijnbaan shopping center in Rotterdam resulted from imaginative planning after the devastation of World War II.

below left: 406. Arcaded walkways and attractive shop fronts have transformed Larimer Square in Denver.

below right: 407. Central plazas filled with flowers are a feature of many European cities. A good example is the square in Harrogate, Yorkshire, England.

model city that provides inspiration to people in all parts of the world. Figure 405 shows the Lijnbaan in the new heart of the city.

A second approach to redesigning downtown areas capitalizes on the history of a city. In some communities the spirit of a colorful past has been re-created by remodeling delapidated sections and developing them into prime attractions. Larimer Street was the "skid row" of Denver until a group of dedicated citizens formed the Larimer Square Association and renovated a block-long segment of the area (Fig. 406). Carefully retaining the oldtime façades, designers built arcades leading back into walkways, opened courtyards where alleys had been, planned shops and galleries where local artists could display their works or shopkeepers could sell imported wares, and encouraged the establishment of restaurants with foreign foods and picturesque interiors. Similar areas have been reconstructed in Old Town in Chicago, in Ghirardelli Square in San Francisco, and in Gaslight Square in St. Louis.

Much about urban beautification can be learned from European cities, where the city center is often built around an attractive plaza (Fig. 407). Some Amerian cities

left: 408. Sidney Simon. Sculptured bronze walls for the Downstate Medical Center in Brooklyn, N.Y. 1967.

below: 409. William A. Garnett. *Mass Production Housing, Lakewood, California.* 1953.

have used planters and hanging baskets along main streets in an effort to regain the lost balance between man and nature. But if civic redevelopment is to have a lasting effect, the owner and builder of each individual building must do his share. Even a parking lot can be softened by a bit of foliage, a touch that indicates that the owner has more in mind than using every possible inch of asphalt for commercial purposes. When new buildings are erected, it is often possible to include landscaping. Other contributions to texture and color can be made through the materials of the buildings themselves. Crushed colored rock imbedded in concrete, tinted concrete, colored building tile, patterned blocks, mosaics, bas reliefs, and murals (Pl. 32, p. 342) all lessen the severity of structural walls. Another possibility is the use of metal sculpture, as in Figure 408. Here added significance is given to a textured door area by the use of symbolism in the design.

410. The houses in Greendale, Wisc., are similar in design, but variety is achieved through different placement of the buildings on their lots.

CITY PLANNING

Since urban renewal implies the renovation of existing areas, city planning as a separate entity would indicate the design of new cities or new sections of present cities. Most new growth inevitably springs up at the perimeter of a city and frequently results in the situation known as "suburban sprawl." All too often a developer buys up tracts of land, divides them into many small lots, and builds literally acres of houses as cheaply as he can. The result is the kind of monotony seen today on the fringes of most large cities in the United States. Builders argue that houses on the same block should have the same roof line and the same setback from the street in order to ensure unity. This theory undoubtedly prevailed in older sections of cities like New York, Baltimore, and Boston, where brownstone fronts and brick buildings in the same block were almost identical. However, while buildings in close proximity should not present a jumbled effect, it is still possible to achieve consistency without monotony.

Figure 409 is an example of uniform building carried to an extreme. Each house is separated from the next by a narrow strip of unusable land, a token show of privacy which has little meaning, for windows look into other windows and voices carry from house to house. The belief that suburban living has fallen into set patterns, with the same standards and the same symbols of status and success, might be attributed in part to the similarity in physical surroundings. Each house has the same attributes as every other one in the block, and each family's life is measured against the pattern they all share.

Quite a different situation is apparent in the town of Greendale, Wisconsin (Fig. 410). In Greendale each house is set on a plot of ground large enough to ensure real privacy and is oriented to its particular lot, thus making the individual home more important than any arbitrary consistency of line along a street. There are no rows of identical houses. Rather, there are individual homes in which people can maintain different life-styles and viewpoints.

The Greenbelt Concept

There is a reason for Greendale's success in breaking away from suburban patterns, for it was designed with innovation in mind. In the depression years of the 1930s

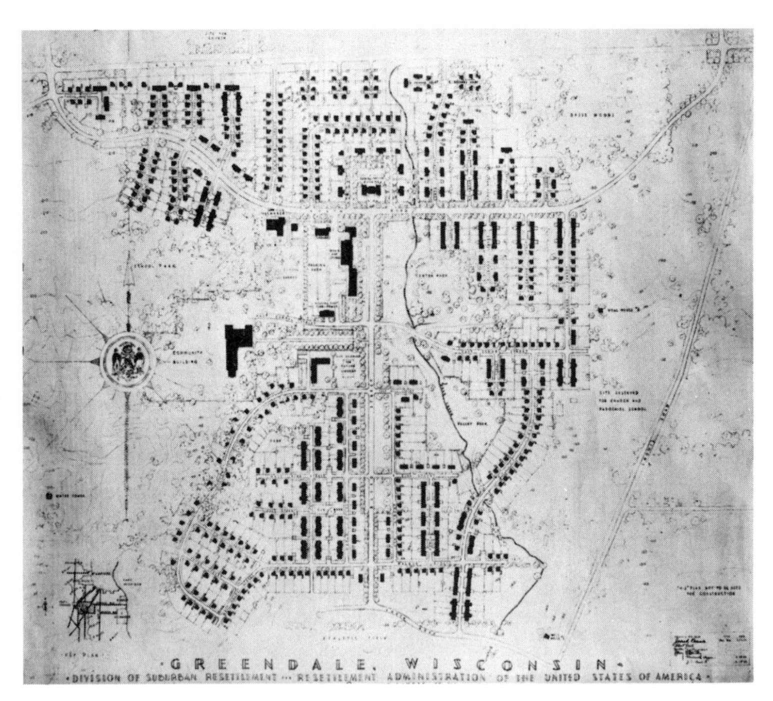

411. The architect's drawing of the city of Greendale shows a pleasant balance between the dark forms of buildings and the open areas of lawn and plantings.

the Federal Government purchased land near three large cities for the purpose of creating jobs by building three model communities that would house workers near industrial areas, yet give them an attractive and satisfying life away from the noise and overcrowding of the city. The three towns constructed were Greenbelt, Maryland, Greenhills, Ohio, and Greendale, which is three miles southeast of Milwaukee. The planners followed the example set by Radburn, New Jersey, the first community anywhere to separate traffic from residential areas in such a way that the pedestrian could move freely without encountering motor traffic. In Greendale open areas and belts of trees curve in biomorphic shapes, which soften the rectangles of the residential streets (Fig. 411). These shapes are interspersed throughout the community in such a way that all living rooms face parks or open country. Bathrooms and kitchens open onto quiet service roads, so that daily chores can be carried out in an unobtrusive manner. Residential streets terminate in dead ends or curve to join other streets adapted to the topography of the land. This solution is an improvement over the plan of most American cities, which are laid out either in rectangular grids or in concentric circles, regardless of topographical features. Wherever possible, sidewalks cross thoroughfares by means of underpasses. Materials for houses have been chosen with variety in mind, and paint colors have been selected to make each home as individual as possible. When the town was first laid out, 366 residential buildings were constructed. By 1967 the population had reached over 12,000 people, many of whom had built their own homes.

As the original designers hoped, these three towns have provided inspiration to other cities seeking a full and attractive community life. Like the early twentieth-century "garden cities" of Letchworth and Welwyn in England, they have established a design adaptable to different situations. Chatham Village in Pittsburgh is a private greenbelt development in which the houses are rented to the residents. Perhaps even more significant are the communities that have undertaken greenbelt developments as civic ventures. The city of Boulder, Colorado, nestled at the foot of the Rockies, was once a quiet university town, but its population quadrupled in a 25-year period because of an influx of large industries, which were attracted to the area by the very features their development threatened to destroy. Determined not to lose the treasured scenic quality of the town, residents voted in 1967 to increase their city sales tax by one percent, with the increased revenue earmarked for greenbelt development. Parks, trails, and mountain areas are to be protected and preserved against the threat of continued growth, thus making it possible for the community to benefit from an expanding economy without losing the natural beauty that had made it a pleasant place to live.

As with all of the greenbelt communities, the preservation of the landscape is largely a matter of texture—the softening textures of trees and shrubbery against the rigid shapes of houses, stores, and factories. This is not an esthetic consideration alone. One of the most effective ways of combating air pollution is by maintaining large areas of green plants that provide fresh oxygen for men to breathe. Psychological effects are equally important to health, for attractive surroundings can overcome dejection, which in turn makes men susceptible to physical disease. The German people recognized this fact when they set up the Schrebergärten movement after World War II. Tenement dwellers in congested German metropolises were each given a small patch of unused land outside the cities for their own cultivation. Lewis Mumford believes that parks are essential in any city designed as a permanent habitat for man, and deplores the lack of attractive places in the United States where young people can conduct courtships without being crowded into cars. The necessity for open spaces and attractive settings is one of the most pressing problems in the crowded, hurried life of today.

THE RHYTHM OF THE CITY

Any city is a dynamic organism throbbing with the pulse of life within it. There is rhythm in the repetition of buildings and the emphasis of large buildings against smaller ones. There is rhythm in the windows of tall buildings, especially at night when some are lighted and some are not. This rhythm can be compared to the pattern in Kay Sekimachi's textile in Figure 51. There is rhythm in the shapes of parks and winding rivers that trace biomorphic patterns through rectangles of concrete and glass. The most vital rhythm of the city, however, is its activity, directed by the flow of streets, the freeways, the avenues, and the drives through parks or along lakes and rivers. This is one of the aspects of the city that has become a major problem—a problem arising from the combination of the machine and overpopulation—for transportation no longer moves through our cities in a smooth, rhythmic flow. The rhythm of the city is seriously impaired.

The city was created for the pedestrian, and the swallowing up of large areas by parking lots and traffic jams is a severe threat. City planners seem unanimous in their agreement that the automobile must be replaced by some other form of urban transportation, if the city is not to become one vast parking lot. It has been estimated that if every customer who shops in Macy's in New York were to drive a car, a parking lot 33 blocks long would be required.[1]

Subways have served many metropolises efficiently, although burrowing underground is not the most attractive solution. Other means of rapid transportation are being studied by designers. Their proposals include individual cars controlled by a center rail, cars without drivers moving on a belt system that runs continuously, vehicles that ride on air cushions, small helicopters, and adaptations of the monorail such as the one built for the Seattle World's Fair in 1963 (Fig. 412). A system similar to the monorail but with cars suspended from a cable was initiated in Wuppertal, Germany, around the turn of the century and has been in use ever since.

The alleviation of downtown traffic is not the only problem confronting transportation experts. Traffic from city to suburbs and from city to city grows increasingly complicated. The design of freeways and traffic interchanges was a new field shortly after World War II, yet within 25 years freeway travel had reached the point of such complexity that many people avoided it whenever possible. When the element of danger overshadows the efficiency and convenience of a traffic system, it cannot be considered totally effective. The alternative seems to be for Americans to forsake the privacy of their own cars for civic transportation. This solution could be interpreted as one more step in the loss of individualism and one more reason for individuality to be encouraged as much as possible in every other facet of city planning.

THE ENTITY OF THE CITY

Throughout this discussion of city design in its various aspects there have been many references to the elements and principles of design. The textures of plants and trees against the smooth concrete and glass of buildings, the colors of flowers and of building materials, the lines of the cityscape and its constructions, the masses of shopping areas, residential sections, and parks, the sizes and shapes of buildings and of landscaped areas—all of these components comprise the total organism that is the city. The balance between man's structures and nature, the form of each city with its individual skyline, the rhythm of repetition in its structures and the rhythm of life flowing through it, and finally the variety of all its parts—these, too, are fundamental to the design of any city.

Variety can be extended, however, to include the distinctive flavor of a city, the identity that distinguishes it from all the other cities of the world. Under the glass and concrete of any city lies the heritage of a group of people with widely diverse origins. Geographical location, too, plays a vital part in the city personality. San Francisco removed from the Golden Gate would lose identity, just as New Orleans

left: 412. Monorails, such as the one built for the Seattle World's Fair in 1963, have been suggested as a possible solution to the parking and commutation problems of the cities.

right: 413. The Getreidegasse in Salzburg, Austria.

414. A sidewalk café in Paris.

would not be the same without its Creole flavor. Any port city moved inland would suffer the loss of its unique spirit, a spirit that comes from the constant arrival and departure of ships, the influx of people and treasures from far places, the smell of the sea and of fish, and the seagulls circling overhead. Chicago would be drab without its lakeshore and the robust activity that results from its position as a hub of transportation. Denver would lose its personality without its crisp invigorating air and the panorama of the Rocky Mountains at its back. Boston, like many other cities the world over, thrives on its particular relationship to history. All of these attributes, tangible and intangible, are the heritage that should be the first concern of any city designer. Yet preserving the heritage is becoming increasingly difficult with the growing need for housing, for transportation, and for parking facilities that threaten historical landmarks.

Many cities conscious of their treasures have taken steps to preserve them through *historic zoning.* Such zoning protects monuments, fine old homes, public buildings, and other landmarks with a tax abatement, overruling the assumption that all property within a city must be taxed to support the city government. A special commission restrains owners from changing or destroying buildings included in the historic zone.

European cities have long protected their heritage in this way, maintaining their links with a long colorful past. In Salzburg one encounters the flavor not only of Austria but of the Middle Ages as well in the Getreidegasse, the winding medieval street where automobiles are allowed only at certain hours for delivery purposes (Fig. 413). Salzburg is a modern city of 100,000 people, yet it is possible to browse in a leisurely manner from shop to shop just as one might have done in medieval days. Many other European cities have "pedestrian streets," where the feeling of the past is preserved. Sidewalk cafés extend the sense of relaxation in Austria and France (Fig. 414), and the same purpose is served by the espresso bars of Italy, the beer gardens of Germany, and the pubs and tearooms of England. These are the gestures of a city's personality, lingering in the memory of the visitor.

415. The Valentine Museum, Richmond, Va.

In the United States as in Europe the preservation of the past is correlated with the tourist trade. In a report made in 1949 before the creation of a historic district in Richmond, Virginia, the situation was stated clearly:

> We must not overlook the fact that the visiting of historic places is of great commercial value. Our tourist trade has been estimated at over $5,000,000. These people did not visit Richmond because it possesses nothing by which it can be distinguished from other cities but because it possesses historical landmarks which are treasured by many.

The enactment of the statute for the district went into effect the following year, preserving such landmarks as the Valentine Museum, a historic home that has been remodeled and donated to the city (Fig. 415).

Devotion to history is even more apparent in Santa Fe, New Mexico. The emphasis is not only on the preservation of historic buildings (Fig. 416) but also on the design of new construction in "the historic styles." All new buildings must give the effect of adobe construction (Fig. 417), and there are such stipulations as: "no door or window in a publicly visible façade shall be located nearer than three feet from the corner of the façade." The results are effective. Santa Fe is often called a world apart, a unique expression of three cultures—Indian, Spanish, and Anglo-American. Preservation of historic areas can be found in other communities, such as the French Quarter in New Orleans and Georgetown in Washington, D.C.

416. Palace of the Governors, Santa Fe, N.M. 1610–14.

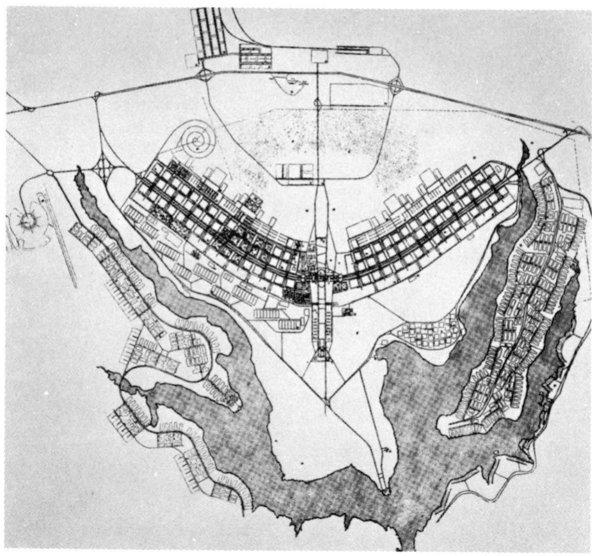

left: 417. New Mexico State Supreme Court Building, Santa Fe, N.M. Completed 1953.

right: 418. The city plan for Brasilia, the new capital of Brazil. The center of the government, the Plaza of the Three Powers, sits on the highest ground on a peninsula extending into an artificial lake.

The cultivation of the past for purposes of the tourist trade is, as pointed out in Richmond's report, of great economic value. Tourism is a kind of mutual admiration society for the cities of the world. Occupants of one city (or country) visit, appreciate, and carry home influences from other cities. The most important reason for holding fast to any city's assets, however, must be for the sake of the city itself. In drawing plans for cities of the future, designers must realize that no city will ever be an abstract entity, but must be a link between past and future, and, like the illuminated manuscripts of the Middle Ages, carry forward the knowledge, the artistry, and the beliefs of the past.

AN EXAMPLE OF CONTEMPORARY DESIGN

Probably the most impressive step toward the city of the future has been the construction of a new capital city for Brazil. For centuries the capital of Brazil had been Rio de Janeiro, a thriving but increasingly crowded metropolis squeezed along the coastal region. Far inland a vast plateau offered a wealth of natural resources, an invigorating climate, and unlimited space and land. For more than a century, successive governments had pledged themselves to move the capital inland, but it was not until 1956, when Juscelino Kubitschek took office as president, that the promise was fulfilled. The result was Brasilia, a completely new city built in a record-breaking four years. In 1960 the government was formally moved into new and dramatically modern buildings, in a city that was planned in every aspect for its specific purpose.

The plan for Brasilia was chosen in a worldwide competition, and the winning design was the work of Lucio Costa. Costa's plan is particularly relevant to a new city in the space age, for it roughly approximates the shape of an airplane (Fig. 418). Buildings and development follow the contours of a large lake that was created as part of the design, and structures are arranged according to function: the ministry and legislative group are placed where the engine of the plane would be; commercial establishments, public parks, and the stadium correspond to the fuselage; and residential structures fill the area of the wings. Architect Oscar Niemeyer designed

419. Oscar Niemeyer. President's Palace, Brasilia. 1960.

all of the public buildings, integrating them into an overall unity of stark modern lines. The president's palace (Fig. 419), with its silhouetted forms like huge paper cutouts across the front, has become the symbol of Brasilia (see also Fig. 355).

Most of the architecture is of concrete block and glass, a fitting contemporary expression that stands between the Portuguese colonial architecture of the coastal area and the primitive art of the Indians of the Amazon Basin. The buildings are set wide apart so that their spacious surroundings preserve the spirit of the frontier. There are no street intersections, for all crossings are cloverleafs, overpasses, or underpasses. The conventional grid pattern of the typical city has been abandoned. Brasilia has no hub with avenues radiating from it; rather, it follows organic arrangement consistent with the contours of a carefully designed location.

Brasilia is an interesting experiment because of its contribution to the art of city design and also because of its sociological implications. When the new city was opened population came slowly, and the lawmakers had a tendency to fly back to Rio immediately after discharging their official duties. The question of whether an entire population can be transplanted from one area to another with lasting success is one that may have to be answered as a foundation for future planning. City growth is an organic phenomenon, involving many personal tastes and needs. The mere planning of an ideal situation on paper, or even the execution of the plan, does not always prove to be the answer to the requirements of a group of individuals who, even in an era of mobility, have a tendency to resist change.

THE CITY OF THE FUTURE

The development of the city is recognized as one of the great problems of the twentieth century, and thus it is a favorite project for designers. The space age and its discoveries make even the most fantastic of man's designs a possibility. Suggestions have been made for platform towns with traffic moving in corridors underneath the ground, and for multitiered cities a mile wide and twenty miles long, that eventually join city to city. Plans have been drawn for satellite cities to be situated

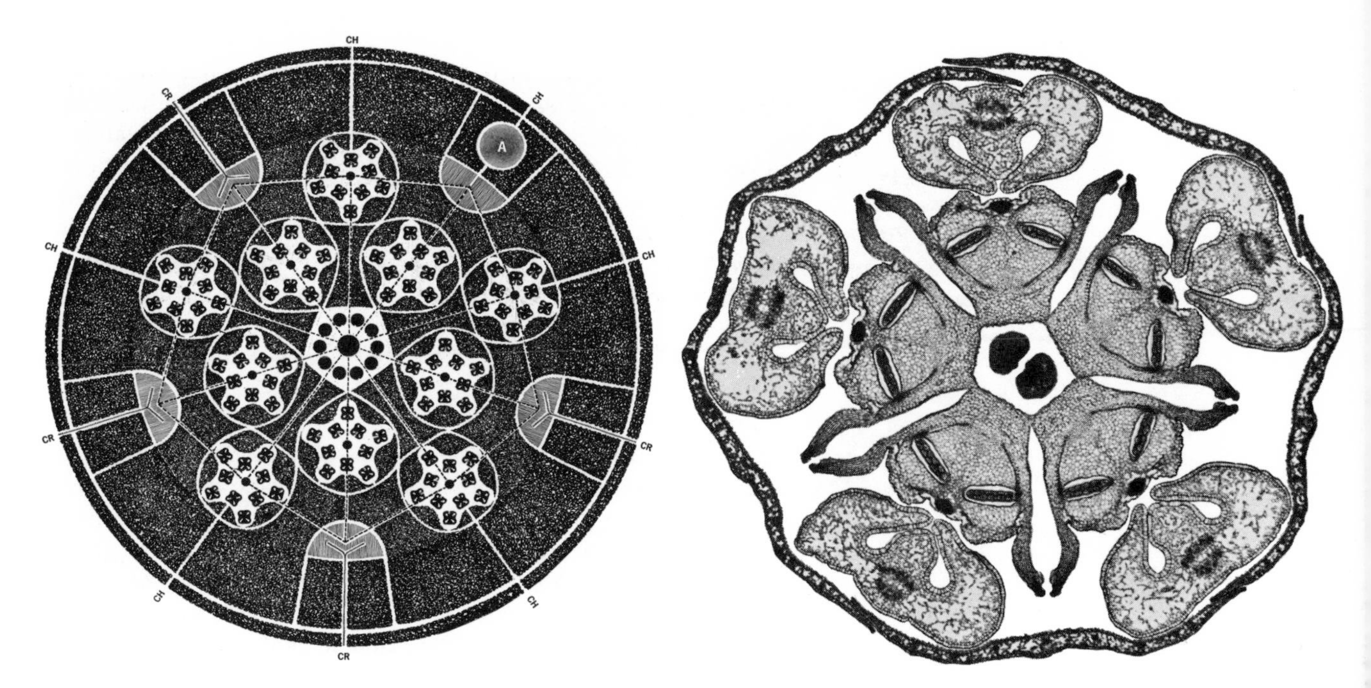

in "rural rings" around existing metropolises, and for cellular cities and towns, in which a number of community units are placed around a central urban core (Fig. 420). The cellular plan of Victor Gruen is remarkably similar to the transverse section of the milkweed flower in Figure 421, for they have in common a central core, five units, and radial symmetry.

Designs for skyscrapers are fascinating and challenging, but there are many other problems of the city that must be solved. This discussion deals with only the surface aspects of city development, those involved with the visual elements and principles of design. There remain innumerable deeper problems—social dissolution, crippling strikes, the provision of adequate pure water, and the disposal of the rising mountain of man's wastes without pollution. Raising money to finance the vast projects needed to keep a city running—from electric light service to civic auditoriums and cultural events—is certain to become an increasingly complex problem for the city of the future. A statement by Lewis Mumford in 1938 seems to grow more significant with time:

> We see that the improvement of cities is no matter for small one-sided reforms: the task of city design involves the vaster task of rebuilding our civilization. We must alter the parasitic and predatory modes of life that now play so large a part, and we must create region by region, continent by continent, an effective symbiosis, or cooperative living together. The problem is to coordinate on the basis of more essential human values than the will-to-power and the will-to-profits, a host of social functions and processes that we have hitherto misused in the building of cities and polities, or of which we have never rationally taken advantage.[2]

This is a field for architect and designer, sociologist and psychologist, biologist and engineer, economist and sanitarian, government and private citizen. It is a problem affecting even those who do not live in cities, for the city is the economic center from which their goods and services must come. The solution to the problems of the city will be found by individuals with the awareness to see the good and

left: 420. City planner Victor Gruen envisions the city of the future as a cellular structure radiating around a central core. In this diagram, the speckled parts denote recreational areas, the broken lines indicate mass transit, and the black dots clustered in the middle are urban centers.

right: 421. Gruen's plan is similar to the radial symmetry of the milkweed flower (*asclepias*), shown here in cross section.

bad in city planning, to prevent opportunists from defacing the city for their own ends, and to overrule designs that may be spectacular or revolutionary without being suitable to the city's needs. Most of all, the fundamental requirement is to reestablish the city on a human scale, providing small informal areas where human contact can be made and human values appreciated, where creative energy may be recharged rather than stifled. For the designer or private citizen, the primary concern must be for balance, balance between imagination and practicality, between technology and nature, between the future and the past, and between science and the living individual.

SUMMARY

The city, which began as the solution to a problem, has become one of the great challenges of the twentieth century. Design for cities falls into two categories: urban renewal or the redevelopment of existing cities, and city planning or the design for new cities. One of the crises confronting the city in recent years has been the move to the suburbs, leaving the hearts of cities in need of new attractions. This has been approached in two ways: (1) by bringing to the center of town the features that have made the suburbs attractive, and (2) by renovating dilapidated sections to restore the flavor of the past.

One of the most successful ideas in city planning is the Greenbelt concept, which balances man's structures against areas of greenery and open spaces and separates the pedestrian from automobile traffic.

Traffic in and around the city is one of the most pressing problems of today, for it leads to the encroachment of parking areas and congestion of traffic. In the future city dwellers will no doubt have to turn to some form of transportation other than the private car.

An important part of any city is its historical and geographical heritage. Many cities are protecting their treasures through historic zoning. Outstanding in present-day city planning is the design of Brasilia, a completely new capital designed for Brazil.

The city of the future will take forms that seem fantastic to us today, but it will not be solely the work of the designer. In order to solve the problems of city living, all kinds of specialists must be involved, and perhaps most important of all will be the concerned citizen who knows the needs of the city and who is willing to work for their fulfillment. The city of the future, like the city today, does not consist only of buildings and parks, but of people and all the aspects of their lives—physical, social, and esthetic.

The Essence of Design

chapter 23

The elements and principles of design span all the centuries of man's existence and are universally applicable. To the artist these elements become a familiar refrain; they reappear in works of art wherever he sees them, and reaffirm his sense of recognition and confidence in his own judgment. In his work they serve as a key to freedom, making decisions easier as he tries to achieve the most effective results. Eventually, they become a part of him and serve unconsciously in all of his creative activity.

The artist observes the world with sensitivity; he absorbs impressions that nourish his imagination. Impressions drop into his subconscious mind like cells that divide and combine to form new entities that could never be created by the conscious mind. Often when he least expects it, the artist becomes aware of these relationships and, seeing them in terms of his own particular medium, he works to give them a form that will make them apparent to others. This, in essence, is the phenomenon called inspiration. When inspiration is guided by the elements and principles of design, consciously or unconsciously, the result is a work of art.

THE ROLE OF THE ARTIST

The artist must be forever alert to opportunities that might contribute to his inspiration. A blade of grass or a trip to Europe may play a part in the storehouse of his impressions, and his imagination may be nurtured through the bare branches of a winter tree or a drama presented in the theater. In the puzzle that is the contemporary world, the role of the artist becomes increasingly important, and his creativity is nourished by conflict as well as by beauty.

In a primitive society the tribal artist decorates weapons and carves totems; in a complex civilization he functions as a prophet, a philosopher, a social critic, and an interpreter of the changing scene. Faced with radically new concepts of art, he still carries the responsibility of endowing his environment with significance. Even in an age of science and technology, the spirit of man must be nourished and his emotional nature expressed.

The Golden Mean

The Greeks based an entire civilization on what Aristotle termed the Golden Mean. In architecture and pottery, they created a beauty of proportion that has been admired and studied for centuries. In philosophy, they sought to achieve an equally balanced proportion in living. The Golden Mean is the ideal between two extremes. Between fear and foolhardiness the mean is courage, between haughtiness and humility it is honest pride. The theory of the Golden Mean teaches that every excess has its price to pay, not only in terms of morality or physical well-being, but also in such matters as sensitivity and self-expression.

Today the Golden Mean represents the balance needed between art and science, but it also has personal implications for the artist. Because he is sensitive, the artist is able to create. He feels trends before they appear, and as a result, his work may show these trends before his audience can comprehend them. In this way, his vision may be met temporarily with scorn and rejection. The increased sensitivity of the artist registers pain and sorrow as sharply as it does the interest and beauty of life, so that for every peak of exaltation he can expect to experience a plunge to despair. In order to work, he must somehow strike a mean between the extremes of his experience, translating them without being devastated by them. The true artist does not work for the end result, because the objective he seeks is never quite attained. His discernment and his aspirations always leap ahead of his skill. This is as it should be, for the art is in the *act* of creating, not in the creation itself. Each new work thus becomes a mean between the artist's noblest hopes and his own self-doubt and is important as an experience that helps him attain a new level of achievement.

The Designer Today

The principles of design often appear in unexpected places. They are just as applicable to the life of a great city as they are to a beautiful piece of weaving. It has been said that the solution to the evils of mankind is for everyone to become an artist in the broad sense of the word. Certainly it is true that the artistic approach can be applied to many of the problems of civilization, and a wide variety of people are, in actuality, called upon to become designers. The expression "the problems of today" has undoubtedly been used since the beginning of the spoken word, and in most periods of history the problems have been monumental. Yet today with the space

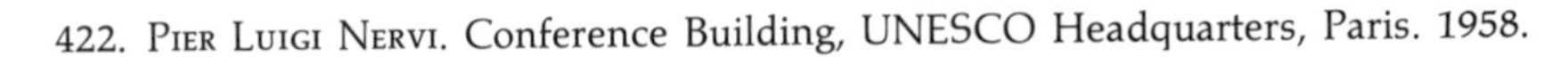

422. Pier Luigi Nervi. Conference Building, UNESCO Headquarters, Paris. 1958.

423. Commercial airliners awaiting clearance for take-off, Kennedy International Airport, New York.

age, a rapidly increasing population, and an explosive international situation, man must face challenges never before encountered. It is quite possible that within this century space-age man may find life on other planets, and this discovery could present unimaginable complications. Solutions to all of these problems will require understanding and, in many cases, an approach that is drastically different from anything known before. Such solutions will undoubtedly require creative imagination.

A PLAN FOR ORDER

Chapter 1 showed that *a design is, first of all, a plan for order.* This is essential if the design is to serve its purpose. The UNESCO headquarters in Paris (Fig. 422) is a particularly eloquent example. It is a large complex including a secretariat and a conference building. The design quality of the buildings springs from simple massive forms that cast lights and shadows without intricate pattern. The adjoining grounds harmonize with the areas of decorative paving. Philosophically, the building has a deeper design; it serves an organization that strives to bring order into world affairs.

Transportation In the past fifty years modes of travel have changed drastically. Just as an ordered system of railroads had become established, the airplane evolved into a forceful contender for first choice in public transportation, a position it has easily attained. Although there is now a system of airports and radar control, the recurrence of air collisions shows that much planning has yet to be done, particularly as more planes take to the air (Fig. 423). The day will come when rockets are commonplace, and new designs for air travel will have to be created, not only for the airplanes and spacecraft themselves but for their movements through an ever-more-crowded atmosphere. Certainly rhythm and balance will play a part in the solution.

Even on the ground all the answers have not been found. In the first half of the century highway travel developed so rapidly that roads sprouted in all directions, forming a hodgepodge of thoroughfares. Only since World War II has a systematic effort been made to create a unified federal highway system, making it possible to cross the country rapidly and easily without having to fight through the traffic of

424. Intersection of the Van Wyck Expressway, Grand Central Parkway, and the Interborough Parkway on Long Island, N.Y.

each town and city along the way. Yet in many localities disputes have arisen over the marring of scenic areas by the construction of superhighways. In an era when wilderness regions are becoming increasingly rare, a new sense of values emerges, in which speed of travel is not always the final criterion. Despite imaginatively handled overpasses and interchanges (Fig. 424) and improvements in base and surface treatment, there are places where any motor traffic is an intrusion. Furthermore, as cars increase in number and in power, the fatalities on highways become appalling. The automobile has created serious problems in many parts of the world. The solution to these problems requires a strong sense of balance and overriding unity on the part of highway planners and car manufacturers.

Another problem related to transportation is the disposal of wrecked or worn-out cars. The junkyard is one of the glaring eyesores of the present time and one of the most unnecessary. Usable parts from old machines of all kinds can be catalogued in storehouses and resold, and the remainder of the junk can be hauled to factories for melting and reuse. Experiments are being carried on with machinery that shreds metal and makes it easily transportable. In small towns across the country the removal of the junkyard at the outskirts would help to restore the order of the landscape.

EXPRESSION OF THE MATERIAL

A second design characteristic is the expression of the material. Just as the traffic interchange is an expression of speed and ease in travel, which are the essentials of modern transportation, so must any design express the substance of which it is composed. Pottery expresses clay in many ways—by solidity, by plastic form, by the texture that proclaims it to be of the earth. Anyone who has worked with damp clay and felt the fascination of its plasticity experiences a keen tactile pleasure just in looking at the stoneware jar illustrated in Figure 425. The shape of the jar has the sense of the material in its own right. It is the kind of full, round form that is satisfying to create from malleable mass. Above all, the handles proclaim the essence of clay. Their texture and the fluidity with which they are shaped and attached to the body of the jar make them look almost as though they were still in the plastic state. One has the feeling that touching them might leave an imprint. This is a particularly articulate expression of the material.

Wilderness In the broader problems of design, one of the most important expressions of material is in the conservation of the wilderness. The material is the natural landscape—the mountains, forests, and rivers with which a country has been endowed. Expression of the material in this case means design that will retain the natural qualities and preserve the beauty that has too long been taken for granted.

The necessity of planning for unpopulated areas has been recognized for the first time in this century. A young country requires taming—felling trees, cutting roads, and leveling ground. The wilderness stretches on endlessly, promising more frontiers beyond each settlement. It takes more vision than most men possess to recognize the point at which the frontier is no longer a challenge but a privilege, beyond which development becomes merely laying waste. It is only after leveling the forests has caused erosion, leading to floods and famine, that trees are recognized as important for more than lumber, or that soil is considered to be vital in itself. Natural resources are not inexhaustible, and man cannot afford to ignore them, much less waste them. Civilization is creeping farther into cherished woods, mountains, and valleys. Mining claims and lumber operations make deserts in the depths of the wilderness, and man's wastes turn rivers into sewers. These things have happened because man's immediate needs have been given more importance than any large design.

The first step toward improvement must be a complete change in outlook. Natural resources are not the property of any one generation but, like knowledge, should be used wisely by each generation and safeguarded for the next. One notable step in this direction was taken in 1916 with the establishment of the National Park Service which set aside 22 million acres of land for ownership by the federal government. Through this action 86 national parks and monuments have now been set up in the United States. Canada has 15 such areas.

Man's earliest gods were closely associated with nature. Sun gods, river gods, gods of fertility and harvest appear repeatedly in the ancient religions and in the primitive expressions of religion today. So long as man lived in harmony with these natural gods, his problems were elemental and simply resolved. It was only when he went forth to conquer nature, to set himself in opposition to the gods, and to declare himself omniscient that complications arose within his surroundings as well as in his mental and physical health.

Because the United States rose from the wilderness, a return to the woods and mountains may seem to be regression. Individually, it is more of an advancement into renewed harmony with nature, appreciation of basic values, spiritual and physical rebirth, and the nurturing of the peace of mind that leads to creativity. Man in a crowd becomes a victim of superimposed human values; he gauges his life to the critical approval of his fellowmen. But man alone in nature has an opportunity to relate himself to a larger perspective. He gains the courage to pursue a goal or an ideal, instead of submitting to the pressure and the leveling influence of the crowd. It is essential that man always be able to find spots like the one

425. Arthur E. Baggs. Covered jar. c. 1939. Stoneware with salt glaze, height 13″. Museum of Contemporary Crafts, New York.

left: 426. ANSEL ADAMS. *Pasture, Sonoma County, California.* 1957.

below: 427. *Lancet,* a textile woven of cotton, linen, and rayon, was designed by Boris Kroll, Inc.

opposite left: 428. Wind-eroded land in the western United States.

opposite right: 429. Hoover Dam and Lake Mead on the Colorado River between Nevada and Arizona. The dam, completed in 1936, provides for flood control, irrigation, and the production of hydroelectric power, and, with the creation of the huge artificial lake, brought recreational facilities to the area.

reproduced in Figure 426. This is one of the responsibilities of the planners of today, for wilderness, once destroyed, can never be salvaged entirely in one generation.

FULFILLMENT OF PURPOSE

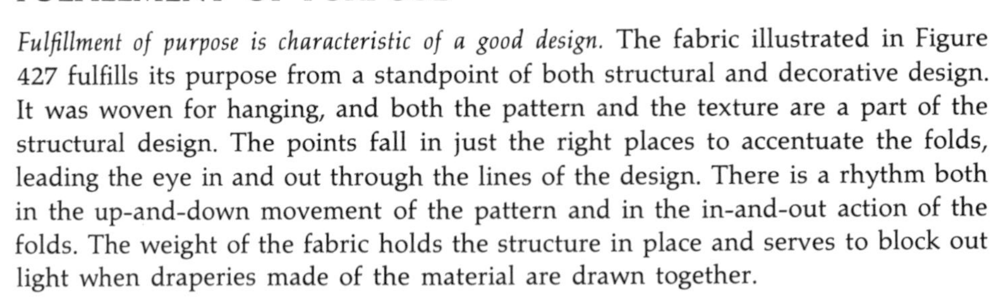

Fulfillment of purpose is characteristic of a good design. The fabric illustrated in Figure 427 fulfills its purpose from a standpoint of both structural and decorative design. It was woven for hanging, and both the pattern and the texture are a part of the structural design. The points fall in just the right places to accentuate the folds, leading the eye in and out through the lines of the design. There is a rhythm both in the up-and-down movement of the pattern and in the in-and-out action of the folds. The weight of the fabric holds the structure in place and serves to block out light when draperies made of the material are drawn together.

Reclamation Man often thinks of natural resources as having been put on the earth to serve his needs. An alternative view considers that man has simply adapted himself to use the resources that were already here. The important point is that man does need the soil and water, the fields and forest, for his sustenance. Even though foods may eventually be manufactured synthetically, no substitute has yet been invented for water. The area of reclamation and conservation requires design that will make it possible for natural resources to fulfill these needs.

Much land has been lost through carelessness and greed. Figure 428 shows an area that was once range land covered with grass. It was then used for crop production without proper care for the binding of the soil and its replenishment. When the land no longer proved fertile, it was simply abandoned. Wind and water carried

away the topsoil, leaving bleak wasteland. Eventually the area will be restored through planting, but this reclamation is an extremely slow process.

Other areas must be reclaimed through reforestation, windbreaks, or irrigation. One carelessly tossed cigarette can destroy acres of valuable timber, and a full generation is required for planted seedling evergreen trees to become large enough to prevent the soil from washing or blowing away.

Reclaiming fresh air and water is a monumental undertaking in the twentieth century, but both are vital to the life and health of people and animals. In July, 1966, Congress passed a water pollution bill and later an air pollution bill. It is estimated that since 1923, when lead alkyls were first used to provide antiknock gasoline, six billion pounds of lead have been burned and spread over the United States. The concentration of lead in the blood of Americans is now one hundred times the normal amount. This is a frightening statistic when it is realized that lead poisoning was one of the methods used by the ancient Romans to destroy their enemies. Congress alone cannot alleviate these conditions. Individuals must be sufficiently interested to take whatever measures are available to control the exhausts from their automobiles, the fumes from their factories, and the smoke from their own backyards.

Water can be fully appreciated only when one has gone without it. When the supply is turned off for an hour, an ordinary household is paralyzed if provision has not been made in advance. The American people now use 400 billion gallons of water daily, 57 percent of the total supply available. By the year 2000 the amount used will be 900 billion gallons—more than the present supply. Ocean water is being considered as a solution to this problem, and experiments are being conducted in purification and desalinization. Projects like Hoover Dam (Fig. 429) contribute to

above: 430. EERO SAARINEN. Pedestal chair. 1958.

right: 431. The use of the hexagon, a basic form in nature, provides effective space for parking DC-8 jets at loading ramps at San Francisco's International Airport.

both the production of power and the harnassing of water supplies for irrigating arid land. The Missouri River has been the site of silt control structures that have cleared its muddy waters, making the river more usable and more attractive. In Iowa the river banks have been landscaped into picnic and recreation areas.

These are some of the projects that show concern for man's future and use design to preserve his needs. However, they are only a beginning. Lake Michigan is said to be dying, and Lake Erie is virtually dead ecologically as a result of sewage and industrial wastes that pollute the waters, kill the fish, and start the cycle known as eutrophication—a complex and deadly process that wipes out all growth. Former Secretary of the Interior Stewart Udall explained the problem as follows: "Lake Michigan has been rich in aquatic treasures for the 5.5 million citizens in its basin. It is a playground for millions. Its waters satisfy the demands of 50 cities—1.5 billion gallons daily. It is a swimming, waterskiing, and boating place for millions. A lake once served hundreds of generations of men. Now one generation of men can destroy a lake—permanently." The Government has done much research and has the authority to take measures to stop the pollution, but it is a long and very costly process.

The great opportunity for design lies in the ability to see overall needs and to design projects accordingly. Most problems have arisen from the selfish goals of local interests. Small groups have been permitted to interfere with large-scale projects that would be of benefit to an entire area or to the country as a whole. No design can be successful unless the designer is backed by an interested, imaginative, and enlightened public, who will accept and promote the designs that have the most lasting effect and the widest application.

LAWS OF GROWTH AND ORDER

An effective design follows the natural laws of growth and order. The laws of growth and order are obvious in designs concerning wilderness and reclamation, where natural resources and natural surroundings are involved. Structural design based on the growth of plants makes possible taller buildings than could otherwise be conceived. A piece of pottery built of coils follows similar laws, as each succeeding coil rests its weight upon the coil below it; without this structural order clay would not hold its form. Pots made on the wheel have a natural order as the result of the centrifugal force of the wheel and the counteracting motions of the potter's hands. There is a rhythmic law involved in weaving a fabric: each row of thread is interlaced with another like the tendrils of vines or the growth of moss. The Eero Saarinen chair illustrated in Figure 430 can be compared with the natural growth of a tree or a piece of driftwood, so rhythmic and organic is its form. The chair is made of plastic and cast-aluminum, molded to follow the contours of the body. Firmly rooted on the ground, it appears to unfold like a leaf, curving upward toward the light. Regarding the pedestal chair, Saarinen said: "I wanted to clear up the slum of legs . . . . I wanted to make the chair all one thing again . . . ." This new interpretation has an emphasis on wholeness that is typical of nature in its seeming growth from the base on which it rests.

Space Utilization Many of the problems of living today center around the utilization of space. This subject is relevant to the design of cities and to methods of transportation. It also applies to the use of wilderness areas. One of the most difficult aspects of space utilization concerns the parking of vehicles when they are not in use. Automobile parking has become a major problem in the United States, and the parking of airplanes may soon become as serious.

One effective solution is being used at the San Francisco International Airport, as shown in Figure 431. Here five DC-8 jets are parked at passenger loading ramps prior to taking off. The design for the ramps is based on a hexagon, one of the fundamental forms in nature; it is a useful space-saving shape, since the six sides offer more surfaces than a rectangle or a square, yet fit together in a more compact manner than a circle. This is the basic shape in a honeycomb and in many tissues, such as the cornea of an insect's eye (Fig. 432). Figure 433 illustrates its adaptation in a floral shape: the six sides are represented by the edges of six petals with a raised center, much like the platform in the center of the loading ramps. Even in areas most closely related to engineering and technology—such as city planning and air travel—solutions still come from designs that are characteristic of nature. Thus, in the most mechanized exploits, man follows the same basic laws of growth and order that are found in a flower or a biological tissue.

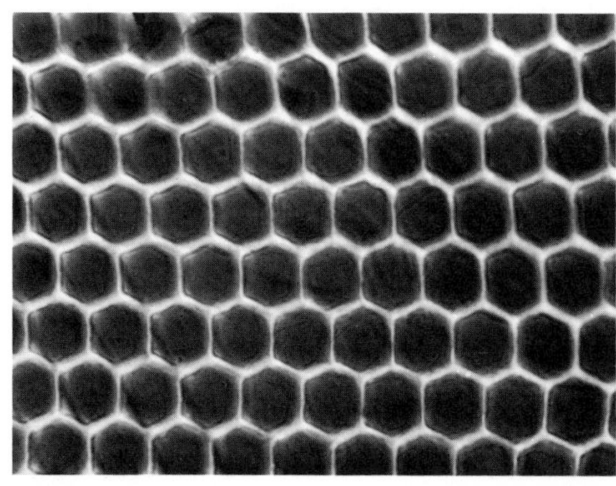

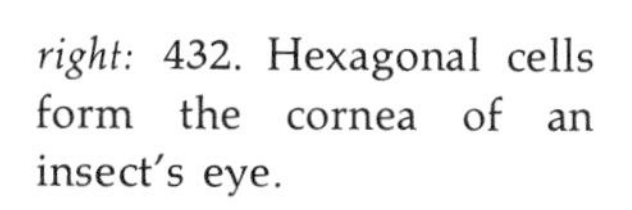

right: 432. Hexagonal cells form the cornea of an insect's eye.

far right: 433. The flower of *clematis Florida bicolor* is also in the form of a hexagon.

434. Edward Hopper. *House by the Railroad.* 1925. Oil on canvas, 24 × 29″. Museum of Modern Art, New York (given anonymously).

INDIVIDUALITY

The concept of individuality is fundamental to the definition of art as expression. Minimal art and art constructed by electricians and plumbers may seem to wander far from this concept. Yet when we look at any of the forms of art that man has created through the ages, we find that, invariably, each form is an expression of something —a religious belief, an emotion, or an experience involving one man's reaction to his environment. The common denominator of art is always man. The factor that makes a personal expression a work of art is the element of recognition that it awakens in the viewer; that is, the viewer feels he has experienced himself what the artist is trying to express. This is known as the universality of a work, a unifying quality that finds utterance through the uniquely personal expression of an individual.

The house reproduced in Figure 434 is not extraordinary, but the highly personal treatment given it by Edward Hopper makes it worthy of attention. When *House by the Railroad* first appeared, people thought it was satirical, that the artist was depicting the eventual emptiness of splendor and material possessions. Later it was interpreted as being nostalgic and romantic, a reminiscence of a cherished past. The artist disavowed both interpretations. He said: "My aim in painting has always been the most exact transcription possible of my most intimate impressions of nature." [1] In this statement Hopper sums up his individuality; he gives us a clue about why his paintings have a distinctive flavor, a flavor filled with memories and associations.

Design in the Intangibles There are innumerable areas that have not been mentioned in which design in its broadest sense is needed. Dedicated men and women are working to solve problems in medicine, in race relations, in international affairs, as well as in the tangible things that can be built of stone and glass. Design in human relationships is the purpose of such organizations as the United Nations, and the problems involved will be ever changing, for human individuality and human attitudes alter continually. In many ways the design of social structures is even more rewarding than the creation of visual forms, and the development of individuals is just as exciting. Human relationships through extrasensory perception offer a field for exploration which has been scarcely touched.

THE ESSENCE OF DESIGN

Design, then, is composed of many factors and is applicable to far more fields than is generally realized. It has been said that as buildings climb higher and higher, man grows farther and farther away from nature. This alienation is easy to believe as one views great cities, where from many angles no tree or patch of grass is visible (Fig. 435). Yet space is also nature, with limits far beyond man's comprehension, and the farther man reaches upward, the farther he extends into space. The basic laws of growth and order are just as much a part of space as they are of the smallest earthbound plant or animal. Furthermore, it is quite possible that in reaching upward physically, man may also be stretching into new realms of intuitive understanding

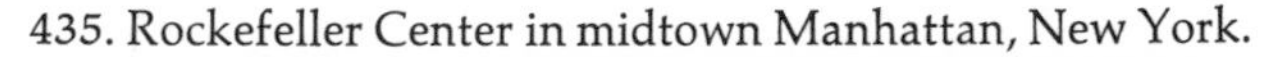

435. Rockefeller Center in midtown Manhattan, New York.

from which traditional concepts of representation may become as outdated as the earliest airplanes. In spite of computers and an increasing dependency upon mechanization, man remains a biological animal, and he cannot be expected to thrive in an environment designed for robots. The most significant frontiers of exploration may well be into the depths of man's mind and emotions, rather than outward into space.

Design lies in a knowledge of materials, of their possibilities and limitations and of the skill required to achieve their fullest expression. It exists in the body and mind of the artist, who receives inspirations through his senses. And it is through the crucible of his creative power that he transforms them into new entities of his own making. Most of all, the essence of design is to be found in the spirit of the designer, who sees the ugliness and confusion around him, but who, even when most repelled by the evils of the world, carries always an overwhelming belief in the dignity and beauty of human life, and a constant recognition of the irrepressible need to express this dignity and this beauty.

SUMMARY

The elements and principles of design are the artist's key to freedom and should become a part of him, augmenting his own sensitivity and making it possible to convert his interpretations into a work of art. The role of the artist is to interpret the changing scene. In this he should try to achieve the Golden Mean between his own aspirations and his despair at not having reached them. The designer today is called upon to work in many fields beyond the conventional reaches of artistic activity, fields that stretch into all areas of existence.

The five characteristics of a good design apply not only to man's visual creations but to many other areas as well. A plan for order includes the need to design methods of handling transportation. Expression of the material is necessary in the design of wilderness areas where the materials of nature will be preserved. The fulfillment of purpose can be related to reclamation, to the preservation of natural resources, and to the understanding of their relationship to man. Laws of growth and order govern even the most highly mechanized projects, such as airports and city planning, and space utilization in an increasingly crowded world. Individuality is being expressed in many fields, and dedicated persons are working to preserve the well-being of men in difficult situations.

Design is composed of many factors and is applicable to more fields than is generally realized. The essence of design will always be found in the spirit of the designer, who sees the wrongs of the world, but who sustains the need to express his belief in the beauty of human life and of human dignity.

Because of his training and sensitivity, the artist is well-qualified to lead the way to greater understanding in the world today. He cultivates variety and unity in his own work and appreciates these characteristics in the work of others. He delights in the individuality of artistic endeavor. These three qualities—variety, unity, and individuality—are basic to the harmonious existence of different peoples in an increasingly crowded world. Only through the realization that there is room for all kinds of people and beliefs, a need for the variety that they express, and a necessity for respect toward their individuality, can the fierce competitive spirit of the modern world be tempered and jealousy and greed be converted into the unity of mutual tolerance. The essence of design, which leads the artist into his varied expressions, can pervade every dimension of living.

Bibliography and Notes

CHAPTER 1

Bibliography

Berenson, Bernard. *Seeing and Knowing.* Greenwich, Conn.: New York Graphic Society, 1968.

Collier, Graham. *Form, Space and Vision.* Englewood Cliffs, N.J.: Prentice-Hall, 1967.

Ehrenzweig, Anton. *The Hidden Order of Art: a Study in the Psychology of Artistic Imagination.* Berkeley, Calif.: University of California Press, 1967.

Fleming, William. *Arts and Ideas.* 3rd ed. New York: Holt, Rinehart and Winston, 1968.

Fuller, R. Buckminster. *Ideas and Integrities.* New York: Prentice-Hall, 1963.

Herbert, Robert L., ed. *Modern Artists on Art.* Englewood Cliffs, N.J.: Prentice-Hall, 1964.

Kepes, Gyorgy, ed. *Vision and Value.* 6 vols. New York: Braziller, 1966–67.

Oeri, Georgine. *Man and His Images.* New York: Viking, 1968.

Read, Sir Herbert. *Icon and Idea.* New York: Schocken Books, 1965.

Notes

1. Alexander Pope, "An Essay on Man," *Pope's Poems* (New York: Lovell), p. 211.
2. Gyorgy Kepes (ed.), *The Visual Arts Today* (Middletown, Conn.: Wesleyan University Press, 1960), Introduction.

CHAPTER 2

Bibliography

Mueller, Robert E. *The Science of Art.* New York: John Day, 1968.

Postma, C. *Plant Marvels in Miniature.* New York: John Day, 1968.

Notes

1. Harlow Shapley, *Of Stars and Men* (Boston: Beacon, 1958), p. 63.
2. F. Ratcliffe, *Flying Fox and Drifting Sand* (London: Anglo Books, 1952).
3. W. Pfeffer, *Abhandl. sachs Akad. Wiss. Leipzig.,* Math-Phil. K-1, 30:259, 1907.
4. F. A. Brown, Jr., *Living Clocks* at Northwestern Medical School, Chicago, Ill. (March 22, 1960); "The Rhythmic Nature of Animals and Plants," *Tri-Quarterly,* Northwestern University, Chicago (Fall 1958).
5. Irwin Edman (ed.), *The Philosophy of Schopenhauer,* Vol. I, *The World as Will and Idea* (New York: Random House, 1956), pp. 357–358.
6. *Ibid.,* Vol. III, p. 267.
7. George Santayana, *Reason in Religion* (New York: Scribner, 1913), p. 273.

CHAPTER 3

Bibliography

Besset, Maurice. *Who Was Le Corbusier?* New York: World, 1968.

Brodatz, Phil. *Textures: A Photographic Album for Artists and Designers.* New York: Dover, 1966.

Jeanneret-Gris, Charles-Edouard. *The Modular: A Harmonious Measure to the Human Scale Universally Applicable to Architecture and Mechanics by Le Corbusier.* Trans. by P. de Francia and A. Bostock. 2nd ed. Cambridge, Mass.: MIT Press, 1968.

———. *Modular 2, 1955 (Let the User Speak Next).* Cambridge, Mass.: MIT Press, 1968.

Ucko, Peter, and Andrée Rosenfeld. *Paleolithic Cave Art.* New York: McGraw-Hill, 1967.

Notes

1. László Moholy-Nagy, *Vision in Motion* (Chicago: Theobald, 1956), p. 36.
2. Aline B. Saarinen (ed.), *Eero Saarinen and His Work* (New Haven and London: Yale University Press, 1962), p. 11.

CHAPTER 4

Bibliography

Arnheim, Rudolph. *Art and Visual Perception.* Berkeley: University of California Press, 1965.

Ehrenzweig, Anton. *The Psychoanalysis of Artistic Vision and Hearing.* New York: Braziller, 1965.

Gibson, James J. *The Perception of the Visual World.* Boston: Houghton Mifflin, no date.

Kuh, Katharine. *The Artist's Voice.* New York: Harper and Row, 1962.

Schaarwachter, Georg. *Perspective for Architecture.* Trans. by E. R. Dawson. New York: Praeger, 1967.

Wyman, Jenifer D., and Stephen F. Gordon. *Primer of Perception.* New York: Reinhold, 1967.

Notes

1. James J. Gibson, "Pictures, Perspective, and Perception," in Gyorgy Kepes (ed.), *The Visual Arts Today* (Middletown, Conn.: Wesleyan University Press, 1960), p. 224.
2. Sigfried Giedion, "The Roots of Symbolic Expression," in Kepes, *op, cit.,* p. 27.
3. Adolf Erman, *Literature of the Ancient Egyptians* (New York: Dutton, 1927), pp. 92–99.

CHAPTER 5

Bibliography

Albers, Josef. *Interaction of Color.* New Haven, Conn.: Yale University Press, 1963.

Birren, Faber. *Color, Form and Space.* New York: Reinhold, 1961.

———. *Creative Color.* New York: Reinhold, 1961.

———. *History of Color in Painting.* New York: Reinhold, 1965.

———. *Principles of Color.* New York: Reinhold, 1969.

Chevreul, Michel Eugène. *The Principles of Harmony and Contrast of Color.* New York: Reinhold, 1967.

Itten, Johannes. *The Art of Color.* Trans. by Ernst van Haagen. New York: Reinhold, 1961.

Judd, Deane B., and Gunter Wyszecki. *Color in Business, Science, and Industry.* 2nd ed. New York: John Wiley, 1963.

Munsell, Albert H. *A Grammar of Color: A Basic Treatise on the Color System of Albert H. Munsell.* New York: Reinhold, 1969.

Ostwald, Wilhelm. *The Color Primer: A Basic Treatise on the Color System of Wilhelm Ostwald.* New York: Reinhold, 1969.

Renner, Paul. *Color, Order and Harmony.* New York: Reinhold, 1965.

Notes

1. Faber Birren, "Color Comes First," *House and Garden* (September, 1957), p. 178.
2. Johannes Itten, *The Art of Color* (New York: Reinhold, 1961), p. 25.

CHAPTER 6

Bibliography

Hambidge, Jay. *Practical Applications of Dynamic Symmetry.* New York: Devin, 1965.

Hartung, Rolf. *Creating with Corrugated Paper.* New York: Reinhold, 1966.

Itten, Johannes. *Design and Form.* New York: Reinhold, 1964.

Newman, Thelma R. *Plastics as an Art Form.* Philadelphia: Chilton, 1964.

Stix, Hugh, and others. *The Shell: Five Hundred Million Years of Inspired Design.* New York: Abrams, 1968.

Notes

1. Paul Weiss, "Organic Form: Scientific and Aesthetic Aspects," in Gyorgy Kepes (ed.), *The Visual Arts Today* (Middletown, Conn.: Wesleyan University Press, 1960), p. 184.

2. George Barford, "Form and Structure, A Pictorial Essay," *Everyday Art* (Winter, 1967).

3. László Moholy-Nagy, *Vision in Motion* (Chicago: Paul Theobald, 1956), p. 45.

4. Alfred H. Barr, Jr. (ed.), *Masters of Modern Art* (New York: Museum of Modern Art, 1958), p. 140.

5. Moholy-Nagy, *op. cit.*, p. 44.

CHAPTER 7

Bibliography

Battersby, Martin. *Art Nouveau.* New York: Book Sales, 1969.

Boas, Franz. *Primitive Art.* New York: Dover, 1962.

Casanelles, E. *Antoni Gaudí.* Greenwich, Conn.: New York Graphic Society, 1968.

Plath, Iona. *The Decorative Arts of Sweden.* New York: Dover, 1965.

Rheims, Maurice. *The Flowering of Art Nouveau.* Trans. by Patrick Evans. New York: Abrams, 1966.

Scheidig, Walther. *Crafts of the Weimar Bauhaus, 1919–1924: An Early Experiment in Industrial Design.* Trans. by R. Michaelis-Jena and P. Murray. New York: Reinhold, 1967.

Schmutzler, Robert. *Art Nouveau.* Trans. by Edouard Roditi. New York: Abrams.

Slivka, Rose, ed. *The Crafts of the Modern World.* New York: Horizon, 1968.

Taylor, John F. A. *Design and Expression in the Visual Arts.* New York: Dover, 1964.

Veronesi, Guilia. *The Rise and Fall of the Decorative Arts.* New York: Braziller, 1968.

Zahle, Erik, ed. *A Treasury of Scandinavian Design.* New York: Golden, 1961.

Notes

1. Johannes Itten, *Design and Form: The Basic Course at the Bauhaus* (New York: Reinhold, 1963).

CHAPTER 8

Bibliography

Arias, Paolo Enrico. *A History of 1000 Years of Greek Vase Painting.* New York: Abrams, 1962.

Donnelly, P. J. *Blanc de Chine: The Porcelain of Tehua in Fukien.* New York: Praeger 1968.

Fisher, Stanley W. *English Ceramics.* New York: Hawthorn, 1967.

Folsom, Robert S. *Handbook of Greek Pottery, a Guide for Amateurs.* Greenwich, Conn.: New York Graphic Society, 1968.

Forms From the Earth: 100 Years of Pottery in America. New York: The American Craftsmen's Council.

Griffing, Robert P. *The Art of the Korean Potter.* New York: Asia Society (distributed by New York Graphic Society), 1968.

Haggar, Reginald G. *The Concise Encyclopedia of Continental Pottery and Porcelain.* New York: Praeger, 1968.

Hughes, Bernard. *English Pottery and Porcelain Figures.* New York: Praeger, 1968.

Jenyns, Soame. *Japanese Porcelain.* New York: Praeger, 1968.

Kenny, John B. *Ceramic Design.* Philadelphia: Chilton, 1963.

Lakofsy, Charles. *Pottery.* Dubuque, Iowa: Wm. C. Brown, 1968.

Nelson, Glenn. *Ceramics.* 2nd ed. New York: Holt, Rinehart and Winston, 1966.

Prodan, Mario. *The Art of the T'ang Potter.* New York: Viking, 1961.

Rhodes, Daniel. *Clay and Glazes for the Potter.* Philadelphia: Chilton, 1957.

———. *Stoneware and Porcelain.* Philadelphia: Chilton, 1959.

Wildenhain, Marguerite. *Pottery, Form and Expression.* New York: American Craftsmen's Council (distributed by Reinhold), 1962.

CHAPTER 9

Bibliography

Bovini, Giuseppe. *Ravenna Mosaics.* Greenwich, Conn.: New York Graphic Society, 1968.

Burton, John. *Glass: Hand Blown, Sculptured, Colored: Philosophy and Method.* Philadelphia: Chilton, 1968.

Johnson, James Rosser. *The Radiance of Chartres.* New York: Random House, 1965.

Kinney, Kay. *Glass Craft: Designing, Forming, and Decorating.* Philadelphia: Chilton, 1962.

Labino, Dominick. *Visual Art in Glass.* Dubuque, Iowa: Wm. C. Brown, 1968.

Neuburg, Frederic, *Ancient Glass.* Toronto: University of Toronto Press, 1962.

Peter, John. *Design with Glass.* New York: Reinhold, 1964.

Revi, Albert Christian. *American Art Nouveau Glass.* New York: Thomas Nelson, 1968.

Steuben Glass. *Poetry in Crystal.* New York: Spiral Press, 1963.

Stribling, Mary Lou. *Mosaic Techniques.* New York: Crown, 1966.

Young, Joseph L. *Mosaics: Principles and Practice.* New York: Reinhold, 1963.

CHAPTER 10

Bibliography

Albers, Anni. *On Weaving.* Middletown, Conn.: Wesleyan University Press, 1965.

Blumenau, Lili. *Creative Design in Wall Hangings.* New York: Crown, 1966.

Erickson, Janet. *Block Printing on Textiles.* New York: Watson-Guptill, 1961.

Hartung, Rolf. *Creative Textile Design: Thread and Fabric.* New York: Reinhold, 1964.

———. *More Creative Textile Design: Color and Texture.* New York: Reinhold, 1965.

Harvey, Virginia I. *Macramé: The Art of Creative Knotting.* New York: Reinhold, 1968.

Kaufmann, Ruth. *The New American Tapestry.* New York: Reinhold, 1968.

Johnston, Meda Parker, and Glen Kaufman. *Design on Fabrics.* New York: Reinhold, 1968.

Krevitsky, Nik. *Batik: Art and Craft.* New York: Reinhold, 1964.

———. *Stitchery: Art and Craft.* New York: Reinhold, 1966.

Laury, Jean Ray. *Appliqué Stitchery.* New York: Reinhold, 1966.

Proud, Nora. *Introducing Textile Printing.* New York: Watson-Guptill, 1968.

———. *Textile Printing and Dyeing.* New York: Reinhold, 1965.

Thorpe, Azalea Stuart, and Jack Lenor Larsen. *Elements of Weaving.* Garden City, N.Y.: Doubleday, 1967.

Notes

1. "Jack Lenor Larsen," *Craft Horizons* (Sept./Oct., 1967), p. 24.

2. Mildred Fischer, "The Weaver as Artist," *Craft Horizons* (Sept./Oct., 1959), p. 14.

3. Nik Krevitsky, "On Stitchery," *Craft Horizons* (Nov./Dec., 1963), p. 18.

CHAPTER 11

Bibliography

Meilach, Dona Z. *Contemporary Art with Wood.* New York: Crown, 1968.

Rottger, Ernst. *Creative Wood Design.* New York: Reinhold, 1961.

Willcox, Donald. *Wood Design.* New York: Watson-Guptill, 1968.

Notes

1. Stanley Kaplan, "The Challenge of a Plank of Wood," *American Artist* (May, 1966), p. 31.

CHAPTER 12

Bibliography

Bedford, John. *Pewter.* New York: Walker, 1966.

Coche de la Ferte, Etienne. *Antique Jewellery from the 2nd to the 8th Century.* New York: Taplinger, 1962.

Garner, Sir Harry Mason. *Chinese and Japanese Cloisonné Enamels.* Rutland, Vt.: Tuttle, 1962.

Granstrom, K. E. *Creating with Metal.* New York: Reinhold, 1968.

Hornung, Clarence P. *A Source Book of Antiques and Jewelry Designs.* New York: Braziller, 1968.

Kovel, Ralph M. *A Directory of American Silver, Pewter, and Silver Plate.* New York: Crown, 1961.

Larkman, Brian. *Contemporary Design in Metalwork.* London: Murray, 1963.
Meilach, Dona, and Donald Sieden. *Direct Metal Sculpture.* New York: Crown, 1966.
Morton, Philip. *Contemporary Jewelry: A Studio Handbook.* New York: Holt, Rinehart and Winston, 1969.
Thomas, Richard. *Metalsmithing for the Artist-Craftsman.* Philadelphia: Chilton.
Winter, Edward. *Enameling for Beginners.* New York: Watson-Guptill, 1962.

Notes

1. Cleve Gray (ed.), *David Smith by David Smith* (New York: Holt, Rinehart and Winston, 1968), p. 54.

CHAPTER 13

Bibliography

Hill, Margot Hamilton, and Peter A. Bucknell. *The Evolution of Fashion, Pattern and Cut, 1066–1930.* New York: Reinhold, 1968.
Levin, Phyllis Lee. *The Wheels of Fashion.* Garden City, New York: Doubleday, 1965.
Sronkova, Olga. *Fashions Through the Centuries: Renaissance, Baroque, and Rococo.* New York: Tudor, 1962.
Volland, Virginia. *Designing Woman.* Garden City, New York: Doubleday, 1966.

Notes

1. H. Dennis Bradley, *The Eternal Masquerade* (New York: Boni and Liveright, 1923), p. 265.

CHAPTER 14

Bibliography

Anderson, Donald M. *The Art of Written Forms: The Theory and Practice of Calligraphy.* New York: Holt, Rinehart and Winston, 1969.
Bewick, Thomas. *1800 Woodcuts.* New York: Dover, 1962.
Biegeleisen, J. I. *The Complete Book of Silk Screen Printing Production.* New York: Dover, 1963.
Bowman, William J. *Graphic Communication.* New York: Wiley, 1968.
Braque, Georges. *Georges Braque: his Graphic Work.* New York: Abrams, 1961.
Chieffo, Clifford. *Silk Screen as a Fine Art.* New York: Reinhold, 1967.
Cleaver, James. *A History of Graphic Art.* New York: Philosophical Library, 1963.
The Complete Woodcuts of Albrecht Dürer. New York: Dover, 1963.
Curwen, Harold. *Processes of Graphic Reproduction in Printing.* Revised by Charles Mayo. New York: Dover, 1963.
The Graphic Art of Mary Cassatt. Museum of Graphic Art, Smithsonian Institution (distributed by Random House), 1968.
Heller, Jules. *Printmaking Today.* New York: Holt, Rinehart and Winston, 1958.
Hlavsa, Oldrich. *A Book of Type and Design.* New York: Tudor, 1962.
Ivins, William M. *Notes on Prints.* New York: Da Capo, 1968.
Johnston, Edward. *Writing and Illuminating and Lettering.* New York: Pitman, 1962.
Lumsden, Ernest S. *The Art of Etching.* New York: Dover, 1962.
Michener, James A. *The Modern Japanese Print, an Appreciation.* Rutland, Vt.: Tuttle, 1968.
Narazaki, Muneshige. *Hokusai: The Thirty-six Views of Mt. Fuji.* English adaptation by John Bester. Palo Alto, Calif.: Kodansha, 1968.
Robertson, Ronald G. *Contemporary Printmaking in Japan.* New York: Crown, 1965.
Rothenstein, Michael. *Frontiers of Printmaking.* New York: Reinhold, 1966.
Senefelder, Alois. *A Complete Course of Lithography.* New York: Da Capo, 1968.
Sotriffer, Kristian. *Printmaking—History and Technique.* New York: McGraw-Hill, 1968.
Weaver, Peter. *Printmaking: A Medium for Basic Design.* New York: Reinhold, 1968.
Wingler, Hans M. *Graphic Work from the Bauhaus.* Greenwich, Conn.: New York Graphic Society, 1969.
Zigrosser, Carl, ed. *Prints.* New York: Holt, Rinehart and Winston, 1962.

CHAPTER 15

Bibliography

Brunner, Felix. *A Handbook of Graphic Reproduction Processes.* New York: Hastings, 1962.
Cardamone, Tom. *Advertising Agency and Studio Skills.* New York: Watson-Guptill, 1962.
Constantine, Mildred, and Alan M. Fern, eds. *Word and Image: Posters from the Collection of the Museum of Modern Art.* New York: Museum of Modern Art, 1968.
Croy, Peter. *Graphic Design and Reproduction Techniques.* New York: Hastings, 1968.
Fletcher, Alan, with Colin Forbes and Bob Gill. *Graphic Design: Visual Comparisons.* New York: Reinhold, 1963.
Goudy, Frederic William. *The Alphabet and Elements of Lettering.* New York: Dover, 1963.
Hayter, Stanley William. *New Ways of Gravure.* New York: Oxford, 1966.
Hutchinson, Harold F. *The Poster: An Illustrated History from 1860.* New York: Viking, 1960.
Longyear, William. *Type and Lettering.* New York: Watson-Guptill, 1962.
Maurello, S. *Commercial Art Techniques.* New York: Tudor, 1962.
Metzl, Ervine. *The Poster: its History and its Art.* New York: Watson-Guptill, 1963.
Nelson, Roy P. *Design of Advertising.* Dubuque, Iowa: William C. Brown, 1967.
Nelson, Roy P., and B. Ferris. *Fell's Guide to Commercial Art.* New York: Frederick Fell, 1966.
Opotowsky, Stan. *TV: The Big Picture.* New York: Dutton, 1961.
Read, Herbert. *Art and Industry.* London: Faber and Faber, 1966.
Shahn, Ben. *Love and Joy About Letters.* New York: Grossman, 1963.
Skornia, Harry J. *Television and Society.* New York: McGraw-Hill, 1965.
Sutton, James, and Alan Bartram. *An Atlas of Typeforms.* New York: Hastings, 1968.

Notes

1. Charles M. Edwards, Jr., and William H. Howard, *Retail Advertising and Sales Promotion* (New York: Prentice-Hall, 1943), p. 378.

CHAPTER 16

Bibliography

Art Since 1945. New York: Abrams, no date.
Baur, John I. H. *Revolution and Tradition in Modern American Art.* New York: Praeger, 1967.
Berenson, Bernard. *The Italian Painters of the Renaissance.* New York: Phaidon, 1968.
Colombo, A., and G. Diehl. *Treasury of World Painting.* New York: Tudor, 1962.
Goosen, E. C. *The Art of the Real: USA, 1948–1968.* New York: Museum of Modern Art, 1968.
Haftmann, Werner. *Painting in the Twentieth Century.* 2 vols. New York: Praeger, 1965.
Janis, Harriet. *Collage.* Philadelphia: Chilton, 1962.
Lassaigne, Jacques. *Chagall Unpublished Drawings.* New York: World, 1968.
Lippard, Lucy R. *Pop Art.* New York: Praeger, 1966.
Masters, Robert E. L., and others. *Psychedelic Art.* New York: Grove, 1968.
Morris, Jerrold. *On the Enjoyment of Modern Art.* Greenwich, Conn.: New York Graphic Society, 1968.
Muller, Joseph-Emile. *Fauvism.* Trans. by S. E. Jones. New York: Praeger, 1967.
Nadeau, Maurice. *The History of Surrealism.* Trans. by Richard Howard. New York: Macmillan, 1965.
New Art Around the World. New York: Abrams.
O'Conner, Francis V. *Jackson Pollock.* New York: Museum of Modern Art, 1967.
Parola, René. *Optical Art: Theory and Practice.* New York: Reinhold, 1969.
Poole, Phoebe. *Impressionism.* New York: Praeger, 1967.
Protter, Eric. *Painters on Painting.* New York: Grosset and Dunlap, 1963.
Read, Sir Herbert. *A Concise History of Modern Painting.* New York: Praeger, 1968.
Rewald, John. *Paul Cézanne: a Biography.* New York: Schocken, 1968.
Rose, Barbara. *American Art Since 1900.* New York: Praeger, 1967.
Rubin, William S. *Dada and Surrealist Art.* New York: Abrams, 1969.

Seitz, William C. *The Responsive Eye.* New York: Museum of Modern Art, 1965.
Weller, Allen S. *The Joys and Sorrows of Recent American Art.* Urbana, Ill.: University of Illinois Press, 1968.

Notes

1. Alexander Eliot, *Three Hundred Years of American Painting* (New York: Time, 1957), p. 42.
2. *Time* (November 24, 1967), p. 64.

CHAPTER 17

Bibliography

Brett, Guy. *Kinetic Art: The Language of Movement.* New York: Reinhold, 1968.
Burnham, Jack. *Beyond Modern Sculpture.* New York: Braziller, 1968.
Craven, Wayne. *Sculpture in America.* Philadelphia: Crowell, 1968.
David Smith by David Smith. Ed. by Cleve
Geist, Sidney. *Brancusi: a Study of the Sculpture.* New York: Grossman, 1968.
Gordon, John. *Isamu Noguchi.* New York: Praeger, 1968.
Gray, Cleve, ed. *David Smith by David Smith.* New York: Holt, Rinehart and Winston, 1968.
Hale, Nathan Cabot. *Welded Sculpture.* New York: Watson-Guptill, 1968.
Hammacher, Abraham Marie. *The Sculpture of Barbara Hepworth.* Trans. by J. Brockway. New York: Abrams, 1968.
Henry Spencer Moore. Photographed and edited by John Hedgecoe. New York: Simon and Schuster, 1968.
James, Philip. *Henry Moore on Sculpture: A Collection of the Sculptor's Writings and Spoken Words.* New York: Viking, 1967.
Jean Arp: Sculpture, His Last Ten Years. Trans. by K. Philippson. New York: Abrams, 1968.
Meauze, Pierre. *African Art: Sculpture.* New York: World, 1968.
Mills, John W. *Sculpture in Concrete.* New York: Praeger, 1968.
———. *The Technique of Casting for Sculpture.* New York: Reinhold, 1967.
———. *The Technique of Sculpture.* New York: Reinhold, 1965.
Noguchi, Isamu. *A Sculptor's World.* New York: Harper and Row, 1968.
Penrose, Sir Roland. *The Sculpture of Picasso.* New York: Museum of Modern Art, 1967.
Pope Hennessy, John. *Essays on Italian Sculpture.* New York: Phaidon, 1968.
Popper, Frank. *Origins and Development of Kinetic Art.* Greenwich, Conn.: New York Graphic Society, 1969.
Rickey, George. *Constructivism: Origins and Evolution.* New York: Braziller, 1967.
Roukes, Nicholas. *Sculpture in Plastics.* New York: Watson-Guptill, 1968.
Selz, Jean. *Modern Sculpture, Origins and Evolution.* Trans. by Annette Michelson. New York: Braziller, 1963.
Trier, Eduard. *Form and Space: Sculpture of the Twentieth Century.* Trans. by C. Ligota. New York: Praeger, 1962.
Weinberger, Martin. *Michelangelo the Sculptor.* 2 vols. New York: Columbia University Press, 1967.
Zorach, William. *Art is My Life: The Autobiography of William Zorach.* New York: World, 1967.

Notes

1. Herbert Read, *The Art of Sculpture* (New York: Pantheon, 1956), p. 73.
2. David Sylvester, *Henry Moore, Sculpture and Drawings, 1921–1948* (London: Percy Lund, Humphries, 1957), p. 34.
3. Alfred H. Barr, Jr. (ed), *Masters of Modern Art* (New York: Museum of Modern Art, 1958), p. 148.
4. *Ibid.*, p. 146.
5. *Ibid.*, p. 181.
6. "The Cool Mind, Notes on Neon from Chryssa," *Arts Magazine* (March, 1968), p. 40.
7. *Time* (November 24, 1967), p. 64.

CHAPTER 18

Bibliography

Adams, Ansel, and Nancy Newhall. *This is the American Earth.* San Francisco: The Sierra Club.
Alloway, Lawrence. *American Action Movies: 1946–1964.* Greenwich, Conn.: New York Graphic Society, 1969.
Bluem, A. William. *Documentary in American Television.* New York: Hastings House, 1964.
De Maré, Eric Samuel. *Colour Photography.* 4th ed. Baltimore: Penguin, 1968.
Eisenstadt, Alfred. *Witness to our Time.* Foreword by Henry R. Luce. New York: Viking, 1966.
Feininger, Andreas. *The Complete Photographer.* Englewood Cliffs, N.J.: Prentice-Hall, 1965.
Huss, Roy, and Norman Silverstein. *The Film Experience: Elements of Motion Picture Art.* New York: Harper and Row, 1968.
Karsh, Yousuf. *Karsh Portfolio.* Camden, N.J.: Nelson, 1967.
Lindgren, Ernest. *The Art of the Film.* New York: Macmillan, 1963.
McLuhan, Marshall. *The Meaning of Commercial Television.* Texas-Stanford Seminar, 1966.
Newhall, Beaumont. *Latent Image: the Discovery of Photography.* New York: Doubleday, 1967.
———. *The History of Photography from 1839 to the Present Day.* New York: Museum of Modern Art, 1964.
Newhall, Nancy. *The Eloquent Light,* Vol. I, *Ansel Adams.* San Francisco: Sierra Club.
Nurnberg, Walter. *Lighting for Photography: Means and Methods.* 16th rev. ed. New York: Chilton, 1968.
Parks, Gordon. *Gordon Parks, A Poet and His Camera.* New York: Viking, 1968.
Reisz, Karel, and Gavin Millar. *The Technique of Film Editing.* New York: Hastings House, 1968.
Rinhart, Floyd and Marion. *American Daguerrian Art.* New York: Potter, 1967.
Rotha, Paul, with Sinclair Road and Richard Griffith. *Documentary Film.* New York: Hastings House, 1964.
Sarris, Andrew, ed. *Interviews with Film Directors.* New York: Bobbs-Merrill, 1967.
Thoreau, Henry David. *In Wildness is the Preservation of the World.* Photographs by Eliot Porter with introduction by Joseph Wood Krutch. San Francisco: Sierra Club, 1962.
Weston, Edward. *My Camera on Point Lobos.* New York: Da Capo, 1968.

Notes

1. Thomas H. Miller and Wyatt Brummitt, *This is Photography* (Garden City, N.Y.: Garden City Books, 1955), pp. 53–56.

CHAPTER 19

Bibliography

Bastlund, Kund. *José Luis Sert: Architecture, City Planning, Urban Design.* New York: Praeger, 1967.
Besset, Maurice. *New French Architecture.* Text in English and French. New York: Praeger, 1967.
Charpentrat, Pierre. *Living Architecture: Baroque, Italy and Central Europe.* Trans. by C. Brown. New York: Grosset and Dunlap, 1967.
Donat, John, ed. *World Architecture.* New York: Viking, 1967.
Doxiadis, Constantinos. *Architecture in Transition.* London: Oxford University Press, 1968.
Faber, Tobias. *New Danish Architecture.* New York: Praeger, 1968.
Fraser, Douglas, and others, eds. *Essays in the History of Architecture Presented to Rudolf Wittkower.* 2 vols. New York: Phaidon, 1967.
Galardi, Alberto. *New Italian Architecture.* Text in English and Italian. New York: Praeger, 1967.
Giedion, Siegfried. *Space, Time and Architecture, The Growth of a New Tradition.* 5th ed. Cambridge, Mass.: Harvard University Press, 1968.
Gropius, Walter. *The New Architecture and the Bauhaus.* Cambridge, Mass.: MIT Press, 1968.
Jacobus, John. *Twentieth Century Architecture, The Middle Years, 1940–1965.* New York: Praeger, 1966.
Korn, Arthur. *Glass in Modern Architecture of the Bauhaus Period.* New York: Braziller, 1968.
Kultermann, Udo. *New Japanese Architecture.* New York: Praeger, 1967.
Le Corbusier. *Creation is a Patient Search.* New York: Praeger, 1966.
———. *Towards a New Architecture.* New York: Praeger.
Nervi, Pier Luigi. *Aesthetics and Technology in Building.* Cambridge, Mass.: Harvard University Press, 1967.

Neutra, Richard Joseph. *World and Dwelling.* New York: Universe, 1962.
Nishihara, Kiyoyuki. *Japanese Houses: Patterns for Living.* Trans. by R. L. Gage. San Francisco: Japan Publications, 1968.
Pevsner, Nikolaus. *The Sources of Modern Architecture and Design.* New York: Praeger, 1968.
Pope, Arthur Upham. *Persian Architecture.* New York: Braziller, 1965.
Rasmussen, Steen. *Experiencing Architecture.* Cambridge, Mass.: MIT Press, 1968.
Redstone, Louis G. *Art in Architecture.* New York: McGraw-Hill, 1968.
Ritchie, Thomas, and others. *Canada Builds.* Toronto: University of Toronto Press, 1967.
Saarinen, Eero. *Eero Saarinen on His Work.* New Haven, Conn.: Yale University Press, 1962.
Sharp, Dennis. *Modern Architecture and Expressionism.* New York: Braziller, 1967.
Stone, Edward Durell. *The Evolution of an Architect.* New York: Horizon Press, 1962.
Tempel, Egon. *New Finnish Architecture.* New York: Praeger, 1968.
Weidert, Werner. *Private Houses, An International Survey.* New York: Praeger, 1967.

Notes

1. C. G. Jung, *The Undiscovered Self* (New York: New American Library, 1960), p. 22.
2. American Public Health Association, Committee on the Hygiene of Housing, *Planning the Home for Occupancy* (Chicago: Public Administration Service, 1950), p. 36.
3. Edgar Kauffman, *An American Architecture, Frank Lloyd Wright* (New York: Horizon Press, 1955), p. 190.

CHAPTER 20

Bibliography

Ball, Victoria Kloss. *The Art of Interior Design.* New York: Macmillan, 1960.
Bernier, Georges and Rosamond, eds. *The Best in European Decoration.* New York: Reynal, 1963.
Faulkner, Ray and Sarah. *Inside Today's Home.* 3rd ed. New York: Holt, Rinehart and Winston, 1968.
Halse, A. O. *Use of Color in Interiors.* New York: McGraw-Hill, 1968.
Miller, Edgar G., Jr. *American Antique Furniture,* 2 vols. New York: Dover, 1966.
Moody, Ella, ed. *Decorative Art in Modern Interiors, 1967–1968.* Yearbook of International Furnishing and Decoration, Vol. 57. New York: Viking, 1967.
Praz, Mario. *An Illustrated History of Furnishing.* New York: Braziller, 1964.
Sweeney, John A. H. *The Treasure House of Early American Rooms.* New York: Viking, 1963.
Verlet, Pierre. *The Eighteenth Century in France: Society, Decoration, Furniture.* Trans. by G. Savage. New York: Tuttle, 1967.
Wilson, José, and Arthur Leaman. *Decoration U.S.A.* New York: Macmillan, 1965.
Zahle, Erik. *A Treasury of Scandinavian Design.* New York: Golden Press, 1961.

CHAPTER 21

Bibliography

Better Homes and Gardens Magazine. *Better Homes and Gardens Landscape Planning.* New York: Meredith, 1963.
Clifford, Derek. *A History of Garden Design.* New York: Praeger, 1966.
Downing, Andrew Jackson. *Cottage Residences. Rural Architecture and Landscape Gardening.* New York: American Life Foundation (distributed by Century House), 1967.
Mock, Elizabeth (Bauer). *Modern Gardens and the Landscape.* New York: Museum of Modern Art, 1964.
Sunset Books and Sunset Magazine. *Garden Pools, Fountains, and Waterfalls.* Menlo Park, Calif.: Lane Books, 1965.

Notes

1. Elizabeth B. Kassler, *Modern Gardens and the Landscape* (New York: Museum of Modern Art, 1964), p. 5.

CHAPTER 22

Bibliography

Aregger, Hans, and Otto Glaus. *Highrise Building and Urban Design.* Text in English and German. New York: Praeger, 1967.
Bacon, Edmund N. *Design of Cities.* New York: Viking, 1967.
Benevolo, Leonardo. *The Origins of Modern Town Planning.* Trans. by J. Landry. Cambridge, Mass.: MIT Press, 1967.
Doxiadis, Constantinos. *Ekistics. An Introduction to the Science of Human Settlements.* London: Oxford University Press, 1968.
Eckbo, Garrett. *Urban Landscape Design.* New York: McGraw-Hill, 1964.
Gruen, Victor. *The Heart of our Cities.* New York: Simon and Schuster, 1964.
Halprin, Lawrence. *Cities.* New York: Reinhold, 1963.
Johnson-Marshall, Percy. *Rebuilding Cities.* Chicago: Aldine, 1968.
Le Corbusier. *Manner of Thinking about Urbanism.* New York: McGraw-Hill, 1967.
———. *The Radiant City.* New York: Grossman.
Meyerson, Martin. *Face of the Metropolis.* New York: Random House, 1963.
Moholy-Nagy, Sibyl. *Matrix of Man.* New York: Praeger, 1968.
Mumford, Lewis. *The Highway and the City.* New York: Harcourt, Brace and World, 1963.
Olmsted, Frederick Law. *Landscape into Cityscape: Fredrick Law Olmsted's Plans for a Greater New York City.* Ed. with an introduction by Albert Fein. Ithaca, N.Y.: Cornell University Press, 1968.
Peets, Elbert. *On the Art of Designing Cities.* Cambridge, Mass.: MIT Press, 1968.
Rudofsky, Bernard. *Streets for People.* Garden City, N.Y.: Doubleday, 1969.
Schneider, Wolf. *Babylon is Everywhere.* New York: McGraw-Hill, 1963.
Smithson, Alison Margaret and Peter. *Urban Structuring: Studies.* New York: Reinhold, 1967.
Tunnard, Christopher. *Man-made America: Chaos or Control?* New Haven: Yale University Press, 1963.
———. *The City of Man.* New York: Scribner's, 1963.
von Eckardt, Wolf. *A Place to Live: The Crisis of the Cities.* New York: Dell, 1967.

Notes

1. Victor Gruen, *The Heart of Our Cities* (New York: Simon & Schuster, 1964), p. 126.
2. Lewis Mumford, *The Culture of Cities* (New York: Harcourt, Brace & World, 1938), p. 9.

CHAPTER 23

Bibliography

Clifford, Derek. *Art and Understanding: Towards a Humanist Aesthetic.* Greenwich, Conn.: New York Graphic Society, 1969.
Ehrenzweig, Anton. *The Hidden Order of Art: A Study in the Psychology of Artistic Imagination.* Berkeley: California Book Co., 1967.
Faulkner, Ray, and Edwin Ziegfeld. *Art Today.* 5th ed. New York: Holt, Rinehart and Winston, 1969.
Hill, Anthony, ed. *Data: Directions in Art, Theory and Aesthetics.* Greenwich, Conn.: New York Graphic Society, 1969.
Hultén, K. G. Pontus. *The Machine as Seen at the End of the Mechanical Age.* Greenwich, Conn.: New York Graphic Society, 1969.
McMullen, Roy. *Art, Affluence, and Alienation: The Fine Arts Today.* New York: Praeger, 1968.
Neutra, Richard. *Life and Shape.* New York: Meredith, 1962.
Feldman, Edmund Burke. *Art as Image and Idea.* Englewood Cliffs, N.J.: Prentice-Hall, 1967.
O'Doherty, Brian. *Object and Idea: An Art Critic's Journal, 1961–1967.* New York: Simon and Schuster, 1967.
Read, Herbert. *Art and Alienation: the Role of the Artist in Society.* New York: Horizon, 1967.
———. *Art and Society.* New York: Schocken, 1966.
Rosenberg, Harold. *The Anxious Object: Art Today and its Audience.* New York: Horizon, 1966.
Rydzewski, Pamela. *Art and Human Experience.* Long Island City: Pergamon, 1967.

Notes

1. Alfred H. Barr, Jr. (ed.) *Masters of Modern Art* (New York: Museum of Modern Art, 1958), p. 111.

Glossary

Abstract. Form originating with a recognizable object, but simplified by the artist to express the essence of the object rather than its physical appearance.
Abstract Expressionism. A movement in painting originating in America, in which the artist divorces himself from the representation of physical reality, in favor of expressing his own feelings.
Achromatic colors. Neutral colors, such as black, white, and gray.
Acrylic. A variety of plastics which are unusually clear and lend themselves to high polishing. Also a painting medium in which the pigments are found in a polymer emulsion.
Additive primary colors. Red, blue, and green, the colors from which any color can be mixed in light.
Additive process. The process of building up forms, as by modeling or welding, as opposed to the subtractive process, in which forms are cut away.
Afterimage. A psychological phenomenon in which the retina of the eye becomes fatigued after viewing any hue for a sustained period of time, causing the complementary hue to be seen.
Analogous colors. Colors that are adjacent on the color wheel.
Appliqué. A type of design made by stitching various shapes and colors of fabric onto a base to form a pattern.
Aquatint. An etching process in which the background is given an allover tone by use of a porous substance applied before treatment with acid.
Arcade. A series of arches supported by piers or columns to form an open passageway.
Arch. A structural device, generally any opening spanned by a curved top supported by two uprights; however, the true arch consists of wedge-shaped blocks placed in a semicircle and in counterthrust, so that they converge at a keystone at the center of the opening.
Art Nouveau. A highly decorative style of the 1890s, based on plant forms, Japanese art, European peasant decoration, and other sources.
Atmospheric perspective. The effect of an intervening body of air between the object and the viewer, causing a softening of outlines, cooling and blurring of colors, and loss of detail at the horizon.
Baroque. A style of art and architecture that flourished from c. 1600 to 1750 in Western Europe, characterized by strong diagonals and a robust swirling quality.
Bas-relief or low relief. Sculpture in which the figures are attached to the background, projecting usually less than two inches.
Batik. A form of resist dyeing in which the dyes are made from the bark of trees. Long used in China and Japan and now associated with Indonesia.
Bauhaus. A school founded by Walter Gropius in Germany in 1919, known for its adaptation of science and technology to art and for the use of glass and metal in unornamented buildings.
Biomorphic. Taken from nature, from the Greek meaning structure based on life.
Bisque. Pottery or other clay ware that has been fired once but not glazed.
Burr. The curl of metal left when a drypoint is cut into a metal plate. It catches the ink along the edge of the cut line, lending a soft and widened line.
Cameo glass. A type of glass made first by the Romans, in which a raised molded design is overlaid on a glass vessel and then fused to it, forming a cameo effect.
Cantilever. A bracket or block projecting freely at one end and firmly supported from the other side.
Cartoon. A drawing made on paper used in transferring designs to walls as a basis for painting, mosaic, or tapestry.
Casein. A painting medium in which the pigment is bound with milk curd.
Casting. The forming of a liquid or plastic substance into a specific shape by pouring it into a mold.
Cavityless mold system. A type of sand casting using styrofoam for a model, around which wet sand is packed. Hot molten metal is poured into the styrofoam, causing it to vaporize, thus replacing the foam model with metal in one step.
Celadon. A Chinese glaze for porcelain, usually in a thick translucent gray, blue-green, or sea green color.
Chasing. A process of decorating or cleaning metal by working with tools of hardened steel on which the tips are smooth and somewhat rounded.
China. Ware made from a clay body usually composed of kaolin, ball clay, feldspar and flint plus a flux.
Chromatic colors. Colors with the quality of hue in them, such as red or blue as opposed to the neutrals, which are black, white, and gray.
Cire perdue or lost wax. A method of casting metal in which a model is coated with wax and a mold built around it. When heated, the wax melts and flows out, leaving a cavity into which molten metal can be poured and allowed to solidify.
Cloisonné. A combination glaze and mosaic technique in which thin strips of metal separate the segments in the design.
Coil pot. A piece of pottery formed by rolling coils of clay and building them into a solid wall, one upon the other.
Collage. A design formed by the pasting of various materials onto a background to create variety in texture and surface interest. Materials such as paper, wood, and cloth are often combined with paint on canvas.
Collotype. A method of printing from photosensitive gelatin spread on sheets of glass or flexible metal.
Color dynamics. The study of the effects of various colors upon each other and of their changing character under different conditions.
Color harmonies. Combinations of two or more colors which are somehow related.
Complementary colors. Colors that are opposite one another on the color wheel, and which, when mixed together in equal parts, form gray, or, in the case of light, form white light.
Conceptual image. An image arising in the artist's mind rather than in his visual experience.
Constructivism. A movement in twentieth-century sculpture in which the emphasis is on architectonic forms built of wires, girders, and the like.
Contact print. A photographic print which is the same size as the negative from which it was made.
Content. The emotional and intellectual structure that the artist incorporates into his work.
Crackle glass. A kind of blown glass which is cooled and then reheated to form a network of cracks over the surface.
Crystallo. A clear Italian glass used during the Renaissance for blowing into elaborate forms.
Cut glass. Glass that is decorated by cutting patterns into the surface by the use of wet sand and turning wheels.
Dada or Dadism. A movement begun during World War I, in which artists expressed their feeling of futility in a war-ravaged world by exhibiting creations designed to shock or ridicule existing standards.
Decorative design. Design of a surface, usually applied after the structure of the object has been completed.
Diaphragm. A part of the camera consisting of overlapping metal leaves by means of which the opening of the lens can be controlled.
Discharge method. A method of dyeing fabrics by removing the dye in certain areas to create a design.
Dome. A vault in the form of an inverted cup, which is formed by the intersection of two or more arches.
Drypoint. A method of intaglio printing in which the metal burr along the cut line catches the ink, making a broad softened line.
Ductility. The capacity of metal for being drawn out or hammered thin without breaking.
Dynamic symmetry. A mathematical basis for composing works of art into a totally related structure.
Earthenware. Ware made from natural clay which is usually soft and porous and fired at a low temperature.
Embroidery. The decorating of fabric by use of colored threads worked in a variety of stitches.
Emulsion in photography. A chemical coating,

usually of silver bromide and various dyes, which forms the substance of a film into which the image is fixed by exposure to light.

Encaustic. A painting medium consisting of hot beeswax and pigment.

Environmental sculpture. Sculpture using materials seen repeatedly in the everyday environment but which are treated or combined in such a way as to remove their usual associations.

Etching. A printing process in which a metal plate is immersed in acid, after first being coated with wax through which a drawing is scratched. The acid eats into the plate where the plate is exposed by the lines.

Expressionism. A movement originating in Germany before World War I, in which the artist gives visual form to his emotions and reactions to reality or depicts the inner nature of his subject rather than the outer aspects of it.

Faïence. A type of Majolica comprising an opaque glaze onto which intricate designs are often painted.

Felting. A method of manufacturing cloth by rolling and pounding fibers together under heat and pressure to form a compact and even sheet.

Fiber. Any material that can be separated into threads or thread-like structures.

Figure-ground perception. The capacity to distinguish between object and background.

Filter. A piece of dyed gelatin or glass that fits over the lens of a camera to modify light rays.

Flexwood. Paper-thin sheets of wood glued to a flexible backing.

Floating yarn. A method of weaving in which either warp or weft threads float over or under several opposing yarns.

Flying buttress. A structural device first used in Gothic architecture to support the vault from the outside.

Focal length. The distance from the lens to the focal plane where the film is located.

f-rating. A symbol to express the speed of a lens by comparing its diameter to its focal length.

Fresco. A method of painting in which pigment is mixed with water and applied to wet plaster walls.

Gemming. A method of decorating glass by applying drops of enamel.

Geodesic dome. A dome first devised by R. Buckminster Fuller, composed of small modules based on the triangle.

Glaze. A vitreous coating fired onto pottery or other clay ware and containing silica, alumina, and a flux. Also a thin layer of paint applied to canvas or other base in one or more layers, in an effort to achieve transparency, translucency, or luminosity in a painting.

Glaze firing. The firing of pottery that has had a glaze applied, resulting in the vitrification of the glaze.

Gouache. Opaque watercolor in which the pigment is bound with gum arabic and a paste of zinc oxide.

Greenware. Pottery that has not been fired.

Grout. A substance composed of glue and cement, which is used to fill the joints in masonry or the cracks between the tesserae in a mosaic.

Happening. An environmental situation related to both sculpture and drama, in which no permanent form is established but an occurrence takes place that is sometimes satiric.

Hard-edge painting. A style of painting developed in the mid-twentieth century in which objects or forms are depicted in a meticulous style, or, in the case of abstraction, with geometric accuracy.

Haut-relief or high relief. Relief sculpture in which the forms project from the background to considerable depth, usually two inches or more.

Hue. The pure state of any color, also the name by which the color is called.

Impasto. The thick application of paint to provide texture.

Impressionism. A movement in painting originating in France in the 1870s, in which paint was used to represent the transitory effects of light and color.

Intaglio. A method of printing in which the part to be printed is cut into a metal plate or other background.

Intarsia. Intricate inlay of wood in furniture to form patterns such as still lifes, scrolls, and arabesques.

Intensity. The amount of purity in a color, also called chroma (from the Greek "color") or saturation.

Iridescence. The effect by which one color seems to contain all of the hues in the spectrum.

Jacquard. A variety of figure weave which includes brocades and damasks.

Kiln. The furnace or oven in which pottery and other clay products are fired.

Kinesthesia. A muscular response to a work of art in which the work inspires a feeling of physical bodily motion.

Kinetic element. The element of movement as it is found in a work of art, relating visual forms to a total experience.

Lacing. A method of manufacturing cloth by fastening a single thread onto itself, as in knitting.

Lattimo. A variety of Venetian glass, milk-like in color and often garnished with gilding, painting, and splash decorations.

Leno. A method of weaving in which weft threads are wrapped around the warp, creating open effects such as in nets.

Lens. Part of a camera, ground from optical glass, to control refraction or bending of light waves as they approach the film.

Linear perspective. A system for depicting distance through the converging of lines at a vanishing point on the horizon line and the foreshortening of objects as they recede from the point where viewed.

Lithography. A printing process using a flat surface and wax crayon, originally done on Bavarian limestone.

Luminal sculpture. Sculpture using light as an element.

Majolica. Earthenware coated with an opaque white glaze onto which is painted a design in metallic oxides.

Marquetry. Veneers inlaid with wood, marble, or ivory that retain a flat surface.

Medium. The material in which a work of art is created.

Mezzotint. An etching process in which the background is given an allover texture by use of a tool called a rocker.

Minimal art. Painting or sculpture which is largely mechanical in conception and construction.

Modular unit. A structural element that is repeated in varying quantities to create a design in which all parts are related to each other and to the whole.

Monochromatic. Referring to the use of one hue in its various gradations.

Monoprints. A planographic process in which ink or paint is applied to a flat surface and paper laid upon it to make a print which will be one of a kind.

Mosaic. An art form in which tesserae—small pieces of glass, ceramic tile, or other materials—are fitted together to form a design and then glued or cemented to a background.

Negative. In photography, the film or plate upon which the image is originally registered and from which a positive print is made.

Negative space. The space not occupied by an object itself but circulating in and around it, contributing to the total effect of the design.

Neoclassicism. A revival of the classic ideals of the ancient Greeks and Romans.

Nonobjective. Having no resemblance to natural forms or objects.

Op Art. A movement in mid-twentieth century America in which painters based their work on the science of optics, depicting eye-dazzling patterns and combinations of colors often in geometric designs.

Papier-mâché. A pulp made from moistened paper mixed with resin, oil, or glue which is then molded into various forms. From the French meaning "chewed paper."

Parquet. Geometric shapes of wood inlaid, mosaic fashion, for flooring or furniture.

Parterre. A designed flower bed in which colorful plantings form geometric or other designs.

Perceptual image. The image seen by the eye but influenced by psychological factors.

Perception. The act of visually gathering knowledge through attention to something the individual considers important and the giving of meaning to the knowledge gathered.

Pigment. A colorant ground into a fine powder and used to color paints or dyes.

Pile weave. A method of weaving with a third yarn in addition to the warp and weft which stands in loops.

Pinch pot. A piece of pottery made by shaping the clay with the fingers.

Plain weave. A method of weaving in which one warp thread is interlaced with one weft thread.

Planography. An area of printmaking which includes lithography and serigraphy.

Plastic. Any of numerous substances composed of organic molecules in certain chemical combinations. Also the ease with which substances can be shaped.

Plate glass. Glass made by rolling and grinding to remove any irregularities.

Plywood. Thin sheets of wood glued together with alternating grains in alternate layers.

Pop Art. A movement in mid-twentieth century, in which artists chose as subject matter the symbols—often the materials as well—of the mass-produced world around them, such as coke bottles, billboards, and blown-up comic strips.

Porcelain. Ware made from a specially prepared body composed of kaolin, ball clay, feldspar, and flint. It fires at the highest temperature of all pottery wares.

Positive space. The space occupied by an object as distinguished from negative space which circulates in and around it.

Post-and-lintel. A structural system in architecture in which beams or lintels are placed horizontally across upright posts.

Pressed glass. Glass made by pouring into molds and pressing the inside by means of a plunger.

Primary color. One of the basic colors on any color wheel, which it is assumed cannot be mixed from other colors, but which serves as a basis for mixing all other combinations on the wheel.

Pylon. A solid pyramidal structure usually of concrete, used for anchoring bridge towers or cantilevers.

Radial symmetry. Balance achieved by the arrangement of elements in a circular pattern around a central axis.

Raising. A method of working metal by hammering it to elevate the outer part of a sheet.

Refraction. The bending of a ray of light as it passes through a prism or a lens.

Relief. A printing process in which portions to be printed stand out, while the background is recessed.

Relief Painting. A combination of painting and relief sculpture in which designs in wood, metal, or other substances are applied to a rigid background and then painted into a total composition.

Relief sculpture. Sculpture which projects from a background to which it is attached, usually projecting three inches or less.

Repoussé. Another name for embossing, in which metal is traced with a tool and then raised from the reverse side to form subtle modelling or relief.

Resist printing. A method of dyeing fabrics by blocking out certain areas with wax or other means and then dipping the fabric in the dye.

Rib weave. A method of weaving in which a thick warp thread is used with a thin weft thread.

Rococo. An eighteenth-century style characterized by delicate curves and pastel colors in painting and architecture.

Rya. A pile weave used in rugmaking.

Sand casting. A method of creating sculpture from molten material by pouring the material into a cavity formed in a mold of wet sand.

Sang de boeuf. A deep brown-red glaze used by Chinese porcelain makers.

Secco. From the Italian term for dry. A method of painting in which pigment is applied to dry plaster walls.

Secondary color. A color created by mixing two primary colors on any color wheel.

Sgraffito. A method of decorating pottery in which designs are cut through the glaze revealing the color of the clay underneath.

Shade. Any variation of a color which is darker than the original hue as a result of the addition of black or of the complement of the hue.

Shutter. The part of the camera which controls the length of time the film within the camera is exposed.

Shuttle. In weaving, the holder for the weft thread.

Slab pot. A piece of pottery formed by cutting flat sheets of clay into pieces.

Slip. Liquid clay of the consistency of cream, used to pour into molds for the making of pottery or for decoration.

Split complementary. A combination of colors involving one hue and the hues on either side of its complement on the color wheel.

Stitchery. The term used for contemporary embroidery techniques in which the stitches themselves predominate in the creating of a design.

Stoneware. Ware made sometimes from natural clay and sometimes from prepared clay bodies. It is hard and vitreous and fires at a relatively high temperature.

Structural design. Design involved with the basic form of an object, as distinguished from decorative design, which usually concerns design of a surface.

Stylization. The simplification of an object to emphasize design qualities.

Subjective vision. The psychological interpretation of color relationships by an individual according to his own peculiarities of vision, of perception, and of past experiences.

Subtractive primary colors. Colors which absorb the light of the additive primary colors, such as, magenta, yellow, and turquoise.

Subtractive process. The process of cutting away to build forms, as from a block of marble or wood.

Successive contrast. The phenomenon by which the afterimage of an object appears to the closed eyes in the complementary color of the original object.

Surrealism. The combining of familiar objects in fantastic ways, as in a dream or the subconscious.

Symbolism. A means of representing what is not known, usually by graphic figures.

Symmetry. Balance achieved through the arrangement of elements in a regular pattern in which each side of a central axis is the exact reverse of the other.

Synesthesia. A simultaneous stimulation of senses, for example, the sensing of color in relation to musical sounds.

Tapestry. A heavy, hand-woven textile in which the weft threads do not usually continue across the full width of the fabric but are woven back and forth in specific areas to form patterns.

Tempera. A painting medium in which the pigment is bound together with egg or with animal or vegetable glue.

Tensile strength. A characteristic of metal or other material which makes it possible for it to be stretched without breaking.

Tesserae. The small pieces of glass, tile, stone, or other material in a mosaic.

Tetrad. Any four colors placed equidistant from one another on the color wheel.

Textile. A fabric that is woven.

Tiffany glass. A style of glass designed in the early twentieth century by Louis Comfort Tiffany, using rich colors and the botanical forms and patterns characteristic of Art Nouveau.

Tint. Any variation of a color that is lighter than the original hue, usually as a result of the addition of white.

Tone. A softened color achieved by mixing pure color with gray or with its complement.

Transparency. The quality of seeing through one layer into layers underneath, achieved in a work of art by use of cellophane, tissue paper, or by skilled painting.

Triad. Any three colors placed equidistant from one another on the color wheel.

Truss. A structural form consisting of rigid bars or beams combined into a framework whose shape cannot be altered without changing one or more of its members.

Value. The lightness or darkness of a color.

Vault. An extension of the arch to form a curved roof over a hallway, a room, or larger space.

Viga. A pole used horizontally as a roof beam, which projects beyond the outside wall. Found in Spanish colonial architecture.

Visual texture. Surface variety that can be seen but not felt with the fingers.

Visual vacuity. Ability to perceive fine differences in details of the visual environment.

Vitro di trina. Lace glass, formed by the Venetian glassmakers, by threading opaque white enamel in multiple threads across the body of the vessel.

Weaving. The process of interlacing two sets of parallel threads to form a web.

Index

References are to page numbers, except for color plates and black-and-white illustrations, which are identified by figure and plate numbers.

Photographic Sources

References are to figure numbers unless indicated Pl. (plate).

Abey, Bob, Fort Worth, Tex. (128, 135); Alinari—Art Reference Bureau, Ancram, N.Y. (44, 109, 285, 299, 307, 385); American Crafts Council, New York (51, 64, 126–127, 158–159, 234); American Forest Products Industries, Washington, D.C. (175); American Museum of Natural History, New York (13, 15, 25); Andrews, Wayne, Grosse Pointe, Mich. (5, 114, 152, 352); Archives of American Art, David Smith Papers, New York (Pl. 19); Archives Photographiques, Paris (45, 241, 287); Archivo Amigos de Gaudí, Barcelona (110); Armstrong Cork Co., Lancaster, Pa. (35, 94, 373, 378); Austrian State Tourist Department, Denver (228); Austrian Travel Agency, New York (413); Avedon, Richard, New York (219); Balestrero, Peter, Tucson, Ariz. (169, Pl. 17); Barford, George, Normal, Ill. (83); Behrens en Consenheim Fotopresbureau, Rotterdam (405); Bergdorf Goodman, New York (229); Berger, Pierre, Photo Researchers, Inc., New York (414); Boesch, Ferdinand, New York, and Museum of Contemporary Crafts, New York (96–99, 106); British Travel Association, Los Angeles (407); British Travel and Holidays Association, London (383–384, 386); Brogi—Art Reference Bureau, Ancram, N.Y. (300); Burkee, Bonnie, Aspen, Colo. (208, 388); Burshears, J. F., La Junta, Colo. (71, 359); Calder, Sam, Los Angeles (60, 130–132); California Division of Highways, Sacramento (345); Canadian Government Travel Bureau, Ottowa (3, 178); Carolina Biological Supply Company, Burlington, N.C. (9–10, 19, 81, 84, 87, 292, 296, 338–339, 349, 351, 433); Leo Castelli Gallery, New York (Pl. 25); Clarke, Henry, Paris (226); Clements, Geoffrey, New York (293); Colonial Williamsburg, Inc., Va. (387); Colorado State University, Fort Collins, Colo. (428); Columbia Broadcasting System, New York (336–337); Columbia Records, New York (282); Corning Glass Works, Corning, N.Y. (139); Corning Museum of Glass, Corning, N.Y. (149, 151); Crowell Collier and Macmillan, Inc., New York (244); Dantzic, Jerry, New York (423); John Day Company, New York (22); Di Liberto, Richard, Fresh Meadows, N.Y. (138); Doyle Dane Bernbach Inc., New York (260–261); Dudley, Hardin & Yang, Inc., Seattle (412); DuMont Schauberg, M., Verlag, Cologne (315); Eberstadt, Frederick, New York (233); Finke, Harold G., Bennet, Neb. (192); Foster, Jack, Cincinnati (65, 168, Pl. 7); Fox, James F., Inc., New York (42, Pl. 4); Franklin Simon, New York (218); Frantz, Alison, Princeton, N.J. (340); Free, William, Agency, New York (258); Freeman, John R., & Co. Ltd., London (Pl. 10); French Government Tourist Office, New York (382); Friedman-Abeles, Inc., New York (236); Gahr, David, New York (317); General Electric Company, Bridgeport, Conn. (102–103); Greene, Milton, New York, and *Life*, New York (238); Greenwood of Glenwood, Glenwood Springs, Colo. (364–367); Grehan, Farrell, Chavannes-Renens, Switzerland, and *Life*, New York (237); Gross, Richard, Los Angeles (187); Gross, Richard, Los Angeles, and California Design/10, Pasadena Art Museum (213); Gruen Associates, New York, and Tidyman Studios, Fresno, Calif. (403–404); Gruen Associates, New York (420); Grumbacher, New York (Pl.5); Hedrich-Blessing, Inc., Chicago (344, 360); Hervé, Lucien, Paris (422); Hill, John T., New York (372, 380); Hirmer Verlag, Munich (91, 225); Holton, George, Photo Researchers, Inc., New York (355, 419); International Silver Company, Meridan, Conn. (198–205); James Foundation, St. James, Mo. (398–399); Japan National Tourist Organization, New York (391); Jensen, Georg, New York (193); Johnson, S. C., & Son, Inc., Racine, Wisc. (278–280); Kidder Smith, G. E., New York (61); King, John, New Canaan, Conn. (248, 325, Pls. 16, 18, 20); King, John, New Canaan, Conn., and Fred Leighton Imports, New York (209); King Photographers, Brooklyn (155); Knoll Associates, New York (430); Landesbildstelle Baden, Karlsruhe (214); Lawrence-Phillips Studios, Chicago (52); Leber Katz Paccione Inc., New York (270); Lee, Christopher, Los Angeles (125); Library of Congress, Washington, D.C. (411); Martin, Dennis, New York, and American Crafts Council, New York (161); Matter, Herbert, New York (16); MAS, Barcelona (Pl. 29); Massachusetts Institute of Technology, Office of Publications, Cambridge, Mass. (281); Mayer, Paul (85); McAllister, Bruce, Denver (363, 406); McGraw-Hill Book Company, New York (77); Miles Laboratories, Inc., Elkhart, Ind. (273); Miller, Herman, Inc., Zeeland, Mich. (183); Milmoe, James O., Golden, Colo. (306, Pl. 14); Moholy-Nagy, Sibyl, New York (2); Moore, James, New York (222–223, 230–231); Multimedia Communications Corp., New York (224); Munroe, Joe, Photo Researchers, Inc., New York (101); Munsell Color Company, Inc., Baltimore (Pl. 6); Museum of Modern Art, New York (113, 397); Museum of Modern Art, Film Stills Archive, New York (334–335); Namuth, Hans, New York (371); Nelson, O.E., New York (191, 309); Nervi, Pier Luigi, Rome (348, 354); New Mexico Department of Development, Santa Fe (416–417); New York City Construction Coordinator (424); Otero Junior College, Biological Sciences Department, La Junta, Colo. (12); Pace Gallery, New York (322); Palade, George E., M.D., The Rockefeller University, New York, and The Upjohn Company, Kalamazoo, Mich. (17); Palmer, Phil, Petaluma, Calif., and California Redwood Association, San Francisco (369); Parade Studios, Inc., Cleveland (89); Parker, Paul, New York; and American Crafts Council, New York (162); Parker, Maynard, Los Angeles (182, 186, 374, 392–393); Pearson, Charles R., Edmonds, Wash. (361); Peterson, Gosta, New York (173); Pettit, Bob, and Studio Two, Newtown, Conn. (206); Photo Ideas, Inc., Chicago (66); Photo Researchers, Inc., New York (356); Pike, Virginia, Hobbs, N.M. (134); Rabin, Nathan, New York (216); Rapho-Guillumette Pictures, New York (70, 122, 323, 327, 330); Revlon Publicity, New York (275–277); Reynolds, Warren, Minneapolis (357); Robinson, Virginia, Tucson, Ariz. (38); Rosenblum, Walter, Long Island City, N.Y. (215); Rudofsky, Bernard, New York (Pl. 31); St. Joseph's Hospital, Denver (11); San Antonio Chamber of Commerce, Tex. (400–402); Sandak, Inc., New York (Pl. 30); Saunders, W. B., Company, Philadelphia (346); SCALA, Florence (350, Pl. 9); *School Arts*, Davis Publications, Inc., Worcester, Mass. (418); Seagram Corporation, New York (92); Shulman, Julius, Los Angeles (368, 370); Siesel, Harold J., Co. Inc., New York (165); Spearman, Jerry, New York (Pl. 32); Steuben Glass, New York (140); Stoedtner—Prothman Associates, Inc., Baldwin, N.Y. (115); © Ezra Stoller [ESTO], Mamaroneck, N.Y. (14); Stuart, John, Inc., New York (184–185); Sunami, Soichi, New York (31, 41, 289, 291, 310, 316); Sutherland, Eric, Minneapolis (318); Swiss National Tourist Office, New York (6); Thomas Airviews, Bayside, N.Y. (435); Tully, Peter A., & Son, New York (434); Uht, Charles, New York (107); United Air Lines, New York (429, 431); United States Rubber Company, New York (263); University of South Florida, Educational Resources Division, Tampa (154); Uris Building Corporation, New York (153); Vatican Photographic Archive, Rome (117); Vine, David, New York (326); Virginia Department of Conservation and Economic Development, Richmond (415); Wagenfohr, Milton, Stone Ridge, N.Y. (176); Ward, Clarence, Oberlin, Ohio (36, 53, 342–343); Watson-Guptill Publications, Inc., New York (59, 68); Wayside Gardens Company, Mentor, Ohio (432); Werner, Oswald, Syracuse, N.Y. (105); Wide World Photos, Inc., New York (347); Zink, Milton C., Toledo, Ohio (93)